International Comparative Education

PRACTICES, ISSUES, & PROSPECTS

Edited by

R. MURRAY THOMAS

University of California, Santa Barbara, USA

BUTTERWORTH
HEINEMANN

Butterworth-Heinemann Ltd
Linacre House, Jordan Hill, Oxford OX2 8DP

A member of the Reed Elsevier plc group

OXFORD LONDON BOSTON
MUNICH NEW DELHI SINGAPORE SYDNEY
TOKYO TORONTO WELLINGTON

First published by Pergamon Press plc 1990
Reprinted 1995

British Library Cataloguing in Publication Data
International comparative education: practices, issues, &
prospects.
1. Education
I. Thomas, R. Murray (Robert Murray)
370

Library of Congress Cataloguing in Publication Data
International comparative education: practices, issues, &
prospects/edited by R. Murray Thomas.
p. cm.
Includes bibliographical references and index.
1. Comparative education. I. Thomas, R. Murray
(Robert Murray), 1921–
LB43.I56 1990 370.19′5—dc20 90-41072

ISBN 0 7506 2831 6

Printed in Great Britain by BPC Wheatons Ltd, Exeter

International Comparative Education

To

COURTNEY MARIE THOMAS

Preface

The primary aim of this book is too introduce readers to the domain of international comparative education by describing key practices and issues that engage the attention of those scholars and educational practitioners who investigate the domain. The practices and issues identified throughout the volume are illustrated with examples drawn from nations all over the world —industrialized and nonindustrialized countries, Eastern and Western civilizations, and the northern and southern hemispheres. A secondary purpose of the book is to provide estimates of how well the matters reviewed in these pages might be resolved in the years ahead.

A brief mention of other types of books in this field may indicate how the present volume differs from them. One popular type offers an indepth study of a given nation's education system, including a chronicle of how the system evolved. A second common variety analyzes education in several nations, with a chapter devoted to each country. Sometimes such analyses focus on a single facet of the educational enterprise, such as curricula, political conditions, finance, ethnic relationships, nonformal learning activities, or the role assigned to schooling in a national-development plan. A third type compares education in several societies from the perspective of a particular theory of social organization or social change.

In contrast to such books, *International Comparative Education — Practices, Issues, and Prospects* offers an overview of representative problems in educational development that are common to many societies, with the problems illuminated by brief examples from a diversity of nations. Our intention in adopting this approach has been to equip readers with a variety of concepts and illustrations that might enrich their future study of education from an international, comparative perspective.

The words *practices, issues*, and *prospects* in the title are used throughout the book with the following meanings. *Practices* are techniques employed in the conduct of education. *Issues* are questions that can have multiple, and ofttimes controversial, answers. One society may respond to a given issue with different strategies than do other societies. The term *prospects* refers to estimates of what the future may hold for the practices and issues addressed in the 12 chapters.

Our authors were selected because of their reputations as experts on the topics their chapters address. The nature of their expertise is suggested by the following sketches of their professional backgrounds and by reference to publications their scholarship has produced.

Jiaying Zhuang Howard (Chapter 3 on Instructional Methods and Materials) is director of the Chinese studies program at the Monterey Institute of International Studies in California. She holds a Ph.D. degree in the field of international education. Her most recent paper on China's policies for sending students overseas appeared in the *Journal of the Association of International Education Administrators.* In addition, she has contributed articles to the *International Encyclopedia of Education, Asian Profile, Foreign Theatre,* and *Journal of the Chinese Teachers Association.* Dr. Howard was formerly on the foreign language faculty of the Shanghai Institute of Foreign Trade.

William Cummings (Chapter 4 on Evaluation and Examinations) is director of the Office of International Education and a lecturer at the Harvard Graduate School of Education He is currently completing a study on the decentralization of Sri Lankan education. He is also analyzing international educational and scientific linkages and soon will finish a book entitled *Overseas Campuses: U.S. and Japanese.* His earlier research and writing have focused on the comparative historical development of education structures and on the evaluation of educational policy options. Among his books are *Education and Equality in Japan* (Princeton, 1980), *The Changing Japanese University* (1981), *Education in Crisis: Japanese and U.S. Perspectives* (1986), *Low-Cost Primary Education* (1986) and *The Revival of Values Education in Asia and the West* (1988). Dr. Cummings received a Ph.D. in sociology from Harvard University in 1972, then taught at the University of Chicago, Tsuda College in Japan, the National University of Singapore, and the East-West Center in Hawaii. He has served as a project officer in educational research and planning for the Ford Foundation in Indonesia and as a senior analyst for the U.S. National Science Foundation.

Noel F. McGinn (Chapter 5 on Forms of Governance) is a professor of education at Harvard University and presently director of the BRIDGES Project, a five-year USAID-funded effort to provide planners and policymakers in Third World countries with increased access to research-based information about the effectiveness of alternative policies and programs for education. Dr. McGinn has worked for the past two decades on issues of educational planning in developing countries, with particular attention to the process of policy formulation. He has coauthored several national studies of education systems (Korea, Mexico, Venezuela) and a series of articles on educational planning and decentralization.

Thomas J. La Belle (Chapter 6 on Delivery Systems) is a professor of education and the dean of the School of Education at the University of Pittsburgh. His scholarship and teaching focus on education and anthropology, nonformal education, and education in Latin America.

Judy J. Sylvester (Chapter 6 on Delivery Systems) is a doctoral student with a concentration in international and development education in the School of Education at the University of Pittsburgh. She has worked for Unicef both as a staff member and as a programming consultant in areas ranging from emergency relief assistance to development programs.

Beverly Lindsay (Chapter 8 on Equity and Access) is the associate dean for academic affairs and a graduate professor of education at the University of Georgia, where she is responsible for academic affairs, international education, educational field services, graduation and certification, and faculty and student affairs. Previously Dr. Lindsay was an administrator/coordinator in the U.S. Information Agency where she directed an education program for 10 African countries. She was also an American Council on Education fellow. While a senior researcher at the National Institute of Education, she served as consultant to the National Commission on Excellence in Education that produced *A Nation at Risk.* In addition to publishing more than 45 journal articles and book chapters, Dr. Lindsay has issued two anthologies of original research entitled *African Migration and National Development* and *Comparative Perspectives of Third World Women: The Impact of Race, Sex, and Class.* She is a past president of the Comparative and International Education Society and member of the executive council of the World Council of Comparative Education. Her Ph.D. degree in administration and management is from American University and her Ed.D. in the comparative sociology of education and higher education/policy studies is from the University of Massachusetts.

Leslie Limage (Chapter 9 on Language and Education) is a program specialist in the International Literacy Year Secretariat in the Education Sector of Unesco. She is in charge of a range of awareness-raising and promotional publications about literacy-related issues. Dr. Limage is also responsible for literacy-related projects in developing and industrialized countries and for liaison functions with non-governmental organizations, international bodies, and governments involved in 1990 International Literacy Year activities. She is the former associate editor of Unesco's international education quarterly, *Prospects.* Earlier she directed a 20-country study on education for linguistic minorities for the Organisation for Economic Cooperation and Development's Centre for Educational Research and Innovation. In addition, she has served as a consultant to the International Labour Office on women's migration and education. Formerly she was also a tutor and organizer in the British adult literacy campaign. Dr. Limage's teaching experience at secondary, adult-education, and university levels was gained in France, the United Kingdom, and the United States. Her publications have been particularly concerned with literacy/illiteracy in industrialized countries and with minority/immigrant education.

Mark Bray (Chapter 10 on The Economics of Education) is a senior lecturer in educational-policy making and planning and a fellow of the Centre of Asian Studies at the University of Hong Kong. His experience in teaching, research, and educational planning has included appointments in Scotland, England, Kenya, Nigeria, and Papua New Guinea. Dr. Bray has also served as an educational consultant for such agencies as the World Bank, Unesco, the Asian

Development Bank, Unicef, and the Commonwealth Secretariat in Indonesia, Pakistan, the People's Republic of China, Botswana, Sudan, Laos, Solomon Islands, Malta, and Fiji. Among books he has written or coauthored are *Educational Planning in a Decentralised System* (1984), *Education and Social Stratification in Papua New Guinea* (1985), *Education and Society in Africa* (1986), *Are Small Schools the Answer?* (1987), *School Clusters in the Third World* (1987), *Community Financing of Education* (1988), and *Multiple-Shift Schooling* (1989).

Gary Theisen (Chapter 11, Research and Education) is Director of International Research and Planning for the Academy for Educational Development. His areas of expertise include educational-systems development, comparative research, and policy analysis.

Don Adams (Chapter 11, Research and Education) is a professor of education and economic and social development in the School of Education at the University of Pittsburgh. His scholarship and research focus on educational planning, policy, and development in an international context.

R. Murray Thomas, the book's editor, heads the program in international education in the Graduate School of Education at the University of California, Santa Barbara. His direct engagement with comparative education spans more than three decades, during which he has served as a researcher, consultant, and teacher in education systems of Southeast Asia and the Pacific, particularly in Indonesia, Malaysia, and American Samoa. He is the author of *A Chronicle of Indonesian Higher Education* (1973) and *Education in American Samoa —1700s to 1980* (1987). He edited *Politics and Education — Cases from 11 Nations* (1983), *Oriental Theories of Human Development* (1988), and *The Encyclopedia of Human Development and Education* (1990). He served as coeditor for *Schooling in the ASEAN Region* (1980), *Schooling in East Asia* (1983), *Schooling in the Pacific Islands* (1984), and *Educational Technology—Its Creation, Development, and Cross-Cultural Transfer* (1987).

Contents

CHAPTER 1

The Nature of Comparative Education

How and why are education systems compared?

R. MURRAY THOMAS

The term *comparative education* in its most general sense means inspecting two or more educational operations in order to discover how they are alike and how they are different. An operation in this context refers to any act associated with learning and teaching. Therefore, we are engaging in comparative education when we analyze two ways of teaching a single mathematics lesson as well as when we simultaneously inspect the entire education systems of two dozen nations.

While the process of inspecting only two classrooms or only two schools does indeed qualify as comparative education, today the term is usually applied solely to analyses of broader scope —matching one nation's schools against another's or one general form of schooling against others. Such a broader meaning is the one intended throughout this book, as the title *International Comparative Education* suggests.

Although from ancient times travelers to foreign lands have always shown interest in how the people they visited were taught, the history of formal comparisons of education systems goes back less than 200 years. With the establishment of nationwide schooling structures in Europe during the 19th century, educators intentionally went abroad to examine schooling in other lands to discover practices they might profitably adopt at home. For example, by the end of the 1800s German universities had provided a model emulated in North America, and the Japanese had adopted a pattern of education found in the United States and in parts of Europe.

Throughout the 20th century, comparative education has increasingly assumed the form of a distinct academic specialization, engaging ever more scholars and practicing educators. This has been particularly true since World War II, which launched a period of history that witnessed a great array of colonized peoples winning their political independence. As the leaders of these new nations set about directing their own affairs, many of them sought to learn what forms of schooling other societies could offer that might serve their needs better than did colonial education. And while newly established governments were inspecting the educational practices beyond their shores, well-established industrialized countries were likewise looking abroad for innovative methods that might improve the literacy, the economic efficiency, and the moral behavior of their populations. The past half century has also marked a period during which worldwide interest in schooling has extended more than ever before to children below age 6 and adults beyond age 20. This expansion of early-childhood education and adult education has been stimulated by the growing expectation that learning should be life-long. As a result, at no time in history has more formal attention been directed at how other peoples seek to meet educational challenges.

Evidence of this heightened interest has appeared in various forms. Beginning in 1956, comparative educationists started establishing professional societies, first in the United States, and thereafter in more than 15 other nations and regions. In 1970 the World Council of Comparative Education Societies was founded as a federation of the individual societies. Periodically the Council holds congresses, with the programs comprised chiefly of panel discussions and the presentation of scholarly papers. Most individual societies also convene annual conferences featuring reports of members' research projects.

To disseminate the results of comparative studies, national societies and such organizations as UNESCO publish journals and books. Among more than two dozen journals devoted entirely to comparative education are such publications as *Comparative Education Review* (USA), *Compare, Comparative Education*, and *The International Journal of Educational Development* (Britain), *Education Comparee* (France), *The International Review of Education* (UNESCO —Hamburg), *Prospects* (UNESCO —Paris), and *Canadian and International Education* (Canada). There are also scores of journals focusing on regional and national education, such as the *Australian Journal of Education*, *Caribbean Journal of Education*, *Chinese Education* and *Soviet Education* (both consisting of translations in English), *Indian Educational Review*, *Scandinavian Journal of Educational Research*, and *Southeast Asian Journal of Educational Studies*.

In recent years the number of books offering comparative studies has grown markedly. However, not all studies reported in either books or journals provide information about more than one education system. For example, an author may describe the structure of the central ministry of education in only one country. Or a scholar may inspect literacy rates within a single nation or in only one region. These one-nation studies are often referred to as national investigations. They serve the purposes of comparative education whenever readers match the contents of such studies against practices in other countries. Because this research is so often conducted and used by comparative educationists, the realm of comparative education in recent years has been broadened, and the label comparative and international education has been adopted so as to accommodate single-nation and single-region research as well as truly comparative studies. Of particular note is the *Encyclopedia of Comparative Education and National Systems of Education* (Postlethwaite, 1988) which provides descriptions of 159 country systems as well as articles outlining major aspects of comparative education.

Further evidence of interest in this field is found in the growth of specialized university programs to prepare both practitioners and researchers in the comparative analysis of educational operations. Many such programs aim at producing scholar-activists, meaning graduates qualified to engage directly in improving a nation's educational operations, basing their efforts on well-informed theory and empirical research.

WHO USES COMPARATIVE-EDUCATION LITERATURE?

The consumers of comparative education are a varied lot. They include educational planners, foreign-aid agencies, educational consultants, university students and professors, business and industrial firms, and the general public.

Educational planners are of several types. Among the most important are government officials responsible for charting the future socioeconomic development of a nation or of a province. In most countries, planning for educational development is centered in a ministry of education which is empowered to direct the conduct of schooling and nonformal programs nationwide. However, in a few nations —such as the United States and Great Britain— the central government has little or no direct authority over most education, so that planning for particular school districts or provinces is carried on at the local level. However, in both centralized and decentralized systems, information about "how others do it elsewhere" is usually valued.

Over the past half century, more foreign aid has been provided for the educational systems of the world than was ever furnished before. In most instances, such assistance has flowed from industrialized nations to ones recently freed from colonial control. There have been four main groups providing such help: (1) international agencies supported by funds from a coalition of nations, (2) individual governments, (3) private philanthropic foundations, and (4) religious denominations. All of these bodies have depended on comparative-and-international-education literature to guide their endeavors.

The most active of the international agencies have been United Nations organizations, such as UNESCO (United Nations Educational, Scientific, and Cultural Organization), UNICEF (United Nations Children's Fund), and ILO (International Labor Organization). However, in addition to such worldwide associations, regional coalitions of nations have also been formed to promote research and assistance in education. Three examples of regional alliances are ASEAN (Association of Southeast Asian Nations), OECD (Organization for Economic Cooperation and Development, consisting of several Western European countries, North American nations, Japan, and a few others), and the Arab Bureau of Education for the Gulf States.

Individual governments have furnished large quantities of educational assistance, usually through their ministry of foreign affairs. Such aid has included sending experts to serve as university professors and consultants to ministries of education, providing funds for school facilities, awarding scholarships that permit people from the recipient nations to study abroad, and supplying volunteers to work in rural-development projects. In most, if not all, cases of such unilateral aid, two motives —compassion and self-interest— have stimulated the donor governments to furnish assistance. The compassion derives from citizens of a "have" society feeling true concern for the plight of people in "have not" societies. Oftentimes this compassion is an expression of guilt which Europeans or North Americans or Japanese feel about their country's having exploited residents of a region held as a colony. The self-interest derives from a nation's desire to attract allies in the world's political struggles and to obtain low-cost sources of raw materials as well as foreign markets in which to sell the goods it produces.

Private philanthropic bodies —such as the Ford, Rockefeller, and Carnegie foundations in the United States— have provided millions of dollars in educational assistance to developing nations over past decades. Their greatest contributions occurred from 1950 through the early 1970s, as formerly colonized countries were struggling to establish educational systems that would offer their citizens schooling opportunities they had never enjoyed before. The amount of aid from secular private foundations has diminished over the past two decades as the cost of such educational ventures has risen and as Third-World nations have become more capable of training their own personnel and planning their own growth.

Beginning in the 16th century, when Western colonization efforts began in earnest, Christian missionaries played a highly significant role in establishing educational institutions in the Americas, Africa, Asia, and the Pacific. Several centuries earlier, Arab traders had already begun traveling into North Africa and to South and Southeast Asia, carrying with them their Islamic educational traditions. As a consequence, by the mid-20th century the educational institutions of the developing regions of the world were to a great extent modeled after European and North American school systems and, to a diminishing extent, after Islamic schools. Since World War II, Christian organizations have continued their efforts, often directing their attention at such neglected, remote regions as the Upper Amazon Basin of Brazil and Peru and the highlands of the island of New Guinea. Through the use of the airplane, radio, and television, religious groups have reached potential adherents who were heretofore inaccessible. Frequently the mission groups have combined medical services with their Christian religious endeavors. In recent times, Islamic educational efforts have also been expanded in Africa, Central Asia, and Southeast Asia, oftentimes funded by monies from oil-rich Arab states.

Consultants are people brought to a formal or nonformal educational project as experts in some aspect of education to offer advice and guidance about how to solve the problems that project personnel are facing. These experts may be permanent employees of the foreign-aid groups described above. But often they are university professors, school administrators, teachers, architects, publishing specialists, computer experts, economists, and the like who have been hired only temporarily by an aid agency or by a developing nation on a short-term assignment to help with an educational project. Effective consultants typically depend heavily on information from comparative-education studies.

Students and faculty members of colleges and universities form another very active group of comparative-education consumers. Their motives are generally of two types. The first type is a general-education or liberal-education goal —to learn more about the educational world and how it operates. The second is a vocational and social-service goal —to learn what forces influence the conduct of education in different societies, and to develop skills that will be of use in promoting the progress of education in those societies. Since World War II, many higher-education institutions in a variety of nations have created degree-granting programs in comparative and international education. Graduates of these programs have become specialists to serve as consultants in the solution of educational problems around the world, to assume positions in foreign-aid agencies, or to occupy permanent posts in ministries of education or in universities. Oftentimes educators from developing nations are sent by their governments to pursue comparative- education studies in Europe, North America, Japan, Australia, and New Zealand so as to improve their knowledge of possible solutions to schooling problems their own countries face.

Business and industrial firms that conduct operations overseas are also interested in comparative education. They wish to know the type and quality of schooling in foreign lands so they can estimate (1) the kinds of skills they can find among employees they would like to hire in the foreign country, (2) the types of training they would need to provide for employees, (3) the kinds of schooling available abroad for the children of the employees their company sends to work overseas, and (4) the general level of education of the foreign country's population, so they can successfully advertise the products they wish to sell.

Finally, there are members of the general public who enjoy accounts of education in various parts of the world. Frequently their desire to read an article or see a television program about schooling is motivated simply by curiosity, an urge to discover how people in different societies gain their skills and knowledge. In other cases, members of the public are seeking to meet a more specific need —to improve their own learning techniques, to select a proper school for their children, to discover efficient ways to teach their children, or to know how to cast a well-informed vote in an upcoming school-board election.

A special segment of the general public is a nation's primary and secondary-school pupils and undergraduate college students. They become consumers of comparative education when they learn about schools in other lands in their study of how people live in different nations, a type of study often called global education.

In summary, comparative education today has a large and variegated audience.

WHO PRODUCES THE LITERATURE OF COMPARATIVE EDUCATION?

Most of the groups that consume comparative-education literature also produce it. However, only a small number within each group function as producers. Furthermore, the groups of producers are not mutually exclusive. A college professor who writes books on education in foreign societies may also serve periodically as a consultant to those societies under the sponsorship of an international-aid organization. Or, an official from a developing nation's ministry of education may be sent abroad to enroll as a graduate student in a foreign university's comparative-education department to conduct research on a problem the ministry faces.

The greatest portion of the literature is created in university settings, principally as masters-degree and doctoral theses, or as journal articles and books written by professors, oftentimes in collaboration with advanced graduate students. Such studies are often small-scale investigations that can be conducted at relatively low cost and with a limited number of participants. The diversity of these studies, in terms of subject-matter and research methods, is very great indeed. They include biographies of important educators, chronicles of a nation's educational development, reports of school drop-out rates, studies of classroom teaching methods, descriptions of ways schools are financed, analyses of the interactions between education and politics, accounts of the competition between private and public education, analyses of the effect of ethnic background on youths' educational opportunities, and far more.

Large-scale investigations that require the cooperation of many school systems, as well as substantial quantities of money, are most frequently conducted under the aegis of one or more governments, of such international agencies as UNESCO or the World Bank, or of a wealthy philanthropic foundation. Sometimes several of these bodies cooperate in sponsoring research. This has been the case of the cross-national studies produced by the International Association for the Evaluation of Educational Achievement (IEA). The body is comprised of major research institutions in more than 40 nations that carry out multinational educational research. Money to support the association's work is furnished both by individual governments and by philanthropic foundations. The people who design and conduct the studies are drawn from the member nations' research centers, ministries of education, universities, international-aid organizations, and the teachers and administrators of elementary and secondary schools.

In conclusion, comparative and international education over the past four decades has become an increasingly important field of scholarly inquiry, with the products of this scholarship guiding educational practitioners' efforts to offer suitable learning opportunities to the world's growing population.

With this overview of the general state of comparative education as a background, we turn now to the contents of the remainder of this book.

THE NATURE OF THIS BOOK

The issues referred to in the book's title are of two types —substantive and methodological. Substantive issues are questions about which ways of solving educational problems or pursuing educational goals are the best. For instance, is it better to finance schools from taxes assessed to the general public or through fees charged to those who attend the schools? Are students better prepared to lead productive lives if they study classical languages than if they take courses in vocational skills? Should everyone be required to complete at least nine years of general education? Should all schools throughout a nation follow the same course of study? Is centralized school administration better than decentralized administration? What kinds of educational research are most useful? In classroom teaching, is an illustrated lecture superior to a reading assignment in a textbook? And the list of such questions goes on and on.

In contrast to substantive issues are those of methods, with the term *methods* referring to the techniques used by researchers to investigate substantive questions. The types of methods applied in comparative and international studies are quite varied. They are often identified by such adjectives as historical, correlational, descriptive, evaluative, and others, or by such nouns as hermeneutics, dependency theory, conflict theory, and more. The matter of methods becomes an issue when a researcher addresses a substantive question and then asks, "Which techniques of investigation should I use to discover the best answer to that question?"

The three-fold aim of this book is (1) to describe a variety of key substantive questions faced by the world's education systems, (2) to consider alternative answers to these questions, and (3) to identify advantages and disadvantages of different methods for investigating the questions.

Each chapter, 2 through 10, centers on a broad substantive question and on a diversity of subquestions that fall under that broad issue. In the description of a chapter's substantive questions, the author illustrates the form which each issue has assumed in particular education systems throughout the world. Therefore, Chapters 2 through 10 not only identify important educational issues, they also provide a host of information about educational problems and attempted solutions in diverse societies. Woven throughout the discussion of substantive issues are analyses of the advantages and disadvantages of investigative methods that can be applied to these issues. Finally, each chapter closes with the author's speculation about the future prospects for the substantive questions and for the investigative methods encompassed by that chapter. Chapter 11, on the other hand, is dedicated primarily to methodological issues.

As a preparation for the rest of the book, the remainder of this introductory chapter offers an overview of perspectives in comparative education.

PERSPECTIVES IN INTERNATIONAL COMPARATIVE STUDIES

Anyone who conducts a comparative-education study does so from a particular point of view, with the point of view different for each type of investigation. It's as if in each new study, the researcher dons a fresh pair of spectacles whose lenses blot out insignificant parts of the landscape and reveal only those features pertinent to the question at hand. Various labels may be used to identify such a point of view —perspective, organizing scheme, plan, approach, paradigm, structure, working outline, or others. When such a viewpoint is organized in a particularly clear fashion, with its elements well integrated, it may be referred to as a formal theory or formal model.

The researcher's point of view can be stated in either a very general and vague fashion or in a manner quite precise and detailed. In its initial vague form it may be only a general topic ["Hungarian vocational education" or "Social class influence on access to secondary education in Sub-Saharan Africa"] or a broad question ["How is language related to schooling in Sri Lanka?" or "How is education financed in East Asian societies?"]. However, it is obvious that before data can be collected and presented in a way that makes sense, the initial vague notion must be amplified into a sequence of subtopics or subquestions that represent an organizing scheme or detailed investigative model. Some researchers lack such a detailed conception at the outset of their study, so they must intuitively evolve a structure as they browse through information related to the topic or as they begin to write their article or report. At the opposite end of the scale of precision, other investigators devise a detailed theoretical structure at the start, then search for the data needed to settle the issues posed in the theory. Still other scholars fall somewhere between these extremes of vagueness and specificity. Reading an author's book or article may not show in which of these ways he or she approached the task, but it does reveal the form that the author's point of view ultimately assumed. In the following paragraphs we consider some of the ways such organizing schemes or theoretical positions can be analyzed and described.

One way to portray the viewpoint represented in a study is to identify it with a label reflecting the author's apparent central purpose. For instance, the term *descriptive study* can be applied to a work that does no more than delineate the components of an educational operation and the connections among the components ["The Organizational Structure of Nonformal Education in Central America" or "Methods of Teaching Science in Yugoslavia" or "A Chronicle of Finnish Higher Education"].

The phrase *analytical study* can be used to identify a work in which the author not only describes components of an educational operation but also seeks to specify cause-and-effect relations, that is, to estimate why the operation functions as it does ["The Influence of Political Groups on Schooling in Zaire and Zambia" or "Educational Residues of Colonialism in the Pacific Islands" or "The Effects of Economic Trends on Private School Enrollment in Britain"]. The terms *interpretive* and *explanatory* may be used to mean much the same as analytical whenever an author attempts to demonstrate relationships not recognized before ["Linking von Humboldt's and Dewey's Theories to West German Schooling" or "Motivational Factors in Japanese Education"].

In an *evaluative study* the investigator assesses how well an educational operation has functioned —its strengths and weaknesses or how close it has come to achieving its goals ["Students' Mathematics Achievement in 14 Nations" or "Administrative Efficiency —A Comparison of Four European Countries"]. Evaluative studies typically include both descriptive and analytical material as the researcher first describes the educational operation, next assesses it, and then estimates what factors have caused the outcomes that were revealed in the assessment.

A *predictive study* usually involves description, an analysis of causal factors, and the assessment of past and present trends as it proposes what is likely to occur in the future ["Prospects for Universal Primary Schooling in the People's Republic of China" or "The Expected Impact of Oil-Price Changes on Educational Expansion in Arab States"].

A *planning model* is an organizational scheme specifying the significant elements of an intended educational operation. The scheme usually estimates the expected effects that these elements exert on each other, and it suggests a sequence of steps for bringing the envisioned innovation to reality. Planning models often begin with a description and evaluation of current and past conditions as a rationale for why such a plan is being proposed ["Designing Literacy Programs in Developing Nations" or "A Method of Determining Children's Vocabulary Command in the National Language"].

Still a different way to characterize studies is in terms of the theoretical stance the author has adopted for interpreting the events on which the study focuses (Altbach, Arnove, & Kelly, 1982; Kazamias & Schwartz, 1977) . The array of theories described in the following paragraphs illustrates some of the approaches which writers on comparative and international topics have used. Additional theoretical positions are found throughout the rest of this book. The types described below can be identified by the labels historical, structural-functional, correspondence, legitimation, conflict, world-systems, dependency/imperialism, liberation, problem-oriented, development, modernization, social-change, and human-capital or human-resource production.

An *historical analysis* can involve inspecting an educational operation during different eras ["The French Ministry of Education: Its Evolution Since Napoleon's Time" or "Elements of Ancient Tradition in Taiwan's Civil Service Examinations"]. Advocates of an historical approach state that its principal advantage is its ability to account for the way unique factors in a given society have converged to produce the educational outcomes that are specific to that society. But critics charge that historical studies fail to produce significant general principles of educational development that are applicable to a variety of cultures. In effect, they claim that historical research is too particularistic. However, defenders of the approach contend that hypotheses about general principles can emerge from an historical analysis of a single education system, and then the hypotheses can be tested in other societies for their general applicability. Furthermore, a comparative dimension is produced when several countries are studied simultaneously ["Parting Company —Divergent Ethnic-Education Policies in Malaysia and Singapore Since 1963" or "The Status of Koran Schools in Egypt, Iran, Nigeria, and Pakistan —1890 and 1990"]. Not only may research be entirely historical, but frequently a detailed report of present conditions in an education system is prefaced by a brief historical introduction to provide the reader a background against which to place the educational operation's current state, even though the title of the piece does not suggest that an historical perspective is included ["Computers in Canada's Primary Grades" or "The Present-Day Influence of Priests in South American Schools"].

Structural-functional theory in the social sciences holds that a society has a given structure and has functions associated with this structure —a particular style of producing and consuming goods, established roles people play (including their place in a social-class system), and established institutions and values. The task of the education system is to perpetuate this structure. Thus, according to supporters of a structural-functional perspective, the kind of comparative research that is most enlightening consists of studies that clarify the way education supports the form of a society. From such cross-cultural research, scholars hope to abstract general principles that account for how and why different education systems operate as they do ["The School's Role in Limiting Social Mobility" or "Vocational versus Classical Education —The Manpower-Supply Controversy"]. Two of the criticisms directed at the structural-functional approach are that (1) it accounts more adequately for societal conservatism and stability than for societal change and (2) it has not explained adequately why daily teaching in the classroom goes on the way it does (Lundgren, 1985:1957-1962).

Correspondence theory is related to structuralism-functionalism in proposing that education and work (meaning occupations and the economic system) correspond in structure and content, and that the role of the education system is to maintain the existing social structure. In a Marxist version of correspondence theory, "the bureaucratic organization of schools parallels that found in business; the hierarchical relations among administrators, teachers, and students are similar to the social relations between managers and workers; the lack of control students have over their education and the alienation they often feel as a result reflect a similar lack of control and alienation that workers find in their adult economic lives; and the extrinsic rewards —grades, test scores— in schools, parallel the use of extrinsic rewards —wages— found in the workplace" (Rumberger, 1985: 1030). Studies conducted from a correspondence-theory viewpoint reflect researchers' belief that it is useful to compare educational operations with the world of work.

Studies conducted from a *legitimation perspective* are founded on the premise that a society's educational policies, school structures, and curricula are employed by those in power to convince the citizenry that the existing political system is the proper one and that the current office holders are the legitimate bearers of power ["Educational Research in Support of Political Actions —West Germany and the USA" or "The Image of Past and Present Regimes in Israel's History Textbooks"].

A *conflict-theory* concept of society contrasts with a structural-functionalist perspective in that it concentrates on divisions within the society, rather than on the mutually supportive aspects that functionalists analyze. From a conflict-theorist's vantage point, dissent and friction are not societal deviations but, rather, are normal conditions that contribute to change ["Social Class Competition for Admission to Colleges in Argentina and Bolivia" or "Women's Desires for Schooling in Asian Nations"]. Conflict theorists try to discover who belong to the groups that are in conflict, what the motives of the dissidents are, the strategies employed by the antagonists, and how successfully the attempts at resolution have been ["Student Demonstrations —Techniques, Objectives, and Results" or "Ethnic Groups in Political Office —Their Influence on Equality of Access to Schooling in Balkan States"].

A *world-systems viewpoint* proposes that the entire socioeconomic-political-cultural world should be considered in any effort to account for the overall condition of any modern-day society, including efforts to explain the operation of the society's educational institutions.

Dependency theory, as a version of world-systems analysis, was developed and diffused during the 1960s to explain how one society relates to others, so that some are at higher levels of socioeconomic development than others, and some must rely on others for their sustenance. One of the progenitors of dependency theory, particularly among Marxist writers, was the concept of imperialism, represented chiefly in the colonial control of most of Africa, Asia, and the Pacific Islands by European and North American powers and by Japan prior to World War II. In Central and South America the imperialism was internal, with a small elite of European heritage controlling the economy and suppressing the culture of native peoples. Since World War II, as so many colonized peoples have attained political independence, their societies have been viewed by dependency theorists as still subservient to the former colonialists ["Neocolonialism in Southeast Asian Education Systems" or "Shadows of the Past —Dysfunctional Classical Education in India" or "Peddling Advanced Educational Technology to Third-World Nations"].

Liberation theory takes a "humanistic approach to questions of development. The underlying assumption is that members of the under-developed societies are oppressed by the powerholders of their own societies, who control the relevant economic resources such as land, industry, and wealth . . . [so] the main remedy for overcoming this oppression lies in the education of the oppressed to be aware of their condition. This practice is called 'conscientizacao' by the Brazilian educationist Paulo Freire" (Fagerlind & Saha, 1989: 25-26).

In a *problem-centered approach*, education is viewed from the standpoint of problems of concern in a society ["Church, State, and the Schools: Problems and Solutions in Western Europe" or "Educational Opportunity and Discontented Minorities in Pakistan and Afghanistan"].

When analyzing education systems from the vantage point of *social change*, scholars attempt to explain the forces that contribute to shifts in a society's form and operation and to specify how education is both influenced by the changes and contributes to them ["Schooling's Contribution to Revolution in the Dutch East Indies" or "Educational Residues of the Japanese Occupation of Korea"].

The word *development* designates one variety of social change. Development studies are intended to answer such questions as: What has been the role of education in determining the nation's socioeconomic, political, and cultural condition? In a nation's plans for the future, how can education contribute to progress, and how can the plans provide educational opportunities for individuals and groups to fulfill their ambitions? Whereas research from an historical or structural-functional viewpoint is intended to explain how and why educational institutions operate as they do, development studies reflect researchers' and planners' faith that institutions can be intentionally wielded as tools to change societies for the better. This faith in the ability of education to transform life is reflected in such phrases as "education is the key that unlocks the door to modernization" and "education is one of the universals in the development of individuals and nations" (Hanson & Brembeck, 1966: iii).

The term *modernization*, as a label for one form of development, identifies studies that focus on the role of education in nations' efforts to adopt increasingly complex forms of technology aimed at enhancing the production and distribution of goods and services. In effect, how does education contribute to, or detract from, the modernization process? ["Industrialization in Taiwan: The Route from School to Work" or "Unemployment Among the 'Over-Educated': India's College

Graduates"].

A *human-capital* or *human-resource* perception of education centers on issues of how education contributes to, or detracts from, individuals' economic productivity ["Cost-Benefit Results of Primary Schooling in Third-World Societies" or "Foregone Earnings —Arab Mothers' Absence from the Job Market"]. "The basic assumption of the notion that education is a form of investment in human capital is that education raises the productivity of workers and that the higher earnings of the educated reflect the value of their product" (Woodhall, 1985: 1503). Economists and political analysts are the types of scholars who most frequently conduct research from a human-capital, human-resource, or manpower-development point of view.

In summary, a variety of special terms have been created to reflect the perspectives that researchers may adopt as they analyze educational operations. It may be apparent that the several vantage points described above are only illustrative and do not nearly exhaust the positions from which either scholars or educational planners approach their task. Furthermore, it should be clear that none of the foregoing types is unrelated to the others. Frequently a single author will include several such vantage points in a given study.

RESEARCH METHODS

People who speak of *the* comparative method run the risk of misleading their listeners, because a wide range of different research methods are used in comparative studies, with each one appropriate for investigating particular types of questions. This point can be illustrated with a brief overview of representative research techniques and of typical titles of studies to which those techniques might be applied. The following sampling of approaches includes historical methods, hermeneutics, content analysis, survey research, correlational studies, experimental research, and ethnography.

The *historical perspective* mentioned in the foregoing section of this chapter leads to the use of historical research techniques. The most common of these techniques consists of inspecting written and printed materials (books, periodicals, newspapers, correspondence, legal documents) and drawing interpretations about what they mean in the evolution of educational operations ["Religious Content in 18th Century Primary-School Readers" or "Laws Governing Schooling in South Africa —1900-1930"]. Historical methods also include interviews with people who were participants in events of the past or with ones that at least were acquainted with those people, now gone, who took part in such events ["Supervising Colonial Schools in French Indochina" or "Teachers' Salary Negotiations During the Great Depression"]. In addition, progress in audiovisual-recording technology over the past century has provided historians with an expanded armory of resources —photographs, motion-picture films, phonograph records, audiotapes, videotapes, videodiscs, computer displays, and others. Furthermore, to investigate past events that are insufficiently represented in written or pictorial form, historians sometimes turn to archeological findings. However, for purposes of comparative education, the remnants of physical culture found in archeological digs are usually not of much use.

One issue faced in the conduct of historical investigations is that of deciding where the past ends and the present begins. In the most liberal interpretation of the word *history*, everything that has happened in the world prior to the present instant is historical. But for the practical purpose of distinguishing the methods of historical research from other methodologies (surveys, experiments, ethnographic studies), historians often choose a point in time for dividing the past from the present. For example, the most recent two or three decades may be regarded as "the present day," so anything that happened prior to this period is dubbed historical. Or the present century may be labeled "modern times" and prior centuries labeled "history."

As valuable as historical research can be for comparative education, the approach suffers from several limitations that can markedly affect the validity of conclusions drawn. Historians are the victims of the vagaries of time —of accidents, of wars, of changes in political systems, of social structures, and of the physical deterioration of written records that occurs with the passing years. When fire destroys the library of a medieval monastery, it may wipe out the last existing records of important events of the past. Victors in war can demolish the books and documents of the vanquished people, then rewrite the region's history in an effort to legitimatize their own right to rule the conquered territory. In societies with a low level of literacy, the written records passed on to succeeding generations are those composed by a select elite who tend to present a biased picture of the society, a picture that may not represent the way of life of the majority of the people. These sorts of influence affect the adequacy of the material that historians have for describing and interpreting educational happenings of the past. Two of the most common tests that practiced historians apply in estimating the accuracy of their material are those of multiple sources and of logical analysis. Multiple sources in this context means finding corroboration for an historical event in more than one place —in the writings of different authors of that period, in legal documents, in letters written by participants in the events, and the like. Logical analysis refers to the procedure of assembling a variety of reported events, then judging the likelihood that they would occur in the assembled pattern. "Is it reasonable to assume that event A would lead to event B and ultimately to C? Does that make good sense?" In this process of analysis, historians may draw several alternative interpretations, then compare the adequacy of the rationales supporting each of the options to arrive at the most likely interpretation.

An important tool in historical research is *hermeneutics* (pronounced her-meh-NOO-tics or her-meh-NYOO-tics). In its broadest sense, hermeneutics can be defined as the art or science of interpretation. But more specifically, it is increasingly being used in the field of education to mean a methodology for explaining the meaning of a document or of a collection of documents —books, newspaper accounts, journal articles, legal papers, personal correspondence, diaries, notebooks, school logs, and such. There are at least six ways this interpretive technique is currently being applied in educational research (Thomas, 1987). The first is to verify a document ("The Authenticity of Little-Known Biblical Texts"). The second is to recreate an author's system of values and assumptions ["The Sociopolitical Backgrounds of Mao Zedong's Educational Philosophy"]. The third is to promote precision of communication by means of the researcher's estimating as accurately as possible what the author of a given educational document was trying to explain to readers. In other words, the investigator attempts to make probability judgments about the author's intention ["Clarifying Ambiguities in Venezuelan Educational Law"].

A fourth function served by hermeneutics is that of establishing the socio-historical foundations of a document through answering two principal questions: (1) What were the factors in the original author's society that significantly influenced her purposes, style of presentation, and line of argument? (2) What societal factors at the time of the document's original publication would have influenced the interpretation which readers of that day might have placed on the work? ["Horace Mann's Purpose in Studying Prussian Schools" or "Popular Response to Comenius' Educational Reforms"]. A fifth use of hermeneutics is that of interpreting symbols, since authors not only may use individual words and phrases symbolically, but they sometimes speak in parables, describing an event or telling a tale whose meaning is not to be accepted literally but, rather, symbolically, as a representation of similar conditions at a different time or place ["Child-Raising Implications of Samoan Proverbs" or "The Boy Who Cried Wolf, and Other Advice to Administrators"]. A sixth application of hermeneutics is that of inspiring new educational ideas, such as by estimating ways that concepts or theories described in a document might be adapted to solving problems in a different educational setting than the original one ["Applying Piagetian Concepts in Korean Preschools" or "Freire's Version of Marxist Doctrine in Brazil and Chile"].

A further technique applied both in historical studies and in certain forms of contemporary research is *content analysis*. This method consists of inspecting written or broadcast material to determine how the material bears on questions of concern to the investigator ["How Ethnic Minorities Are Represented in School Textbooks —France, Spain, and Italy" or "Intimations of Rousseau's Emile in Modern Teacher-Education Curricula"]. A typical way of performing content analysis is for the researcher to prepare a list of questions to be answered, then to read selected documents —law books, school books, newspaper accounts, journal articles, minutes of meetings— to learn what answers are provided in the materials. Or the objects of inspection may not be printed documents but, instead, may be speeches, films, television or radio programs, videotapes, or audiotapes. Content analysis can be exclusively qualitative, with the investigator seeking only to learn if a particular topic or opinion has appeared someplace in the material ["References to Enemies in European History Books" or "The Moral Nature of Children in Hindu Tradition"]. Or it may also be quantitative, so that the investigator tabulates how frequently different topics are mentioned or attitudes are revealed in the material ["The Incidence of Violence in Children's TV Fare" or "References to Royalty in Pre- and Post-Revolution Soviet Texts"].

Survey research, in contrast to historical methods, involves an investigator collecting information from members of a presently existing group —such as teachers, parents, students, school administrators, or textbook writers— and analyzing the results in order to clarify some educational issue ["Peer Teaching Practices in an Israeli Kibbutz" or "Student-Admission Standards in 10 South--Central Asian Universities" or "Nonformal Vocational-Education Programs in Scandinavia"]. Most surveys do not reach all members of the intended group. Instead, they sample only a portion of the members and, on the basis of the responses of that portion, estimate how accurately the sample results might represent the responses that would have been gathered from the entire group (the target population) if the entire group has been queried. In terms of purpose, there are two main types of surveys. One is to describe the way significant characteristics are distributed within the target population, such as levels of literacy in a nation, years of schooling among factory workers, languages spoken by immigrants, drop-out rates in secondary schools, or the frequency of use of microcomputers in three nations' primary-school classrooms. The other purpose is to examine relationships among various factors in an effort to explain likenesses and differences among people or institutions in the target population. Examples of such *correlational studies* are surveys that focus on such relationships as the linkage between achievement in mathematics and time spent on homework, between families' socioeconomic status and students' success in secondary school, between a college's library holdings and its reputation in the academic world, or between the amount of money spent on schools and students' scores on standardized achievement tests. As Rosier has proposed:

> Sometimes a researcher may wish to fulfill both purposes in a single survey: for example, in evaluating an innovative educational programme, the researcher may wish to describe characteristics of students and teachers and levels of student achievement (the descriptive purpose), and also to examine the ways in which these characteristics are related to achievement (the explanatory purpose). Such a dual-purpose survey is valid, and may be less expensive than conducting two separate studies. However, the structure of the survey may be

more complicated, especially in terms of sampling designs and analyses. An efficient sample used to provide descriptive characteristics of a population (population parameters) may not be as efficient for estimating the strength of the relationships in an explanatory model (Rosier, 1985: 4942) .

The kinds of research devices employed in surveys include questionnaires, opinionnaires, interviews, tests, attitude scales, check lists, and rating scales. A survey may also be made of documents, such as of education laws or financial statements, with the results tabulated as lists or charts showing the frequency of selected characteristics.

Experimental research is a term applied to studies in which an effort is made to control certain variables so that the amount of effect exerted by one or a few other variables on an educational outcome can be estimated with some degree of precision. A variety of research designs have been created to accomplish this purpose, with each design suited to the conditions of particular experimental situations. For example, a two-group pretest/post-test design could be used for estimating the effect of a computer program compared to a textbook for teaching German-language reading skills. In such a design, all students will take a reading pretest in German. Then pairs of students with similar scores are divided, with one of each pair assigned to the computer-program group and the other assigned to the textbook group. As a consequence, the two groups are assumed to be alike in reading skill at the outset of the experiment. Then, for a period of time the students in the first group study German by means of programs on microcomputers, while those in the second group study the same material in a textbook. The two different modes of instruction are often referred to as the treatments. After the period of study, both groups are post-tested with a test similar in content to that of the pretest. Then pretest and post-test scores are compared to reveal how much the groups' reading skills changed during the treatment period. Conclusions are thereby drawn about the comparative effectiveness of the two treatments for promoting German reading competence among these kinds of students. Not only can judgments be made about how effective each mode of study seemed to be for each group (by comparing the average amounts the two groups gained), but conclusions can also be reached about how effective each mode was for particular students (by comparing the change between any given student's pretest and post-test scores). A further comparative dimension could be added to such a study by extending the experiment to include additional samples of learners, such as students whose home language is English compared to ones whose home language is Spanish.

In the foregoing example, the procedure of matching students on the basis of their pretest scores before assigning them to the two experimental treatments was applied in an attempt to control the influence of variables other than the two instructional methods. A more common way of accomplishing this same purpose is that of randomly assigning students to the different experimental treatments, on the assumption that extraneous factors (socioeconomic class, parents' levels of schooling, knowledge of other languages) which might influence the outcome of the experiment would be distributed rather evenly between the two groups so that these factors would have no more effect on the success of one group than on the success of the other.

Whereas the above example has centered attention on instructional media, experiments are conducted on a wide range of other variables as well —centralized versus decentralized administrative systems, classrooms with teacher-aides versus classrooms without aides, private versus public financing of schools, harsh versus lenient discipline, large versus small schools, "new math" versus "traditional math," and many more. And while our illustrative case of teaching German language has involved only one experimental variable (computers versus textbooks), many studies include two or more variables so as to reveal how they may interact to produce the educational outcome. For instance, we could study the interaction of age, gender, and science-instruction method (a discovery approach versus a lecture approach) by forming three age groups (10-year-olds, 13-year-olds, 16-year-olds), with each group divided further by gender and science-instruction treatment to make 12 subgroups whose success we would compare.

As suggested above, the main purpose of experimental methods is to provide a basis for estimating causes, that is, for proposing how much a given variable will affect an educational outcome. This purpose is fostered by the experimental design's ability to control certain factors so that the effect of one or a few others can be isolated for study. However, the conditions that obtain in many educational settings render the settings unsuitable for controlled experimentation. First, the desired controls often cannot be applied in the work-a-day world of the school, administrative system, or community, since the experiment would unduly disrupt normal operations. Second, the conclusions that can validly be drawn from an experiment may be limited to the particular group of students or the school system or culture on which the study focused. This is because certain influential variables present in that experimental setting are different in other settings, so generalizations derived from the study cannot, with any degree of confidence, be extended to other places. Third, controlling particular variables may cause the experimental conditions to differ so radically from the natural state of affairs that the results of the experiment are over-simplified, not representative of normal life in a classroom or administrative system.

Observation techniques are procedures researchers use for collecting information either in natural or in experimental settings ["Time-on-Task versus Wasted Time —Classroom Behavior in the United States and Japan" or "The Social Function of Teasing among Adolescents" or "Norwegian Pupils' Persistence with Difficult Problems"]. The investigator's task is to watch what goes on and to record the observations in a manner that permits accurate conclusions to be drawn about the question being studied. Two of the traditional problems with observation methodology are those of recording-efficiency and of intrusive-influence. The recording-efficiency problem is caused by the demands of the investigator's dual task of carefully observing the flow of events while, at the same time, taking accurate notes about what has transpired. One way researchers have sought to solve this problem has been to use more than one observer. When two investigators watch an event, anything missed by one may be noted by the other. In recent years the accuracy of the simultaneous observing-and-recording task has been advanced by the use of video-recording devices. When the sights and sounds of an event are captured on videotape, researchers can later review each scene time and again to ensure that the details are faithfully transcribed.

The intrusive-influence problem concerns the effect that an obvious observer may exert on an educational event. A researcher sitting in the back of a classroom may alter the behavior of both the teacher and the students so much that the happenings witnessed by the observer fail to reflect the way the class typically operates. One way to cope with this difficulty in a laboratory setting is to install a one-way-vision screen or mirror in the wall, so observers can view the scene from behind the mirror without disturbing the social atmosphere in the room where the activities are taking place.

A special type of observation methodology is called *ethnography*. It entails the use of participant-observer techniques traditionally employed by cultural and social anthropologists in their field studies of groups and communities. In an ethnographic study, the researcher attempts to (1) observe and faithfully record the behavior of individuals and their interactions within a delineated social setting —such as a classroom, a family, an educational administrative organization, or a community— and (2) interpret what these interactions mean for the culture of that group. Because ethnographic investigators are seeking to obtain an insider's perception of the social unit, they typically live as participants in the group for an extended period of time in an effort to achieve partial acculturation. Such participation is intended to equip them with tacit knowledge that can be combined with data gathered through interviews and documents so as to furnish a more accurate picture of life in the group than would be available to outsiders who collected data solely through tests, interviews, and questionnaires ["Indian Pupils' Experiences in Three Mexican Schools" or "Child-Rearing Methods and Rationales in a Ponape Village"]. Ethnographic methods are more qualitative than quantitative. They are naturalistic, in the sense of focusing on people who are pursuing their normal daily activities in their natural settings, in contrast to experimental studies which place people in controlled environments (Taft, 1985; Wilson, 1977).

It should be obvious that the research methods described above are not necessarily independent of each other. Frequently an investigator will employ several of the techniques at different points in a study. It may also be apparent that the foregoing descriptions have focused on only a few of the methods available for comparative and international-education studies. Further methods, and variations of those inspected above, are to be found throughout the rest of this book, and especially in Chapter 11.

ISSUES TO BE ANALYZED IN DETAIL

Following this introductory chapter, the remainder of this volume is devoted to a more detailed inspection of issues of special importance for the realm of comparative and international education. Every chapter elucidates a broad issue whose essence is initially reflected in a general topic question. Then, within the chapter the topic question is analyzed into constituent subissues as they have been manifest in educational systems throughout the world. To provide a suggestion of what the key issues will be, the following paragraphs offer a brief preview of the subject matter treated in each chapter, 2 through 12.

The chapters are organized under three sections. Section I, entitled *The Process of Instruction*, depicts the teaching-learning process as consisting of three stages —the identification of educational goals, the application of instructional methods and materials that enable learners to pursue the goals, and the assessment of how well the goals have been achieved. In keeping with this pattern, Chapter 2 (The Goals of Education) is designed to answer the topic question: How do different societies compare on their intended educational outcomes? Chapter 3 (Instructional Methods and Materials) addresses the issue of: How are decisions made about which teaching procedures are most appropriate? Chapter 4 (Evaluation and Examinations) answers the question: Why and how are educational outcomes assessed?

Section II, entitled *Educational Structures and Personnel*, concerns the way educational operations are administered, what organizational forms instruction can assume, and the sources of teachers for the schools. The topic questions for the three chapters comprising Section II are —Chapter 5 (Forms of Governance): How can the control and guidance of education be organized, and which of these modes are most suitable? Chapter 6 (Delivery Systems — Formal, Nonformal, Informal): In what forms is education offered, and which of these forms are the most desirable? Chapter 7 (Teacher-Supply Systems): How do school systems provide effective teachers?

Section III, bearing the title *Influences on Educational Operations*, focuses on four diverse factors that can affect the conduct of education. These factors may vary markedly from one society to another. Chapter 8 (Educational Equity in Cross-National Settings) treats issues at the core of controversy throughout the world about fairness and justice in the distribution of education: How do nations build educational bridges and dismantle educational barriers? Chapter 9 (Language and Education) analyzes problems concerning language as a tool in the teaching-learning process: How will the language —or languages— used in an educational setting influence the welfare of individuals and groups? Chapter 10 (The Economics of Education) focuses on the question: What key economic issues concern educational planners? Chapter 11 (Comparative Education Research) reviews the relationship between the study of education and the way education is managed: What are the methods and uses of comparative education research?

Finally, the volume closes with a summary chapter (Postscript —Into the Future) as an exercise in speculating about the upcoming decades, with the speculation based on observations about future population growth, treatment of the environment, and technological developments.

REFERENCES

Altbach, P. G., Arnove, R. F., & Kelly, G. P. (1982) *Comparative education.* New York: Macmillan.

Hanson, J. W., & Brembeck, C. S. (Eds.) (1966) *Education and the development of nations.* New York: Holt, Rinehart, and Winston.

Fagerlind, I., & Saha, L. J. (1989) *Education & national development* (2nd Ed.). Oxford: Pergamon.

Kazamias, A. M., & Schwartz, K. (1977) Intellectual and ideological perspectives in comparative education: an interpretation. *Comparative Education Review*, 21 (2-3): 153-176.

Lundgren, U. P. (1985) Frame factors and the teaching process. In T. Husen & T. N. Postlethwaite (Eds.), *International encyclopedia of education*, (Vol. 4, pp. 1957-1962). Oxford: Pergamon.

Postlethwaite, T. N. (1988) *Encyclopedia of comparative education and national systems of education.* Oxford: Pergamon.

Rosier, M. J. (1985) Survey research methods. In T. Husen & T. N. Postlethwaite (Eds.), *International encyclopedia of education*, (Vol. 8, pp. 4942-4948). Oxford: Pergamon.

Rumberger, R. W. (1985) Correspondence theory. In T. Husen & T. N. Postlethwaite (Eds.), *International encyclopedia of education*, (Vol. 2, pp.1030-1031). Oxford: Pergamon.

Taft, R. (1985) Ethnographic research methods. In T. Husen & T. N. Postlethwaite (Eds.), *International encyclopedia of education* (Vol. 3, pp. 1729-1733). Oxford: Pergamon.

Thomas, R. M. (1987) The advent of hermeneutics in educational parlance. *Perspectives in Education*, 3 (1): 5-14.

Wilson, S. (1977) The use of ethnographic techniques in educational research. *Review of Educational Research*, 47: 245-265.

Woodhall, M. (1985) Earnings and education. In T. Husen & T. N. Postlethwaite (Eds.), *International encyclopedia of education*, (Vol. 3, pp.1495-1505). Oxford: Pergamon.

SECTION I:

THE PROCESS OF INSTRUCTION

This section is comprised of three chapters, each representing a stage of the teaching-and-learning process. In a sense, instruction can be likened to phases of a journey. The first phase involves identifying a destination —"Where should we go?" In teaching, this is the stage of setting goals, as described in Chapter 2. The second phase involves choosing ways to reach the destination —"How can we best get there?" For the teacher, this means selecting instructional methods and materials, as analyzed in Chapter 3. The third phase consists of assessing progress —"How close have we come to the destination?" In the process of instruction, this is the stage of evaluation, as depicted in Chapter 4.

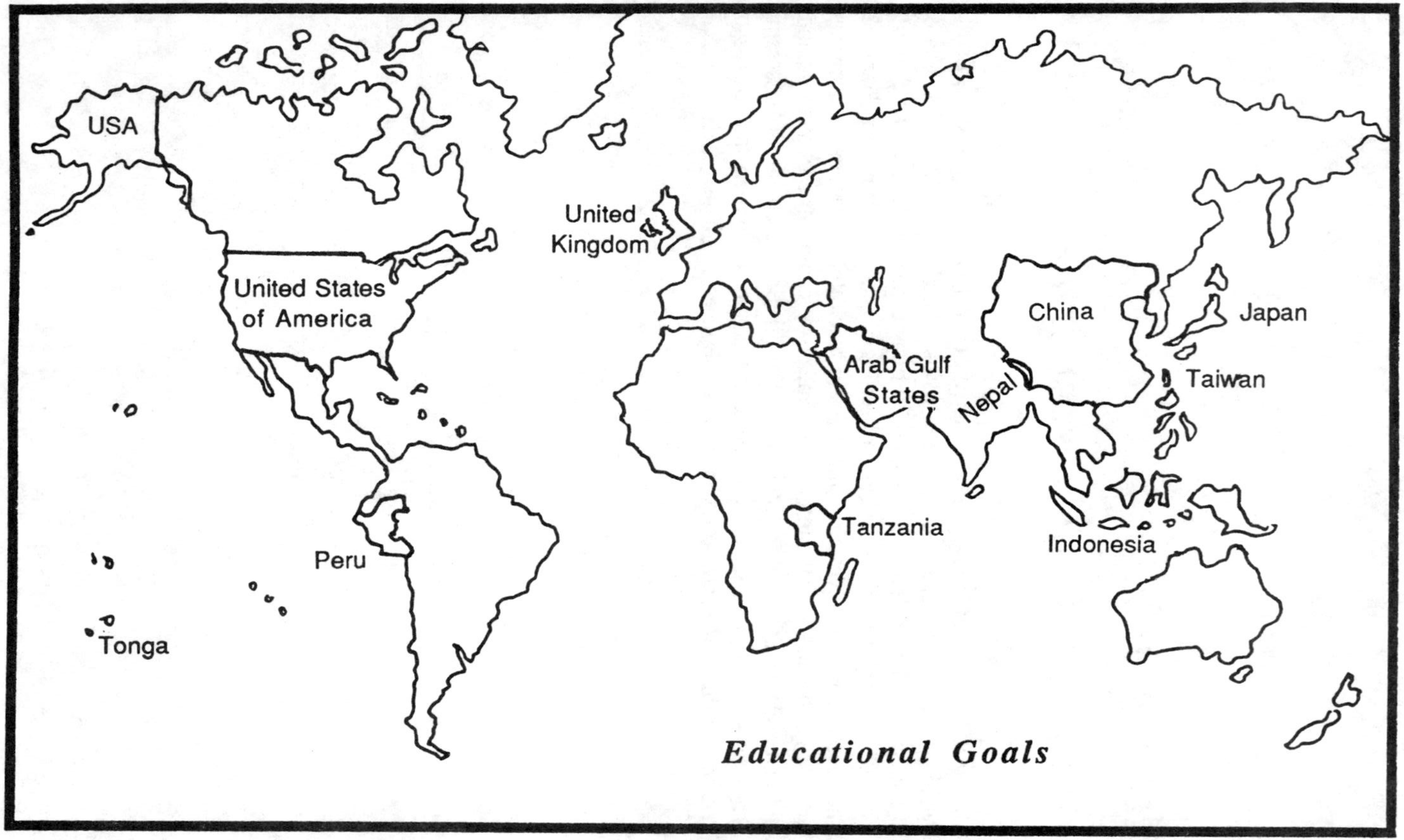

Educational Goals

CHAPTER 2

The Goals of Education

How do different societies compare in their intended educational outcomes?

R. MURRAY THOMAS

Over the years there has been considerable disagreement among educators about which labels are most suitable for identifying the results that education systems are expected to produce. The disputed labels include goals, aims, objectives, intended outcomes, ends, purposes, targets, functions, desires, and ambitions. Often the disagreements revolve around the matter of how general or how specific the speaker wants to be. For example, some people use *goals* or *aims* when referring to very general educational outcomes —"The goal of the schools is to graduate good citizens" or "The aim of education is to produce people who are well-informed problem-solvers." Then they reserve the term *objectives* to identify specific, detailed outcomes that would be the focus of a particular day's lesson or a particular homework assignment —"Accurately conjugating the Spanish verb *vivir* in present and past tenses" or "Locating Uruguay, Paraguay, Bolivia, and Chile on a world map." Because the distinctions drawn among such labels are founded on personal preference rather than logical necessity, throughout the following pages I avoid the debate by using the labels interchangeably as synonyms. Then, when it is appropriate to differentiate among types of intended outcomes, I append an adjective to the label to produce such phrases as general goals, daily-lesson aims, nationwide educational objectives, moral-education purposes, vocational-education targets, and the like.

This chapter does not simply aim to list the learning goals adopted in different nations. Rather, it aims to inspect issues relating to four questions about educational goals and to illustrate ways the issues have been addressed in representative societies around the world. The issues are connected with questions of (1) which agencies in a society assume the responsibility for achieving which goals, (2) what conditions may cause changes in goals, (3) how detailed instructional objectives may differ from one society to another, and (4) how decisions are reached about which learners pursue which goals.

WHICH SOCIETAL AGENCIES ARE RESPONSIBLE FOR WHICH EDUCATIONAL OUTCOMES?

For the purpose of comparing nations' educational systems, one useful way to categorize goals is in terms of seven aspects of human development on which a society's instructional institutions may focus. The goals are those of (1) producing good people (social/moral education), (2) preparing skilled communicators (basic education in reading, writing, speaking, listening, calculating), (3) developing well-informed people who understand the physical and social universe (liberal or general education), (4) promoting individuals' physical and mental health (health and safety education), (5) developing faithful supporters of the society (citizenship, civic, or political education), (6) producing efficient workers (vocational education), and (7) equipping individuals to realize their self-selected destinies (self-fulfillment education). In one way or another, every society intends to provide for all seven types. However, societies can differ on the specific objectives they choose to promote within each of these types. They also can differ in regard to which agencies are held responsible for which kinds of goals. In most nations, the principal agencies are the family, the neighborhood, the church, the formal school, community groups, apprenticeship programs, and such mass-communication media as television, radio, and the press.

The cases of Peru, the United States of America, and Nepal demonstrate ways that societies have dealt with the issue of which principal agencies furnish instruction in the several aspects of human development.

Peru

Peru is South America's third largest country in area and fourth largest in population, with an estimated 22 million inhabitants by 1990. The territory is divided into three parallel strips, north to south. The Andes mountains form the strip in the middle. West of the Andes is a dry coastal plain bordering the Pacific Ocean. East of the Andes is a dense lowland jungle around the headwaters of the Amazon River. The three regions differ not only in their climate, but also in the cultural, economic, and political complexion of their populations.

In terms of ethnic affiliation, Peruvian society is comprised of three particularly significant groups and a few minor ones. The major groups are referred to as *Indians, mestizos* (those of mixed Indian/Spanish heritage), and *criollos* (descendants of the original Spanish colonists). The minor ones are comprised of blacks and Asians. Figures on the percentage of the population in each of these categories are inconsistent, partly because of difficulty in determining what proportion of Indian-versus-Spanish genetic and cultural inheritance qualifies an inhabitant as mestizo rather than Indian or criollo.

Published estimates of the number of Indians range from 32 to 45% of the total population. Speculation about the mestizos places their number between 37 and 45% of the inhabitants. Criollos account for another 6 to 10%. Blacks and Asians are found in far smaller numbers (Krugmeier, 1985: 3848; *World almanac*, 1989: 707).

The Indians are descendants of the Incas whom the Spanish conquered in the 16th century. Most continue to live in villages distributed throughout the Andes. For a livelihood, they engage in herding and small-scale agriculture (potatoes, corn, barley, and the like) and speak traditional Quechua and Aymara dialects. The extensive jungle territory east of the Andes is sparsely settled, primarily by Indians living in isolated villages. Mestizos populate the larger cities on the Pacific Coast and towns of the mountain regions, where they engage in business, in trade, or in farming the more fertile plots. They normally speak Spanish and hold a higher position in the social-class structure than do the Indians. Criollos are found mainly in the urban areas along the coast. Like their Spanish ancestors, they maintain a position of wealth, political power, close in-group ties, and Spanish culture that keeps their group at the apex of the society's social-status structure. These differences among the three main ethnic groups significantly influence which agencies in the society assume responsibility for promoting the group members' progress toward our seven types of educational goals.

Economically Peru is one of the poorest nations in South America, with most of the labor force engaged in subsistence agriculture. Despite the country's financial constraints, the government has managed to furnish educational opportunities for a major portion of the school-age population, as well as for a growing number of adults. In the following overview of agencies that assume responsibility for the goals of our seven areas of human development, we begin with the formal schooling structure.

For nearly two decades, Peru's formal education system has operated under a plan inaugurated in 1972. According to the plan, official concern for children's development begins in early infancy as parents and their children are encouraged to become involved both formally and informally in the country's several thousand child-care centers and nursery schools. By the 1980s, around three-quarters of the centers were public and the rest private. The goals of programs during the first four years of the child's life are to detect learning disorders the children might suffer and to promote constructive nutritional, health, and social-environment practices in the home. After age four, children may enter a two-year kindergarten sequence that prepares them for entrance into the primary school (Krugmeier, 1985: 3849).

Formal basic schooling (*educaciòn bàsica*) is intended to be compulsory for children ages 6 through 15. It comprises three cycles, the first covering four years, the second two years, and the third three years. At each of these levels, the Ministry of Education prescribes general goals and guidelines for the fields of language, mathematics, social and natural sciences, art, physical education, religion, and manual arts. Within these guidelines, school personnel are expected to provide variations of specific instructional objectives to suit local conditions.

> The reformed curriculum follows more practical objectives than did the previous course of study, with the new goals including (a) the development of a critical conscience and a sense of self-reliance, (b) basic preparation in scientific, technological, and humanistic knowledge, (c) the development of an ability to perceive and take part in the transformation of Peruvian society, and (d) preparation for a useful occupation (Krugmeier, 1985: 3849).

Paralleling the basic school program attended by children and young adolescents is a series of evening courses that focus on the same basic goals but enroll youths and adults over age 15 who have not already completed the nine-year basic-education cycle. The government also operates a series of nonformal vocational-education centers that provide flexible curricula and encourage self-instruction and the formation of study groups. Private business and industrial organizations are likewise encouraged to sponsor vocational programs.

Beyond the nine years of basic education, high schools designed for professional preparation offer studies in basic skills and in one specialization as preparation for a particular occupation. Specializations include such fields as accounting, animal husbandry, auto mechanics, chemistry, electronics, mining, nursing, statistics, and textiles. Following high school, selected candidates may enter the university where they can earn a *licenciatur* degree after four years of successful study and *maestria* or *doctorado* degree after two or three additional years.

In summary, the formal schooling structure is intended to foster learners' progress in communication skills, knowledge of the physical and social world, health practices, citizenship, and occupational preparation. The goal of producing "good, moral people" is expected to be part of the citizenship and required religious classes of the schools. No self-fulfillment goal is listed as an explicit aim of education. But perhaps the formulators of the curriculum would assume that success in the other areas of development would be self-fulfilling.

The foregoing overview of Peru's schooling structure might suggest that the formal and nonformal education systems bear the chief responsibility for promoting Peruvians' progress in all of our seven aspects of human development. However, a closer inspection of Peruvian social structure demonstrates that such is not entirely the case.

The traditional culture of the Indians, the remote location of their villages, and their typical occupations have meant that informal instruction in the family and community has been far more important than formal schooling in fulfilling their needs. Until 1972, Spanish was the sole language of instruction in all schools. Pupils were not permitted to speak their native Quechua or Aymara, and there were no instructional materials in these dialects. By the 1960s, only 67% of the nation's inhabitants were Spanish speaking (Cowen & McLean, 1984: 762). The remaining 33% spoke Quechua or Aymara dialects. And while Spanish is more widely understood today, language continues to be a barrier to the schooling progress of a substantial portion of the Indian population. In an effort to remedy this situation, formulators of the social reforms of the early 1970s made Quechua and Aymara official national languages along with Spanish, and programs were initiated to produce instructional materials in these native tongues.

> [However,] despite a 1975 law mandating the rapid phasing in of Quechua or other appropriate primary languages of instruction in indigenous areas and their use as secondary languages in urban areas, Spanish remains the language of dominance in classrooms. Apart from experimental programs in isolated highland areas, the use of Quechua and Aymara appears to be limited to ad hoc judgments as to their need and appropriateness by individual teachers. Only in the experimental programs is such instruction accompanied by Quechua, Aymara, or other language-specific curricular materials and supported by teacher training programs (Nakamoto, White, & La Belle, 1985: 81).

As a consequence, among the Indians the family and neighborhood still bear the primary obligation to teach a large proportion of their population the communication skills, conceptions of the physical and social environment, handicrafts, and occupational skills that are of practical value in their daily lives.

In addition, two agencies — the home and the church— play a more significant role than the school in furthering the typical Indian's moral development. In religious affiliation, Peru is 90% Roman Catholic. In most localities the church continues to serve as an important source of moral education. The church also promotes a traditional Catholic conception of such matters as family planning and the proper basis of authority for resolving social issues.

To conclude, schools in Peru are intended to address most of the aspects of human development listed earlier. However, the nature of the curriculum, as it relates to people's everyday lives, means that schools perform this service far more adequately for the upper social classes (*criollos* and the *mestizos* who identify with Spanish culture) than they do for the indigenous peoples. The traditional Indian segment of the population continues to depend primarily on informal participation in family and community life for instruction in how to achieve goals of personal development. The church functions as one of the important community agencies.

The United States of America

Schooling in the United States, unlike schooling in most nations, does not operate under the direction of a central ministry of education which dictates learning objectives and curriculum content. Instead, each of the 50 states operates independently, establishing its own rules for the conduct of schools. Furthermore, within a given state, local communities retain at least partial control over what will be taught and the amount of time dedicated to various objectives. Yet, with all of this freedom of decision among regions and communities, there is substantial unanimity throughout the nation about which agencies in the society should be held responsible for which types of educational aims.

For instance, the entire population of U.S. American children and youth attend elementary and secondary schools that are expected to produce graduates highly literate in an American version of the English language, mathematically competent, well informed about the physical and social world, and faithful supporters of the U.S. form of democracy. It is assumed that in the process of attending school, students will also become "good" people by learning to respect and cooperate with others. However, no special classes are set aside for teaching moral behavior, and public schools are forbidden by national law from advocating religious beliefs. Therefore, the task of producing "good" people in a religious sense has been assigned chiefly to the home and the church. The goal of promoting physical and mental health is shared by the home and school, and to a lesser extent by such community institutions as social-service agencies. Responsibility for preparing workers with specific job skills is divided mainly among employers and schools of various types. A strong strain of individualism in U.S. American culture has meant that more emphasis is placed on the goal of self-fulfillment than in many nations. In other words, in the U.S. the choice of what goals learners will pursue, particularly at the secondary and post-secondary levels, is to a great extent left up to the individual learners. Opportunities for choices among diverse learning programs and for options within programs (elective classes) are usually rather generous.

So far, I have centered attention mainly on educational agencies which, by design or tradition, have intentionally been assigned instructional tasks. However, in recent times mass-communication media outside the control of education officials and parents have, without any real planning, assumed a major educational role. Television has become the most influential of these media, with newspapers, radio, and magazines assuming subordinate functions. Only a small portion of U.S. television programs have been created to provide instruction. By far the greatest number have been designed to entertain and to sell commercial products. However, the effect of such broadcasts has extended far beyond the purposes of entertaining and selling, since the programs' content —either intentionally or unwittingly— can influence what the viewing audience comes to believe about the nature of the physical world, the operation of societies, peoples' ideals and ambitions, and what kinds of behavior are proper. In effect, mass-communication media in the United States produce important learning outcomes, some of them desired and some not. Although the mass communication media also influence people's knowledge and attitudes in such countries as Peru, the far higher percentage of the population owning television receivers in the United States results in that medium's impact being greater than in societies with a lower incidence of television viewing.

In conclusion, the means by which people in the United States seek to achieve the seven categories of learning goals described earlier include a combination of the formal school system, the home, the church, employment sites, and mass-communication media. Which agencies in U.S. American society contribute to the pursuit of various types of learning outcomes is determined by a combination of (a) conscious planning on the part of political leaders, parents, and educational personnel, (b) tradition, (c) individuals' preferences, and (d) such societal functions as entertaining the populace or selling products, functions which do not have constructive learning goals as their central purpose but which inadvertently alter people's knowledge, skills, and values.

Nepal

The Kingdom of Nepal is located in the Himalayan mountains between India and China. The population of nearly 19 million is divided among such diverse tribal groups as the Bhote, Brahmin, Gurkha, Gurung, Limbu, Magar, Maithili, Muslim, Thakuri, and Tharu, all of them descendants of migrants from India, Tibet, and Central Asia. The nation's official language is an Indic tongue called Nepali, which is the basic medium of instruction, while English is studied in secondary schools. Twelve other languages are also spoken in different sections of the country. Over 88% of the work force is engaged in agriculture, with the chief crops being jute, rice, and grain. In religious affiliation, the populace is Hindu (90%), Buddhist (6%) Muslim (3%), and Christian (1%) (*Europa year book*, 1988: 1924; *World almanac*, 1989: 701).

To identify which agencies in Nepalese society assume responsibility for promoting the seven goals of human development, we can first consider the place of the present-day formal education system. Primary schooling lasts five years, lower-secondary two years, and upper-secondary three years, followed by three to six years of vocational training or general college studies. The official aim of the primary school, as found in the country's national socioeconomic development plans, is to teach reading, writing, and arithmetic and to inculcate habits of disciplined and hygienic living. Lower-secondary education stresses character formation, a sense of the dignity of labor, and habits of perseverance. Upper-secondary education prepares students to enter higher education. The stated purpose of tertiary education is to produce the personnel required for national development (*The sixth plan*, 1981). Thus, the schools have been assigned the task of fostering moral, communication, health, civic, and certain vocational outcomes. Furthermore, for adults the government has sponsored six-month functional-literacy courses whose goals focus on agriculture, nutrition, family planning, health, and personal hygiene. However, if schooling is to accomplish its assigned aims for the entire population, it is necessary that everyone regularly attend school, at least through the primary grades. A review of formal-education trends over the past four decades can suggest how likely this has been the case.

Nepal is one of the world's most recently modernizing societies. Planned socioeconomic development did not begin until the 1950s. Since that time, marked advances have been recorded in education. For example, in 1950 there were only 320 primary schools and 11 secondary schools. By 1980, primary schools had increased to 10,120 and secondary schools to 785. As a result, the estimated national literacy rate of 1% in 1950 had reached 24% by 1980 and 29% by 1989 (Shrestha, *et al.*, 1986: 509; *World almanac*, 1989: 701). Despite this dramatic progress, there remain significant shortcomings in consistent school attendance among the school-age population and in the growth of literacy among adults. Although enrollment in primary schools in the latter 1980s was reported at 79% of the age group and in secondary schools at 22%, attendance among those who were enrolled was often erratic, and the school drop-out rate was high (Kasaju, Pande, & Matheson, 1985: 3500).

> [Thus] the problems of an abbreviated education in childhood and a resulting illiteracy in adulthood remain massive and resist ready solution. Of men aged 15-49 in 1980, only 40% had ever attended a primary school, and of women the same age range, only 9 percent had ever been enrolled. Furthermore, even though the relative number of nonliterates has been declining, the absolute number has actually been increasing. Because of the steadily expanding Nepalese population (with a growth rate near 2.7% per year), the number of illiterates in the country has been expanding even as the illiteracy rate has been shrinking. Thus in 1951 the nonliterate population numbered 7.8 million, and by 1981 it had reached 11.3 million (Shrestha, *et al.*, 1986:510).

School attendance and literacy are lowest within three segments of the population —women, the poor, and people living in remote mountainous regions. A study conducted in 1979 showed that among children aged 6-15, 63% of the boys were enrolled in school as compared to 23% of the girls, a discrepancy reflecting a widespread cultural attitude about the comparative value of the two sexes. The rural population is widely dispersed across terrain "that may be the most rugged in the world...and many children must walk 1-2 hours, often traversing hazardous hillside paths, to reach their classroom" (Shrestha, *et al.*, 1986: 511-512).

In effect, a large portion of the populace receives little or no formal education. Consequently, agencies other than the school assume the responsibility for fostering individuals' progress in our seven categories of human development. The most significant of these agencies is the family. From family members children learn to speak their mother tongue, to abide by moral rules, to adopt habits of hygiene and nutrition, and to understand the physical and social world around them. But because so many of the parents are illiterate, children's command of the language is limited to speaking, a limitation that is a significant handicap in a modernizing society. Since so many Nepalese are employed in agriculture, most youths' training for a vocation is also acquired informally from the family as the young labor beside their parents in the fields.

The agency second to the family is the community, where children learn from their peers and from the elders who serve as models and supervise the behavior of the young. This informal family and community instruction includes a body of belief derived from a deep-seated Hindu-Buddhist tradition which promotes a world view that in many ways conflicts with the democratic social-egalitarianism and the science taught in the formal school. Although the Hindu caste system was officially outlawed in 1963, the convictions underlying a centuries-old social-caste structure are not readily dispelled by government fiat. Caste prejudices persist. Furthermore, the cause-and-effect logic of secular science runs contrary to a Hindu lore that accounts for events in the world of nature by how well people perform rituals intended to placate the gods (Thomas, 1988).

To summarize, not only do agencies other than the school assume responsibility for promoting many Nepalese children's growth in the seven areas of development, but the specific content and objectives toward which instruction is directed in each of these areas can differ significantly from what is taught in school.

WHAT CONDITIONS ALTER THE SELECTION OF EDUCATIONAL GOALS?

A further way societies differ is in how, when, and why they change their educational aims. One important source of goal-change is a shift in the political control of a society. Such a shift can be precipitated by various events, including a foreign military force conquering the country, an armed revolution within the society, or the election of a new government to power. Goal-change can also derive from an economic crisis that calls for new priorities in educational investment, from the peaceful immigration of large quantities of foreigners, from the popularization of a new educational philosophy, or from technological innovations that require new skills on the part of the nation's work force. In addition, a change in goals can result from social demand, as when an influential group in the society seeks educational opportunities to pursue ends the group's members wish to reach. The issue of which forces can be held responsible for altering educational aims is illustrated in the cases of Japan, Tanzania, Arab states bordering the Arabian (Persian) Gulf, and the People's Republic of China.

Japan

Over the past century and a half, two major changes in Japan's educational goals have been precipitated by invasions of Western nations' military forces. The first and most dramatic event came in the mid-19th century when Japan's policy of strict political, commercial, and cultural isolationism was broken by insistent Western intrusions that brought an end to the Tokugawa era (1603-1867) and inaugurated the Meiji period. The second major shift in educational aims came nearly a century later when Japan's defeat at the close of World War II led to the occupation of the country by an interim U.S. military government which ordered revisions in school curricula. In the decades between these two external obtrusions into the country's affairs, Japanese leaders directed schooling outcomes toward strengthening their people's national identity and their society's industrial and military capabilities. The sociopolitical settings in which these changes occurred is reviewed briefly in the following paragraphs.

For more than two centuries prior to the mid-1800s, Japan was governed under a feudal system, with a ruling shogun and his samurai warriors comprising about 6 percent of the population, and commoners the remaining 94 percent. Separate schools were conducted for sons of rulers and sons of commoners, while daughters were kept at home to learn domestic skills. Schools for the ruling samurai class taught Chinese Confucian literature, calligraphy, history, self-discipline, and the martial arts. Schools and apprenticeship programs for commoners taught reading, writing, calculating with an abacus, moral precepts for the common man, and suggestions for daily conversation. Although formal education was moderately widespread, it was far from universal (*Japan's modern educational system*, 1980: 4-8).

The inability of the last Tokugawa shogunate to repulse the thrust of Western military and commercial interests caused a political crisis in the 1860s, resulting in the end of Tokugawa rule and the beginning of the Meiji period. In 1867 the emperor was restored as the head of government, and the new leadership sought help from the West in renovating Japan's military, commercial, and educational establishments. Radical educational reforms were instituted on the recommendation of a commission which founded its proposals on detailed studies of the education systems of Europe and North America. The Meiji government announced that the function of the schools would no longer be to further Confucian scholarship, but rather to impart practical knowledge and develop talent. The educational plan included providing universal primary schooling for boys and girls and expanding opportunities in secondary and tertiary institutions. By the mid-1880s, 46% of primary-age children were in school. By 1906 this figure had risen to 97% and by 1916 to 99% (*Japan's modern educational system*, 1980: 464-465).

Throughout these years, a growing spirit of national pride and ambition became evident among Japan's educational aims. An Imperial Rescript on Education issued in 1890 identified the development of national identity as a prime goal of education. A Royal Message on the Enhancement of National Spirit in 1923 urged the creation of a vigorous spirit of national glory, of prosperity founded on industrial production, and of strong soldiers.

By the 1920s, the elementary-school curriculum included Japanese language, arithmetic, geography, moral development, drawing, singing, physical education, and handicrafts, plus sewing for girls. By the 1930s greater stress was placed in secondary schools on citizenship and vocational training, with the addition of compulsory classes in "civic virtue" and industrial arts at each grade level, and military training became required. It was apparent that the education system was being viewed as an essential instrument for achieving the political aim of military leaders who now dominated government policy. Their purpose was to construct a Greater East Asia Coprosperity Sphere, uniting all territories from Korea in the north to Indonesia in the south to form an immense commercial empire under Japanese rule.

The dream of the Coprosperity Sphere ended with the defeat of Japan at the close of World War II, when the U.S. American military took control of the government.

> The Allies hoped that Japan would be transformed into not only a peace-loving nation, but also into a democratic state, for it was believed that a democratized Japan would contribute to international order. Thus, the occupation became one of the most enormous experiments in "social engineering" ever conducted in any nation.... A new constitution was written, which in many respects was more liberal than the American Constitution. Article 23 simply read, "Academic freedom is guaranteed." Women were given the franchise, and were to have other rights equal to those of men. The constitution drastically altered the position of the Emperor and created a new governmental system that was intended to be more responsive to the populace. War was renounced as an instrument of national policy, and the creation of military forces was forbidden (Kobayashi, 1968: 93-94).

As for educational goals, the occupation government required the elimination of militaristic topics and the suspension of moral courses which were judged by the Americans as too nationalistic. A new emphasis was placed on teaching skills deemed vital for citizens to participate fully in a democratic society —skills of problem-solving, of cooperating in group efforts, and of communicating with each other.

However, with the termination of the occupation in 1952, Japanese policy-makers began to reinstitute certain learning goals the Americans had removed.

The most significant were the ones that traditionally formed the core of the schools' required class in ethics, morality, and national pride. By the early 1960s a one-hour-a-week moral-conduct course was required in all compulsory schools, guided by a Ministry-of-Education manual of essays and stories emphasizing moral qualities. Many intellectuals and leftists:

> viewed the events with alarm and criticized the move of the Ministry as another step backwards into Japan's ultra-right past when morals had been a course that aimed to indoctrinate youth into chauvinistic and authoritarian values. Most Japanese, however, did not share the fear and, on the contrary, appeared to feel that Japanese youth needed greater aid from the schools in developing stronger characters. They also saw the need for the schools to aid in reversing the rising trend of juvenile delinquency (Kobayashi 1968: 112).

In conclusion, the Japanese case depicts a society which in the mid-19th century voluntarily imported educational objectives from the West so as to enhance the process of industrialization. Then in the early 20th century, political leaders placed increasing emphasis on goals of patriotism and of aggressive national self-interest. Military defeat in World War II forced uninvited changes in both the Japanese system of government and its educational institutions, changes that included altering certain educational aims. With the end of American military occupation, some post-war innovations were retained, while others were altered. Among the most notable alterations was the reinstatement of compulsory classes in morality and national identity, reflecting educational ideals rooted in such deep-seated cultural values that they could not be erased by a few years of military occupation.

Tanzania

Prior to 1961, the territory occupied today by the East African nation of Tanzania contained the British colonies of Tanganyika and Zanzibar. In 1961 Tanganyika gained independence, as did Zanzibar two years later. When the pair united in 1964, they coined the name of Tanzania to reflect the merging of their earlier identities.

Tanzania provides an example of a nation's top political figure proposing drastic changes in the objectives and form of education in order "to create a socialist society which is based on three principles: equality and respect for human dignity; sharing of the resources which are produced by our efforts; work by everyone and exploitation by none" (Nyerere, 1967:5). The case also illustrates (1) the influence exerted by educational tradition and social demand on the fate of the plans devised to achieve such objectives and (2) the differing goals for the education system that can be held by different segments of society.

Tanganyika and Zanzibar had been under British rule for seven decades before gaining control over their own political destiny. Following independence, the visionary who charted the course for the country's future was its president, Julius K. Nyerere, a former teacher in Tanganyika's colonial school system. In a pamphlet entitled *Education for Self-Reliance* (1967), Nyerere announced a change in educational aims from stressing high-level skills for a selected minority to emphasizing basic education for the entire populace. Schools were to equip young people to function effectively as adults in their home villages so as to achieve a sense of self-reliance, to improve the leaders' communication with the citizenry, to build national unity, and to encourage popular participation in community development (Samoff, 1987: 339).

In President Nyerere's proposal, the schools were to play a dual role in regenerating society along the lines of an African family-oriented rural tradition. First was the social role, that of teaching pupils to live and work together for the common good. "This means that the educational system of Tanzania must emphasize cooperative endeavor, not individual advancement; it must stress concepts of equality and the responsibility to give service which goes with any special ability, whether it be in carpentry, in animal husbandry, or in academic pursuits.... Our education must therefore inculcate a sense of commitment to the total community and help the pupils to accept the values appropriate to our kind of future, not those appropriate to our colonial past" (Nyerere, 1967: 2, 7). Second was the vocational role:

> Particularly in the primary school, where the majority of children who go to school at all will be educated, the pupils should learn those vocational skills that will prepare them for their roles as better farmers in a predominantly agricultural society. Through the development of such skills at school, the farmers of the future will be able to contribute substantially to that improvement of agriculture which is at the heart of economic improvement through "self reliance" .... The social role of the school bears upon the attitude toward farming and the recognition of its importance for the future (Dodd, 1969: viii).

Primary education was to be universal, both as a human right and as an instrument for improving rural life (Gillette, 1978: 66). Secondary and higher education would be controlled, with the government limiting the types of training and numbers of pupils so as to produce at a proper rate the more specialized human resources needed for the society's evolving self-reliance. The first six aspects of human development described early in this chapter (communication techniques, social skills, health, knowledge of the physical-social world, support of the political system, vocational skills) would be fostered both in the formal school and in such nonformal programs as those offered through radio broadcasts and village work projects. Individuals' self-fulfillment would be achieved by each person realizing that his or her role in the predominantly agricultural society was essential to the general good. Self-fulfillment would be realized in the form of pride individuals felt in carrying out their assigned tasks.

During the latter 1960s and well into the 1970s, the Tanzanian plan was lauded by many observers of African education as a show-case experiment, a model of post-colonial education that could profitably be emulated by other nations. Foreign-aid agencies invested large sums in support of the venture. And by the early 1980s the nation had gone a long way toward providing the desired universal primary education, since nearly all Tanzanian children were able to find school places.

However, in other respects the earlier euphoric hopes for the success of Nyerere's plan had turned to doubt and disappointment. For one thing, the campaign to stimulate self-reliance among the citizenry yielded some unintended results. During colonial times there had been significant numbers of Christian missionary schools in certain regions of the country, enabling those regions to produce far more educated people than did districts relatively untouched by missionary influence. Following independence, the government sought to remedy this unequal distribution of educational opportunity by concentrating new primary schools in the less developed areas. However, community leaders in the more developed regions displayed their self reliance by starting increased numbers of private schools, oftentimes under church auspices. Thus, the missionary tradition of colonial times offered a model Tanzanians could follow in organizing schools under private sponsorship. Nor were parents content to limit their children's schooling to primary education, especially to an education aimed solely at rural life. Hence, contrary to the government's plan to control the type and amount of secondary education, parents also set up private secondary schools. It therefore became clear that parents' self-reliance included a large measure of self interest —a desire to provide their offspring a good chance for individual achievement that extended well beyond the satisfaction of contributing to the group good by staying on the farm (Samoff, 1987).

As a response to this tide of popular demand for advanced schooling, government leaders sought to maintain their image of legitimacy and of control by making it official policy to further extend secondary and post-secondary facilities well beyond projected manpower needs. Hence, while the "rhetoric of planning has been retained, popular demand has prevailed over centralized planning in the recent expansion of secondary education in Tanzania" (Samoff, 1987: 351).

In effect, people's perceptions of what type of education would promote their personal interests obviously influenced the goals they held for the education system. And because different segments of society had different interests, by the latter 1980s it was apparent that not all Tanzanians subscribed wholeheartedly to the educational outcomes proposed by Nyerere two decades earlier.

> Socialists expect schools to mold new attitudes. Planners expect the schools to produce required skills and increase productivity. Employers expect the schools to do the hiring preselection as well as to provide training and instill discipline. Politicians expect the schools to reinforce legitimacy both

> through the expansion of the schools themselves and through political education within the schools. Students and their parents expect the schools to offer a route off the farm and into higher income. All expect schools to matter —to make the future quite different from the present (Samoff, 1987: 360).

The Arab Gulf States

The Gulf-states example illustrates (1) how the discovery of a highly profitable economic resource can motivate a nation's leaders to add new objectives to the education system's goals and (2) how the resulting events may change which agencies are assigned responsibility for achieving the goals. The economic resource in this case was the world's largest regional petroleum deposit.

Whereas Japan's most radical change in the goals and forms of schooling was launched in the mid-19th century, similar changes have come only recently for seven Arab Gulf states (Bahrain, Iraq, Kuwait, Oman, Qatar, Saudi Arabia, and the United Arab Emirates) that occupy an area 1.3 times the size of Europe with a population of 30 million. Until the mid-20th century, the dominant —and nearly exclusive— type of formal education in these countries was the Quran school, located at a mosque, where youths studied the holy book of Islam. The chief goal of such education was to produce faithful adherents of Islam —moral individuals, adept at the Arabic language, with a Quranic perception of life. Little if any attention was given to teaching about the broader social and scientific universe, to training youths for vocations, or to providing instruction in the arts as media for self-expression. The Quran school was an ungraded institution conducted by an Islamic scholar. Students could enroll and depart whenever they wished.

However, as the mid-20th century approached, immense oil reserves were discovered in the territories around the Gulf, bringing to the region an influx of Western industrial technology for exploiting the petroleum resources. The resulting sale of oil on the world market earned the nations immediate riches. In tandem with the technological intrusion from Europe and America, Western forms of schooling were introduced into most Arab Gulf states between 1940 and 1970, so that today the great majority of schools in the region are organized much like those in Western societies. Most Arab Gulf schools feature a hierarchy of grades (kindergarten through the university), entrance requirements, diplomas for completing each segment of the educational ladder, and a range of studies that covers secular science and social studies, Arabic and foreign languages, and various types of vocational and professional training as well as religious subjects.

For the first two or three decades of the modern era, each state worked individually to expand and reorganize its schools. Then in 1983 the ministers of education from the seven nations decided to unify their educational efforts by agreeing on a common set of learning goals. The result was a compilation of 48 educational aims. The following examples, selected from the 48, demonstrate the diversity of aims the states' educational systems have since been obliged to follow. It may be apparent that, in contrast to the exclusively religious objectives of the traditional Quran schools, the goals of the states' modern schools address all seven types of educational outcomes described early in this chapter. Furthermore, the new goals represent additions to, rather than substitutes for, the original Islamic learning objectives:

1. To inculcate the Islamic faith in the younger generation on the basis of understanding and conviction.
8. To develop reason based on the scientific method and to develop sound judgment.
12. To instill the sense of belonging in the family and to develop strong family ties with emphasis on the consciousness of family rights and duties.
21. To gain mastery of the Arabic language and make it a foundation in all fields of thought, culture, and practice.
26. To teach about problems and challenges facing the region, as well as international covetousness, and to prepare the individual to meet such challenges by developing his:
    (a) Work motivation, skills, and expertise.
    (b) Attitudes suitable for a citizen of the Gulf, with pride in his Arab and Islamic links.
    (c) Moral values and behavioral patterns as a cooperative and responsible citizen.
32. To produce efficient persons who have the information, skills, and tendencies necessary for utilizing the resources and methods of modern technology in order to fulfill the needs of societal development.
39. To promote open-mindedness toward other cultures and benefit from the experiences of others as long as the experiences are in conformity with the principles of Arabic Islamic culture.
43. To create sublime sentiments which give integration to the personality of an individual, as they lend him will-power, a sense of security, and self-confidence.
47. To develop a taste for art and aesthetic expression, so that an individual may feel and enjoy the beauty and novelty in the creations of Allah (Rasheed, 1989)

The People's Republic of China

It is not unusual for changes in emphasis on goals to assume a cyclical or alternating character in response to changes in political and socioeconomic conditions of the society. A dramatic instance of such back-and-forth shifting in emphasis has been observed in the People's Republic of China over the past three decades. The issue at stake has been the red/expert conflict.

For some years prior to 1949 the two political factions that vied for control of China were the Nationalists (Kuomintang Party) and Communists (Chinese Communist Party). In 1949 the Nationalists, suffering military defeat at the hands of the Communists, retreated to the island of Taiwan, leaving the Communists free to establish a People's Republic on the mainland. The two chief educational goals set by the Communist government were those of producing thoroughly dedicated adherents of Marxism (politically *red* citizens) and highly skilled, diligent workers (vocational *experts*) (Chen, 1981: 79, 121-152). Other aims, such as extending literacy throughout the populace, were to support these primary goals.

Between 1949 and the mid-1960s, Chinese officials occasionally altered the emphasis between the red aspect and the expert aspect in both formal and nonformal education programs. Throughout most of the 1950s there was clearly a need to prepare skilled scientists and engineers to implement China's socialist modernization program, so the stress in the education system was on producing experts. However, concern over a decline in political fervor led to the Great Leap Forward in 1958 and a consequent shift in the field of education to the "red" component. Economic problems identified with the Great Leap led to a retrenchment, and in the 1960s the educational system shifted to an emphasis on expertise. The code words of the early 1960s period were "quality, expertise, and evaluation" (Hawkins, 1983: 142).

Then suddenly the pendulum swung back to an extreme red position as the nation's top leader, Mao Zedong, introduced the Great Proletariat Cultural Revolution in 1966. His stated purpose was to root out the elements of antirevolutionary revisionism which he claimed were rampant in the schools and were endangering the achievement of his Marxist ideal of creating a classless society governed by peasants and workers. Over the next decade, until Mao's death in 1976, Marxist political aims that featured social-class struggle, and the dominance of the proletariat over the intelligentsia, overwhelmed the goal of producing experts. Thus, during the latter 1960s, higher learning institutions closed, intellectuals were discredited, and entrance to educational programs was based on applicants' Communist Party connections rather than academic aptitude. Some years later, the Party's Central Committee in retrospect condemned the Cultural Revolution for bringing "domestic turmoil and catastrophe to the party, the state, and the whole people" (Kwong, 1988: 1). As a result, in the latter 1970s the social and economic wreckage produced by the red dominance during the Cultural Revolution motivated government officials to stress the opposite goal, that of producing experts, particularly in science and technology.

It is true that in the 1980s the nation's leaders continued to affirm their commitment to the red portion of the dual educational aim by urging that "ideological work of schools must be strengthened so as to build up students' confidence in socialism and foster in them the communist spirit and morality" (Zhou, Cai, & Liu, 1983: 24). However, in practice it was obvious that the stress was no longer on political fealty but, instead, on producing experts. Elite key schools were founded, admission to advanced educational opportunities now depended on passing stiff competitive examinations, diplomas and academic titles were restored, and curricula were comprised of both theoretical and practical studies. As demonstrated in the educational provisions in China's national socioeconomic development plan initiated in 1985, concern for expertise was clearly overshadowing fidelity to Maoist Marxism.

Then in the spring of 1989, massive public demonstrations, led by university students, were aimed at convincing the government to permit more freedom of speech, exert greater control over rising prices, and reduce government corruption. The government responded with military force and returned to emphasizing the red factor, requiring students who participated in the demonstrations to attend political indoctrination classes in order to receive their diplomas.

HOW MAY THE DETAILED OBJECTIVES DIFFER FROM ONE SOCIETY TO ANOTHER?

When the general aims of two education systems are compared, it may appear that the systems are nearly identical in what they expect schooling to achieve. However, analyses of their specific classroom objectives may reveal that the two societies differ significantly in the kinds of educated people they hope to produce. To help illustrate this point, we turn to a further way of categorizing educational outcomes. So far we have viewed goals from the perspective of seven aspects of human development that may become the foci of educational aims. Now we adopt a scheme devised by Bloom and his colleagues labeled *A Taxonomy of Educational Objectives* (Bloom, 1956; Krathwhol, Bloom, & Masia, 1964). In analyzing educational outcomes, these authors first divided learning objectives into three general domains —the cognitive, affective, and psychomotor. Within the cognitive domain, they identified six subareas of objectives comprised of:

(1) kinds of knowledge and (2) five varieties of intellectual abilities and skills:
- (a) comprehending (interpreting, translating, and extending what has been studied),
- (b) applying learning to new situations,
- (c) analyzing material into constituent parts,
- (d) synthesizing diverse information,
- (e) evaluating the desirability of information or proposals.

Each of these subareas was then further analyzed into its components. For instance, the category of knowledge contained:
- (a) knowledge of specifics, isolated bits of information,
- (b) knowledge of ways to organize, study, judge, and criticize specifics,
- (c) knowledge of abstractions, theories, and generalizations in a field.

In the affective domain, the authors proposed a series of emotional objectives of schooling:
- (a) paying attention to instruction,
- (b) responding to instruction and gaining satisfaction in responding,

(c) adopting values,
(d) organizing values into a system (Bloom, Madaus, & Hastings, 1981: 331-337).

The psychomotor domain was likewise analyzed into constituent objectives.

Examples comparing Eastern Europe with North America and Indonesia with Taiwan illustrate ways that societies can differ in regard to which of these instructional objectives are emphasized in the schools.

Eastern Europe versus North America

Tibor Frank, an Hungarian professor of history, became a careful observer of education systems in Europe and North America during his teaching career in Hungary and the United States. His analysis of textbooks and of students' assignments in the two settings led him to conclude that primary and secondary schools in Eastern Europe place far greater stress on the acquisition of large quantities of factual knowledge than do schools in North America. In comparison, schools in North America place greater emphasis on how to learn, including how to organize, study, judge, and criticize specifics and generalizations.

Frank has proposed that these differences in emphases over the years of later childhood and adolescence tend to produce two noteworthy results. First, pupils in North America more often enjoy school, or at least they do not feel oppressed by the types of objectives they are expected to pursue, whereas pupils in Eastern Europe frequently fear school because of the heavy load of factual knowledge they are required to memorize. Second, the typical student who enters the highly selective university system in Eastern Europe has a significantly more detailed command of bodies of knowledge and communication skills than does the typical student entering the less selective university system in North America (T. Frank, personal communication, August 21, 1989).

Indonesia versus Taiwan

Throughout the world, most classroom teachers base their instruction on the content of textbooks. As a result, the most convenient source of information about detailed objectives of typical educational programs is the set of textbooks students use, especially if the texts are accompanied by a teacher's guidebook that describes the objectives. The use of textbooks for comparing programs that bear the same general title can be illustrated with materials from two Asian nations, the Republic of Indonesia in Southeast Asia and the Republic of China on Taiwan.

The textbooks analyzed here are ones currently used in the moral-education classes that all students must take in the elementary and secondary schools of both Indonesia and Taiwan. We direct attention first to similarities in the objectives that are reflected in the textbook contents, then consider differences between the two nations in their instructional aims.

The Indonesian and Taiwan books are alike in several respects. First, the instructional objectives that the texts were designed to promote derived from each government's basic philosophical precepts. In the case of Indonesia, the values espoused in the books were drawn from five concepts adopted as the nation's moral guidelines when the Republic was founded after World War II. The five —referred to as the *pancasila* (pahn-cha=five, see-lah=principles)— are belief in God, nationalism, humanitarianism, social justice, and sovereignty of the people. The values taught in Taiwan's *Life and Ethics* texts represent an array of virtues that evolved in the Confucian tradition over a period of more than 25 centuries. Lin's (1985) analysis of the Taiwan *Life and Ethics* texts for grades 1 through 6 of the primary school showed that 18 such virtues formed the objectives pupils were expected to master.

The primary-school books from the two societies are also alike in their almost exclusive emphasis on only two types of objectives in Bloom's taxonomy. The objective from the cognitive domain is *comprehension*, that is, comprehending the virtues exemplified in the stories that comprise the majority of the texts' contents. The objective from the affective domain is *adopting values*. Rarely do the texts encourage readers to exhibit skills of organizing, judging, analyzing, or synthesizing concepts or values. In the case of the Taiwan books, Lin has questioned the desirability of limiting cognitive objectives to comprehension:

> The decision-making process is very important for children's acquiring morality. We found that a moral dilemma was seldom utilized in the textbooks to present a [moral] trait. In other words, the trait was always presented in a nonconflict situation. Under this circumstance, children hardly learn how to take such factors as their needs, their previous values, or the events of a situation into account to make a moral judgment. As a result, children perhaps merely accept rules of what is right or wrong without knowing how to judge what is right or wrong. We wonder if such a lack of practice will become an obstacle for children developing their independent moral-reasoning capacities (Lin, 1985: 140).

Although the Indonesian books for grades 1 through 6 focus almost entirely on comprehension, those at the junior-secondary level (grades 7-9) include activities for students that represent additional objectives in Bloom's scheme —extending what has been studied, applying learning to new situations, and evaluating the desirability of information or proposals.

The two nations' textbooks are also alike in many of the values they intend to impart. Table 2-1 shows which values appear on numerous occasions in the two sets of primary-school books. The first 18 values are listed in the order in which they are presented in each of the Taiwan texts.

Although the *Life and Ethics* series from Taiwan gives nearly equal space to each of the 18 virtues, Lin's analysis of an additional broad array of story books used in school and at home suggests that some virtues are considered more important than others. The story books, intended for children ages 6-12, contained 1,590 brief tales. In a list of 26 moral virtues displayed in the stories, the 10 most common —in the order of their frequency—are filial piety, humanity (friendliness), diligence, trying hard, patriotism, honesty, humility, prudence, thrift, and cooperativeness. Of the 26 traits, *independence* is the least frequently mentioned (Lin, 1985: 87-90).

Most of the moral virtues espoused in the Indonesian elementary-school texts are identical to those in Taiwan's *Life and Ethics* series. A notable exception is the strong emphasis in the Indonesian books on belief in God. The Indonesian population is 88% Muslim, and three other religious groups (Christians, Hindus, Buddhists) enjoy equal rights. A second marked difference between the two sets of texts is the stress in Indonesia on tolerance of others' religious beliefs, ethnic origins, and social-class status. The fact that Indonesia has a far larger and more heterogeneous population than Taiwan is perhaps the most significant reason for this difference. By the 1990s, Indonesia's population exceeded 190 million compared to Taiwan's 21 million. In Indonesia, more than 300 languages were spoken by the different ethnic groups, whereas in Taiwan there were no more than three principal languages. Therefore, the effort to maintain national unity has been a more serious problem in the Republic of Indonesia than in the Republic of China.

A further difference between the two nation's textbooks is the degree of emphasis placed on values that are included in both columns of Table 2-1. For example, filial piety plays a far larger role in the books from Taiwan than in the books from Indonesia, whereas patriotism (including knowledge of the government) is accorded far more space in the Indonesian texts than in those from Taiwan.

The final value in Table 2-1, *freedom*, refers to Indonesians' rights to organize and to express their opinions. This virtue appears in only the sixth-grade textbook. Its description also includes a warning about the limitations that such freedom entails. In both the Indonesian and Taiwan texts, frequent emphasis is placed on the importance of the group's good over the individual's desires or needs. In each series, whenever a conflict appears between responsibilities and personal rights, responsibilities always take precedence.

In conclusion, textbooks can be useful sources of information about an educational programs' specific instructional objectives. Thus, the analysis of texts from various societies can reveal likenesses and differences in the outcomes the societies' educational programs are expected to foster.

Table 2-1

MORAL VALUES IN TEXTBOOKS — INDONESIA AND TAIWAN

The Moral Values	*Taiwan*	*Indonesia*
1. Diligence in study —Try hard in school.	X	X
2. Politeness —Follow rules of social intercourse.	X	X
3. Patriotism —Support the nation.	X	X
4. Forgiveness —Be kind to others, forgive them.	X	
5. Public-mindedness —Care for the environment.	X	X
6. Honesty —Tell the truth, never cheat.	X	X
7. Cooperativeness —Help others, work together.	X	X
8. Lawabidingness —Obey the rules.	X	X
9. Fraternal love —Sympathize with & help others.	X	X
10. Righteousness —Be fair, stand for justice.	X	X
11. Courageousness —Be brave, do not fear difficulties.	X	
12. Filial piety —Respect and obey parents.	X	X
13. Friendliness —Respect and help neighbors.	X	X
14. Thrift —Save money, do not waste materials.	X	
15. Sense of shame —Work hard, correct your faults.	X	
16. Responsibility —Fulfill obligations, don't complain.	X	X
17. Persistence —Never stop trying.	X	
18. Peacefulness —Do not quarrel, respect others' rights.	X	
19. Godliness —Honor and obey God.		X
20. Tolerance —Respect others' social status & opinions.		X
21. Freedom —Freely organize and express opinions.		X

Sources: Lin (1985: 74-77); *Pendidikan moral pancasila* (1982-83).

WHICH LEARNERS PURSUE WHICH OBJECTIVES AND WHY?

When general educational aims are dissected into their detailed components, it becomes clear that not all learners in a society are expected to achieve exactly the same objectives. For example, different expectations are held for the mentally retarded than for the intellectually gifted. Furthermore, specific objectives for students preparing to be electronic engineers are not identical to the objectives for youths intending to be farmers, shopkeepers, or teachers. Also, learners living in a bilingual region of the nation can be expected to pursue more ambitious language-usage goals than are learners in a monolingual region.

The issue of what factors determine which students pursue which specific objectives can be addressed by our analyzing ways that societal conditions interact with characteristics of individual learners to influence the goals students will pursue. Three important conditions are (1) the complexity of the society, (2) the diversity of its educational programs, and (3) the system by which learners are distributed among those programs. Four important characteristics of learners are (1) their talents, (2) their interests and ambitions, (3) their family's position in the social-class structure, and (4) their mental and physical health. An impression of how these variables may combine to determine who is expected to achieve which goals can be derived from the cases of the United Kingdom and the Pacific-island Kingdom of Tonga.

The United Kingdom

The United Kingdom —comprised of England, Scotland, Northern Ireland, and Wales— is a society of considerable complexity with a marked diversity in types of educational programs. Part of the diversity results from decentralized administrative control of education. The functions of schooling are not under the direct jurisdiction of a central body, such as a Ministry of Education. Rather, the aims and curricula of schools and nonformal programs have been more directly the responsibility of local public authorities or of sponsors and headmasters of private schools, a situation resulting from a long tradition of non-interference by the central government in most aspects of education (Booth, 1985:5353). Consequently, unlike most countries, whose education systems operate under a central government agency, traditionally there has been no official statement of goals which all educational institutions in the United Kingdom are expected to adopt. Any statements of desired aims that infrequently were issued by central officials were traditionally cast in suggestive, non-binding, and very general terms. The following illustrates such a statement from a government document.

(a) to help children develop lively, inquiring minds, giving them the ability to question and to argue rationally, and to apply themselves to tasks;

(b) to instill respect for moral values, for other people, and for oneself, and tolerance of other races, religions, and ways of life;

(c) to help children understand the world in which we live, and the interdependence of nations;

(d) to help children to use language effectively and imaginatively in reading, writing, and speaking;

(e) to help children to appreciate how the nation earns and maintains its standard of living and properly to esteem the essential role of industry and commerce in this process;

(f) to provide a basis of mathematical, scientific, and technical knowledge, enabling boys and girls to learn the essential skills needed in a fast-changing world of work;

(g) to teach children about human achievement and aspirations in the arts and sciences, in religion, and in the search for a more just social order; and

(h) to encourage and foster the development of the children whose social or environmental disadvantages cripple their capacity to learn, if necessary by making additional resources available to them (Secretary of State for Education and Science, 1977).

However, the Education Act of 1988 inaugurated a new era in the nation's planning of instruction by establishing a nationwide primary- and secondary-school curriculum organized around a core of mathematics, English, and science. The core was supplemented by seven foundation subjects —history, geography, technology, music, art, physical education and, for secondary pupils, a modern foreign language. The national curriculum was intended to comprise two-thirds of a pupil's program, with the remaining third created at the local level. Religious education has been compulsory since 1944, with the content determined at the local level.

It may be apparent that when general aims are translated into specific instructional objectives, great variability can occur among educational institutions in their detailed objectives. Not only does a decentralized administrative structure contribute to the diversity of specific learning goals, but so also do such factors as (1) the British social-class structure, (2) the nation's variety of occupations, (3) the increasing ethnic/linguistic diversity of the population, (4) an expanding sensitivity to individual differences among students in their ability to succeed in educational programs, and (5) a commitment to life-long learning. A brief inspection of these factors will illustrate how they can affect who pursues which educational goals.

In regard to social-class structure, over the centuries distinctions among upper, middle, and lower social classes in Britain have been reflected in educational provisions. Children from families in the top social strata have traditionally attended elite private schools —Eton, Harrow, Rugby, Winchester, and the like— that are incongruously labeled *public schools*. The aim of these institutions has been to produce "gentlemen" to serve as the society's top scholars, church dignitaries, and professional and political leaders. An inordinately large proportion of people holding distinguished positions in British life today are products of such schools, whose curriculum was traditionally heavy on mathematics and the classics (including Greek and Latin), while "innovations (like science, modern languages, or geography) were stoutly resisted" until well into the 20th century (Judge, 1984: 32). On a slightly lower tier of the socially stratified secondary-education system are grammar schools catering to middle-class aspirations for upward social mobility through a curriculum modeled after that of the public schools. Before 1965 a third level of institution, secondary-modern schools, enrolled most middle- and lower-class pupils who followed a less academic curriculum. Since 1965, the major trend has been to replace the secondary-modern type with comprehensive schools intended to cater for children of all abilities and social classes. But despite the attempt to reduce social-class differences by introducing comprehensive schools, it remains the case that the secondary-school system is still socially stratified, and learning objectives of one type of school are not identical to those of another.

Consider next the diversity of occupations in the United Kingdom. Great Britain has traditionally been identified as the key instigator of the industrial revolution that began in the mid-18th century. One dramatic consequence of industrialization was the accelerating rate of technological change and the diversification of occupations. In Britain, as in other highly industrialized nations, occupational specialties now number in the thousands, with each specialty requiring its own skills and detailed knowledge that must be acquired through education —whether the education is acquired in a formal educational program, through on-the-job apprenticeship, or by self-study. In short, the detailed learning objectives for each of these occupations differ to some degree from the objectives for other occupations.

A third stimulus to the diversification of specific educational goals has been the rapidly growing ethnic/linguistic variability in the British population as the result of the influx of immigrants from former British colonies in Asia, Africa, and the Caribbean to settle in the United Kingdom. New learning objectives have been required to care for the needs of students whose home language is not English and whose religions and customs are not the traditional varieties found in the United Kingdom.

A fourth source of differentiated educational objectives has been the practice of drawing ever-finer distinctions among kinds of learners who appear to deserve special education. In Britain over the past century, the types of students officially designated as needing exceptional instructional goals and teaching methods have grown from two types to nearly two dozen. According to Tomlinson (1982: 55-56), in 1886 the only two categories of individuals officially designated for special attention were those of idiot and imbecile. By 1913 five more categories had been added —moral imbecile, mentally defective (feeble-minded), blind, deaf, epileptic, and physical defective. By the 1980s the official types numbered 14, with several additional kinds suggested but not officially adopted, including children with learning difficulties (severe and mild) and those who were partially sighted, partially hearing, maladjusted, disruptive, speech defective, delicate, dyslexic, autistic, neuropathic, inconsequential, psychiatrically crippled, or aphasic. Special goals and teaching techniques were defined for each type. The British also have recognized giftedness in the arts and sciences that warrants advanced learning objectives and special instructional approaches. As a result, the percentage of school-age learners qualifying by the 1990s for special-education opportunities under the British conception of exceptionality could be as high as 25 or 30 percent.

A growing commitment in British society to life-long learning has also stimulated additional diversification of objectives. At the lowest end of the age continuum are a growing number of infant centers and nursery schools for children ages 2 through 5. In the upper ranges of the age scale —from late-adolescence throughout adulthood— programs furnished by traditional universities and vocational institutions were augmented in 1971 with courses at the new Open University. Since the university has no true campus, students study at home at their own pace. Course work is offered in the form of reading materials (65%), radio and television broadcasts (10%), individual and group tutoring and counseling (15%), and assignments and evaluations (10%). By the early 1980s, 78,000 working adults were enrolled in a wide range of courses in both general education and occupational specialties. Thus, for learners at both ends of the schooling ladder —young children and adults— new learning goals have been added in recent decades.

To conclude, a variety of social forces have contributed to the increasing complexity of British society, with the result that educational goals have been increasingly differentiated to serve the needs and desires of the members of such a variegated society. While the foregoing brief overview of learning opportunities in the United Kingdom falls far short of identifying the entire range of educational programs available, it should be sufficient to illustrate two points:

1. Specific learning objectives in a complex, advanced industrialized society can vary markedly from one type of program to another.

2. The decision about which set of objectives a given individual will pursue is influenced by such characteristics as the person's social-class status, cultural characteristics (ethnicity, gender, religion, home language), talents, mental health, and physical condition.

The Kingdom of Tonga

Like Britain, the Kingdom of Tonga in the South Pacific is an island nation. Furthermore, the two nations share common features in their formal education systems as a result of the work of Christian missionaries in the 19th century.

Tonga's educational history is much like that of most Pacific islands. There was no written form of the native tongue until Christian missionaries —principally from the British Isles— arrived in the early 1800s. They learned spoken Tongan and cast it into a written form, thereby creating the means for translating the Bible, Christian hymns, and other religious writings into the local language. Missionaries organized teacher-training classes and established schools in an ever-increasing number of villages, a venture greatly enhanced when King George Tupou I adopted Christianity in 1826 and added his eager support to expanding the Europeans' style of schooling. Before many years had passed, virtually all Tongans were Christians and were literate in their own language, as they are today (Thomas, 1984: 240-243).

Tonga was never directly a colony of a European power. Instead, it held the status of a protectorate of the United Kingdom and thereby maintained close political and cultural ties with that country. Schooling in Tonga originally followed patterns imported from the British Isles, and in more recent times has followed practices from New Zealand. By 1990 the curricula of both primary and secondary schools were still academic and foreign, except for the use of the Tongan language as the medium of instruction and a modicum of homemaking skills for girls and agricultural studies for boys. The New Zealand examination system rather than the requirements of daily life in Tonga has been a principal determinant of what is studied in school, although lately efforts have been made to focus the social studies more on issues of direct concern to islanders and to devise examinations better suited to the needs of life in the South Pacific.

Compared to British society, Tongan society is dramatically less complex in social-class structure, in ethnic/linguistic composition, in educational organization, in occupational diversity, and in perceptions of personal abilities. These differences have had a marked influence on the degree of differentiation among educational goals that are pursued by members of Tongan society.

In terms of ethnic origin, the population of 108,000 is comprised of 98% Tongans and 2% other Polynesians and Europeans. Thus, virtually no adjustments need be made in the schools' objectives for variations in learners' cultural backgrounds.

Rarely do Tongan children attend a nursery school before they enter the primary grades at age 6. Thus, all preschool education is furnished by the nuclear family (parents and their children), the extended family (grandparents, aunts, uncles, and cousins), and the neighborhood. The six-year primary curriculum is preoccupied with teaching reading, writing, and arithmetic, accompanied by some natural science and social studies, with upper primary grades emphasizing topics useful for passing the secondary-school entrance examination. Learning goals at the secondary level also derive primarily from British tradition. The Tongan language continues to serve as the principal medium of instruction, and English is studied as a foreign language.

The occupational structure of Tongan society is simple compared to that of Britain. Over 70% of Tongans engage in farming and fishing, with the skills required for these activities generally learned at home. To furnish adolescents a modest introduction to general vocational skills, industrial arts for boys and home economics for girls are included among the subjects in the junior secondary school. There is little post-secondary schooling in Tonga, with most of the available programs aimed at a few vocational specializations —nursing, primary-school teaching, police science, theological studies, and agriculture. During a given year, several hundred students would enroll in such courses.

While the great majority of primary schools are government operated, nearly all secondary schools are sponsored by church groups, so Christian religious goals form an important part of secondary-school fare.

In contrast to the complex provisions in Britain for children with learning disorders, Tongan schools recognize only the most obvious handicaps, such as blindness and deafness, and are ill prepared to differentiate learning objectives and instructional methods very much to accommodate for these disabilities.

In summary, as the cases of Britain and Tonga have shown, a variety of factors combine to influence the kinds of specific learning objectives available to a populace and to determine who pursues which of the objectives.

PROSPECTS FOR EDUCATIONAL GOALS

The aim of this chapter has been to offer four ways of perceiving educational goals and to illustrate how such viewpoints can help elucidate the nature of goals in representative nations. The four have concerned issues of (1) which agencies in a society assume responsibility for various educational goals, (2) conditions that cause nations to change their general educational aims, (3) ways that detailed instructional objectives may differ from one society to another, and (4) how decisions are reached about which learners pursue which goals. The chapter has also illustrated two methods of classifying goals. The first method identified goals under seven aspects of human development. The second —a taxonomy of educational objectives created by Bloom and his coworkers— divided objectives into three major categories (cognitive, affective, psychomotor) and defined sub-goals within each category.

In speculating about the likely future of educational objectives from a comparative international perspective, I would estimate that in the years ahead:

1. International communication about educational goals will continue to expand.

In all fields of endeavor, the past half century has witnessed an accelerating growth in communication among the world's societies. As a consequence, political leaders and educators in virtually all nations are increasingly well informed about the educational goals pursued in other countries. Significant sources of this information have included radio and television programs, conferences and publications sponsored by such bodies as United Nations organizations, consultants sent overseas on educational-aid projects, educators who visit or study in foreign lands, and scholarly publications in the field of comparative education. New developments in technology that promise to extend and quicken such communication are computer networks, data bases on compact disks, international educational radio and television networks via satellites, and personal-computer desk-top publishing that places low-cost, high-quality book and journal publishing potential in the hands of nearly any school system or individual educator. As a result, more people can know more than ever before about developments throughout the world in the realm of educational goals.

2. Governments will make further public commitments to educational objectives that bring greater relevant education to an increasing number of subgroups in their populations.

A further phenomenon of the past half century, and particularly of the most recent decades, has been the increase in the number of international alliances whose roles include furthering educational cooperation among alliance members. Typically a key feature of these groups is their dedication to fostering particular educational goals. The organizations' members become signatories to the groups' mission and thereby incur a moral obligation to promote the mission in their own nations and communities. After publicly placing themselves on record as supporting the aims of the group, the members can then be held accountable —both by their constituents and by the other members of the organization— to carry their promises into practice. Commitments that have been effective in stimulating expanded educational opportunities throughout the world are exemplified by such widely endorsed documents as the United Nations *Universal Declaration of Human Rights* [1948] and *Declaration of Rights of the Child* [1959] and by the UNESCO *Convention Against Discrimination in Education* [1960] (Tarrow, 1987: 237-248).

By 1990 the number of international organizations that had at least a peripheral interest in educational goals was very large, extending into the thousands. The most inclusive of the groups have been such United Nations organizations as UNESCO (United Nations Educational, Scientific, and Cultural Organization), UNICEF (United Nations Children's Fund), WHO (World Health Organization), and ILO (International Labor Organization). Each contains dozens of member nations.

Other groups are regional coalitions, such as the European Community (12 Western European governments), ABEGS or the Arab Bureau of Education for the Gulf States (7 nations), ASEAN or Association of Southeast Asian Nations (5 nations), Communist-bloc countries of Eastern Europe, and the Organization of American States (35 countries of South, Central, and North America).

Some alliances focus on particular aspects of socioeconomic development that include educational components, such as OECD or Organization for Economic Cooperation and Development (industrialized Western European and North American nations, Japan, and Australia).

Still other coalitions are concerned solely with educational matters. Examples are IEA or International Association for the Evaluation of Educational Achievement (more than 40 education systems) and the ACU or the Association of Commonwealth Universities (over 200 member institutions in 30 Commonwealth countries).

If past trends can be trusted as harbingers of the future, the foregoing types of organizations will increase in number, in membership, and in their influence over the expansion of nations' commitments to objectives of relevant life-long learning for all of their inhabitants.

3. In educational practice, the realization of societies' goal commitments will continue to be limited by philosophical, economic, political, cultural, personnel, and geographic constraints.

Despite the desires of nations' political and educational leadership and of the general citizenry to achieve ambitious educational aims, the ability of many nations —if not all— to realize their ambitions is bound to be restricted by a variety of influences that are not readily controlled.

According to the widely held dream following World War II, the peoples of the world could now achieve political independence, freedom from armed conflict, good health, prosperous economies, and just social treatment, including opportunities for universal education. While most formerly colonized regions did, indeed, become self-governing over the period of 1945-1975, the other elements of the dream have, at best, been only approximated in most regions of the globe. And in many respects, matters are worse than they were prior to the Second World War. Forces preventing societies from achieving their educational goals have included high population growth rates, economic disorder leading to inadequate public funds and personal income, conflicts among ethnic and religious groups, philosophical disagreements about the proper function of the schools, corruption among public officials and employees, personnel with too little training or dedication, the diminished attractiveness of teaching as a profession, the inadequacies of communication and transportation facilities to serve geographically isolated segments of the population, and more.

Renewed efforts to reduce the effects of such forces are clearly required if societies are to more adequately realize their educational ambitions.

REFERENCES

Bloom, B.S. (1956) *Taxonomy of educational objectives: Handbook I, cognitive domain.* New York: McKay.

Bloom, B. S., Madaus, G. F., & Hastings, J. T. (1981) *Evaluation to improve learning.* New York: McGraw-Hill.

Booth, C. (1985) United Kingdom: System of education. In T. Husen & T. N. Postlethwaite (Eds.), *International encyclopedia of education* (Vol. 9, pp. 5351-5359). Oxford: Pergamon.

Chen, T. H. (1981) *Chinese education since 1949 —Academic and revolutionary models.* New York: Pergamon.

Cowen, R., & McLean, M. (1984) (Eds.) *International Handbook of Education Systems —Asia, Australasia, and Latin America.* (Vol. III). New York: Wiley.

Dodd, W. A. (1969) *"Education for self-reliance" in Tanzania.* New York: Teachers College Press.

Europa year book (1988) London: Europa Publications, Vol. 2.

Gillette, A. L. (1978) *Beyond the non-formal fashion: Towards educational revolution in Tanzania.* Amherst, MA: University of Massachusetts.

Hawkins J. N. (1983) The People's Republic of China. In R. M. Thomas & T. N. Postlethwaite. *Schooling in East Asia.* Oxford: Pergamon.

Japan's modern educational system (1980) Tokyo: Ministry of Education, Science, and Culture.

Judge, H. G. (1984) *A generation of schooling: English secondary schools since 1944.* Oxford: Oxford University Press.

Kasaju, P. K., Pande, B. D., & Matheson, W. M. (1985) Nepal: system of education. In T. Husen & T. N. Postlethwaite (Eds.), *International encyclopedia of education* (Vol. 6, pp. 3499-3501). Oxford: Pergamon.

Kobayashi, V. N. (1968) Japan under American occupation. In R. M. Thomas, L. B. Sands, & D. L. Brubaker (Eds.), *Strategies for curriculum change: Cases from 13 nations.* Scranton, PA: International Textbook Co.

Krathwohl, D. R., Bloom, B. S., & Masia, B.B. (1964) *Taxonomy of educational objectives —Handbook II: affective domain.* New York: McKay.

Krugmeier, C. J. (1985) Peru: System of education. In T. Husen & T. N. Postlethwaite (Eds.), *International Encyclopedia of Education* (Vol. 7, pp. 3848-3851). Oxford: Pergamon.

Kwong, J. (1988) *Cultural revolution in China's schools, May 1966—April 1969.* Stanford, CA: Hoover Institution Press.

Lin, H. Y. (1985) *Moral development and children's literature in Taiwan.* Unpublished doctoral dissertation, University of California, Santa Barbara.

Munro, D. J. (1977) *The concept of man in contemporary China.* Ann Arbor: University of Michigan Press.

Nakamoto, J. M., White, P. S., & La Belle, T. J. (1985) Education and white/mestizo-Indian relations. In J. N. Hawkins & T. J. La Belle (Eds.), *Education and intergroup relations* (pp. 60-86). New York: Praeger.

Nyerere, J. K. (1967) *Education for self-reliance.* Dar es Salaam: Government Printer.

Pendidikan moral pancasila, Vols. 1-6. (1982-83) Jakarta: Departemen Pendidikan dan Kebudayaan.

Rasheed, M. A. (1989, April) Sources of educational goals in the Arab gulf states. Paper presented at the meeting of the Comparative and International Education Society, Cambridge, MA.

Samoff, J. (1987) School expansion in Tanzania: Private initiatives and public policy. *Comparative Education Review,* 31 (3): 333-360.

Secretary of State for Education and Science (1977) *Education in schools: A consultative document.* London: Her Majesty's Stationery Office.

Shrestha, G. M., Lamichhane, S. R., Thapa, R. K., Chitrakar, R., Unseem, M., & Comings, J. P. (1986) Determinants of educational participation in rural Nepal. *Comparative Education Review,* 30 (4), 508-522.

Tarrow, N. B. (1987) *Human rights and education.* Oxford: Pergamon.

Thomas, R. M. (Ed.) (1988) *Oriental theories of human development.* New York: Peter Lang.

Thomas, R. M. (1984) Tonga. In R. M. Thomas & T. N. Postlethwaite (Eds.), *Schooling in the Pacific Islands.* Oxford: Pergamon.

Tomlinson, S. (1982) *A sociology of special education.* London: Routledge & Kegan Paul.

World almanac (1989) New York: Pharos Books.

Zhou, Y., Cai, G., & Liu, H. (1983) *Education and science.* Beijing: Foreign Languages Press.

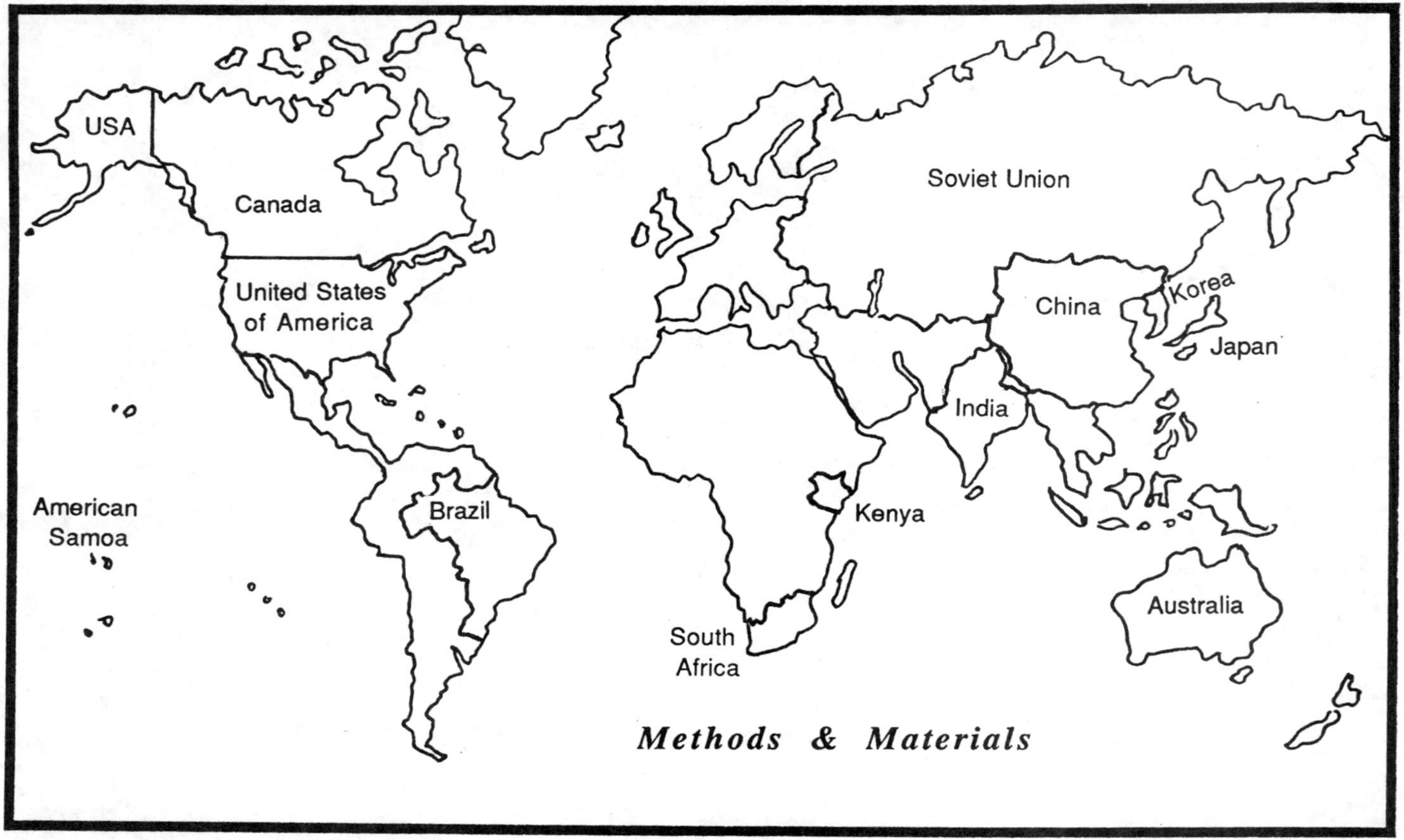
USA
Canada
United States of America
American Samoa
Brazil
Soviet Union
China
Korea
Japan
India
Kenya
South Africa
Australia
Methods & Materials

CHAPTER 3

Instructional Methods and Materials

How are decisions made about which teaching procedures are most appropriate?

JIAYING ZHUANG HOWARD

Instructional methods and materials are the vehicles designed to convey learners to the instructional goals. Methods are the processes of teaching —lectures, discussions, question-answer sessions, demonstrations, experiments, dramatic presentations, excursions, and the like. Materials are physical objects used as part of instructional methods. Although textbooks, as the most traditional of materials, are still widely used, the supplies and equipment found in today's classrooms also assume a variety of other forms —magazines, newspapers, audiotapes, videotapes, films, typewriters, microcomputers, simulation games, photographs, drawings, charts, maps, microscopes, lathes, sewing machines, exhibits of real-life objects, and far more.

A question teachers often ask is whether one method or one material is generally better than others. Is a TV program better than a straight lecture? Is role-playing better than a demonstration? Is a radio program better than a film? Efforts to settle these issues have produced a great quantity of research. However, attempts to draw a clear conclusion from the results of such research have proven disappointing, for the studies too often yield mixed outcomes. Consider, for example, studies comparing the effectiveness of lecturing with the effectiveness of small-group discussion. In some cases, lecturing yields greater learning results, while in other instances small-group discussion produces better outcomes, and in still other cases there is little or no difference between the two. To a great extent, such inconsistency is caused by researchers failing to ask the right question. Instead of wondering whether one method or material is *generally* better than another, they should phrase their query in a form that recognizes the multi-faceted nature of instruction. In effect, any learning outcome is the result of a combination of significant variables, not just one. Factors other than the general method or material will influence how well students learn. Hence, the research question would more suitably be phrased in the following manner:

> In this particular instructional environment, which of the methods and materials under consideration will be most suitable in view of: (1) the specific learning objectives being pursued (skill-oriented, knowledge-oriented, value-oriented), (2) the

available technology (the facilities and supplies at hand), (3) sociopolitical conditions that can influence instructional methods, (4) the maturity levels, educational backgrounds, abilities, and interests of the learners, (5) teachers' skills, knowledge of subject matter, and preferred instructional style, (6) the place in which the students and the teacher are located, and more?

The following conviction, then, becomes the central theme of this chapter —*that multiple factors determine the suitability of a teaching method or material.* No attempt is made here to analyze all possible teaching methods and materials. Instead, the aim is to illustrate how this multiple-factor principle explains why particular instructional approaches and materials may be adopted in specific teaching situations. The illustrations are organized under six categories, each of them featuring a different variable from the foregoing set of conditions that affect the selection of teaching methods. The first category focuses on the types of learning objectives being pursued, the second on influential socio-political conditions, the third on the availability of instructional materials, the fourth on the variability among learners (individual differences), the fifth on teachers' skills and preferred instructional style, and the sixth on the location of teachers and their students.

THE NATURE OF THE LEARNING OBJECTIVES

Obviously, the purpose of schooling is not simply to equip students to perform well in the classroom. The more important aim is to prepare them to succeed well in settings beyond the school. This means that methods of instruction should be ones which maximize the transfer of students' learning to those situations in life that require such skills and knowledge. In other words, instructional techniques and materials should promote attainment of the learning objectives as those objectives will be needed in real-life settings. Three ways that instructional approaches have been designed to achieve this transfer-of-learning goal are illustrated in examples from Canada and Japan.

Simulation Activities in Canada

The terms *simulation games* and *simulation activities* have been used to describe instructional experiences that approximate as closely as feasible the significant real-life situations in which the learning is expected to apply. Two examples from Canada illustrate the application of such activities at the kindergarten and at the secondary-school or college level.

The instructional objective in this kindergarten class was to have children follow safety practices when playing out-of-doors or when walking or riding around the neighborhood. Instructional materials included a large game board placed on a low table. Streets, sidewalks, crosswalks, and people's yards were painted on the board. Toy buildings and houses were also located there. Small puppets represented pedestrians who might walk through this neighborhood. There was also a pile of *scenario cards* placed face-down at the side of the board alongside two piles of *face cards* (one pile with smiling faces, the other with sad faces). Each scenario card described something a child was supposed to do, such as: "Look at the game board. Decide where you like to live on it. Now, [have your puppet] leave your house and go to school" (Renaud & Stolovitch, 1988: 333).

To carry out the activity, the teacher and six children gathered around the game board. Each child took a turn drawing a scenario card, which the teacher read aloud. As the child performed the actions described on the card, the five classmates judged whether the player's puppet-pedestrian properly followed safety practices. The classmates displayed their appraisals by holding up either a smiling-face card or a sad one.

Follow-up evaluations of the success of the traffic game as a teaching method led the authors of the activity to conclude that:

> the findings of this study support the contention that the use of attitude- and behavior-triggering elements (role playing/group dynamics and behavior modeling/training) in a simulation game with 5- to 6-year olds does definitely modify their attitudes and lead them to adopt and maintain proper traffic safety habits,... [thus] promoting transfer of learning with respect to traffic safety (Renaud & Stolovitch, 1988: 344).

The second of the Canadian simulation games, designed for use with adolescents and older youths, utilizes a microcomputer to teach key concepts in the field of anthropology. Specifically, it is intended to "help students discover the organizational structures of a society different from their own. A foreign society often appears illogical, even ridiculous, and it is essential that students understand the rationality of other cultural systems" (Corbeil, 1988: 228).

This game, called *Les Chasseurs-Cueilleurs* (Hunters-Gatherers), was designed in Quebec, the principal French-speaking region of the nation. It is played on a microcomputer by one person at a time. As the player follows the directions that appear on the computer screen, he or she takes on the role of leader to a family of hunters and gatherers.

> The player must make the decisions to see his family through one year made up of three seasons and played in weekly turns. During that time, he must make cultural decisions, such as to whom he will marry the young people, and with whom will they live. This deals with such social values as exogamy and patrilocality (marrying outside the clan and living with the groom's family). He must also interact with the environment, deciding when to migrate to the fishing and trapping grounds, when to move to the hunting groups, when to move back to the seashore, and when communal fishing will guarantee survival (Corbeil, 1988: 229).

At the close of the game, the computer prints out an evaluation of how the player succeeded with different tasks and according to different criteria. For example, the player may have earned a score of 60% percent on survival rate but only 40% on social conformity. In effect, the game not only engages learners in the sorts of decisions faced by people in a culture far different from their own, but it also provides an assessment of how well they might have fared in such a culture.

One obvious intention of such a simulation experience is that the skills of analysis and the attitudes fostered by the game will transfer to the student's perceptions of other cultures he encounters in his own life

On-the-Job-Training in Japan

Training on the job is often used in vocational education because, as La Belle (1986) has noted, learning at the work site is generally more cost-effective and practical than classroom lectures in vocational education. By training on the job, students not only directly discover which skills and attitudes are necessary to be successful in their vocation, but the work site also provides them with immediate opportunities to apply what they have learned to actual job conditions. Furthermore, the education system's problem of furnishing expensive equipment is solved by placing the learner where equipment is already available rather than having to place the equipment in a school.

An efficient application of on-the-job training is demonstrated in Japan where that nation's industrial complex has achieved such remarkable productivity over the past four decades. According to Cantor (1985), 75% of Japan's vocational education is furnished by private industry as authorized by the government. Four major types of industrial training are provided: (1) basic training which supplies initial instruction for new employees; (2) up-date training to keep experienced employees current with new developments; (3) up-grading preparation for experienced workers by means of courses linked to national trade tests; and (4) occupational-capacity redevelopment training that enables redundant workers to acquire new skills suitable for reemployment. Although some training consists of traditional classroom lectures, direct on-the-job experience under guidance is the main approach used.

The country's on-the-job training is designed to offer employees a variety of preparation through structured experiences which involve (1) a progression of tasks from the simple to the difficult, (2) linking an employee's learning progress to promotion in the company, and (3) planned rotation of employees among jobs to broaden the range of experiences and deepen the complexity of tasks (McCormick, 1989). Such opportunities are not limited to new employees. Supervision and support are provided also for experienced workers.

An example of an on-the-job approach is the Toyota automobile company's program that finds 100 instructors in charge of training for the company's

45,000 employees. A typical new employee's studies during the first year consist of a seven-month program on theory, three months working on the production line to understand the direct process of manufacturing cars, and three months of sales experience with one of the nation's privately-operated automobile dealerships (Cantor, 1985)

Among the principal techniques used in Toyota's on-the-job programs are group work, job rotation, and multi-skilled job experience. For instance, at times, trainees are assigned to work in small groups on a project so as to facilitate the exchange of ideas and information and to help them acquire skills of cooperating in team efforts. Trainees are also rotated from job to job, so they experience a wide range of tasks, thereby enhancing their ability to adjust to new working situations and increasing their awareness that through their contributions they complement each other. Multi-skilled work experience is intended to avoid narrow specialization and to increase employees' desire to learn more.

Such training is necessarily lifelong vocational study because of the rapid development in modern technology. Many enterprises provide a two-step training process. Each time an innovative technology or new type of equipment is adopted by a company, key workers are selected for intensive training by production engineers. Later, the trained key workers are responsible for diffusing their skills to other members of the labor force. Although this practice varies between large and small enterprises, the variation is not in kind but only in degree (McCormick, 1989). Japan's economic achievements reflect not only the effectiveness of on-the-job-training methods but also the success of lifelong vocational education.

Although on-the-job training has been an effective approach to vocational education in Japan, other countries may experience difficulty in achieving simlar success. One reason appears to be the quality and skills of trainers. Unlike Japan, where highly-skillful and experienced vocational educators are available in almost all large private industries, many developing nations lack such human resources. Another reason seems to be the organization of such programs. Japanese vocational education is usually organized by employers, thus fully integrating vocational training with specific needs of the industrialists. In contrast, in many other countries vocational schools and industries are separate. As a result, schools may contribute to the problem of turning out educated unemployable students. La Belle (1986) notes that the principal problems associated with vocational training can be traced to a lack of articulation between the training and work opportunity. He further notes that the success of vocational programs is not determined entirely by the quality of training but also by the nature of the economy. In other words, the strategies for training should begin with the opportunities available for work, rather than beginning with training and then trying to find jobs for graduates. For many developing nations whose economies are in great difficulty, the success or failure of vocational education, or of a specific training method, cannot be as easily measured as in Japan.

TAKING ADVANTAGE OF THE AVAILABLE TECHNOLOGY

As the pace of technological progress continues to quicken, the variety and sophistication of instructional materials advance at an increasingly rapid rate. However, this progress is not enjoyed in equal measure by all societies. The pair of cases in the following section contrast two societies, showing the way instruction in the two settings was influenced by the nature of materials at hand.

Applying Advanced Technology to Health Instruction in the United States

In a nation such as the United States, where modern technology and highly-trained human resources are easily available, educators increasingly apply sophisticated technology to solve unique educational problems. The case described in the following paragraphs demonstrates how the analysis of significant conditions of a population of learners resulted in the creation of specialized teaching methods and materials made possible by the available technology.

In view of the high death rate caused by diabetes-related complications among elderly Hispanics in the state of Texas, the University of Texas Health Service Center in San Antonio designed a pilot series of programs to educate diabetes patients in how to care for their health. Several previous investigations had indicated that there was an urgent need for such educational intervention as approximately 300,000 Hispanics in Texas were diabetic patients. Diabetes and complications from the disease had become the number-one cause of death among Hispanics over the age of 40. It was also discovered that the incidence rate of Type II Diabetes (non-insulin dependents) among Hispanics was 300% higher than among non-Hispanic Americans in that state. Therefore, educators intended to provide Hispanic patients with instructions on how to take responsibility for controlling their blood pressure and blood sugar level (Marshall & Richard, 1989).

In order to reach a large audience at a relatively low cost, university personnel decided to rely on television and video technology. Before the program was designed, educators conducted a learner analysis which included an assessment of each learner's academic level, age, language background, reading ability, ethnicity, and curriculum placement of material prerequisites. The educators decided that the program should target elder Hispanics. Because many such people spoke a language other than English at home (usually Spanish) and had no formal education, they were unable to speak or read English. A large number of them could not read their native language either. Furthermore, the patients were located in different geographic areas. Based on these findings, the educators concluded that tele-education was probably their most cost-effective approach, because it could reach a large audience who represented different backgrounds and lived in different regions. The planners also decided to depend primarily on nonprinted audio-visual materials specially developed for their project.

Before designing the teaching materials, the educators also conducted a content analysis of books on nutrition, ophthalmology, podiatry, internal medicine, and community nursing to provide the information to be conveyed to the diabetic population. In recognition of the patients' cultural and language backgrounds, the program planners prepared family-life dramas with actors who spoke Spanish. In other words, the program was cast in a *novella/soap opera* format, that was recognized as being a favorite type of entertainment among older Hispanics. Since television sets and videocassette recorders were available in most of the patients' homes, the learners would have easy access to the educational materials.

Project personnel created a fictional extended Hispanic family for their soap serial. The stories and situations were generally based on actual cases that the program designers had previously discovered when interviewing patients. From this source, the script writers obtained rich, realistic resources for their stories. Within a dramatic sketch, various situations evolved that enabled the authors to convey information about diabetes and health care. Organizing the drama around an extended family that included several generations made it possible to cover many types of life situations. Because traditional Hispanic culture promotes respect for the elderly and for authority, the drama featured several highly esteemed authority figures, usually doctors and nurses, as the characters providing patients with the desired health information (Marshall & Richard, 1989).

Locally Produced Visual Aids in India

In advanced industrialized societies that have a wide range of audio-visual instructional aids available in the market place, a teacher's task of locating suitable photographic or diagrammatic materials is often simply a matter of ordering the items from a catalog. But the problem of finding appropriate materials is not so easily solved in most developing nations, where teachers have to depend more heavily on their own initiative to provide visual aids. Such was the case in the irrigation-supervisors training institutes in India.

To improve the operation and management of India's irrigation system, the government's Central Water Commission, with financial assistance from the World Bank and the U.S. Agency for International Development (USAID), established training centers called State Training Institutes to provide inservice education for government staff members engaged in irrigation, water management, and land development. The centers provided short workshops and seminars of a duration of three days to two weeks, and long-term training as long as four to six weeks. Typical training programs included technical specifications for water-management devices and processes as well as abstract management concepts. Most instructors were irrigation engineers (Maughan, 1989).

In the beginning, instructors typically used the existing content and materials in the irrigation management organizations as well as the textbooks, technical specification charts and tables, and a few video tapes supplied by the World Bank or USAID. But as the program matured, faculty members devised additional visual devices to promote trainees' learning. Specifically, a demand arose for more appropriate course notes, handouts, worksheets, overhead transparencies, slides, audio programs, and video programs. Because appropriate training aids were not readily available from media-production services, instructors were called on to develop their own materials. Since the centers varied in facilities and personnel, the teaching aids that were produced varied from one place to another. In some centers, instructors or draftsmen on the staff produced specialized overhead-projector transparencies. In other centers, faculty members used their personal collections of photographic slides. In still other regions, the staff began experimenting with the on-site production of video programs. Thus, while the principal teaching method in all upgrading centers consisted of the presentation of information in lecture and printed form, the instructional materials varied from one center to another, depending on the available materials and the ingenuity of the staff. The most popular materials were diagrams and drawings shown via an overhead projector and photographs displayed by means of a slide projector.

SOCIOPOLITICAL CONDITIONS AFFECTING THE CHOICE OF METHODS

The term *sociopolitical conditions* in the present context refers to social traditions and political actions that influence the selection of teaching methods. The two cases offered in way of illustration concern language instruction. The first example, drawn from the People's Republic of China, focuses on the effect of traditions on the choice of a teaching method. The second, from the Republic of South Africa, describes a type of language-instruction material intended to promote both political goals and literacy.

Exporting a Language-Teaching Approach to China

The Chinese case shows what may occur in the attempted transfer of a method from one culture to another when there are significant differences between the two cultures in their instructional goals, educational traditions, social attitudes, available materials, and teachers' skills.

grammar methods which are intended to equip Chinese to translate English reading matter into Chinese rather than to converse in colloquial English.

Language and Politics in South Africa

Compared to the case of the People's Republic of China, the example from the Republic of South Africa pictures a very different set of conditions affecting language instruction. The South African case portrays an attempt by anti-aparteid forces to foster English-language literacy among speakers of tribal languages by adapting a nontraditional literary form (the comic book) to produce an appealing textbook. The case also illustrates the way a political decision can prevent further use of a successful teaching approach.

Our example is derived from Pierce's (1989) study of a project that the South African Council of Higher Education carried out to promote English education among black South Africans. In the country's population of 30 million, less than 20% speak one of the nation's two official languages, English and Afrikaans. The majority, mainly blacks, speak one tribal language or, in many instances, more than one tribal dialect. During the recent movement against apartheid in South Africa, a National Education Crisis Committee (NECC) was set up to address issues of black education. NECC intended to promote English education among the blacks but argued that because of the special conditions in South Africa, English education for black South Africans should be based on the principles of teaching English as a second language that have been generated by British universities. Instead of emphasizing the formal rules of the language in a proper British society, English teaching should recognize the political nature of language, thereby improving learners' ability to say and write what they mean, to hear and understand what is said and what is implied, to defend their viewpoints, and to make their voices heard. Pierce notes that this recent conception of English instruction uses the *pedagogy of possibility*, which involves an exploration of the informal rules of the English language used in South Africa and examines the conditions that give rise to these rules. Pierce contends that the social conditions in South Africa strongly suggest that issues of teaching English are not simply those bearing on linguistic features of the language but, instead, are the political issues of how English should be taught in school, who has access to the language, how English is reflected in power relations in South Africa, and how the language can serve to produce changes in that society.

One effective example of teaching English in a manner that supports the anti-apartheid movement is a project of the South African Council of Higher Education, which produced a special kind of English textbook for black learners, *Down Second Avenue: the Comic*, based on the novel with the same title by a famous South African writer, Ezekial Mphahlele. The comic book describes in pictures the experience of the writer growing up under apartheid. The first half of the text contains the pictorial story. The second half provides many interesting exercises which help readers understand the text and develop writing and reading skills in imaginative and interactive ways. The exercises were designed not only to improve learners' language skills but also to stimulate critical thinking, thus enabling readers to recognize both what is said and what is implied, to explore relationships, and to create responses. The writers of the textbook specifically encouraged readers to compare their exercises with those of friends so as to share and pool ideas. According to Pierce's account, this form of teaching English to the general black public has proven very effective. It has motivated learners to study the English language, has made the writings of a black writer accessible to a wide audience, and has taken advantage of the popularity of the comic-book format.

The South African apartheid government, apparently anticipating the effectiveness of *Down Second Avenue: the Comic*, banned the book from distribution soon after it was published.

ACCOMMODATING FOR INDIVIDUAL DIFFERENCES AMONG LEARNERS

Perhaps the most difficult task teachers face when instructing a group of students is that of suiting the instructional methods to the individual variations represented within the group. Among the variations that most seriously affect how well students progress are their differences in background knowledge, intellectual aptitude, language skills, learning style, physical maturity, interests and motives, diligence, and study habits. The instructional setting in which such individual characteristics can most easily be accommodated is the tutorial or apprenticeship situation where one instructor teaches one student. Such a condition, however, is the exception rather than the rule. Education usually must be conducted in groups. Three approaches that offer some measure of individualized instruction within group settings are described in the following cases from South Korea, the Soviet Union, and Australia.

Mastery Learning in South Korea

In recent decades the term *mastery learning* has been widely used throughout the world for identifying methods designed to provide all of the learners in a group a fair chance to achieve the instructional objectives. In the traditional classroom, both past and present, teachers have aimed their instruction at the group as a whole, making little or no adjustment for differences among pupils in their ability, speed of comprehension, motivation, or learning style. The most common traditional approach has been referred to as *talk and chalk*. It involves the teacher lecturing and explaining, then writing material on the chalkboard for pupils to copy into notebooks and memorize. The oral explanation is typically given only once, with the expectation that students will grasp the content during that first pass. Sometimes a review session is also provided, so that anything students missed the first time through might be retrieved during the review. Finally, to assess how well pupils have learned the material, the teacher poses oral questions or gives a written test and assigns students marks according to how well they have succeeded. Then they move on to the next unit of study.

In contrast to this traditional tack, mastery-learning approaches are planned in ways to offer pupils a better opportunity to attain the instructional goals. An example of such a mastery plan at the junior-secondary-school level is one devised in South Korea for teaching mathematics and English. Curriculum planners began by dividing the semester's program into short instructional units. The aim of the scheme was to have all students in a given class advance through each unit together, but to differentiate instruction within a unit in ways that might accommodate for variations among the learners in their abilities and background knowledge. The instructional strategy adopted to implement the scheme was comprised of the following seven steps.

1. A brief written test is administered to the class to determine whether the pupils have the background knowledge needed for succeeding with the upcoming unit. Pupils who display deficiencies on the test are given a printed up-grading exercise to complete in order to fill-in the missing knowledge.

2. The new unit begins with the teacher describing to the class the exact objectives that they should master by the end of the unit.

3. Instruction is now provided. This usually consists of the teacher explaining and illustrating the concepts and skills to be mastered.

4. Supplementary instruction is offered in the form of review materials involving concepts and exercises that furnish pupils practice with the unit's contents.

5. A formative test is given to students when they have completed the exercises. (*Formative test* here means diagnostic evaluation to determine strengths and weaknesses in the pupils' command of the unit's contents.)

5-A. For students who still exhibit weaknesses in their grasp of the material, remedial teaching is provided. The remediation can assume several forms, depending on the nature of the lesson contents and the types of errors pupils have made. Sometimes students who display a particular type of error meet in a small group with a classmate who has mastered that material, and the classmate reteaches the material. In other instances, the remediation takes the form of written instructions and exercises cast in a simpler form than that of the original instruction.

5-B. For students who have already mastered the unit objectives, enrichment activities are provided. These can be supplementary printed materials that expand on the basic objectives of the lesson, or they may be puzzles and creative activities that can embellish the learner's knowledge of the subject-matter.

6. A summative test is given as the final step in the unit to determine how well all members of the class have achieved the objectives. Following the summative test, the class moves on to the next unit in the series.

The success of this mastery approach compared to the traditional teaching method of teacher explanation plus exercises was tested in an eight-week experiment with 5,800 first-year junior-secondary students in nine schools in the city of Seoul. Half of the group followed the mastery system and the other half the traditional approach. Students were judged to have attained sufficient mastery of the unit objectives if they answered at least 80% of the items correctly on the final test.

Results of the experiment showed that, on the average, 72% of the students in the mastery-learning English classes exceeded the 80% standard compared to 28% of those under ordinary instructional conditions. In mathematics, an average of 67% of the students in the mastery classes compared to 39% in the traditional classes attained the achievement-test criterion. In effect, even though this mastery approach did not equip every pupil to pass the final tests above the 80% level, it did substantially increase the number who succeeded with the unit (Block, 1971: 124-126).

A Personality Approach in the Soviet Union

A traditional assumption in the Marxist sociopolitical philosophy of the Soviet Union has been that the differences among people in their success in life's activities are caused chiefly, if not exclusively, by the opportunities that society offers. In other words, most people are much alike in terms of inborn talents and native ability. When this assumption is applied to the formulation of educational policy, it can be interpreted to mean that all learners, in keeping with their similar innate abilities, can profit equally well by the same sort of teaching methods. Likewise, all teachers, if properly trained, can implement a given instructional method equally well. From such a viewpoint, *equal learning opportunities* means identical instruction for all, including identical instruction from one classroom to another.

Suddaby (1989) reports that at the outset of the 1960s the official mode of instructional improvement in the nation was *the correct scientific approach*.

> The aim of...research was the construction of an ideal or model lesson which would, after thorough testing, be recommended for use in all schools.... The attitude [appeared] to be one entirely consistent with educational philosophy generally throughout the Soviet Union [at that time]; that is, that there is just one right way to do anything in the classroom. The high degree of supervision in the first stage of a student's practice teaching [was] to ensure the development of exactly the right method of teaching the particular lessons that he [was] teaching (Suddaby, 1989: 248).

Then, from the mid-1960s into the 1970s, official recognition of pupils' differences in learning aptitude led to the introduction of an *individual or differentiated approach*, which involved group work, project work, individual work sheets, and some freedom of choice on the part of the pupil in educational tasks. The method was tried out in experimental schools with reported success before it was recommended for widespread application. However, the realities of the traditional Soviet system of pedagogy mitigated against the application of differentiation as it was found in other nations. Teachers apparently did not understand how to individualize their instruction. They continued to consider the teacher-centered lesson as the only proper approach to use. In addition, students were still required to pass examinations in order to advance to the next higher grade, so that the individual approach

> in any Western understanding of the term was not practicable. This meant that the 'individual approach' (when it was not totally ignored or misunderstood) acquired its own peculiar Soviet interpretation. For example, Strezikozin, director of the Institute for Research into Curriculum Content and Method, described differentiation as a means to help backward pupils to catch up while brighter ones study the topic in greater depth.... Stezikozin has stated that the entire lesson should never follow a differentiated approach and the teacher's initial exposition must be at a general level accessible to all students.... The aim is therefore to equalize the class rather than to develop the full potential of each individual with the result of an ever-increasing gap between the weakest and the strongest (Suddaby, 1989: 250).

The difficulties met in attempts to apply the Soviet version of differentiation with large classes, with a compulsory curriculum and with the vestiges of the scientific method, led to dissatisfaction with the individual approach. Under these conditions, attention turned in the 1980s to the work of a variety of educational innovators, most of them classroom teachers not officially associated with the Soviet Academy of Pedagogical Sciences that coordinates all educational research in the USSR. The innovators began with a concern over the way pupils' motivation to learn appeared to decline as they progressed through primary and secondary school. Children who began as eager participants in the lower grades gradually discovered that, in teacher-led lecture and recitation lessons, they were forced to play the generally passive role of listening to others, with the result that their enthusiasm for learning dissipated. The innovators' solution was the introduction of a new pedagogy whose principles were articulated in two manifestos, the first in 1986 and the second in 1987. The new tack was labeled a *pedagogy of cooperation* or *the personality approach*.

> The pedagogy of cooperation must become the pedagogy of the development of the personality, not just of intellectual development.... Our concern is the content of the moral, cultural, professional, and political world-outlook of the personality of the teacher and of every pupil (Suddaby, 1989: 252).

Although proponents of the personality approach have not been of entirely the same mind about what their pedagogy should entail, some elements suggested as desirable components of this pedagogy are that: homework should not be obligatory, there should be some choice of activities so pupils develop initiative, pupils need some free time in which to develop their interests, methods of teaching through play should be introduced, and attention should be focused on developing the learners' self-concepts.

By the close of the 1980s, the enthusiasm that many teachers expressed for the personality approach was not shared by the leadership of the Soviet Academy of Pedagogical Sciences, which continued to advocate instructional methods representing the correct-scientific and individualized approaches (Suddaby, 1989: 255).

Reading-Miscue Analysis in Australia

An example from Australia illustrates the use of detailed research as the basis for recommending how individual differences in reading skills among primary-school pupils might be accommodated.

The study addressed the problem of why certain children become *disabled* readers, in the sense of their falling at least two years behind their agemates in reading skills. The research question was: Are disabled readers simply delayed in their development or are they different in the way they approach the task of reading? To find an answer, the investigators studied two groups of pupils whose reading skills were at the average for grade two of the primary school. One group was comprised of seven-year-old second-graders who were considered to be *normal readers* for their grade. The second group was comprised of fourth graders, age nine, who read no better than the average second grader and thus were judged to be *disabled readers*.

To discover how the two groups differed in their approach to reading, the researchers inspected the miscues pupils made when they met a new passage of reading material. The study led the investigators to conclude that adept "normal" readers intuitively and informally have discovered word-analysis skills (phonics, structural analysis of words, the use of context for understanding a new word, picture clues) that had not been taught to them directly. Therefore, they had acquired multiple techniques for estimating the meaning of new words they met in their reading. In contrast:

> Those children who become disabled readers limit their attention to the cues to which they have been directed in formal reading instruction and, in the absence of training in the recognition and use of linguistic cue systems [word and sentence structural analysis], fail to acquire the meta-knowledge which characterizes their non-disabled peers. This may have been the case for the children participating in this study who had received initial reading instruction that emphasised phonics. Alternatively, the reading disabled child may

> begin to read without the necessary linguistic skills upon which to build word and print specific knowledge, i.e., he (usually he) is asked to run before he can walk and learns only to limp. If these early and basic differences are not remedied via reading instruction, then this may result in the more restricted use of strategies seen in disabled readers in this study (Willich, Prior, Cumming, & Spanos, 1988: 324).

The authors' recommendation for treating such individual differences among learners was that "an important component of reading remediation, at least at this age level, should be a language experience-based approach, with provision of opportunities for disabled and 'at risk' readers to acquire the kinds of deeper knowledge of language which is evident in their non-disabled peers" (Willich, Prior, Cumming, & Spanos, 1988: 325). Such an experienced-based approach can include having children dictate to the teacher their own stories or experiences, which the teacher then prints on a chart so the pupils can read familiar material that is printed in their own words.

TEACHERS' SKILLS, KNOWLEDGE, AND PREFERRED INSTRUCTIONAL STYLE

We are uttering a truism when we propose that teachers prefer to use those instructional methods which they feel they can carry out with some measure of skill. Equally apparent is the observation that most teachers will not adopt a new teaching technique unless they have had enough preparation with the new approach to feel they can manage it with confidence in the classroom. And they also need to be convinced that the new method is more effective than the old, so that adopting the innovation is worth the time and bother required to master it. One example of the influence of teacher skills and preferences was our earlier case of the attempted importation of an English-language instructional method into China. Another illustration is the following one from American Samoa.

From Teacher to TV and Back to Teacher: The Case of American Samoa

The American Samoa example demonstrates the way a cluster of factors can result in the transfer of instructional decisions from the hands of the classroom teacher to a centrally controlled medium, such as textbooks or television. But as time passes, significant conditions can change again, and the control may be shifted once more. In the present instance, control was taken from the teacher, given to television, and returned to the teacher.

American Samoa is a South Pacific possession of the United States of America. The territory is comprised of seven small islands just south of the equator, populated by around 30,000 indigenous Polynesians and recent immigrants. The islands have been held by the United States since 1900.

During the first six decades of this period, the education system was a mixture of public and private schools, most of them in primitive buildings and staffed by local teachers who had meager professional preparation and a relatively poor command of English, which was the intended medium of instruction.

This situation changed suddenly in the 1960s when an investigative commission from the U.S. Congress reported that the island people's educational welfare had been badly neglected by the U.S. government. To remedy the unsatisfactory conditions, officials in Washington appointed a new governor for the islands, H. Rex Lee, who judged that the best way to improve schooling in American Samoa would be to establish a television-instruction system for the territory's two dozen public schools. Modern buildings would replace the schools' crude quarters, and a television-studio complex with transmission facilities would be constructed on Pago Pago Bay to beam daily lessons from the central Department of Education to classrooms throughout the islands. Lee and his staff envisioned in 1961 that such a system, "through the use of a dozen outstanding teachers in the studio, could bring the best teaching to some 300 classrooms that are now being staffed by poorly trained local teachers" (*Report of the governor of American Samoa*, 1962: 3).

From the early 1960s into the early 1970s, the typical lesson in virtually all subject-matter fields for the eight-grade elementary schools consisted of 20 minutes of televised instruction from the central studio, followed by 20 minutes of related activities directed by the classroom teacher. The activities provided pupils the opportunity to apply the content of the televised lesson by completing work sheets, participating in discussions, conducting experiments, preparing exhibits, or the like. In effect, the classroom teacher was no longer the central actor in presenting information but, instead, became a supervisor of children's application of the information. Classroom teachers were expected to learn instructional skills by observing the techniques of the television teachers. In addition, inservice workshops and courses were organized through the territory's new community college to upgrade classroom teachers' skills.

The 1970s, however, witnessed the decline of the television-instructional system so that by the 1980s TV had become only an occasional supplementary or enrichment medium in both elementary and secondary schools. The classroom teacher was once again in command of instruction. The decline, and near demise, of television as the core medium of instruction was caused by the following array of interrelated conditions, some of them technical and professional, others political and economic (Thomas, 1980).

One of the most important influences on the transfer of instructional control back to the classroom teacher was the marked improvement in teachers' instructional skills over the 1960-1980 era. This improvement was chiefly the result of strong preservice and inservice teacher-education programs instituted in the 1960s and 1970s. Preservice teacher-education candidates now earned college degrees (associate of arts, bachelor of arts) before entering full-time teaching. Inservice teachers not only advanced their instructional skills and command of English by viewing the television models, but intensive training in modern instructional techniques was provided by experts from the U.S. mainland. Furthermore, a host of innovative instructional materials were imported. As a consequence, by the 1980s, Samoan teachers commanded a far wider array of instructional skills than ever before.

Linked to the teachers' improved classroom methods was a characteristic of the television lessons that made them ill suited to caring for pupils' individual differences in ability, pace of comprehension, and learning styles. Television programs move ahead at their own pace and offer their fare in a single form. In contrast, a skilled classroom teacher can alter the form and pace of learning tasks to suit individual differences among pupils. Unlike a typical TV presentation, the classroom teacher can continually assess how well pupils are grasping information and then can repeat material that pupils have missed on the first presentation. In effect, the inability of television broadcasts to match its form and pace of presentation to individual needs of students was a significant reason for returning instructional control to teachers.

Additional causes for the abandonment of television as the principal instructional mode were the high costs of preparing new TV programs, problems of keeping equipment in proper working order under tropical atmospheric conditions, and serious financial belt-tightening that the government of American Samoa suffered in the 1970s.

Whereas some observers of the Samoan experiment interpreted the decline of television to mean that instructional TV in such a setting was a mistake —that the experiment had failed. However, others concluded that television did indeed succeed, but not as the central permanent instructional tool. Rather, the TV system succeeded as an emergency measure to upgrade instruction and as a catalyst that mediated broad improvements in the islands' instructional system.

> Few if any members of the Samoan educational establishment seem to think that installing the instructional television project in the 1960s was an error, even through they believe sustaining it today in its original form would be a mistake. The system furnished islanders far better opportunities for learning English and better models of teaching, planning, and evaluating than they had had before. The system also stimulated controversies about educational goals and methods —controversies that brought to Samoa additional teaching methods that could be compared with instructional television for their appropriateness in the Samoan setting. Numbers of these alternative approaches in science, mathematics, health education, the language arts, and bicultural education have since been adopted [so that]...many innovations now in the schools have no necessary connection with instructional television, yet they are in the schools as the result of a catalytic function of the educational television experiment (Thomas, 1980: 166).

ACCOMMODATING FOR WHERE INSTRUCTORS AND THEIR STUDENTS ARE LOCATED

In many Asian, African, and Latin American countries, the schools, inhibited by limited resources and insufficiently trained teachers, cannot expand to meet the educational demands of the populace. Numerous social groups, including rural people, the poor, and those who have had to leave school for economic reasons, suffer from inadequate access to education. To help solve these problems, open-learning programs and distance teaching, as described in Chapter 6, have been viewed as alternatives to traditional instructional approaches for providing programs that extend the access to education to widespread populations that lack nearby educational facilities. Distance education can also reduce educational costs and improve the quality and relevance of instruction. This form of education has emerged largely because so many societies have not been able to satisfy needs through traditional educational structures (Pelton & Filep, 1984).

Distance education assumes several popular forms, each featuring particular instructional methods, equipment, and materials. The most traditional form is written correspondence that is exchanged between teacher and students through the public mail. Teachers at a central location post reading materials to students. The students complete exercises, write essays, conduct experiments, and take quizzes at home, then return these responses to the teacher by mail.

More recently, radio and television have come to play a crucial role in linking instructors with their students. Radio has become the more popular of the broadcast media, particularly in developing nations, because of the low cost and small size of radio receivers and the relatively modest expenditure for equipment and preparation required at the source of the broadcasts.

Although television is a far more expensive medium than radio, its advantages in providing both sight and sound have made it the preferred distance-instruction tool in societies that can afford the necessary investment of funds and personnel. As a consequence, many nations are currently engaged in satellite-based tele-educational program development to provide both basic and vocational education to people of all ages who live in widely dispersed geographic areas. A satellite system permits the establishment of quality educational programs far more quickly than is possible by conventional means of building and supplying new schools. This is a significant advantage for developing countries which lack extensive ground infrastructure (roads, school buildings) in rural and remote areas. Through radio or television, a single teacher can offer instruction simultaneously to hundreds of students who live hundreds of kilometers apart.

Examples of distance education in Brazil and Kenya illustrate two ways instruction has been provided for widely distributed populations of learners.

Distance Education in Brazil

As early as 1961, Brazil recognized the potential of radio for educational purposes and developed a project called *Movement de Educacao de Base*, which used a combination of radio, print, and interpersonal communication to train illiterate rural farmers. The basic unit in this particular educational program has been the rural farmers' study group. Apart from studying together in a small group, farmers have been furnished books and required to listen to radio broadcasts that have supplemented direct personal interaction. The radio broadcasts not only have taught farmers how to read but have also disseminated information on agriculture, nutrition, labor practices, and other practical topics.

Starting from 1969, Brazil began to apply television technology in its public education. To combat the severe lack of public-school facilities beyond the fourth grade, television was used to present secondary learning materials, while trained teachers provided the instructional support for learning. The program was directed to students in grades five through eight. Later, Educational Television Maranhao gradually expanded its activities and now includes a secondary school course for out-of-school adults, a literacy program, and cultural programming for more advanced students.

With the help of specialists from abroad, particularly from the United Kingdom, Brazil has evolved an expert group of educational-program designers trained in instructional skills, production techniques, evaluation, and system analysis. Typical of the staff's products is the series entitled *The Wonderful World of Mathematics* in which everyday situational problems are dramatized with a humorous approach to keep students interested. Another program targeting teacher trainees has focused on instructional methodology in which classroom situations have been dramatized while a narrator isolates, emphasizes, and explains classroom events for the audience of student teachers.

In sum, Brazil, over the past 30 years, has progressed from broadcasting fairly simple radio teaching programs to producing educational fare for both private and governmental TV channels (Lauffer, *et al.*, 1984).

Instruction via Radio in Kenya

Educational planners in the East African nation of Kenya have depended chiefly on radio rather than television to serve the educational needs of a scattered population of learners. Radio has been adopted in preference to television, not only because of the very limited availability of TV receivers and production facilities, but also because radio represents a continuation of the oral tradition in Africa. An example of a typical series in Kenya's array of broadcast offerings is the *Radio Language Arts Project* (RLAP). The RLAP program was devised for teaching English to primary school students so as to prepare them for secondary school, where English is the language of instruction. Each day a 30-minute lesson is broadcast as the pupils' major instruction in language arts, with the programs focusing on improving students' oral skills.

Instead of directly importing foreign materials, the program planners developed their own lessons that assist the student in learning skills related to needs and interests in their rural environments. The daily broadcasts also engage classroom teachers in preparing their pupils for each lesson and, following every broadcast, in providing pupils with additional language exercises, both oral and written. Thus, RLAP has offered quality instruction in English at lower cost to a greater number of students than would be possible with direct classroom teaching. The design of the instructional materials makes them adaptable to various instructional contexts. In other words, the practice exercises can be altered to suit local needs (Lauffer, *et al.*, 1984).

FUTURE PROSPECTS

In the years ahead, marked advances in educational technology will open a wide range of new possibilities for educational methods, yet a great proportion of the world's instructional programs will remain bound to traditional, outmoded teaching techniques. An examination of the areas of technological innovation and of instructional traditions demonstrates the reasoning behind such a prediction.

First, consider the state of communication electronics. Present-day computer and video technology has made possible the following vision of the well-equipped classroom, which includes a microcomputer at each student's desk, a teacher's master computer console, a learning-resource center within the school system, and remote resource centers that may be reached either via telephone lines or via communication satellites.

> The microcomputer at each student's desk is small —6-by-8 inches in length and width, and 2-inches high. The student can enter information into the computer either by voice (by a microphone/headset unit) or by means of a keyboard. In addition, the computer is equipped with a flip-up 6-by-8-inch video screen that can be laid flat on the desk so the student can write or draw on it with a stylus.
>
> For transmitting to, and receiving from, distant computers, a student's microcomputer can be connected to any telephone by means of a tiny clip-on microphone/receiver. Or, alternatively, the microcomputer can be connected to a matchbook-size transmitter/receiver that permits direct interaction with a communication satellite. However, such communication with information sources outside the classroom is permitted only under direct teacher supervision. A silicon chip inside the microcomputer provides storage capacity for millions of elements of information.
>
> There are several options available to students for displaying information that is already in their computer's memory or that arrives from some outside

> source, such as from the teacher's master computer at the front of the classroom or from a telephone line or satellite. These options include the 6-by-8-inch video screen, a headset and an audio amplifier for music or speech, a remote-controlled laser printer, and a remote-transmitter switch that permits the microcomputer to display the computer's printed or graphic output on any regular television set (accompanied by sound, either music or speech). Each desk-top computer can also run compact disks that contain large quantities of information from a wide range of fields —the language arts, natural and social sciences, the humanities, and creative arts.
>
> A computer complex at the teacher's desk offers wireless transmission to, and reception from, students' microcomputers, the school's learning-resource center, and remote communication satellites. The ability to connect with students' microcomputers allows the teacher to transmit the same material simultaneously to all students' computers, or, by means of a special entry code assigned to each student's computer, to communicate only with selected individuals or groups. In addition, it gives the teacher the means to "tune in" the display of any student's microcomputer.
>
> The ability to connect directly with the school system's learning-resource center gives the teacher access to a wide variety of learning materials and evaluation devices. In similar fashion, the ability to tie into communication satellites that furnish access to national and international banks of information puts the teacher in touch with countless other resources with which to enrich students' learning opportunities. The teacher also can display printed and graphic material on a 4-by-6-foot video screen at the front of the classroom. Anything that she writes or draws on an 8-by-10-inch plate on her desk can be shown simultaneously on the large video screen or on the students' individual screens, thus making classroom chalkboards unnecessary.
>
> The school system's learning-resource center stores great quantities of information in a mainframe computer, with each segment of material retrieved by teachers via telephone lines. The stored materials include (1) reading matter, such as textbooks, worksheets, novels, encyclopedias, biographical dictionaries, atlases and (2) videodisc recordings of science demonstrations, maps, travelogues, musical performances, art exhibits, vocational activities, historical events, recent news, athletic contests, and the like (Thomas, 1987: 12-13).

In parallel with these advances in technology, a rapidly increasing body of research and development on instructional methods today furnishes teachers with better information than ever before about the application of a wide array of teaching procedures. Furthermore, improved modes of information exchange among nations have made this body of knowledge available to more education systems than at any time in the past. As a consequence, the potential for improving instruction throughout the world has never been as great as in the 1990s.

The question now may be asked: To what extent are such bright possibilities for instructional progress likely to be realized in practice over the coming years?

The answer, I believe, is that the degree to which improved teaching methods are adopted will vary dramatically from one nation to another. Furthermore, even within a particular nation, the extent to which innovations are applied will differ significantly from one educational program to another. This marked variability will be caused by such conditions as (1) educational programs' financial support, (2) societies' educational traditions, (3) facilities and personnel available for preservice and inservice teacher training, and (4) the complexity of decisions about when a given instructional approach will be the most suitable.

Present-day differences in the level of financial support of educational programs can be expected to continue in the future. Such affluent societies as those of Japan, the United States, Canada, oil-rich Arab countries, and the more advanced industrial nations of Western Europe, Singapore, Australia, and the like are in a far better financial position to apply technological innovations in both formal and nonformal educational programs than are those countries whose schooling is supported by either a modest or weak economic base. Impoverished countries cannot even afford to supply enough minimally-qualified teachers, classrooms, or textbooks to serve their populations, much less introduce such electronic gadgetry as computers and television systems. It is also the case that within many countries —and particularly in developing nations— financial support and attitudes toward innovation are usually greater in urban than in rural areas. Because so many regions of the world experience serious financial limitations, we can expect that the most efficient instructional methods available today will not be found in most of the world's classrooms and nonformal programs. Although more and more countries will take advantage of distance education via radio and television, in-classroom teaching methodology will continue to be of the more traditional, less efficient types —nonillustrated lectures and pupils memorizing material from textbooks or the chalkboard.

Educational traditions will also continue to be an important factor retarding the use of newer instructional approaches. If teachers are to adopt innovations, they must be willing to spend the time and effort to change their established practices. They also need to admit that their present methods are inferior to the proposed new ones. In other words, they must acknowledge that they have not been doing a particularly good job of teaching in the past, so a change to something better is called for. But, for most teachers, such an admission is ego-deflating. It is more self-satisfying for them to assume that they have been doing their job efficiently, so there is no need to change. Therefore, sticking with their traditional methods enables teachers to save time and energy and to maintain their established self-satisfied self-image. Likewise, by continuing in their familiar teaching style, they avoid risking the embarrassment they might suffer in front of their students if they failed to use the new approach skillfully. The influence of tradition is readily observed in higher-education classrooms throughout the world. Most college instructors in both economically advanced nations and developing societies continue to lecture crowds of students, even when their lecture material is readily accessible to students in printed form and when other instructional procedures would profitably engage students in actively applying the subject matter (experiments, group discussions, problem-solving tasks, individual and group projects, simulation games, computer applications, field trips, and the like).

A third factor affecting the adoption of efficient teaching procedures is the shortage of facilities and personnel needed for equipping preservice and inservice teachers with the skills required for applying improved practices. The inertia of tradition that retards the adoption of new methods in typical schools also operates in teacher-training institutions. Instructors in teacher-education programs, like their counterparts in regular schools, are often reluctant to learn innovative teaching practices. And even when they do introduce such methods in their teacher-training program, it takes years before the effect of the innovations is felt in a nation's primary- and secondary-school classrooms.

In summary, because of the above factors (finances, traditions, teacher-education conditions) the widespread adoption of improved instructional methods is a slow process. An additional factor, described in the opening paragraphs of this chapter, is the variability of teaching situations from one classroom to another. It is often difficult for even the best-qualified teachers, equipped with sufficient finances and advanced technology, to arrive at a clear answer to our multi-faceted question about teaching methods:

> In this particular instructional environment, which of the methods and materials under consideration will be most suitable in view of: (1) the specific learning objectives being pursued (skill-oriented, knowledge-oriented, value-oriented), (2) the available technology (the facilities and supplies at hand), (3) sociopolitical conditions that can influence instructional methods, (4) the maturity levels, educational backgrounds, abilities, and interests of the learners, (5) teachers' skills, knowledge of subject matter, and preferred instructional style, (6) the place in which the students and the teacher are located, and more?

REFERENCES

Block, J. H. (1971) *Mastery learning, theory and practice.* New York: Holt, Rinehart, & Wintson.

Burnaby, B., & Sun, Y. L. (1989) Chinese teachers views of Western language teaching: Context informs paradigms. TESOL Quarterly Vol 23, 2: 219-238.

Cantor, L. (1985) Vocational education and training: the Japanese approach. Comparative Education Vol. 21-1: 67-76.

Corbeil, P. (1988) Les chasseurs-cueilleurs (hunters-gatherers). *Simulation & Games*, 19 (2): 228-230.

La Belle, T. J. (1986) *Nonformal education in Latin America and the Caribbean.* New York: Praeger.

Lauffer, S., Douglas, S., & Casey-Stahmer, A. (1984) National capacities for tele-education. In W. Blume & P. Schneller (Eds), *Toward international tele-education* (pp. 99-113). Boulder, CO: Westview Press.

Marshall, C. E., & Richard, J. (1989) Developing culturally based patient education materials for non-reading elderly Hispanics. *Techtrends: for Leaders in Education and Training,* 34 (1): 27-30.

Maughan, G. R. (1989) India: Implications of communication infrastructure on the production of media in state training institute. *Techtrends: for Leaders in Education and Training,* 34 (1): 17-21.

McCormick (1989) Towards a lifelong learning society? The reform of continuing vocational education and training in Japan. *Comparative Education,* 25 (2): 133-150.

Pierce, B. N. (1989) Toward a pedagogy of possibility in the teaching of English internationally: people's English in South Africa. *TESOL Quarterly,* 23 (3): 401-420.

Pelton, J. N., & Filep, R. T. (1984) Tele-education via satellite. In W. Blume & P. Schneller (Ed.), *Toward international tele-education,* (pp. 149-188). Boulder, CO: Westview Press.

Renaud, L., & Stolovitch, H. J. (1988) Simulation gaming. *Simulation & Games,* 19 (3): 328-345.

Report of the governor of American Samoa (1962) Pago Pago: Department of Education.

Suddaby, A. (1989) An evaluation on the contribution of the teacher-innovators to Soviet educational reform. *Comparative Education,* 25 (2): 245-256.

Thomas, R. M. (1987) Advanced information systems and the goals of schooling. *Andrew Seybold's Outlook on Professional Computing,* 5 (12): 12-15.

Thomas. R. M. (1980) The rise and decline of an educational technology: Television in American Samoa. *ECTJ (Educational Communication and Technology Journal),* 28 (3): 155-167.

Willich, Y., Prior, M., Cumming, G., & Spanos, T. (1988) Are disabled readers delayed or different? An approach using an objective miscue analysis. *British Journal of Educational Psychology,* 58 (3): 315-329.

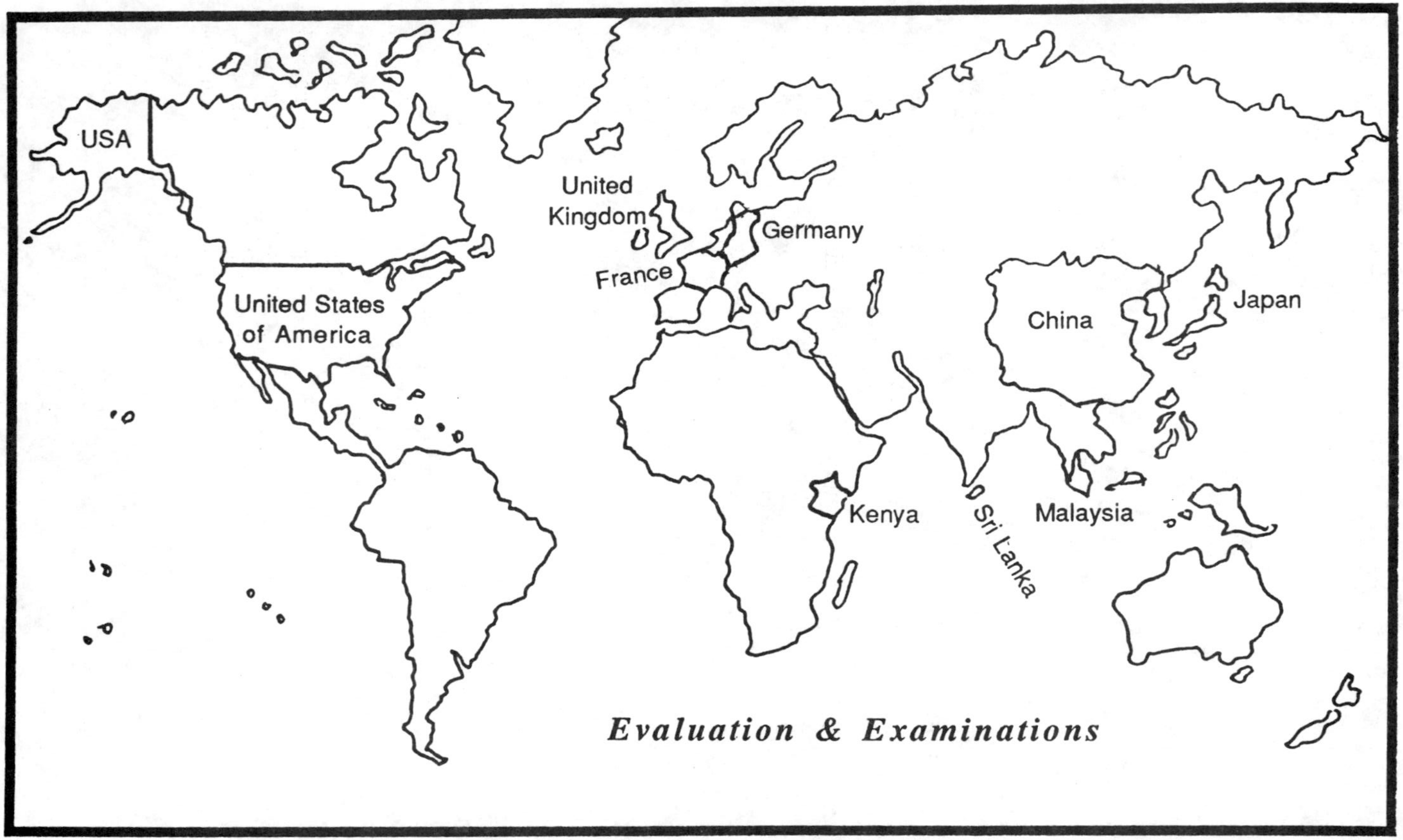
USA
United States
of America
United
Kingdom
France
Germany
China
Japan
Kenya
Sri Lanka
Malaysia
Evaluation & Examinations

CHAPTER 4

Evaluation and Examinations

Why and how are educational outcomes assessed?

WILLIAM K. CUMMINGS

Evaluation in education assumes diverse forms and serves many purposes. The procedures for evaluating pupils and other participants in education systems have become progressively elaborated since at least the middle of the nineteenth century to the point where they now command substantial resources. Upwards of ten percent of instructional time is devoted to such procedures in many systems, and as much as ten percent of educational expenditures may go —either directly or indirectly— for evaluation.

Educators' evaluation activities are of many kinds. Policy makers appraise the schools' learning goals to determine whether such goals are the ones most suitable for the society and for the learners' aptitudes. Administrators assess the schools' management system to decide how effectively it promotes educational outcomes. Governing boards appraise the sources of school funds to judge if those are the most appropriate sources. The personnel who operate the education system —teachers, headmasters, school psychologists, support staff— are also evaluated to determine how well they perform their functions.

However, among all the types of assessment, the most frequent and pervasive is that which focuses on the learners. Students are evaluated to determine how much they know (knowledge), how efficiently they perform (skills), what convictions they hold (values, attitudes), and how much potential they have for further learning (aptitudes). Assessments of student performance are often categorized as either *formative* or *summative* evaluations. Formative evaluation is the kind continuously conducted during the students' learning activities. It consists of day-by-day teacher judgments of how well pupils are mastering each step of the learning process. The resulting information is typically used to guide teachers' decisions as they help students overcome learning difficulties and as they determine when sudents are ready for new learning tasks. Among the techniques used for deriving formative information are: written tests that accompany a textbook, teacher-made quizzes, standarized tests, workbook exercises, oral questions that students answer during group discussion, pupils' essays, the teacher's judgments of products students create (charts, graphs, maps, models, exhibits, experiments), observations of pupils' performance (their use of a computer, their skill in games, their participation in group work), and more.

Summative evaluation, on the other hand, refers to assessment conducted at the end of a lengthy period of study, such as at the end of a semester, of a year, or of a major segment of the schooling hierarchy (the end of elementary school, or of junior-secondary school, or of senior-secondary school). Information dervied from summative evaluation is typically used for deciding what final mark or grade a student deserves, whether the student should receive a diploma or certificate, and where the student will go for the next stage of his or her schooling.

Reviewing all of the foregoing facets of educational evaluation is far beyond the scope of this chapter. Thus, one aspect that is currently of key international interest has been selected for analysis. That aspect is the use of summative evaluation —in the form of written or oral examinations— for guiding decisions about the next step in students' school careers. Although the focus will be primarily on examinations, we will also direct some passing attention to the assessment of the value of educational innovations, the assessment of teacher and school performance, and the generation of information to help decision-makers plan ahead (Lewy, 1981: 4; Bloom *et al.*, 1971: 7).

While evaluation pervades the educational system, many of its characteristics become most evident through the role it plays in shaping the linkage of schools and universities (Clark, 1985), so the major focus of this chapter will be on that transition. Some recent studies tend to look for commonalities in national evaluative styles (Eckstein & Noah, 1989), but there are also marked differences. And these differences in evaluative styles provide some striking revelations of how education systems vary. Some national systems evaluate selected subject-matter areas or skills, while other focus on a broad range. Evaluative procedures take many forms, ranging from verbal to written assessments, from predetermined to open formats, from pretest to posttest, from aptitude to achievement. Similarly, the institutional locus of evaluations varies widely: in some systems national governments supervise evaluation, in others special independent examining bodies perform this function, while yet in others teachers have extensive responsibilities.

In this chapter we seek to understand (1) why has evaluation become progressively more prominent in educational systems, (2) what are the major variations in evaluation, (3) how can this variation be explained, and (4) what are the educational implications? The discussion begins with a brief review of the history of examinations, then describes how this history helps explain the present-day role of examinations in Germany, France, Britain, the United States, and Japan. The chapter closes with comparative reflections on systems of evaluation and speculation about what might be expected in this field over the years ahead.

THE ORIGINS OF EXAMINATIONS

Rigorous forms of evaluation of formal educational achievement are generally believed to have first been developed in China by the Sui (589-618 A.D.) emperors (Miyazaki, 1981). Prior to that, during the Han period, informal means of evaluating the qualifications of members of aristocratic families had been employed to select those who would assume key posts in the Imperial household. But in the earlier evaluations, which tended to focus on attributes of character and style, relatively little attention was focused on specific content taught in schools.

Two major factors account for the introduction of formal examinations by the Sui emperors. Perhaps most important was a tactical need, in that the Sui were outsiders attempting to establish control over an entrenched aristocratic system, so they developed a means of selecting officials that would provide legitimacy for a new ruling group. Recognizing the high prestige of the Confucian intellectual heritage, the Sui leaders hit upon the idea of testing aspirants in terms of their knowledge of this presitigous heritage. They reasoned that the aristocrats would have no special advantage in these tests over other candidates from, for example, their own society. The crucial determinants of success would be natural ability and effort in mastering the prescribed subject matter.

Secondly, as Shigeru Nakayama (1984) observes, China by virtue of the special characteristic of its intellectual heritage, was uniquely in a position to devise a formal examination. Nakayama suggests that two major approaches have emerged for the development of knowledge, the documentary and the rhetorical. In the rhetorical tradition, which was characteristic of the Judeo-Hebraic tradition and received its highest development in Classical Greece, knowledge was developed through verbal assertions and argumentation. The standard of proof was success in convincing a group of peers of the soundness of a particular viewpoint. Plato's *Dialogues* are an example of this form of knowledge creation; significantly, the *Dialogues* were written down by Plato's student long after their original presentation. The rhetorical tradition did not depend on a written record.

In contrast was China's documentary tradition where knowledge was developed and recorded on paper rather than expressed in debate. Additions to knowledge made reference to antecedents either directly or through symbolism. The core documents in the Confucian tradition were the Five Classics and the Four Books. The later books in this corpus made consistent reference to their precedents as they explored new themes. Professional scholars working in such areas as medicine, astronomy, or even poetry observed the same discipline.

There are extensive debates on the relative merits of these two forms of knowledge development (Needham, 1956; Lach, 1977; Boorstin, 1983). Regardless of the conclusions, undisputed is the much earlier development in

China of a flexible writing system and an extensive body of recorded knowledge. Thus, China was in a position, at a much earlier time than the West, to develop written knowledge-based examinations.

The Chinese exam system was designed to test the pupil's comprehensive mastery of all this written material. Aspirants were expected to prepare for the exams on their own in private schools run by able scholars or through private tutorials. It has been estimated that an exceptional youth who could memorize 200 new characters a day (the equivalent of a page in this book) might be prepared for the first round of examinations by the age of 15; most aspirants took much longer, continuing their studies even into their thirties. A system of regional testing was devised to screen out poorly prepared students. Those who survived these hurdles were invited to travel to the capital city to take the highest exam over a continuous period of three days. The candidates' answers were evaluated by a special examining board appointed by the emperor, focusing their appraisal on correct referencing, literary quality, and penmanship. Each time the exam was offered, a fixed number of aspirants were accepted into the imperial bureaucracy.

EXAMINATIONS IN THE WEST

There are various accounts concerning the origins of examinations in the West (Durkheim, 1966; Montgomery, 1965; Amano, 1990). An enduring theme in the Western societies, drawing from the rhetorical tradition, has been the reliance on oral and other less-structured forms of evaluation, such as recommendations and practical achievements. For example, in continental Europe, most secondary school-leaving examinations have an oral component; and the interview is a major component of evaluation for entry to top English universities. Through the seventeenth century, evaluation in the West relied almost exclusively on such criteria. But from about that time, written examinations became progressively more prominent, and it is generally assumed that this was due to admiration for the Chinese example.

It is not altogether clear how the West became aware of the Chinese system. For example, Matteo Ricci, a Jesuit missionary, was said to have provided glowing descriptions of this system in the letters he sent from his China post. His letters and subsequently the prominence of Matteo Ricci in the Jesuit order are pointed to as factors behind the introduction of rigorous examinations into the Jesuit schooling system from the early eighteenth century (Durkheim, 1966). The quality of Jesuit schooling, it has been suggested, eventually led to imitation by other educational institutions.

Ikuo Amano (1990), who has written the most comprehensive study of the role of examinations in modern education, suggests that Prussia was the first European society to rely on such assessments for the selection of public officials. From as early as 1748 Prussia depended on examinations for filling all government administrative posts. University education became a prerequisite for seeking a government office, thus leading to competition for university entrance (Ringer, 1974). In 1788 the *abitur* examination was introduced as a means for determining who was qualified to graduate from the middle schools (and thus have claim to a place at the university). Over the succeeding years, examinations were introduced at lower levels.

The German example was the inspiration for selective reforms in other nations of Continental Europe during the late eighteenth and early nineteenth centuries.

Another account (Montgomery, 1965) suggests that the British East India company admired the Chinese examination system, and decided from the early nineteenth century to introduce a similar method for the selection of its local-hire personnel. Eventually the system was elaborated to become the basis for all new appointments to the East India Company. And following this example, in 1872 the British government introduced competitive examinations for all civil service appointments.

Amano observes that, while there are various accounts of the origins of exams, what stands out is the pervasive interest from about the middle of the nineteenth century in examinations as a means of social selection. Thus, he calls this period the *Age of Examinations*. The key background factor in this era is the emergence of large public bureaucracies to collect revenues and administer various services. These bureaucracies sought effective means of selecting staff. One after another, they turned to some form of examination for this purpose. Exams were also used for entry to other important positions, including those in medicine, the judiciary, and even the clergy. In some areas, the professions introduced examinations ahead of the civil service. But especially from this period, the examinations for entry to the professions became more rigorous, and often the state played some role in the administration of the exams.

Because schools had been the traditional source for supplying staff to the bureaucracies, the schools themselves began to introduce examinations, in part, at least, as a means of preparing students for the official examinations. There are interesting national peculiarities in the structure of school examinations of that time which persist in considerable degree down to the present, as demonstrated in the following examples.

The German Pattern

In Germany, which pioneered in the introduction of civil service and professional examinations, students move at a relatively early age into one of several tracks. Currently these are the *hauptschule* (main school) leading to terminal vocational training at about age 18, the *gymnasium*, which provides preparation for universities, and the *realschule*, which directs youth to intermediate positions in the occupational hierarchy (Teichler, 1985: 46). Once students are in these tracks, there are relatively few examinations until their conclusion; and, even at that point, the pressure of the examinations is not insufferable, for there is reasonable balance in the number of openings in the next respective stages (Teichler & Sanyal, 1982). The *abitur*, which covers only certain subjects, is the examination administered at the conclusion of the gymnasium. Students who pass this test are entitled to continue studies at their local university, and in principle are qualified to attend any university throughout Germany.

The French Pattern

In France there are frequent exams at every stage over many subject-matter areas, and many pupils fail, with the result that they have to repeat grades and even drop out. For those experiencing difficulty, various terminal vocational educational opportunities are provided. Those who endure the gauntlet of academic tests enter a lycee where they can pursue either a science or arts course (Neave, 1985: 24). At the conclusion of each year, students are required to take year-end tests, and the failure of a test in any subject area necessitates the repetition of the entire school year. At the completion of the lycee, students are tested with both a written and an oral examination as a condition for further study. In contrast with Germany, where the universities are paramount, the most prestigious concluding step to educational careers in France is one of the *grandes ecoles* which specialize in fields of practice, such as engineering, finance, or education. Only a small fraction of lycee graduates are able to gain entry to these institutions. Relative to other European systems, the French system is viewed as highly competitive and singularly shaped by the series of selective examinations devised by the Central Ministry of Education.

The Anglo Pattern

The United Kingdom was a late entrant to the Age of Examinations. England's great universities and her well-known public schools were managed by the Anglican Church for the benefit primarily of the upper classes, and many of the places in these institutions were reserved for the descendents of these special groups. Under such circumstances, there was natural resistance to testing the qualifications of students. However, in the mid-eighteenth century, Cambridge University introduced an honors examination to confer recognition on those students who applied themselves with special vigor. Oxford followed suit in 1800, and this practice also was emulated in several of the public schools.

In contrast to Prussia and France, schooling in the U. K. was much more decentralized, and the state had a minimal role in the popular educational system which was quite diverse. To bring some unity to this system, in 1861 the state proposed a special national test with the provision that local governments whose students did well would receive certain subsidies. Thus, a pattern was introduced linking state involvement in local educational systems with the examination performance of the students of these systems. So in the U.K., exams were introduced from above as a means of promoting quality in certain subject areas offered by the schools of a highly decentralized system and not as part of a monolithic program for realizing a fully integrated system under the control of the Center. This same principle was manifest in later exam reforms. Especially noteworthy after World War II was the 11+ exam which schools were encouraged to use as a means for selecting young adolescents for university preparatory courses (Young, 1958). As the secondary school system expanded, it became necessary to devise a means for selecting individuals for those university places not allocated on the basis of heredity. In response, the major universities formed an examining board which devised a series of subject specific examinations. These became known as the ordinary examinations (O-levels) and advanced examinations (A-levels). Students could take as many of these as they wished, but a high performance on at least three A-levels came to be essential for advancement to university studies.

The reforms associated with the U.K.'s Educational Act of 1988 are, at least in the views of some, a further extension of the traditional principle of limited state intervention, with reward tied to evaluation (Johnson, 1989). The main difference in the current round is that the state has prescribed a fixed national curriculum, and the state's evaluation will focus on the success of local educational authorities in implementing that curriculum as measured by student performance on national exams tied to this curriculum. The local educational authorities, however, retain the autonomy to implement the curriculum in whatever way they wish.

Evaluation in the United States of America

Until the middle of the nineteenth century, U.S. American education was largely modeled on the U.K. pattern, with a minimum of formal evaluation of student performance. However, as a new nation that was conscious of its backwardness, America was highly alert to the latest trends on the Continent, including the use of written examinations. Thus, as early as 1850 systematic testing began to appear in the school systems of large urban areas, and in 1865 in the state of New York the Regents Examinations were introduced along the lines of the German *abiteur*. But these examinations were peculiar to New York.

Two other traditions that emerged during this period had a more enduring influence on the selection of college students. According to Wechsler (1977), the University of Michigan pioneered in the identification of reputable high schools and in reliance on their recommendations as a basis for admitting students. Eventually this approach was modified to take account of the averaged grades received by their students (GPA or grade-point average). But the elite colleges of the East Coast, while also maintaining special relations with selected high schools and preparatory schools, did not want to be solely tied to such a principle. Nicholas Murray Butler of Columbia University was particularly firm in pressing for some form of entrance exam. Eventually this led him in 1901 to take the lead in forming a small consortium known as the College Entrance Examination Board. This Board devised an essay-style entrance test to be used jointly by participating schools as one means for evaluating prospective entrants. While the first examinations followed the English pattern of essays, over the early decades of the twentieth century the philosophy changed under the influence of the emerging discipline of psychology. To understand this shift, it will be helpful to consider important developments of that time in American society.

At the turn of the century, America was just moving into a stage of rapid growth of industrial and governmental organizations, with their needs to recruit employees and make good use of them. For example, the new factories for the mass production of cars needed to evaluate the applications of several thousand employees in a short period of time and make appropriate assignments of their work force to a great diversity of jobs. The new discipline of psychology was turned to for assistance in making these decisions, and it responded with various tests of ability, personality types, and intelligence. Noting that new Southern European immigrants and Blacks generally faired poorly on these tests, some critics suggested that the tests served as a means of providing "scientific" legitimacy for discriminatory personnel practices. Subsequently, psychological testing achieved a new level of legitimacy in World War I when it was used as a means of screening recruits for military service (Young, 1958).

With this background, it was only a matter of time before educational institutions would turn to psychological testing to assist them in making various decisions. Indeed, as we will indicate in the next section, some American school systems have institutionalized psychological testing as a key element in virtually all decision-making areas. But prior to outlining that comprehensive approach, it will be helpful to point out some of the distinctive features of American testing.

In contrast to Continental Europe, where schools were oriented to conveying a commonly accepted curriculum, American educators were less certain about what should be taught at the various levels. In the absence of agreement on content, they tended to look at schools as settings for the stimulation of thought processes and overall human development. Thus, in thinking of ways to evaluate students, they were as much concerned with measuring the students' ability or aptitude as their achievement. Indeed, many of the educational tests developed over the twentieth century had this character.

Perhaps most notable among these is the *Scholastic Aptitude Test*, which was developed after World War II under the sponsorship of the College Entrance Examination Board. Following World War II, a large number of Americans returned from their military duties with the intent of seeking further education. As the soldiers had been away from their studies for a long time, it seemed unfair to examine them on the basis of what they knew. Thus a new test was sought which would measure their aptitude for collegiate study. This test was to be divided into two sections, one for verbal aptitude and one for mathematics aptitude. To develop the SAT, the independent non-profit Educational Testing Service was established, and over time this organization has developed impressive sophistication in the design of various other tests. Most such tests take a multiple-choice format which, while costly to produce, as they require considerable expertise for the framing and selection of questions, they can be efficiently graded. Thus, they are suitable for the common evaluation of large numbers of students.

The SAT was first administered in 1947 and rapidly became institutionalized as one of the principal criteria that American colleges use for deciding on the admissibility of applicants. The test supposedly taps basic aptitudes and thus ostensibly is not one that individuals can study for or that teachers can teach to. It is not tied to the study of specific subjects, so the particular curriculum a student has covered should not have great bearing on their results. The test also is supposed to be culturally unbiased so that students of different ethnic and racial backgrounds have an equal chance to do well. These "supposed" characteristics are highly attractive, and thus have caught the attention of educators around the world who are concerned with such issues as cultural bias, teaching to the test, diverse academic backgrounds of students, and inefficient testing procedures. Therefore, a number of countries, ranging from Japan to Indonesia, have attempted to introduce elements of the U.S. model into their procedures for university admissions.

Not all American educators have been as enamored of the aptitude tests as are personnel of the Educational Testing Service. Many obserervers question the appropriateness or accuracy of numerical measures of an individual's worth, especially when these measures are based on multiple-choice questions. Critics can point to other possibilities for evaluation that are equally sensible (Owen, 1985). And they ask whether some areas of knowledge can be meaningfully measured with multiple-choice questions. They also ask if the tests measure the full range of aptitudes or intelligences that American education seeks to cultivate (Gardner and Hatch, 1989).

Over the past several years, the "supposed" characteristics of the SAT have further been called into question by a number of researchers who show that, despite the efforts of the ETS to construct culture-fair measures, many of the test questions retain a strong cultural bias. A number of private tutoring or "cram" schools have achieved excellent results in raising the test scores of students (Slack & Porter, 1980). And the academic preparation of students has been shown to have a strong relationship to aptitude as measured by the SAT. So the

SAT's reputation has been in decline as a panacea for educational evaluation. Many American educators are urging a shift back to more curriculum-specific achievement-based tests as a fairer way of evaluating student progress. And many leading colleges are deemphasizing their reliance on the SAT as a criterion for admissions.

A Comprehensive Educational Evaluation System

Another important American contribution has been the vision of a comprehensive educational evaluation system. In no other country have schools shown such an interest in testing as in the U.S. For example, the *Ninth Mental Measurements Yearbook* (Mitchell, 1985) describes 1,409 published tests in current use. Furthermore, in no other country have computers been so extensively mobilized to store and analyze test results. Tests have been used by American schools not only for measuring student aptitutes and achievement but also for assessing student personality profiles, teacher aptitudes, school climate and management styles, and a host of other characteristics. In recent years, some educational evaluators have begun to see how these various pieces of information can be linked so as to produce a comprehensive system for the evaluation of education. Perhaps the best way to illustrate this vision is to cite the example of the state of North Carolina, where considerable progress has been made towards the realization of the formal testing portion of this goal.

In the state of North Carolina, all children in all grades are administered an achievement test in selected subjects each year. The test results are coded in such a manner that the scores of a student during one year can be compared to that student's results for the previous year, thus providing an indicator of how much he or she has gained during the year. The results can also be analyzed to determine how much the students of particular schools or particular classes in schools have gained in a year. Such results also enable comparison of the relative level of achievement of individual children, classes, and schools. Information of this kind can be put to a variety of uses, including the mobilization of remedial work for individual students, classes, or schools where insufficient progress is shown. Other uses could include linking teacher salary increases to the tested performance of the students they teach, or keying principals' salaries to the test scores of their schools.

In North Carolina, the system thus far has been used only for student-related decisions. However, the possibilities for applying test results appear great indeed, and that is one of the concerns of watchful educators. For instance, is the information in this system appropriate for making all sorts of decisions about students, teachers, and administrators? Might the privacy rights of students and teachers be violated by certain uses of such a system? These are some of the disturbing questions raised by that type of comprehensive testing program.

EXAMINATIONS IN MODERN JAPAN

Japan, which wakened from a deep feudal slumber in the mid-nineteenth century, was much impressed by the technological advances of the West and concluded that the key to catching up would be the rapid development of Western style education (Spaulding, 1967: 23). Thus, in 1872 the new government proposed compulsory primary education and took rapid steps to develop a university system of high quality.

The Japanese began the development of their education system just at the time the West was at the peak of its Age of Examinations. Hence, a major theme in the early Japanese thinking about education was the use of examinations to stimulate learning. In local areas, a series of learning competitions was set up between primary schools. Top government officials would attend day-long sessions in which young students competed in jousts of mathematics or literary prowess. Through such competition, the young government sought to fan enthusiasm for modern learning (Amano, 1990).

Distinct from these popular competitions were the principles for evaluation built into the formal educational system. The early Japanese model was founded on European precedents, especially the French example with a centrally prescribed curriculum and textbooks, frequent tests throughout each school year, and a final test at the completion of the year. Passage of the year-end test was, in principle, a precondition for moving on to the next level. But in the Japanese case, schools were often small, and able students found ways to complete the year-end tests ahead of schedule, thus accelerating their progress. At least in the early stages, most of the tests were devised by the teachers of the particular schools.

The critical tests that emerged in Japan were those determining who could move from one school level to the next. And concerning this transition, the Japanese eventually resolved on a different principle from that practiced in Europe —the use of entrance exams to the higher level rather than school-leaving exams from the lower level. As the system now operates, in the transition from middle school to high school, middle-school marks receive equal weight with the high school entrance test. But in transition to higher education, the exams administered by the universities are the sole criterion. The final decision on a student's admission to a university is based on his or her performance on an examination prepared and marked by the faculty of that particular institution.

The formal reasoning behind this practice is that the content for the two levels is not always adequately articulated, so it is important for the receiving institution to insure that entrants have adequate preparation for the institution's program. Indeed, to insure adequate preparation, some of the middle and higher-level schools have created special preparatory courses. However, it has been argued that this modification reflects a strong theme in Japanese culture of setting strict conditions for the initiation of new social relations on the assumption that once a commitment is made it should be a lasting one. That is, the system is designed to preclude the failure of a student by a teacher or a school (Cummings, 1985).

Another interesting feature of Japanese evaluation is the comprehensiveness of the subject-matter covered. For example, to enter upper secondary schools, students are required to take an exam in every subject, including physical education. Entrance examinations to universities typically cover five subjects. Even schools of music include the standard subjects of English language and mathematics in their entrance tests. Especially at the university level, Japan's entrance examinations are difficult, and quite a few students fail. Those who fail are not considered unworthy for the next level, but the cause is assumed to be insufficient effort in their preparation. Therefore, a student who has failed once can try again the following year —and again and again. In other words, the system recognizes and even applauds the value of hard effort.

Diploma Disease

The various measures of the Japanese government to promote education have resulted in extraordinary popular enthusiasm for schooling, such that universal primary education was achieved by 1900 and the numbers seeking entrance to the middle schools soon exceeded the number of available places. Over subsequent decades, additional middle schools were established so the competition shifted upwards to focus on entrance to the higher schools and the universities (Kinmouth, 1961). The intensity of this competition came to be described as *examination hell* by some social observers. Students studied long hours, often with the aid of tutors or teachers at special "cram" schools. Many of the aspirants, known as *ronin*, dropped out of school a full year or more specifically to prepare for the exams, and a few who failed committed suicide. Yet even those who succeeded were not always destined for a job fitting a university graduate.

Ronald Dore (1976), a leading Japanologist, found even more extreme examples of the same pattern in a number of developing societies he had occasion to observe, notably Sri Lanka and Kenya. He expressed his concern that the chase for diplomas was turning the schools of these nations into factories for exam-cramming. Schooling in such late-developing nations was "ritualistic, tedious, suffused with anxiety and boredom, destructive of curiosity and imagination; in short, anti-educational" (Dore, 1976: ix).

Dore observed that the problem derives from the use of the evaluative activites in schools to double as society's mechanism for social selection. To relieve schools of their "diploma disease," he urged such approaches as the use of aptitude tests (or forms of lottery) for social selection and a reliance on apprenticeship and mid-career education and training in place of the pre-career pattern.

Dore's views on the impact of testing on "late-developers" has since been questioned by other educators. For example, a careful analysis of Kenya's revised Certificate of Primary Education, with its related feedback system, suggests that is has provided important "insight into the reasons for pupils' cognitive difficulties" and has had "a major impact in improving the overall quality of education and in reducing quality differences among schools" (Somerset, 1988: 194). A number of educators believe that their educational systems can benefit from a strong dose of the diploma disease.

Regardless of whether one accepts Dore's analysis, it is certainly true that the evaluation practices of particular developing countries have tended to be modeled on those of their colonial mentors. Thus, in Sri Lanka and Malaysia, even though the languages of instruction are no longer English, the content of instruction is much as it was during the colonial period, and the same O-level and A-level examinations continue to be administered. Similarly, most Francophone African countries employ an evaluation system identical to that found in France. It is reasonable to ask if these classical European approaches fit the new circumstances of these new nations.

COMPARATIVE REFLECTIONS ON SYSTEMS OF EVALUATION

While each of the evaluative systems we have reviewed has its strengths, we have also seen that these systems are the focus of much criticism. Indeed, it seems that, just as in the developing world, several of the advanced educational systems are searching for more suitable modes of assessment. As part of this effort, in recent years there has been a new wave of policy-oriented research on evaluation systems (Somerset, 1987; Heyneman, 1987; Heyneman & Fagerlind, 1988; Madaus, 1988). The following appear to be some of the major findings that have emerged from these studies.

1. Systems of evaluation have to be judged not only on technical criteria but also in terms of their political and cultural compatibility. We have outlined some of the characteristics of the examination approaches found in several of the more prominent advanced societies. The approaches have evolved over the course of development of these societies to the point where they have highly distinctive styles. Each reflects special concerns of the society —for local autonomy in the U.K., for insuring intellectual breadth in the case of France, for encouraging diligent effort in the case of Japan, and for insuring the fair treatment of a diverse citizenry in the case of the U.S.A.

2. Conceptions of the knowlege that schools should impart become important determinants of the style of evaluation systems. Berlach and Berlach (1981) have characterized differences in the way knowlege is perceived. In the

classical view, knowledge is content, given, and holistic. In the modern view, knowledge is process, problematic, and molecular. Evaluation following the classical view is best carried out with essays, while the modern view is more amenable to short open-ended or multiple-choice questions. These differences are reflected in the evaluation procedures used by different fields as well as by different countries. Newer fields of knowledge and newer countries seem more comfortable with the short-answer approach.

3. Uniform evaluation systems are more easily developed in programs with a clearly specified curriculum. Most educational systems with national curriculums have developed some form of acceptable national exam for key transition points, while in more decentralized systems, such as the U.K. and the U.S.A., much of the evaluation work is school-based.

4. Evaluative formats involving multiple-choice questions may or may not be more efficient than essay exams. Multiple-choice tests can usually be graded more quickly than essays, but they tend to take more time to prepare. Moreover, special skills are required for the preparation of questions and for their effective presentation in test papers. The additional time required for preparation may equal the time saved in grading. Sometimes the issue is not whether gross efficiency results, but whose energy is saved. It makes a difference to teachers whether it is their time or someone else's time that is required to prepare tests and mark them.

5. Careful analysis and preparation are required for the development of a fair and effective evaluation system. Concerning the development of evaluation material, an extensive technical literature has emerged to guide the preparation of evaluative procedures that use multiple-choice formats, with the literature stressing such issues as bias, scope and balance, difficulty level, coverage of the full range of skill hierarchies (from recall to synthesis or higher reasoning), validity, and reliability. All of these issues have equal relevance for formats using other procedures. Whatever the format for particular questions, extensive planning is required to insure an appropriate procedure for the presentation and the assessment of the evaluation materials.

6. It may be impossible and even unwise to devise an evaluation system that provides no encouragement for students to prepare their answers outside of school hours. In evaluation systems where the criteria are well known and are perceived to have consequences for the child's future, children do spend more time on homework and at special cram schools. Some critics, expressing concern that such children are robbed of their youth, urge the development of an evaluation system that cannot be studied for. While it once was assumed that carefully prepared aptitude tests could meet this need, recent experience indicates that it is even possible to provide cram-school courses that will help children signficantly improve their aptitude-test scores. Thus, it seems difficult to develop a study-free test. But it is just as difficult to develop a study-free learning process. No

pill has yet been developed that enables a child to become brilliant and mature overnight. The acquisition of societally approved personal habits and critical knowledge still requires study, the more the better. Under the circumstances, it makes sense to publicize the goals and general structure of tests and to encourage children to study for them.

7. It is not clear that children in societies afflicted by the diploma disease receive a "poor" education. Critics charge that the children who attend exam-oriented educational systems focus so narrowly on the task of passing the exams that they experience boredom and their minds fail to be stimulated. But comparative studies suggest that children who study in such systems learn more than children in schools with more diffuse educational objectives. Moreover, the former children are more adept in answering questions that require higher reasoning skills. While children in exam-oriented systems take up their studies with the extrinsic motivation of passing exams, they seem more likely to eventually develop a genuine love of learning than do children in less demanding systems.

8. The locus of critical evaluative assessments has a profound influence on the climate of relations in educational institutions. In most European educational systems, evaluation comes at the end of an extended period of schooling. The same teachers that are trying to motivate students in the classroom during the school year are the ones who determine the learners' fate at the end. The overlapping of the pedagogic and selection roles tends to encourage formal interpersonal relations. In contrast, in Japan and China, the critical examinations are administered at the stage of entrance to schools by the very teachers who will be receiving the students. Once the students are admitted, the teachers appear to feel a special responsibility to help the entrants complete the educational program. The separation of the pedagogic and selection roles seems to lead to more intimate interpersonal relations.

9. There are rich possibilities for the expansion of the functions served by evaluative systems, but there are also important constraints. As illustrated in the North Carolina example, many local school systems in the United States have taken bold strides toward linking different evaluative functions in a comprehensive system. When similar procedures were proposed in Japan in the 1960s, the Japan Teachers Union voiced its firm resistance, arguing that such information, in the hands of administrators, could be manipulated to discriminate against particular teachers or students. Thus, the proposal for a comprehensive approach was abandoned.

10. Evaluation methods have an important and visible impact on the way teachers and students use their time in class. In countries with explicit testing systems, government agencies or commercial firms are likely to develop and publish special exercises and tests. Teachers can rely on these externally created materials for many of their routine assessments. If the materials are well

prepared, the amount of time that teachers and students need devote to such assessments may be modest. In systems with less explicit evaluation methods, teachers may have to devote considerable time in the preparation and marking of tests and quizzes. Moreover, such teacher-made tests tend to absorb a considerable amount of class time while teachers write them out (perhaps on the chalkboard) and while students participate in correcting the tests.

With these ten comparative observations as a background, we turn now to what might be expected in the field of educational evaluation in the coming years.

FUTURE PROSPECTS

Recent experience would seem to raise major questions about the value of systematic and comprehensive evaluations, whether of student learning or of other aspects of the educational process. Each new system of evaluation adds costs to the educational system while, at the same time, inviting compensatory adjustments for what may be undesired side effects —such side effects as pupils studying just for the tests or educators manipulating the material entered into data files so as to produce the results the educators seek. These adjustments then invite further refinement of assessment procedures by the evaluators, leading to yet another spiral of innovative manipulation and response. One might assume that after so many cycles of this kind, educators would be tempted to discard the process of evaluation all together. But far from it —the current trend is towards a progressively more solid institutionalization of evaluation in education systems.

One prospective trend today is towards more centralized standards for evaluation. The British Education Act of 1988 for the first time placed on the shoulders of the central ministry of education the responsibility for formulating a national curriculum and for developing procedures for evaluating how well schools achieve curriculum goals. Considerable sentiment has also become evident in the United States for the creation of national achievement standards, or at least for more uniform standards across the nation, along with uniform ways of measuring progress toward the standards. And in most other societies, a system of national standards and assessment procedures is already in place, with the desirability of their continued use generally unquestioned. Thus, agreement seems to be emerging across the world on the value of establishing national criteria for educational achievement. At some distant date in the future, the next stage may well be the widespread recognition of international standards. A very early step in that direction is the *International Baccalaureate* program adopted by schools in various countries.

A second prospective trend is towards linking educational evaluation with levels of support or reward for individual actors in the education system —a process sometimes referred to as *accountability*. A variety of formulas have been tried over time to attach rewards to the quality of individual educators' and individual schools' performance. Among these formulas are merit pay for superior teachers, opportunities for parents to choose which schools their children will attend, and promotion in the schooling hierarchy for effective administrators. However, the outcome of such schemes has often proved disappointing, partially because of the difficulty of assessing personnel and schools in a just and convenient manner. In recent years, there has seemed to be a hunger for new and more acceptable accountability procedures, ones that will produce accurate and fair assessment results with an economical expenditure of staff time and money.

As part of the trend towards greater accountability, more school systems may shift toward publicizing evaluation results so as to mobilize public participation in schools and to stimulate public action toward promoting educational improvements. As suggested by those who advocate publishing test results, teachers who repeatedly failed to educate their students effectively could be exposed through public records, and schools that continually displayed poor results in standardized examinations might find able students departing for schools with better test outcomes. Such an approach opens the road to a variety of accountability that lies outside the normal bureaucratic processes which heretofore have dominated the use of summative assessments in nearly all education systems. However, the difficulties and potential dangers in implementing such plans are formidable. For example, all children do not have the same aptitude for academic success, so a teacher who has a quantity of less adept learners will be blamed for the low test scores that such pupils earn. Furthermore, schools can differ markedly in the level of support for academic efforts that is provided by the families from which the schools draw their clientele. Nor can all schools furnish the same learning facilities or have the same numbers of pupils per class. In addition, paper-pencil exams do not provide suitable evidence about students' progress toward many of the schools' goals, particularly in the arts and in character traits and moral values. These barriers to the fair implementation of accountability schemes are not easily dismisssed. As a consequence, the proper role for evaluation in promoting educational accountability will continue to be a highly controversial issue.

A further future prospect is for the increasing involvement of work-places in the evaluation of educational processes. Employers have traditionally relied on schools as a means of selecting highly educated personnel, with this reliance reflected in companies making an effort to encourage and recruit the best of the college graduates. At the same time, employers have tended to neglect the educational fate of those students who have not fared well in school. However, as the numbers of positions in the job market for unskilled and semi-skilled workers diminish, employers face the need to become more active in their search for lower-level employees who can perform well in job assignments requiring literate, well-trained personnel. Thus, increasingly employers find it in their best interest to focus attention on all levels of the education system, rather than solely on tertiary education. It seems likely that employers will increasingly tie incentives to the indicators of success provided by educational evaluation. An example of such incentives in the United States is the offer by certain industrial benefactors to pay the full costs of education to all workers who complete their high-school studies. Another incentive is the provision of monetary rewards for good school reports. What is clear, in these efforts, is that the results of education are more and more seen to be closely linked with the success of national economies. As economic leaders become increasingly convinced that better schooled employees in all jobs foster productivity, they are seeking new ways to establish compacts or partnerships with education systems, while not excessively intervening with the actual educational process. One means of accomplishing this is to provide attractive incentives to learners who receive positive evaluations.

Finally, at no time in the world's history has the field of educational evaluation been so active as in recent years. This activity has involved an unprecedented number of researchers and practitioners proposing innovative means of assessment, devising improved methods of analysis and interpretation, and critically appraising the use of evaluation techniques. Never before has there been so much international transfer of assessment methods and of student-achievement results. Therefore, despite the many problems associated with assessment procedures, it is likely that evaluation will become an ever more prominent feature of education systems in the decades to come.

REFERENCES

Amano, I. (1990) *Examinations and modern society,* (F. Cummings & W. K. Cummings, Trans.). Tokyo: University of Tokyo Press.

Berlak, A., & Berlak, H. (1981) *Dilemmas of Schooling.* London: Methuen.

Bloom, B. S., Hastings, J. T., & Madaus, G. F. (1971) *Handbook on formative and summative evaluation of student learning.* New York: McGraw-Hill.

Boorstin, D. J. (1983) *The discoverers.* New York: Random House.

Clark, B. R. (Ed.) (1985) *The school and the university.* Berkeley: University of California Press.

Cummings, W. K. (1985) Japan. In B. R. (Ed.), *The school and the university* (pp. 121-159). Berkeley: University of California Press.

Dore, R. (1976) *The diploma disease.* Berkeley: University of California Press.

Durkheim, E. (1966) *The evolution of educational thought.* London: Routledge & Kegan Paul.

Eckstein, M. A., & Noah, H. J. (1989) Forms and functions of secondary-school-leaving examinations, *Comparative Education Review*, 33 (4): 295-316.

Gardner, H., & Hatch, T. (1989) Multiple intelligences go to school: Educational implications of the theory of multiple intelligences, *Educational Researcher*, 18 (4): 4-10.

Heyneman, S. P. (1987) Uses of examinations in developing countries: Selection, research, and education sector management. *International Journal of Educational Development*, 7 (4): 251-263.

Heyneman, S. P., & Fagerlind, I. (Eds.) (1988) *University examinations and standardized testing: Principles, experience, and policy options.* Washington: World Bank.

Johnson, R. (1989) Thatcherism and English education: Breaking the mould, or confirming the pattern?, *History of Education*, 18 (2): 19-121.

Klitgaard, R. (1985) *Choosing elites*. New York: Basic Books.

Kinmouth, E. H. (1981) *The self-made man in Meiji Japanese thought: From samurai to salary man.* Berkekey: University of California Press.

Lach, D. F. (1977) *Asia in the making of Europe: Vol. 2: A century of wonder. Book three: The scholarly disciplines.* Chicago: University of Chicago Press

Lewy, A. (1981) The scope of educational evaluation: An iIntroduction. A. Lewy & D. Nevo (Eds.), *Evaluation roles in education* (pp. 1-8). London: Gordon & Breach.

Madaus, G. (1988) The influence of testing on the curriculum. In L. Tanner (Ed.), *Critical issues in curriculum* (87th Yearbook of National Society for the Study of Education, Part 1. Chicago: University of Chicago Press.

Mitchell, J. V. Jr. (Ed.) (1985) *The ninth mental measurements yearbook.* Lincoln: University of Nebraska Press.

Miyazaki, I. (1981) China's examination hell: The civil service examination of imperial China (C. Schirokauer, Trans.). New Haven: Yale University Press.

Montgomery, R. J. (1965) *Examination.* Pittsburgh: University of Pittsburgh Press.

Nakayama, S. (1984) *Science in Japan, China, and the west* (J. Dusenbury, Trans.) Tokyo: University of Tokyo Press.

Neave, G. (1985) France. In B. R. Clark, (Ed.), *The school and the university* (pp. 10-44). Berkeley: University of California Press.

Needham, J. (1956) *Science and civilization in China.*

Owen, D. (1985) *None of the above: Behind the myth of scholastic aptitude.* Boston: Houghton Mifflin.

Ringer, F. K. (1974) *The decline of the German mandarins.* Cambridge: Harvard University Press.

Slack, W. V., & Porter, D. , (1980) The Scholastic Aptitude Test: A critical appraisal, *Harvard Educational Review*, 50: 154-175.

Somerset, A. (1988) Examinations as an instrument to improve pedagogy. In S. Heyneman & I. Fagerlind (Eds.), *University examinations and standardized testing: Principles, experience and policy options* (pp. 169-194). Washington: World Bank.

Somerset, H. C. A. (1987) *Examination reform in Kenya* (World Bank Education and Training Series No. EDT 64). Washington: World Bank.

Spaulding, R. M., Jr. (1967) *Imperial Japan's higher civil service examination.* Princeton: Princeton University Press.

Teichler, U. (1985) The Federal Republic of Germany. In B. R. Clark (Ed.), *The school and the university* (pp. 45-76). Berkeley: University of California Press.

Teichler, U., & Sanyal, B. C. (1982) *Higher education and the labour market in the Federal Republic of Germany.* Paris: International Institute for Educational Planning.

Wechsler, H. S., (1977) *The qualified student: A history of selective college admission in America.* New York: Wiley.

Young, M. (1958) *The rise of the meritocracy: 1870-2033.* Harmondsworth: Penguin.

SECTION II:

EDUCATIONAL STRUCTURES AND PERSONNEL

Among the factors that obviously influence the kind of instruction learners receive, two of the most important are the way a society's education system is organized and the qualities of the people who operate the system. Section II is dedicated to an inspection of these factors. Issues of organization are considered in Chapters 5 and 6, while the matter of providing teachers is the concern of Chapter 7.

Although the two chapters on organization are interlinked, the issues treated in them are not identical. Chapter 5, entitled *Forms of Governance*, focuses on how the educational enterprise is structured for the purposes of decision-making and control. Chapter 6, entitled *Delivery Systems*, focuses on the forms in which learning opportunities are offered to the populace.

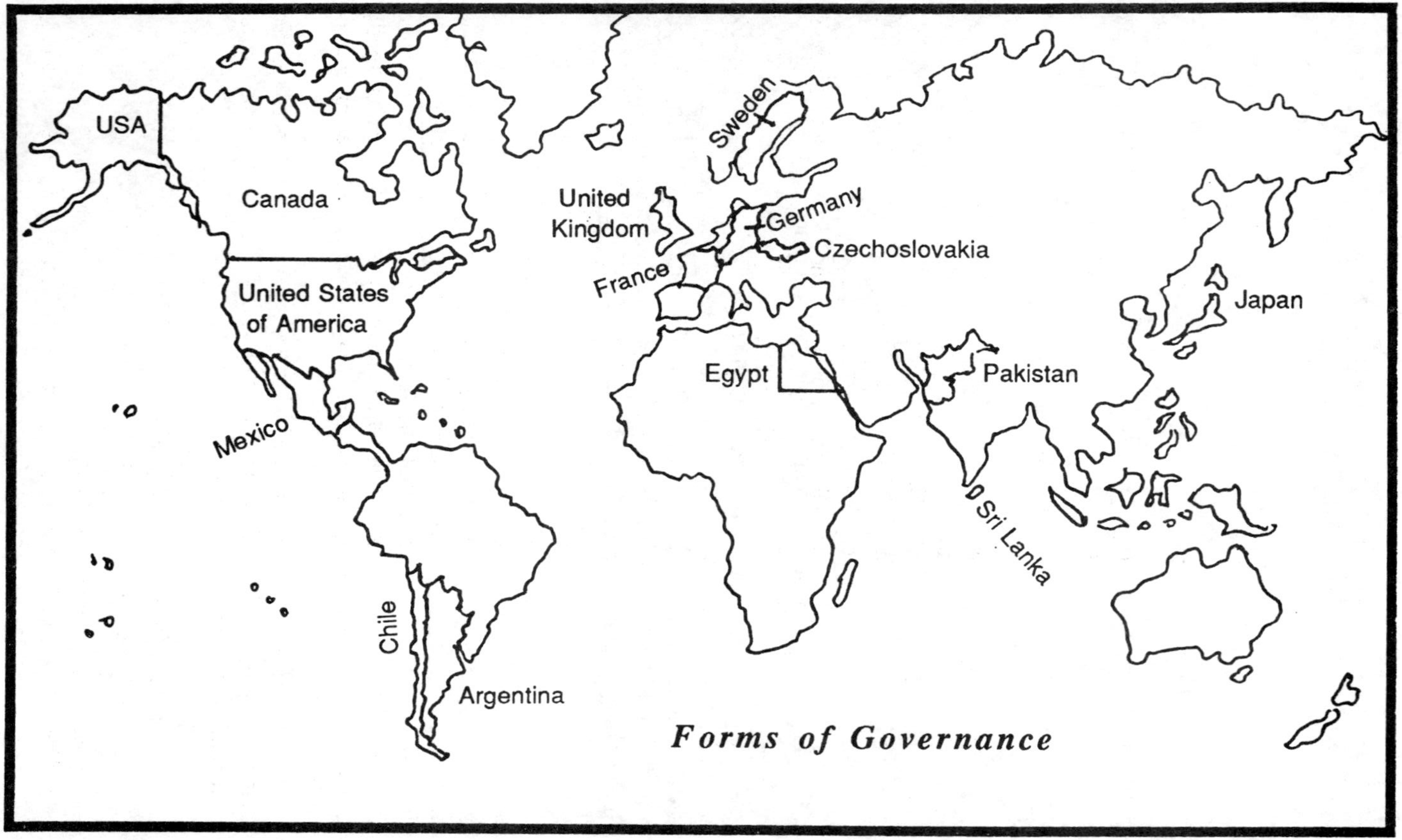
USA
Canada
United States of America
Mexico
Chile
Argentina
United Kingdom
France
Sweden
Germany
Czechoslovakia
Egypt
Pakistan
Sri Lanka
Japan
Forms of Governance

CHAPTER 5

Forms of Governance

How can the control and guidance of education be organized, and which modes are most suitable?

NOEL F. MCGINN

Control over education has always been a prime concern of the community. Among many historical examples is the case of Socrates, sentenced to death by the citizens of Athens for his failure to teach their youth the right values. All systems of education have mechanisms established by the state or its representatives for the control and guidance —or governance— of the system.

This chapter describes the major forms of governance of education systems, and where necessary provides some background to account for differences among them. The chapter is divided into six parts. Part 1 traces historical trends in the control of education. Part 2 identifies three important aspects of governance that can vary from one society to another, with the aspects reflected in the question: *Who* controls *what* and *how*?

Part 3 illustrates how the three aspects may function in the primary-secondary systems of seven nations —Czechoslovakia, France, Mexico, Pakistan, Chile, Sri Lanka, and the United States of America. Part 4 describes patterns of higher-education governance, drawing examples not only from countries in Part 3 but also from Argentina, Canada, Egypt, Germany, Great Britain, Japan, and Sweden. As will be shown, patterns of control for primary-secondary schooling and for higher education are quite different in their historical construction. The illustrative cases demonstrate that the form of governance which is most effective depends on the context in which schools and universities currently operate. The long-term trend, however, has been toward increased central control over education.

Part 5 assesses the effectiveness of different types of governance, and the closing section —part 6— offers an estimate of what the future may hold for the control and guidance of education systems.

HISTORICAL DETERMINANTS OF THE GOVERNANCE OF EDUCATION SYSTEMS

Should we expect to find the same forms of governance in all places? After all, it could be argued that the logic of education is well-known and its variations limited, so that forms of organization and control should also be limited. In fact, education systems around the world are similar in many respects, in terms of general goals, in terms of structure of grades and levels, and in terms of content (Ramirez & Boli, 1987). But does the existence of these similarities mean that we should expect to find similarities in forms of governance?

One perspective argues that similarities in goals, structure, and content occur because of factors internal to education; there are only a limited number of ways to organize an effective school. Proponents of this perspective claim that increasing world consciousness of the "logic of education" has led to similarities across countries. If education systems around the world are similar because of factors internal to education itself, then we might expect to find the same degree of similarity in forms of governance.

A second approach attributes what similarities are found to the imposition, through colonial expansion of the European nations, of a small number of models of education. The colonized people in the main acquiesced to the concept of schooling, but not to its control by the colonizers. Different forms of governance emerged, even though what was subject to control was similar. This argument is elaborated in the paragraphs that follow.

All but a tiny handful of countries in the world now have a national system of mass schooling with European origins (Ramirez & Boli, 1987). These systems were built as part of the development of the nation states of Europe in the late 18th and 19th centuries. Powerful groups in the European countries saw in education a means to create national political systems that would command the loyalty of factions that earlier gave allegiance to local elites. The earliest move toward creation of a mass education system is attributed to Frederick William I of Prussia in 1716. Other countries soon followed suit.

In all these systems the state assumed primary responsibility for education. Control over schooling was seen by the groups controlling the State as essential to the realization of their vision of national development. State control was justified in terms of national objectives that transcended local, regional, or social-class interests.

The process of creating national systems of education was marked by conflict. At first the struggle was to wrest power from family and regional elites that competed with central rulers. A coalition of the church and national mercantile elites successfully created the beginnings of a national system of schools, with elites and masses separated. As national secular leaders increased their power, they broke with the church and struggled to secularize the education system. Finally, with the industrial revolution in full swing, the emerging capitalist class beat back attempts by workers to establish their own school systems (Curtis, 1988). This process took more than a century, so that universal mass education was not achieved in any European country until near the end of the 19th century.

The mechanisms of control and guidance developed for Europe [e.g., in France under Napoleon (McGinn, 1987)] were also applied in colonies in Latin America, Africa, the Middle East, and Asia. This process of transference was not without conflict. In some cases, the struggle was between colonial masters and national patriots (Kelly, 1987). In other cases it was between national elites and local groups (Curtis, 1988). The struggles were over who would be in control, but they crystallized around specific issues of content. In many cases these conflicts were resolved through compromise, in which even the losers (seldom the national elites) came away with some of their objectives met.

As the examples reviewed in this paper will indicate, conflict over governance continues, as new groups emerge seeking control over some aspect of education, and as changes occur within the system of education itself. Most conflict is resolved through adjustment of some part of the governance structure, rather than by complete redesign. The result is a patchwork quilt of modes of governance of national education systems which cannot be explained solely by reference to the logic of what constitutes a reasonable educational enterprise.

FORMS OF GOVERNANCE

There are three major dimensions with respect to the structure and operation of mechanisms of guidance and control of national education systems. These are:

1. the location of persons authorized to exercise control;
2. the actual mechanisms of control; and
3. what is controlled.

Each of these dimensions can be broken into sub-dimensions.

Location of Persons

One way of looking at governance focuses on who makes the rules or evaluates the performance of the system. We can refer to groups of persons in terms of their location with respect to the education system. The case studies that appear in the next section are examples of systems of governance in which control is exercised primarily by:

—(a) government officials who are not educators, that is, who do not work within the education system; or by

—(b) educators; or by

—(c) non-educators outside the government, e.g., owners of capital, religious bodies, parents' organizations.

Governance is exercised at the national, provincial, and local levels. Within each level we can distinguish between forms of governance in which the actual control is exercised outside the educational system itself (for example, by the President, by a ministry of planning or finance, town council) or within the system by a specific bureau (such as a ministry of education or school board).

Educators sometimes exercise control through their domination of a ministry of education, sometimes through authority delegated to them at the level of the district or school. Non-educators may be represented on boards that have authority over education, at any level, but generally at the level of the institution (that is, school or university).

Mechanisms of Governance

The control and guidance of an education system, as any other organization, is carried out in three major ways:

—(a) through the promulgation of laws, decrees, regulations and other statements of the policies of the organization. These policies typically contain statements of objectives and of the kinds of methods to be used in the pursuit of those objectives. Some objectives are stated at the level of the broad goals of education described by Thomas in Chapter 2. Others are more specific, referring perhaps to one level of the system, or to one particular content area. The broad goals of education are changed infrequently, and are for that reason of less interest here. When we talk about governance through policy-formulation, we refer to policies that are likely to change when a particular government changes, a new national plan is written, or perhaps when a new minister takes office.

—(b) through the translation of policies into plans and programs. The work of organizations is controlled through plans and programs that specify the specific objectives to be met, the methods to be pursued in carrying them out, the resources and time that are to be used, and the persons responsible. Organizations vary in the extent to which these plans and programs are formalized, but education systems around the world are famed for their high degree of formalization. They are organized as bureaucracies, in which the achievement of the system's objectives is expected to follow from compliance with rules, carried out by interchangeable occupants of positions whose activities are coordinated through layers of hierarchy. Plans and programs are the means by which rules of the organization are adapted to meet changing circumstances or goals. The preparation of these plans and programs, requiring interpretation of broad policy statements, can be a powerful mechanism for the governance of an education system.

—(c) through the translation of plans and programs into specific activities. Here it is important to distinguish between control and guidance or governance, and the actual execution of the tasks of the education system. Those who govern will design the plan, and then may grant others, such as the teacher, autonomy in choice of means to carry out the plan. The governance system remains distinct from the individual creativity of the teachers and permits, as in the case of ancient Athens, the correction of teachers who fail to achieve desired objectives.

The governance position closest to teachers is that of the school administrator (department chair, headmaster, etc.) whose major responsibility is to insure that plans and programs developed at the level above are actually carried out. Countries vary widely in terms of the authority of school administrators.

The impact of policies, plans, and programs on the performance of the education system is checked in two ways. Most common, those with authority monitor the actual implementation of policies, plans, and programs. Administrators and supervisors have this as their major responsibility. Their focus of attention is on what is done, more than on the consequences of what is done.

Less common, but growing in use, is exercise of control over the system through observation of the outcomes of the behavior of the workers in the system. In this case, emphasis shifts from attempting to control inputs into the system (teacher and student attendance, use of specific textbooks, adherence to the official curriculum), to control over achievement of goals (learning of specific curriculum objectives). All systems evaluate achievement levels of students, but some systems are now beginning to evaluate teachers, schools, and regions in terms of level of achievement, then to reward or punish teachers and administrators in terms of their organization's performance. Where governance is localized, the mechanisms of evaluation may be relatively informal, such as, an administrator may assess the level of parent satisfaction. In more centralized systems reliance is on standardized achievement tests. As we will see, the shift from monitoring of inputs, to monitoring of outcomes, has important implications for the most effective location of the governance mechanism.

What is Controlled

Systems of education also vary in terms of what elements of the system are controlled by whom. For convenience, let us consider as important elements teachers, students, curriculum, administration, and finance. Every system specifies the requirements to be a teacher, sets teacher salaries and benefits, provides training, and supervises teacher performance. Control over teachers is in some countries national, in other countries provincial or even local.

Every system has regulations that affect students. There are specifications with respect to admission (such as age), proper behavior in school, requirements for promotion, and awarding of degrees.

Countries also vary in terms of who sets curriculum goals, who specifies methods, who prepares materials, who evaluates student and/or teacher performance.

Although every country may have some administrative official responsible for the local school, the extent of authority of this person varies widely, as does the authority of functionaries and officers in the national bureaucracy. Finally, countries vary in terms of who controls the level and method of finance of the education system, the allocation of resources across the system, and actual disbursement of those resources.

There are a number of combinations of levels of control and content of control. Most systems have national curricula, which in most cases are constructed by professional groups operating under the supervision of the ministry of education. Within those same systems, however, training of teachers may be a provincial responsibility. Supervision may be either a national or a provincial responsibility. In some countries local groups provide significant proportions of the funds required for school operation, but disbursement of those funds is controlled by the State. In short, there is considerable variation in patterns of control and guidance of education systems, the result of a series of negotiated settlements between opposing groups.

Although there are important differences across countries, authority for some aspects of education is most frequently located at the national rather than the local level. This is shown in a study that used data supplied by 100 national governments to rank the degree of regulation of the following aspects of education:

(a) general responsibility for education
(b) general control over education
(c) control of student admissions
(d) control over curriculum
(e) control over examinations
(f) source of funding for students
(g) source of funding for schools.

Ratings for all seven scales were summed and averaged to provide an average overall scale rating that could range from 1 = total local control to 7 = total national control. Missing in this analysis was a rating of authority for control and guidance of teachers and for administration.

The average rating for the primary level was 5.46, for secondary 5.41, and for higher education 3.81 (Ramirez & Rubinson, 1979). These data indicate that governance of primary and secondary education is more centralized than is governance of higher education.

In the section that follows we look at specific examples of the forms of control and guidance for primary-secondary education in these seven countries —Czechoslovakia, France, Mexico, Pakistan, Chile, Sri Lanka, and the United States of America. In a subsequent section we consider governance of higher education in most of the same nations as well as in Argentina, Canada, Egypt, Germany, Great Britain, Japan, and Sweden.

GOVERNANCE OF PRIMARY AND SECONDARY EDUCATION SYSTEMS

The sequence of cases that follows is arranged in an approximate order on the dimension of location of governance, ranging from more to less centralized. Within this order, however, there are important variations in the mechanisms of control and guidance that are used and in what is controlled.

Czechoslovakia

The governance system of this country (as of October 1988) illustrates how authority held by a national political organization can be distributed down through the system without loss of control by leaders of the organization. This arrangement appears to maximize local participation in actual administration of the system, while at the same time minimizing inequities or deviations from central philosophy.

The maximum authority for control and guidance of the education system of Czechoslovakia has been the Communist Party Central Committee. The Party has exercised control in two ways: through formal review of decisions and actions by organizations at lower levels in the system, and by placing members of the Party in positions of leadership at all levels.

The major administrative apparatus are ministries that have been located in the capitals of the Czech and Slovak republics, Prague and Bratislava. A Council for Education has made general policy, coordinated the decisions of the two ministries and reported to the Central Committee's Department of Schools, Science, and Art.

The two ministries have appointed all teachers (there are no private schools in Czechoslovakia[9]; set salaries, benefits and qualifications; and provided training. Admission to secondary schools is determined by examinations controlled by the ministries. The number of students to admit is based on forecasts by the national planning office of the numbers of graduates required from each discipline to meet the requirements of the national economy. The ministries have authority for curriculum, and they choose the textbooks to be used in the system.

The administrative apparatus corresponds to the civic divisions of the Republic: regions which are subdivided into districts and municipalities, and cities divided into wards. Committees at the regional and city level administer both the basic nine-year schools and secondary schools. Each district has a committee of education and culture, from which operate inspectors who monitor secondary schools; inspectors at the municipal level are responsible for primary schools. A national inspectorate compares the performance of the various regions and cities. Pedagogical research institutes in each region and city carry out research, advise on textbooks produced in Prague and Bratislava, and train teachers. The institutes in Prague and Bratislava have major responsibility for curriculum revisions; combined groups of scientists and teachers are appointed to write the curriculum (Petracek, 1988). All finance is provided by the central government, but disbursed through the budgets of the regions and cities.

Given the vertical organization of the Party, and central control over curriculum and finance, almost all conflicts over education in Czechoslovakia have been resolved at the national level. The ability of the Party to influence centrally-made decisions has depended on its ability to command the loyalty of local officials. The major means to accomplish this has been involvement of local officials in national conferences and assemblies that formulated the Party position on issues of policies and programs.

France

The governance system for primary and secondary education in France exemplifies how a government can, by locating its delegates at all levels of the nation, achieve high levels of uniformity in application of detailed plans and programs. These delegates are employees of the State and are not members of a political party. Their conformity to State regulations is more limited than that of political party members. The system is centralized but has limited scope.

The French system was initiated as a bureaucracy. Control was exercised by insistence on rules and regulations designed and promulgated by national authorities. All regions of the country were expected to implement identically these prescriptions. Nationally-designated supervisors monitored compliance and administered sanctions. State examinations controlled admissions to the next level of schooling.

Recently the French system has begun to use examination results to monitor system performance. Additional resources are provided to regions that perform at low levels. This is an attempt to stimulate regional innovation that might raise overall levels of achievement, and at the same time to reduce disparities between regions.

Authority for the control and guidance of French primary and secondary education is held by the minister of education, who is appointed by the prime minister. A separate ministry exists for universities. The ministry of education is organized in nine directorates, responsible for planning and coordination, preschool and primary schools, secondary education, teachers in lycees, administrative staff, general administration, equipment and buildings, and finance. The top officials in the directorates are often career bureaucrats and not educators. A national higher council of education, with representatives from professional groups, parents, and students, provides advice on policy issues.

The ministry has authority over all public education and oversight over private education. Administration of education is delegated to 26 academies, corresponding to geographic regions. Each is headed by a rector who is assisted by a permanent professional staff, an inspectorate, and advisory councils. Authority is delegated from the ministry to the academies for the training and management of teachers, but the central ministry sets salaries, benefits, and qualifications.

Policies and regulations with respect to curriculum are made by the Academic Inspectorate. Curriculum goals and content are determined, in conjunction with professional academies linked with the university, by 15 specialist groups (Halls, 1976). The specialists are renowned scholars, generally members of the universities. Classroom teachers have no influence over curriculum content. All public schools in France use the same curriculum. The curriculum is highly detailed in both objectives and methods. In effect, the curriculum is intended to insure that all teachers teach the same material at the same pace in the same way.

Private education in France (largely Catholic) enjoys considerable autonomy. Teachers need not meet State qualifications and may be paid more or less. Private schools are free to select curriculum materials and methods, and are not subject to inspection by the State. At the same time, some private and church schools receive subsidies from the State, for the most part to supplement teacher salaries and benefits. In some instances private schools sign contracts with the State that result in increased State control over the schools' operation.

Conflict over education in France is worked out both through negotiated settlements between institutions and the national government, and by public political action. In its most severe form, this action includes national demonstrations against government policy. Recent conflicts have been over proposed legislation to reduce government subsidies to private schools.

Mexico

This country is another example of governance through regulation and inspection. The unique feature of the governance of Mexican education is the participation of the leaders of the teachers' union in administration of plans and programs. As in Czechoslovakia, control is exercised both through official mechanisms and through the apparatus of the ruling party. As in both France and Czechoslovakia, a national curriculum insures uniformity of content.

The public primary and lower secondary schools of Mexico, which enroll more than 80 percent of all students, are under the control of the national ministry of education. In the last decade the government has moved to delegate administration of primary education to provincial ministries of education. At the same time, Mexico has created a system of upper secondary schools (*colegio de bachilleres*) under the control of the ministry of education, in competition for students with the *preparatorias* controlled by either autonomous or provincial universities.

The control and guidance of teachers is shared with the national teachers' union, which is a major partner in the ruling party that has controlled the government for more than 60 years. This form of power-sharing means that while the government has authority for all policy and regulations, in fact the union participates in much of decision-making, either through formal negotiations or through its link with colleagues in the ministry who prepare plans and programs. The union also shares power in the appointment of delegates and heads of regional institutions and schools, and in some states it is dominant in the administration of plans and programs. Teachers are selected and trained following policies of the ministry of education. Salaries are common across the 32 states, with differentials for teachers in rural service. The ministry of education until recently controlled the normal schools but now has limited influence over the national pedagogical university, and less over state universities which train teachers.

Students are promoted from one grade to the next and from primary to lower secondary to the ministry's *colegio de bachilleres* on the basis of teacher evaluations. These upper secondary schools send their graduates to non-autonomous universities. Autonomous universities design and administer the examinations which admit students into their upper secondary schools or *preparatorias.* Students who graduate from *preparatorias* are admitted into the sponsoring university. All other upper secondary graduates must take a national examination controlled by the ministry of education.

Curriculum is the province of the national ministry of education, and uniform throughout Mexico. Under recent reforms public schools are allowed to supplement the curriculum with regionally-appropriate materials, but these are subject to central review. All schools use textbooks designed and printed by the national ministry. In earlier years, the government frequently intervened in private schools, citing Article 3 of the Constitution of the United States of Mexico which promises that all education will be free and secular. Today, private primary schools are still required to use the national textbooks, but private and church schools no longer are subject to the strict governmental supervision of previous years, and in general it can be said that these are autonomous institutions.

The national ministry is headed by the secretary of education, who is appointed by and responds directly to the nation's president. Many top-level officials are career bureaucrats, not educators, who are transferred to other ministries with the change of the president. Those officials who are educators are generally also high-ranking officers in the teachers' union.

The secretary of education appoints the province-level delegates. Many of these are not educators. Under the current system delegates submit annual budget requests to the central ministry and receive block grants for primary schools on the basis of enrollments. The creation of a system of block grants increased the autonomy of the delegates, but increased autonomy also meant that the delegates became subject to pressures from regional groups. Prior to the decentralization reform, education had been controlled by out-of-reach officials in the national capital; now the delegate is accessible, and political bargains can be made without reference to national policy.

In recent years, the major conflicts in Mexican primary-secondary education have been over teacher salaries and working conditions. The government-aligned teachers' union is no longer able to control its provincial affiliates. Strikes and protests begin at the provincial level, but when met with government repression or lack of response, may culminate in massive demonstrations in the national capital.

Pakistan

When Great Britain left the Indian subcontinent in 1947, Pakistan ended up with only the skeleton of an education system. Many Muslims had resisted British rule by refusing to send their children to public schools. After the partition that separated Pakistan from India, Pakistan had few teachers and few educated persons. There were marked ethnic and linguistic differences and rivalries among the four provinces. A common education system was required to contribute to the creation of national identity, but the political structure of the country made that difficult (Saqeb, 1985).

In the governance of education in Pakistan, there are divisions of authority between the federal government and governments of the four provinces, and there are conflicts between (a) appointed and elected officials from political parties and (b) members of the permanent civil service. Pakistan can be said to have three ruling factions —the military, the landowners, and the bureaucrats— which form unstable coalitions in their contention for power. The combination of political instability and regional conflict has limited the effectiveness of efforts by both federal and provincial governments to build an education system that contributes to national unity.

Primary education in Pakistan is considered a "concurrent subject," administered jointly by provincial and federal governments. Governance of teachers and students is assigned to the provincial level while control over curriculum is maintained by the federal government. Secondary education is under the control of the federal government. The federal minister of education is appointed by the prime minister, and in turn selects, from the education civil service, a federal secretary. The secretary of education for the province is designated by the chief minister of the province, who has been chosen in popular elections. Staff of the department are members of the national civil service and have career tenure, but both federal and provincial governments (illegally) fill positions on the basis of party loyalties.

There is a rigid hierarchy of seniority in the education system. Officials in the education service begin as teachers, then become headmasters or supervisors, next district officers, then provincial officials, and eventually reach the federal ministry. Promotions in grade depend on formal qualifications and years of service but are also attached to specific positions. The creation of cohorts of officers who move through training and promotions together contributes to the formation of strong personal bonds, which sometimes transcend political party loyalties and differences in provincial policies, but which also contribute to protecting officers who do not perform well in their positions.

Policies with respect to teacher qualifications, salaries, benefits, and supervision are generally set at the provincial level, but the federal government has from time to time attempted to affect provincial policy by the creation of new programs funded at the federal level. For example, it used a loan from the World Bank to fund the creation of a number of *learning coordinators* who were trained to provide classroom teachers with inservice education on the job. At the end of the loan, the provincial governments were obliged to fund salaries for these new officers from their recurrent budgets.

Primary teachers are trained in colleges controlled by the federal ministry but located in the provinces, or through the federally-controlled Open University. Secondary teachers are trained in the provincial universities.

Policies with respect to admission of students, and promotion from grade to grade and primary to lower secondary, are also set at the provincial level, and the polices are administered through instructions to district officials who devise their own examinations.

Broad curriculum policies are formulated as part of the five-year planning process by committees chosen by the ministry of planning and composed of heads of universities and teacher training colleges, representatives from state enterprises, officials from federal and provincial education, and other public officials. Curriculum objectives consistent with these broad guidelines are generated by committees of discipline experts (generally from the universities) organized by the national curriculum wing in the federal ministry.

Each province has its own curriculum bureau responsible for preparation of textbooks which present the curriculum. These textbooks are printed by each province, but must be approved by the federal curriculum wing. The texts are identical in objectives and coverage, but they vary in presentation. All public-school students use the official provincial textbooks.

The federal ministry carries out research on all aspects of education and provides training for officials in federal, provincial, and district offices. Salaries of primary teachers are provided by provincial governments. The federal government provides most of the funds for school construction, in response to provincial submissions to the five-year plan, but also supplements federal allocations with provincial funds. Grants and loans to the federal government from international assistance and lending agencies can also be targeted for a single province, and disbursement of those funds is controlled by the provincial ministry of education.

The Pakistan governance system divides authority in such a way that little can be accomplished unless federal and provincial authorities work together. Because there are many layers in the organization, messages from policy makers at the top are often distorted by the time they reach teachers in classrooms. Information from teachers often reaches policy makers at the top too late or too aggregated to be of use. Intermediate (district) officials have great administrative authority but insufficient resources to monitor compliance with their orders. Local and provincial-level pressure groups act to resist government policies (as when landowners refuse to grant land for schools) or to bend them to their benefit (as when relatives are appointed as teachers or supervisors). Efforts at reform from the federal government have generally failed to reach even half the schools (Warwick, Reimers, & McGinn, 1989).

Chile

The governance system for education in Chile combines features of strong central control over content with local control over teachers, students, and administration. The system, established after the military coup in 1973, is inspired in part by the doctrine of national security, in which the central state assumes responsibility for protection of society from even its own citizens, and by the doctrine of supply-side economics, in which the consumer is allowed to choose between varieties of schools (Programa Interdisciplinario de Investigación Educativa, 1984). This case illustrates how it is possible to decentralize control over some aspects of education in order to increase effective central control over others.

Chile has long been a leader in education, beginning with the establishment of the first teacher training institution in Latin America in 1832. Education was a priority policy area for each of the three democratic governments (conservative, Christian Democrat, and socialist in that order) that preceded the recent military regime, and public and teacher participation in education was high. The military junta that overthrew the elected government in 1973 dissolved the parliament and banned all political parties in an effort to "purge the nation" of undesirable elements. The effects of the purge were felt especially in the education system.

Qualifications, salaries, and work rules for public school teachers are now set by municipal governments appointed by the nation's president. Private schools essentially set their own requirements and salaries for teachers. A once-powerful national teachers' union has been dismantled, as teachers cannot organize except within their own municipalities. Teachers are trained in both public and private universities, with little or no intervention from the ministry of education. Regional centers run by provincial authorities appointed by the ministry provide inservice training and supervision of public schools, and organize research and conferences with both public and private school teachers.

The ministry contracts a university to develop and apply a diagnostic achievement test, aggregated results of which are shared with participating schools. Private schools apply admissions tests to applicants, beginning as low as the first grade. There are no external examinations for schools until high school. Graduates of high schools can apply to one of the more than 40 tertiary-level institutions. The reputations of individual schools, both public and private, depend on both their selectivity of students and on the rate of admission of their students into more prestigious universities.

The curriculum is set by the ministry of education, which monitors its application in classrooms. Schools are allowed to choose from ministry-approved textbooks, and both municipal and private schools can supplement their curriculum with additional materials and subjects. All schools teach the same national history, but there are marked differences across municipalities in terms of the amount of material presented in classes and in the quality of teaching.

The ministry of education provides a financial subsidy based on enrollment in the compulsory level (grades 1-8) to municipal and to private schools that accept all students who apply. Both municipal and participating private schools can also charge fees that amount to up to 50 percent of the per-student cost. Given larger class sizes and lower teacher salaries, schools can now generate a financial surplus, a fact which has stimulated the establishment of a large number of private establishments. At least one municipality has "privatized" its education system by turning over management of schools to a private firm. During the first five years after the implementation of this policy in 1979, private expenditures as a percentage of total expenditure on education increased from 16 to 26 percent, but total national enrollments declined, from 51 to 48 percent of the 0-24-year age group. Enrollments in autonomous or non-subsidized private schools declined, while enrollments in government-subsidized private schools increased.

Parent and teacher participation in management decisions in public schools in poor communities also declined as a result of the new policy, but participation in private subsidized schools increased, as many of the new institutions were created by groups of middle-class parents and teachers who wanted some involvement in the organization of the education of their children. Management of autonomous private schools remained in the hands of the organizations that owned them, which includes church and secular groups.

It is clear that one effect of the new governance system in Chile has been to increase differences in quality between best and worst public schools. Not clear is whether the overall average level of quality has improved. Decentralization in this case increased the control of some groups —middle-class families— over the education of their children, but perhaps at the expense of lower-income families.

Sri Lanka

On achieving independence from Great Britain in 1948, this country had approximately 3,000 schools, most of which were either run by religious bodies or by privately-owned plantations. Only 30 percent of the age group was in school. The creation of a national government meant also the creation of a national, public education system. Under a socialist government this included the nationalization in 1960 of many private schools.

Although Sri Lanka today continues to have a highly centralized curriculum, recent administrative reforms have greatly increased the authority of headmasters over the organization of their schools and the actual practices of teachers in classrooms. This case is an example of decentralization of program and administrative authority to professionals at the school level.

Teachers in Sri Lanka are governed under policies set by the national ministry of education and administered by district officials. Headmasters have administrative responsibility for teachers, but their control is exercised primarily through persuasion rather than coercion. Teacher training is provided through programs controlled by the ministry of education or by the autonomous universities which are located in most regions of the country. A national teachers' union plays an important role in party politics but has relatively little influence in control and guidance of the system.

Curricula are formulated in the ministry of education, but ideas for innovations generally originate at the level of teachers, and teachers participate in curriculum design and evaluation. Districts, and especially school clusters, are encouraged to modify the curriculum to match characteristics of students and the local community. Cluster headmasters and district officers prepare annual plans in which they state both enrollment and learning objectives, and they indicate the activities that will be carried out to meet them. Experiences with innovations are collected in periodic regional and national meetings of teachers, headmasters, and district officers.

Academic achievement is important in Sri Lanka, but schools also are evaluated in terms of the performance of athletic teams in interschool contests, and by communities in terms of schools' reputations for teaching moral values to students. A national examination controlled by the ministry is applied at the end of the compulsory cycle to determine admission to upper secondary and to award scholarships, and schools are recognized in terms of the numbers of their students who score high on the examination. Another national examination at the end of the secondary level determines admission to universities.

The minister of education and a national education council make broad policy statements, but operating policies are the responsibility of the ministry of education, which is staffed by education civil-service officers. All educational administrators, including headmasters, are trained in a national academy run by the ministry of education.

Several patterns of control of schools exist, as the latest reform has not completely replaced earlier reforms. These patterns vary in the number of units or span of control that each administrative officer must monitor. Cummings (1989) indicates that academic achievement is higher in those school clusters in which there is greater communication and sharing of resources between teachers in the various schools. This occurs in those regions in which each officer has relatively few units to supervise. In areas in which span of control is high, officers rely on the regulation and monitoring of inputs, such as attendance and expenditures. In areas in which span of control is low, officers rely on monitoring of outcomes.

Funds for public schools in Sri Lanka come from the national government, but many regions have systems of voluntary fees (monitored by the ministry) which supplement income. Especially important are contributions to the school by local communities, usually in the form of labor for school construction and maintenance, but also of furniture and equipment. Community contributions to schools are highest in school clusters in which headmaster activity and teacher participation is high and in districts in which span of control is small.

Decentralization of authority for administration of schools has had a noticeable positive impact on the morale and innovative behavior of headmasters and teachers. Although community control over schools has not increased, community participation in support of schools has grown.

United States of America

The governance system for education in the United States is unique in both its history and current direction. Its inclusion here serves purposes of contrast rather than as the standard toward which other systems are likely to evolve. In the 17th and 18th centuries, the education system in the northern American colonies was begun by educated protesters against the traditions of their homeland, England. Schools were controlled by local communities bound together by a common religion which insisted on democratic participation in governance. As population density was extremely low, each community operated with considerable autonomy under a charter from the colony.

The U. S. American war for independence in 1776 was fought in part against a central government. So in the federal constitution that followed, control over education was reserved to each of the states. For the most part, these in turn relied on local governments to finance education, to choose teachers and curricula, and to award diplomas. States created public normal schools for teacher training, and eventually they imposed statewide certification requirements for teachers, but did not set salaries or specify working conditions. Local control of education has continued as a dogma of American education, although in fact both state and federal governments now participate in major aspects of the governance of American schools.

The long term trend in governance is clearly toward centralization. The number of school districts (or units of local control) has been reduced from more than 100,000 in 1900 to about 25,000 today, as communities and states have found it convenient to consolidate districts. As the population and enrollments of districts have increased, so have struggles for control of schools. Early in this century professional educators in large cities, in league with liberal members of the middle and upper classes, moved to wrest control from lay school boards, often dominated by political parties. Under the banner of professionalization, teachers in many districts were given great authority in the selection of curricula and methods of evaluating students. School administrators in many instances were members of the same professional association as teachers, and therefore as responsive to teachers as they were to local school boards. Tenure for teachers insured teacher influence over not only administration but also programs. States set some minimal requirements for health and safety and for the inclusion of English and American history in the curriculum.

The challenge to American world hegemony in the 1950s by the Soviet Union was met in part by attacks on the U.S. education system, and led to moves by the federal government to stimulate states and local school districts to modify their curricula. Although federal finance of education generally was less than 10 percent of total expenditures, it was federal funds that generated new programs, leading to greater homogeneity across school districts. A subsequent push for civil rights and federal court intervention into schools to require desegregation took control over admissions away from local school boards. Since the 1960s, federal and state courts have used a series of decisions to require local school districts to alter policies that affect who will be admitted (minority-group members, handicapped, mentally retarded), how students will be taught, how they will be evaluated, and what facilities will be provided for them. State and federal courts became involved in disputes over curriculum, eventually limiting the right of local communities to choose particular forms of religious observances or to teach alternatives to Darwinian evolutionary theory (Mitchell, 1982).

These events have occurred in a context of increased interest and participation in school governance by individual citizens, civil rights groups, religious organizations, unionized educators, and others, with their lobbying focused on state and federal legislators and courts. Efforts to improve equality of opportunity and school effectiveness have resulted in a diminution of local control and to increased control by regulations imposed from outside the local community. In some states, local communities have backed legislation to limit levels of expenditure on education. The effect has been to increase the state government's share of total expenditure on primary and secondary education, thereby increasing state control over policies and programs in schools.

Most recently, continued dissatisfaction with the performance of American schools (especially in terms of achievement scores in mathematics and science compared to schools in other countries) has led to calls for national curriculum standards.

GOVERNANCE OF HIGHER EDUCATION

In this higher-education rubric are included all post-secondary institutions. Only some of these are universities. Those that are not universities generally have the same governance system as primary and secondary schools. In the United States, for example, most two-year post-secondary institutions, called community colleges, are controlled by the same school board as primary and secondary schools. Mexico operates a series of post-secondary technological institutes that are controlled by the federal ministry of education. In Sri Lanka the ministry controls the two-year colleges. In some countries (for example, Egypt and Pakistan) teacher training is given in post-secondary institutions controlled by the ministry of education.

In this section we focus on universities, because these institutions were in general constructed in a different context than were primary and secondary schools, and often therefore are governed under a different set of rules. Some universities existed before the creation of mass national education systems, and university members were important actors in the struggle to take control of the new nation-states. In general, existing European universities have continued as important bases of power in those countries (such as Great Britain) where the new state was not powerful enough to take complete control of primary and secondary education (Archer, 1979). Such universities are said to be autonomous or self-governing (Knowles, 1977). Members of the university have control over their curriculum, teachers, students, and administration. Although most or all of the finance comes from the state, the university has control over how it will be spent.

In other countries (such as France), the university became part of the state education apparatus. University members were considered employees of the state, and significant control over curriculum, teachers, and students was exercised by external governing boards or councils. This also has been the dominant model of governance in European universities created after the appearance of the strong central state. In Sweden, for example, prior to 1977 professors were responsible for the immediate administration of the university, but government agencies appointed tenured staff, made broad policies for the curriculum, built facilities, and decided on numbers and criteria for student admission.

Universities in the colonies followed the model of the colonial master. In many cases the local university was created as a dependency of a metropolitan university. Curricula, criteria for selection and promotion of faculty, patterns of administration and regulation of students were, as in the colonizers' homeland, established and administered principally by members of the university faculty. Even with colonies' gaining independence, many of their universities continued to have strong links with a metropolitan university, which acted to protect its autonomy.

In other cases, university autonomy was won through political struggle by groups within the university in opposition to the government. This is the dominant model in Latin America, where most universities were begun by the Catholic church, but later taken over by anticlerical forces who had seized control of the state. For many years these public universities were arenas for struggle between factions of the ruling class, but self-government was limited. Elites circulated in and out of universities according to whether their faction was included in the coalition in control of the government at that time. In the first third of this century, alliances between faculty and students were powerful enough to force the government to extend autonomy to the university for management of all its affairs, first in Argentina, later in other countries.

In some cases autonomy was won by progressive elements seeking to take control of the university from conservative elements linked with the Church. In other cases, it was conservative groups in the university that sought autonomy to protect their power base (Mabry, 1982). Autonomy granted the university control over appointments, curriculum, and expenditure of resources guaranteed by the government.

Autonomy is not the same as independence. Autonomous universities continue to operate within a political and social system in which external groups, both within and without the government, see in the university resources to help in the achievement of their particular projects. Mexican public universities receive more than 90 percent of their revenues from the federal government, but retain control over selection of students, professors, and administrative personnel, including the university rector or president (Levy, 1980). But these universities are highly penetrated by national political groups, including the government. Most public universities in Mexico support the ruling party line, because ruling party support of candidates in internal political struggles has insured that government supporters gain key administrative and professorial positions. In only a small proportion of universities do groups in opposition to the government control the governing apparatus of the university. The government need not be concerned about university autonomy when most universities are controlled by supporters of the government.

Even when individual universities are granted considerable autonomy in the administration of their internal affairs, states seek to coordinate or control the overall operation of the university system. Clark (1983) suggests three sources of coordination or integration of universities. The most common source is that of state regulation. The more unitary and coherent the state apparatus, the less self-government by universities. Sweden is an example of a "tight" system of state coordination; its small size has allowed the state to exercise control with relatively few organizations. Universities in France enjoy slightly more autonomy because of multiple and sometimes competing bureaus. On the opposite end of this dimension Clark places the United States, in which the control of federal authorities over universities is limited to that exercised through grants and student-aid programs. Control by state governments in the United States varies widely from state to state, with some states appointing rectors or chancellors, controlling budgets, and from time to time legislating particular academic programs.

Where universities enjoy relatively little control by provincial and federal governments, integration of the university system is achieved by non- or quasi-governmental organizations. Clark distinguishes between those dominated by members of the universities and those in which a variety of non-governmental groups and interests act to shape university policies.

In some countries university faculty have control over national organizations responsible for the appointments of faculty, design of curriculum, and finance of research and general administration. For example, German professors dominate the national science council, the West German Rectors Conference, the association of universities, and research organizations with control over grants. The University Grants Committee (UGC) in Great Britain is controlled by prominent academics (Clark, 1983). In some instances these academics are able to command sufficient support from their membership and other groups in society to act independently of the government. Eustace (1984) shows how the UGC mechanism took a different form when transferred to colonies in West Africa. In Egypt, university presidents control the Supreme Council of Higher Education, which makes all regulations for universities.

Finally, Clark argues that integration can also be achieved by the participation of a variety of groups with an interest in the products of universities —teaching, research, and services— in governmental and non-governmental organizations that advise individual institutions and state-level governments on allocations to public and private universities, admission and evaluation of students, and curriculum content. These kinds of organizations are more likely to occur in large university systems, such as that of the United States, Canada, and Japan, in which both public and private universities compete for students, faculty and finance. This may be seen as a form of decentralization, in that government authority is shared with outside groups, but it may reduce faculty self-governance as well as community participation in governance through elected government officials. Nor is it guaranteed that shared decision-making leads to consensus and "integration." When the French state decided to reduce its own authority over universities, the relative power of other groups increased enough to stimulate a series of confrontations between faculty, political and trade unions, students, and state authorities (Dry, 1983).

State influence is also exerted through the creation of segmented public higher education systems (two-year colleges, mass four-year colleges, and elite research institutions). The expansion of opportunities for higher education comes about through increased government funding, which in turn generates increased tension over autonomy (Eurich, 1981). By varying the amount of subsidy to different kinds of programs, the central government can influence the admission to higher education of different social groups and to some extent determine the programs offered. How these mechanisms work is seen in the case of Sri Lanka.

Sri Lanka

In Sri Lanka —when it was known as the British colony of Ceylon— university colleges linked to Cambridge University and the University of London were established as early as 1870, but the first university was not organized until 1942. The first principal and vice-chancellor came from Oxford University, and instruction was in English. The University of Ceylon initially enjoyed complete autonomy; neither the colonial governor nor the ministry of education had authority over any aspect of the institution. Authority over academic matters was held by the Senate in which faculty members predominated. The council was responsible for all administrative matters; its members came from the University. A university court met once a year to elect the vice-chancellor (chief executive officer of the University) and approve the annual budget and proposals by the council. The court included members of parliament and elected representatives, along with officials of the University. The governor was named as chancellor and chairperson of the court.

Following Sri Lanka's independence in 1948, nationalist political movements pushed to replace English with Sinhala as the only official language of the country. The University of Ceylon was at best uncooperative. Elected to power in 1956, the nationalists created two more universities, with instruction in Sinhala, but also with autonomy.

By 1966 all three universities were crowded, as the campaign to expand education at the primary and secondary levels came to fruition. Students protested large classes and low quality of instruction. A faculty group that had dominated governance of the University of Ceylon was increasingly alienated and unable to control students. The government intervened to reorganize the governance system of all three institutions. A National Council of Higher Education, composed of persons from outside the universities, replaced the court. The NCHE allocated funds, set standards for quality of the institutions, coordinated the admission of students into programs in the three universities, and nominated candidates for vice-chancellor to be named by the minister of education. The NCHE also appointed all members of a board of regents, which replaced the council as the governing body of the university. The faculty senate retained control of academic matters. The minister of education was given authority at times of crisis to close universities or take over their management.

The autonomy of the universities was over, but autonomy became a national political issue. Progressive parties backed legislation in 1971 and 1972 to include student participation in both academic and general governance of the universities, but high levels of unrest were used by the government to justify defeat of the proposals. A government proposal in 1975 to appoint student and faculty representatives to governing boards was defeated by the combined protest of universities and opposition parliamentarians. Centralization of the universities was now so complete that the Vice-Chancellor approved even the appointments of casual laborers.

In 1978 a ministry of higher education was created, and in 1979 legislation restored a measure of autonomy to the universities. A Universities Grants Commission of five members appointed by the nation's president now allocates funds and appoints university administrative officers (vice-chancellor and campus rectors). The university court was re-established, but the UGC was given authority to appoint most of its 50 members from the community. Most of the members of the university council are appointed by the UGC. A 100-member faculty senate chaired by the appointed vice-chancellor maintains control over existing programs, but new programs and faculty appointments have to be approved by the UGC (Gamage, 1983, 1987).

THE EFFECTIVENESS OF DIFFERENT FORMS OF GOVERNANCE

The long history of conflict over how and by whom schools and universities should be governed demonstrates the wisdom of beginning an evaluation of forms of governance with a specification of the perspectives to be taken into account. What works for one group may be seen as ineffective or harmful by another. Objectives for governance vary by group and by the subject of the control mechanism. Academics may be concerned principally about distribution of resources to maintain or improve the quality of education, while a ministry of finance worries about levels of expenditure. Local communities may be more concerned about the extent to which schools reproduce cultural values, while employers are concerned about training in skills for production using their technologies.

Within a given nation or local community, criteria for the evaluation of the governance system vary with changes in the external environment (such as the world or national economy) or with changes in the balance of forces of groups within the ruling coalition. Federal intervention in American schools was generally condemned by local politicians and educators until the sound of Sputnik was used to mobilize educators and communities into reforming science and mathematics instruction, financed principally by the federal government. Self-governance of Sri Lankan universities was considered appropriate by the government until student violence appeared to threaten the stability of the state, or at least of the government.

From this perspective, it does not seem prudent to recommend one form of governance over another. We can, however, attempt to trace out some of the conditions that would make one form more effective than another for a given group in power, and to indicate which form should be preferred by groups not in power.

A new government that cannot assume a long term in power (such as an elected government or a military group fearing a counter-coup), but which wishes to bring about a radical or revolutionary reform of society, should seek centralized control of the education system. Selective admission of students will be an effective device to redress inequalities in access and graduation. Tracking and streaming of children on the basis of abilities or values associated with desired outcomes will enhance the effectiveness of the system. Control over curriculum will be essential to insure that content matches societal goals. For the short term, existing teachers can be used if their classroom behavior is closely monitored; for the long term it will be necessary to reform teacher-training institutions. School administration, as in the routine implementation of predetermined tasks, should not be a major concern except as linked with supervision. Parents and other community members who support the changes can also contribute to supervision of teacher performance. Government control over the schools is increased by eliminating other sources of finance. Teachers and administrators can be defined as employees of the government, denied the right to strike, and encouraged to participate in the ruling party.

These kinds of control mechanisms are ones used when a group in power has a clear objective that is not supported by all members of the current school system. Such mechanisms characterize the governance system of countries that have experienced radical reform of education (such as Czechoslovakia) but also of many of the newer nations of the world in which there is low consensus about core political and social values.

When education is controlled by factions that limit the power of another group which wishes to rule, then some form of decentralization can be used by the group seeking to rule to force a redistribution of power to its benefit. This was the strategy of a modernizing group in Mexico that sought to reduce the power of the central teachers' union in order to push through reforms of curriculum and administration. The modernizers, backed by the President of the Republic, seized control of personnel appointments and construction contracts in the federal ministry, thereby cutting off a major source of power for the central union.

But a redistribution of power may have unintended consequences. The weakening of Mexico's central union leadership by the reforms of the modernizers strengthened the position of local, democratic teachers' unions. Teachers began to take power from local administrators appointed by the ministry-union coalition, to participate directly in governance of their schools, and to clarify demands for participation in governance at the provincial and federal levels. The modernizers were forced to renew their alliance with the central union in order to stifle local movements (Street, 1988).

As a system grows more complex, central control becomes increasingly difficult. Although the central ministry may continue to exercise its authority to make regulations, its capacity to monitor actual compliance with those regulations declines. Constant supervision of teachers becomes impossible. Achievement of objectives declines. Some degree and form of decentralization is necessary to regain achievement of system objectives.

Decentralization moves the locus of control for the implementation of programs and policies "down the line" from center toward periphery, or from larger to smaller units. In the Sri Lanka school reform, district and school administrators were given authority originally held by ministry officials. In Chile, authority over hiring and firing of teachers was given to municipalities. In Mexico, the secretary of education sent his delegates to the various states with complete authority over teachers and finance. The 1968 reform in France gave universities the right to devise their own curriculum (given broad national objectives), carry out their own research, and to some extent set up their own evaluation of student performance. The reform also increased regional participation in the universities' advisory councils (Neave, 1985).

From a technical perspective, the most effective governance system is one that gives the persons with most information about the situation the authority to devise methods to carry out objectives set at a higher level. In general, that means that a governance system will be most effective when teachers have autonomy in their classrooms to devise methods of teaching, including sequence of subject matter, and methods of evaluation in response to assessments of student interests and abilities. But individual teachers, and even teachers as a group, are not likely to have full information about labor-force requirements or national political goals. Choice of academic programs, therefore, should be made outside of individual institutions. Teachers are better qualified than parents to decide on methods of teaching, but parents have more information about the value orientation and economic requirements of the community. Hiring of teachers should be done at the institutional level, but the total number of teachers to be hired should be decided at a community or regional level, taking into consideration resource constraints. The more geographically mobile the community served, the less local teachers or parents should control content of the system.

From an equity perspective, the most effective governance system is one that minimizes differences across communities or regions. This means that control over admission to school and assignment of resources should be carried out by central rather than local bodies. Local mobilization of resources is important from a technical effectiveness point of view, but central bodies should act to make up the differences between richer and poorer regions.

An over-emphasis on technical efficiency can lead to inequities in the education system. One definition of decentralization makes the smaller unit —which is the right-hand extreme of the dimension— the "private citizen." In the Chilean application of this concept, citizens were encouraged to choose between different municipal and private schools. The U.S. American voucher scheme, which would provide parents with a school-expenditure voucher, was an attempt to provide citizens with an opportunity to choose where they would educate their children. Both of these schemes relied on public funds. By exercising control over student admission, parents are supposed to eventually control teachers, curriculum, and administration. Another variation of the concept of "privatization" suggests reduced public expenditure on education, arguing that private finance will have more impact on the quality of education.

Evidence for the "effectiveness" of this kind of decentralization is still limited. Decentralization in general, and especially privatization, are not likely to have uniformly positive effects when fiscal resources are committed and skilled persons are in short supply and/or concentrated in some regions. Municipalization and subsidization of private education in Chile has not had any demonstrable effect on overall levels of quality of education, although individual institutions and their clientele have benefited greatly. The imbalance of distribution of resources to urban and rural students has grown more marked (Magendzo, Egaña, & Latore, 1988). Greater reliance on community support for schooling in Kenya, according to Lillis (1988), tends to result in lower quality of education. Communities lack experience in school construction and build poor physical facilities. Teachers with qualifications are hired out of rural areas by richer urban communities, so that private rural schools have poorly qualified staffs. With poor quality staff and no supervision, community supported schools deviate from the official curriculum, and fall back on less effective teaching methods. Variations across schools result in inequalities related to the income levels of the communities and students' families. There is no evidence that overall efficiency or quality improves. If the general level of human resources and organizational capacity in a country is low, as in Kenya, shifting the source of finance and control of education from the central government to communities is likely to reduce quality and increase inequality.

Another definition of decentralization names the school or district as the smaller unit of the system. The central government assumes the responsibility of equitable distribution of its human and fiscal resources throughout the system, but relies on local schools or districts to adapt centrally-designed materials and curricula to local conditions. The success of one experiment of this kind was described in the section on Sri Lanka.

Local control of schools is the U.S. American model, but it may not seem reasonable to use the United States as proof that a decentralized system is best, given the unique history of the country and current widespread dissatisfaction with achievement scores in comparison with those of other, more centralized systems. The American model was tried in Japan, but eventually abandoned. Local school boards were mandated for Japan by the American military occupation forces in 1947, but beginning in 1954 conservative governments have systematically reduced local control. Boards of education are now appointed by the provincial governor rather than elected directly by citizens. The ministry of education specifies employment practices and rules for school attendance and intervenes in curriculum development. It controls budgets and provides staff development programs. Education is seen as having too much national importance to be entrusted completely to local authorities.

> The ministry of education justifies the central control of education as necessary to modernize the Japanese society. Lacking confidence that local boards can make educational policy in the best interests of the nation, centralization assures that all schools have similar offerings and standards. If a local school board is confronted with a discipline problem or curriculum question, usually the Ministry of Education is contacted. The ministry distributes a *Handbook on School Administration*, which contains detailed specifications that must be followed in all schools (Aoki & McCarthy, 1984: 446).

In the past few years there have been efforts to move control over education closer to schools and local communities, but also increased numbers of education cases brought before national courts.

FUTURE TRENDS IN GOVERNANCE

Proponents of the concept of an emerging world system of education argue that belief in the myths of the individual (as opposed to the concept of the person who derives meaning from membership in a community) and the nation as an aggregate of individuals (as opposed to an organic whole) are essential to explain the worldwide institutionalization of the European model of schooling (Ramirez & Boli, 1987).

Paradoxically, the increasing emphasis on the individual as opposed to family or community will, in those countries in which the state is strong, act to increase some aspects of central control of education. This will occur because as community organizations decline in importance, higher-level organizations will step into the vacuum to regulate social and economic affairs. The trend has been observed by Kogan (1988) for higher education in industrialized countries. Central intermediary agencies created to protect individuals take power away from local groups. Democratic control of education will be especially weakened, as it has in the United States and in Japan, by increasing reliance on the courts —over which local voters have no control— as the source of education policy and even management.

Current interest in decentralization by governments and international agencies reflects a shift in ideology away from emphasis on equity toward emphasis on efficiency. Two schemes are likely to be increasingly chosen by conservative governments. The first scheme (like that of Chile) attempts to strengthen local government and private control of education. This reduces the participation of teachers and therefore may lead to declines in overall efficiency while improving quality for some.

A second scheme decentralizes to the level of the school, which increases the influence exerted by individual teachers but reduces the overall influence of teachers as an organized group. In Great Britain this is being accomplished by centralizing control over curriculum while decentralizing further control over management and fund-raising. Prior to the British Education Act of 1988, Local Education Authorities (county and municipal boards, often elected) chose their own curriculum and hired teachers. Central government subsidies were used to pay teacher salaries according to a national scale. The National Teachers' Union exercised influence at the national level through collective bargaining, and at the local level through its association with the Labor Party which controlled a number of local education authorities. Now the government has established a single national curriculum, and given authority to individual schools to hire teachers, using central subsidies to pay teachers whatever the school wants. Headmasters and teachers in a given school have more influence on practices of their particular institution than before, but teachers as an organized group now have little voice in the national educational debate. In both schemes, the central government ends up with more control over curriculum. Both schemes reduce central control over distribution of resources, which can lead to greater inequity.

In those countries in which the state is weak or weakening, decentralization reflects the capture of local and regional organizations by groups seeking to change the composition of the state. In Sweden, for example, central authorities now accept the value of decentralization and are moving to devolve control of highly centralized primary-secondary and university systems back to local government. Critical to this process are the education professionals, who resent the earlier usurpation of their power by central government, but are not sure whether local control promises them more autonomy (Lane & Murray, 1985). In general, education professionals will increase their influence over the practice of education, but have less influence over setting broad goals for education.

Decentralization of administration and finance will reduce the power of those in central government who rely on regulations and monitoring of inputs as major mechanisms of control. They will be replaced by groups that exercise control over education through monitoring of outcomes. Installation of procedures for rapid detection of failure by local school districts to achieve system objectives will allow central governments to take corrective measures, including application of incentives to raise levels of performance. We are just now beginning to see the adoption of this method of governance by national governments interested in the improvement of local education. This mechanism may lead to greater efficiency in education. Whether it will lead to increased equity will depend on the objectives of the groups that employ it.

REFERENCES

Aoki, K., & McCarthy, M. (1984) The right to education in Japan. *Journal of Law and Education*, 13 (3): 441-452.

Archer, M. S. (1979) *Social origins of educational systems*. London: Sage Publications.

Clark, B. R. (1983) *The higher education system: Academic organization in cross-national perspective*. Berkeley: University of California Press.

Cummings, W. K. (1988) *The decentralization of education*. Cambridge: Harvard Institute for International Development, BRIDGES.

Curtis, B. (1988) Patterns of resistance to public education: England, Ireland and Canada West, 1830-1890. *Comparative Education Review*, 32 (3), 318-33.

Dry, J. (1983) Patterns of authority in the higher education system in France. *International Journal of Institutional Management in Higher Education*, 7 (2), 31-35.

Eurich, N. P. (1981) *Systems of higher education in twelve countries: A comparative view*. New York: Praeger.

Eustace, R. (1984) The export of the UGC idea to Africa. *Higher Education*, 13 (5), 595-612.

Gamage, D. T. (1983) The struggle for control of higher education in a developing economy: Sri Lanka. *Comparative Education* 19 (3): 325-339.

Gamage, D. T. (1987) Vicissitudes in the administration of higher education in a Third World country: Four decades--seven reforms. *Educational Administration and History*, 19 (1), 47-61.

Halls, W. D. (1976) *Education, culture, and politics in modern France*. Oxford: Pergamon Press.

Kelly, G. P. (1987) The transfer of an education operating system: French educational management organization in the colonies. In R. M. Thomas & V. N. Kobayashi (Eds.) *Educational technology: Its creation, development and cross-cultural transfer* ((233-252). New York: Pergamon.

Knowles, A. S. (1977) Governance and administration. In A. S. Knowles (Ed.), *The international encyclopedia of higher education* (Vol. 5, pp. 1880-1901). San Francisco: Jossey-Bass.

Kogan, M. (1988) Government and the management of higher education: An introductory review. *International Journal of Institutional Management in Higher Education*, 12 (1): 5-15.

Lane, J. E. & Murray, M. (1985) The significance of decentralisation in Swedish education. *European Journal of Education*, 20 (2-3): 163-170.

Levy, D. C. (1980) *University and government in Mexico: Autonomy in an authoritarian system.* New York: Praeger.

Lillis, K. (1988) Issues of quality. In M. Bray with K. Lillis (Eds.) *Community financing of education: Issues and policy implications in less developed countries* (75-93). Oxford: Pergamon.

Mabry, D. J. (1982) *The Mexican university and the state.* College Station, TX: Texas A&M Press.

Magendzo, A., Egaña, L., & Latorre, C. L. (1988) *Privatización de la educación: La educación y los esquemas privatizantes en educación bajo un estado subsidiario (1973-1987).* Santiago, Chile: Programa Interdiciplinario de Investigación Educativa.

McGinn. N. (1987) The creation of an education operating system: The bureaucratic organization of the French national system of education. In R. M. Thomas & V. N. Kobayashi (Eds.) *Educational technology: Its creation, development and cross-cultural transfer* (209-232). New York: Pergamon.

Mitchell, D. E. (1982) Governance of schools. In H. E. Mitzel (Ed.) *Encyclopedia of Educational Research* (Vol. 2, pp. 730-738). New York: Free Press.

Neave, G. (1985) Strategic planning, reform, and governance in French higher education. *Studies in Higher Education*, 10 (1): 7-20.

Petracek, S. (1988) Czechoslovakia. In T. N. Postlethwaite (Ed.) *The encyclopedia of comparative education and national education systems* (pp. 223-228). Oxford: Pergamon.

Programa Interdisciplinario de Investigación Educativa (1984) *Las transformaciones educacionales bajo el regimen militar.* Santiago, Chile.

Ramirez, F. O., & Boli, J. (1987) The political construction of mass schooling: European origins and worldwide institutionalization. *Sociology of Education*, 60 (1): 2-17.

Ramirez, F. O., & Rubinson, R. (1979) Creating members: The political incorporation and expansion of public education. In J. W. Meyer & M. T. Hannan (Eds.) *National development and the world system* (pp. 72-82). Chicago: University of Chicago Press.

Saqeb, G. N. (1985) The effects of tensions between nationalism and provincialism on educational administration in Pakistan. In J. Lauglo & M. McLean (Eds.), *The control of education* (pp. 33-44). London: Heinemann.

Street, S. (1988) *Organized teachers as policymakers: Domination and opposition in Mexican public education.* Unpublished doctoral dissertation, Harvard Graduate School of Education, Cambridge.

Warwick, D. P. Reimers, F., & McGinn, N. (1989) *The implementation of educational innovations in Pakistan.* Cambridge: Harvard Institute for International Development, BRIDGES.

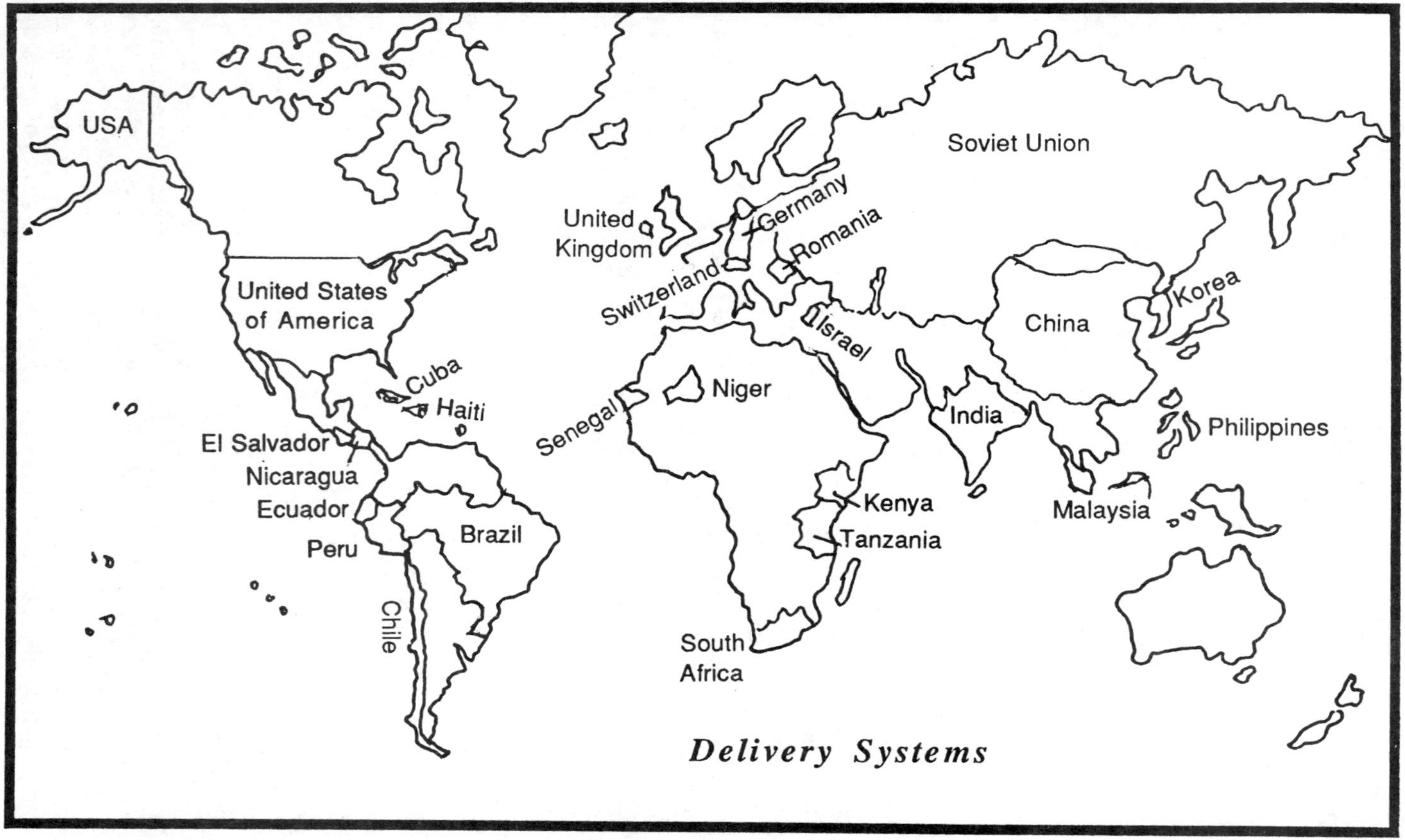
USA
United States of America
Cuba
Haiti
El Salvador
Nicaragua
Ecuador
Peru
Brazil
Chile
United Kingdom
Switzerland
Germany
Romania
Israel
Senegal
Niger
Kenya
Tanzania
South Africa
Soviet Union
China
Korea
India
Malaysia
Philippines
Delivery Systems

CHAPTER 6

Delivery Systems —Formal, Nonformal, Informal

In what forms is education offered, and which of these are the most desirable?

THOMAS J. LABELLE & JUDY J. SYLVESTER

Teaching and learning occur in many different settings. From street corners, peer groups, and families to organized youth groups and school classrooms, most of our individual lives is composed of experiences from which we learn. In recognizing this diversity in teaching and learning, it is important that we think about education as extending beyond schools into other settings. Collectively, these educational processes and settings constitute the teaching and learning delivery systems available to a society.

Taking this broad view of education necessitates the availability of words and concepts to help us think and talk about, as well as classify and use, this range of resources. While there is a tradition of conceptualizing education as occurring either in schools or in the home, we will argue that this bipolarization fails to recognize a middle ground of systematic teaching and learning (La Belle, 1981). Thus, we will use definitions for three types of education —informal, nonformal and formal— introduced by Coombs and Ahmed (1974). Informal education is seen on a continuum as "the lifelong process by which every person acquires and accumulates knowledge, skills and insights from daily experiences and exposure to the environment." Hence, informal education is learning through day-to-day living as we carry on our normal activities. Nonformal education, the second form of teaching and learning, is defined by the authors as "any organized, systematic educational activity carried on outside the framework of the formal system to provide selected types of learning to particular subgroups in the population, adults as well as children." A major difference between the informal and nonformal processes is the deliberate instructional and programmatic emphases in the latter but which are absent from informal education. Finally, Coombs and Ahmed describe formal education as the "institutionalized, chronologically graded and hierarchically structured educational system spanning lower primary school and the upper reaches of the university."

In practice, informal, nonformal, and formal education should be viewed as predominant modes of learning rather than, as Coombs and Ahmed's definitions imply, discrete entities. The three modes of emphasis — formal, nonformal, and informal— may exist simultaneously, sometimes in concert with one another and sometimes in conflict. For example, in a formal education situation, the classroom reflects not only the stated curriculum of the teacher and the school but also the more subtle informal learning associated with how the classroom is organized, the rules by which it operates, and the knowledge transmitted among peers. In this case, simple participation in the school process fosters informal learning, but that learning may have little to do with the deliberate and systematic teaching associated with the preplanned curricula. Similarly, the school fosters nonformal education through extra-curricular activities which may have little to do with credits, grades, or diplomas, yet reflect deliberate and systematic ways to facilitate teaching and learning (La Belle, 1982).

THE INTERACTION OF FORMAL, NONFORMAL, AND INFORMAL EDUCATION

The three modes of education are interactive such that all individuals at all times are engaged in one or more of them, thereby learning from planned, compulsory, and intentional activities to unplanned, voluntary, and incidental activities. Although age, sex, social class, and ethnic-group patterns can be detected and are common across these modes, each individual also composes his or her own configuration of educational influences. The unique patterns that emerge will likely find that one mode will be dominant for a period of time. For example, there may be a tradition in certain situations of pursuing formal or nonformal education at various points in a lifetime to receive training for either a new career path or for mobility within the same career. The particular contact made with differing educational modes or with the interactions within those modes depends to a considerable extent on the social class of the individual and his or her ability to exercise educational options throughout the life span.

There are many cross-national and cross-cultural characteristics of educational processes that can be studied to gain insight into differing patterns of teaching and learning. For example, one can concentrate on the content (environment, values), the methods of teaching, who educates, how the person being educated behaves, how the educator behaves, how some things are taught to some groups but not to others, forms of discipline, the kinds of self-conceptions that are reinforced, the length of the process, and so on (Henry, 1960). In the discussion which follows, a number of these characteristics are highlighted, with special attention to who controls education and how the educational process is implemented.

INFORMAL EDUCATION

The combined effect of informal, nonformal, and formal education is the preparation of individuals to behave appropriately in the culture to which they belong. Informal education through day-to-day activity is likely to be the most powerful contributor to this kind of learning. The particular nature of what is learned and how it is learned will vary, but each society must produce individuals who will adapt to, and make productive, a way of life that interacts within and preserves an ecological niche. Over time, the transmission of this cultural information, whether it is in a small town, a rural area, or a large city, leads to an agreed upon view of reality —from naming and carrying the newborn to taking one's place in a family and community and eventually being married and buried. This kind of learning, mostly by copying and imitating, enables each of us to learn behavior that ultimately becomes habitual. Thus, we learn to act in particular ways because that is the way it has always been done. Such learning makes life secure and predictable as we grow up conforming to and creating rules that guide our own as well as others' behavior.

Table manners, personal hygiene, exchanging appropriate salutations with friends and acquaintances, and obeying traffic laws and signals are examples of ways that our daily lives take on a habitual, reinforcing character. The way each is manifested, of course, is subject to the acceptable patterns of behavior in a given culture and society.

Family, Community, and the Media

The family and community, as well as a wide variety of media, are at the center of this kind of education. In the family and community it is often the role models and mentors rather than what is taught that is most important. While schools standardize activity and what is learned, out-of-school learning is determined more by time and place, is reinforced day after day by the same individuals, and leads to language, values, and cognitive patterns which may be at least partially unique to neighborhoods, social class and ethnic groups. For example, the daily activities of the family —cooking, shopping, planting, harvesting, living in urban or rural areas and in apartments or single-family dwellings— influence the problems an individual within that family is asked to solve. Also, the nature and extent of communication within the family —instructions, discussions, questions— shape the vocabulary and verbal skills acquired by any of the family members. Similarly, the extent to which the family adheres to religious, dress, or dietary practices will help determine how effectively the family transmits the ethnic heritage of its members.

In this regard, Resnick (1987) argues that whereas schooling focuses on the individual's performance, fosters unaided thought, focuses on symbolic thinking, and teaches general skills and knowledge, out-of-school mental work is often socially shared, involves cognitive tools, engages directly objects and situations, and encourages learning that is more likely to involve situation-specific competencies. Resnick contends that out-of-school activities link objects directly to events in an individual's reasoning, whereas school learning must use symbols, often unsuccessfully, to make connections to real-world events and objects. Further, she sees out-of-school work and recreation taking place in interactive social systems, whereas schooling requires individual work, often separated from the same work being done simultaneously by others. Because of these out-of-school and in-school teaching and learning characteristics, Resnick believes that school programs should redirect themselves into the socially shared mental work and more direct engagement with the real world that is characteristic of out-of-school activity, thus more successfully carrying out the achievement of the school's objectives.

Such observations suggest that the organization and structure of communities and families are influential in shaping how and what is learned. In the community, for example, the existence of definable roles and statuses for members and the particular expectations for behaviors that are defined, often by age and sex, can influence greatly the nature of learning by each member. In the family, there is evidence that the ways in which leadership, child care, and decision-making are carried out or the extent to which particular functions are shared within primary groups are influential for learning language structure and the methods of thinking about self, things, and ideas (Cohen, 1969). For instance, in some families older siblings have responsibility for child care, providing potentially strong bonds among offspring and requiring the assumption of adult caretaking roles early. In other families, parents or grandparents assume most of these responsibilities, thereby providing a slower transition into adulthood for children and less shared responsibility for day-to-day functioning among primary family members. Such alternative family structures and behavior patterns, with their distinct requirements for functioning successfully, give rise to different task and problem-solving skills and thus shape the cognitive and socio-emotional characteristics of family members.

The family and community are especially important because early learning is the most powerful and because it takes place primarily through interactions with parents, siblings, kinsmen, and other members of primary groups. Informal education lays the initial groundwork in areas of language, values, and cognition that is acquired by individuals as they move into schools. While this early learning takes place in the family and community, it is heavily influenced through other interventions which become part of daily behavior. These other interventions may come in the form of non-kin relationships but are most likely to involve items that can be manipulated, like toys, or be associated with the mass-communication media in the form of print, video, and audio transmissions, often tied to commercial sponsorship and which serve to extend an individual's sense of what is most important and of most worth. Examples of agents outside the family influencing children's gender identification are found in the ways that adults assign blue and pink colors or footballs and dolls to the young, and in the ways that mass-communication media influence people's tastes for products to wear or consume.

Many of us fail to realize the nature of the multi-media environment within which we grow up. While the radio remains the dominant medium in families and communities world wide, an increasing percentage of the world's population is now born into homes where television is a natural part of household furnishings. In the United States, where television has been commonly found in households for forty years, a typical youngster now views some 22-28 hours of television programming per week. In more affluent homes throughout the world, books and other printed media are major influences on teaching and learning, and more recently the advent of personal computers brings to the home an additional variety of educational resources. Finally, the kinds of toys that children play with often reflect the anxieties, behaviors, visions, prejudices, and roles and statuses common in a society and thereby provide reinforcement to children of appropriate ways of patterning their own ways of life. Many such characteristics are embodied in the depiction of traditional heroes based on sports or military figures, in children's stories portraying competition or cooperation, in computer video games and the special arcades in which to play them, and in such board games as *Monopoly*.

As an individual grows older and learning for behaving in the wider society becomes more complex, the rules that govern behavior undergo change. Non-kinship and more universal bases of social interaction come into play so that economic, political, and social relations can be made productive and predictable. As this process occurs, schools, and often nonformal education, become more important because these more systematic contexts are where societies institutionalize such learning.

FORMAL EDUCATION

As McGinn pointed out in Chapter 5, schools appear when political entities known as nation-states become a reality. Such collectivities emphasize universalistic values, criteria, and standards of performance needed for the execution of laws, the management of revenue, and the maintenance of law and order. It is through schools that more standardized and stereotyped knowledge, skills, and values are fostered and through which the larger political and economic system is maintained. As the nation-state seeks the allegiance and loyalty of the population and a uniformity among the polity through ideology, what goes on inside schools often subverts or is in competition with what goes on in families and communities. The essence of this process is a universalistic orientation to performance and expectation as there is a limited range of acceptable behaviors within the society to which all are expected to conform.

The Control of Schools

From a control perspective, schools are not expected to foster creativity or to challenge the status quo. Instead, they are intended to socialize the new generation to stand for and against the principles upon which the society is based. Thus, schools are always for some things and against others. They are intended to maintain the society as it is or to be used to achieve the kind of society that is envisioned. Schools are also designed to recruit and select individuals to participate as knowledgeable members in the society. To capture this thrust, one might imagine what it would be like to be a student in a school located in the Middle East but attended only by Arabs or only by Jews, or located in Northern Ireland but attended only by Catholics or only by Protestants, or located in South Africa but restricted to only Blacks or Whites. In each instance, although the learners are in close geographical proximity, the ways in which they would be drilled in the political, economic, and cultural orientations of the dominant population would be very different.

Both private and public formal education can be characterized in this way because each is typically sanctioned by the government of a given nation, state, or city. As such, the schools in a particular political entity serve to socialize in standardized ways the individuals of a region into economic and political participation as productive citizens. As will be pointed out below, this centralizing and government-oriented nature of formal education in many countries is different from the local and often private sponsorship associated with nonformal education. In both instances, however, the systematic teaching offered through organized and preplanned programs may be at odds with the informal education coming from families and communities. This potential conflict results primarily from the particularistic values embodied in religious or ethnic backgrounds that parents desire for their children in contrast to the more universalistic values justified by governments as providing a common set of skills and behaviors for a diverse population.

Educational programs which build on the informal learnings of the student's past provide continuity in cultural conditioning while those which do not are discontinuous with that background. Such discontinuities are seen when a child learns one language at home and is taught through a different language in school, or when the child holds particular religious beliefs at home that are not reflected in the belief systems adopted in school textbooks.

The extent to which formal education serves to maintain and perpetuate or to reduce and ameliorate divisions in society is a major issue as one looks to schools as the primary means of delivering teaching and learning (La Belle & White, 1980). In most countries, formal education is a responsibility of the federal government, with curricula, decision-making, and policies remaining in the hands of central authorities. Even where there is considerable decentralization, as in the United States, much of what goes on inside of schools is heavily influenced by the fiscal, legal, and legislative actions at the national level. Among the many factors contributing to this worldwide trend toward administrative centralism are authoritarian traditions in social, economic, and political life, the impact of nationalism and modernization, the use of schooling as an instrument of national policy, and the effort to attain social goals efficiently through coordinated planning and supervision.

In some cases this centralization is associated with authoritarian and totalitarian regimes, while in others there is space allowed for participation in at least some decision-making at the local levels. In South Africa, for example, education operates along racial lines, with cultural prestige, political power, and economic control in the hands of the minority white population. In such a country, centralization means controlling who has access to schools and at what levels, how students are tracked, the curriculum that is planned, the personnel who teach, and the language of instruction. Somewhat similar patterns can be seen in Haiti and Peru. In Haiti such centralization assures a near monopoly of cultural prestige, political power, and economic power in the hands of an urban, French-speaking mulatto minority over a primarily rural, creole-speaking majority. Educational policies find the creole population in schools with few and dated materials, poorly-trained staff, and curricular tracking which channels the students into dead-end and low-status occupations (Layne, 1985). In Peru, similar urban-oriented educational policies favor a dominant, Spanish-speaking white and mestizo minority over a rural, Quechua-speaking Indian majority. Curricula, language of instruction, and related school practices place the Indians at a severe disadvantage (Nakamoto, White, & La Belle, 1985).

A much less authoritarian approach to centralization can be seen in Kenya. Since independence in 1963, the government there has used schooling to build national unity among its more than 30 distinct ethnic groups. Despite a tradition of ethnic diversity in language, customs, and even homeland, policy statements have consistently called on the schools to inculcate into children a sense of belonging to, and support of, the nation. The school system has been expanded, free and universal primary education has been furthered, and national control over curricula —including the identification of Swahili and/or English as the languages of instruction— has been implemented (Urch, 1985).

A far different model of delivering formal education, with shared decision-making and considerable influence exercised at the local level, is seen in Switzerland. Here there are efforts made to provide learners a balance in cultural prestige, political power, and economic control by offering opportunities for various constituencies to participate in the decisions which affect the ways in which schooling is conducted. Although complicated in recent years by the influx of migrant labor from Southern Europe, the traditional focus of the curricula, the language of instruction, who does the teaching, and so on, are negotiated among the constituents, with the interests of regionally oriented ethnic groups specifically addressed.

There are many other examples of countries where decisions about formal schooling involve some combination of centralized and decentralized organizations and structures. The state-oriented system in the United States is one variant on this theme, and the more ethnic-based systems in India and Malaysia provide other variants (La Belle & White, 1980). Whatever the combination, however, it is important to note that schooling usually remains a mechanism for the delivery of teaching and learning for the collective good of the nation, rather than for a region or group within that nation. If a region or particular interest group promulgates educational experiences which are found to be in opposition to the nation's collective interest, it is likely that a compromise will be worked out or the school closed down. Arabs in Israel and the Amish in United States are examples in which some level of compromise has had to be worked out but where the results have nearly always favored the more dominant population.

While it should not be surprising to learn that all nations require some centralization of structure and culture to exist over time, it is important to note that compliance and coordination of the processes to achieve such a goal differ across nations. As indicated above, in some there is greater tolerance of linguistic, religious, and other group-specific practices and beliefs. These societies appear to place more positive value on cultural pluralism and horizontality in power and prestige rather than assimilation and absorption to dominant group preferences. Whatever the orientation, however, schools are central to the struggles over power and influence as both subordinate groups and those which have power vie to use them as vehicles to achieve their own specific interests.

School Process and the New Technology

It is common for the formal school bureaucracy at the national or state level to reach into the classroom in many ways, including, for example, the certification of teachers and the review and approval of curricula. As seems to be universal, most schooling centers on an individual, the teacher, who orchestrates and coordinates the learner's experiences. Students, in turn, are typically placed at individual desks where they are expected to dutifully follow the instructions of those in charge. While there are obviously variants of this standard classroom model, in most countries, whether they are less developed or industrialized, there is remarkable uniformity in the conduct of the teaching and learning process. When diversity is present, it often comes in two areas. One is in the growing use of alternative technology and the other is in linking education more closely with the interests and activities of the community.

Teacher talk or lecturing, combined in the more affluent countries with print media, constitutes the mainstay of the formal teaching-learning process.

However, as indicated in Chapter 3, more advanced media and technology, have continued to find their way into the classroom with mixed reception and, relative to cost and student learning, with mixed results. There is evidence, for example, that the use of radio in combination with instruction by teachers and print media can be a cost-effective means to increase student achievement (Anzalone, 1988). A project which combined these three elements effectively is the Radio Mathematics Project in Nicaragua, a radio-based instructional education program begun in 1974 for 10,000 students in the first four primary school grades. The project involved a minimum of teacher training and limited printed materials. Testing showed that the students, especially those from rural areas, who received in-class radio instruction learned more mathematics than comparable students in traditional classrooms (Gonzalez, 1980). Television, however, has not demonstrated such benefits worldwide, primarily because of the costs of program production and the costs of television sets. It is still too early to determine the effects of such devices as hand-held computers for instruction in subjects like mathematics and spelling, other uses of personal computers, or other technology, such as video disks and interactive video.

Technology has also been used outside of the classroom to bring schooling to outlying areas or to foster self-instruction among older youth and adult populations. As also noted in Chaper 3, this mode is often referred to as *distance education* or *distance teaching and learning* and is used by private for-profit schools, missionaries, adult education, and high school or university extension efforts. Many programs of this sort have used audio cassettes and radio in combination with print media as a form of correspondence instruction. Most of these programs operate on a multi-media principle, are broadcast in sequence, and are tied to a package of printed instructional materials, including workbooks, and involve the training of discussion leaders. Homework is assigned and completed individually or in groups and then sent to the broadcast headquarters to finish the two-way communication process. Sometimes there are direct audio link-ups between the broadcaster and the learners, and the programs become the source of access for many rural communities to the outside world. Many of these efforts have demonstrated both learning gains and cost effectiveness in their approaches. The Open University in Britain is probably the most widely known case of distance education, but there are many other universities throughout the world using this method to reach a variety of audiences, from school teachers to the adult illiterate. In Israel, for example, there is the Everyman University, which offers primarily vocational courses to members of the defense forces and to practicing teachers, but also includes other individuals whose access to the regular system may be limited (Melmed, Ellenbogen, Jamison, & Turniansky, 1982). Other examples are the two-year Korean Air and Correspondence University that is oriented to poor adults and the Open University in Sri Lanka intended for students not admitted to regular higher-learning institutions (Unesco, 1985).

The nature of the new technologies has often changed so dramatically in recent years that they outstrip our ability to use them efficiently and effectively in helping to solve educational, information, and development problems (Spaulding, 1986). This can be seen in the United States as technology there is altering, for example, the way in which college distance education is carried out. In this instance, some colleges have updated the traditional correspondence concept by offering courses via electronic mail systems. Students who have home computers that can be connected to the telephone line via a modem simply dial up computers on campus to receive course assignments and directions, read text material, and communicate with their professor. The instructor's responses to questions asked by students may be stored in the computer until forwarded at a more convenient time to the student. Also, some colleges are beginning to use digital compressed video. This relatively new technology allows distant classrooms to be interconnected via full-motion video with two-way capability so that teachers and students at all locations can hear and see one another as the lesson progresses. Communications are also being dramatically improved among two-year colleges with the development of a national satellite network, called the Community College Satellite Network (CCSN) which is providing an efficient method for receiving and delivering telecourses and teleconferences (English, 1988).

Schools and Their Communities

As schooling reaches out beyond the classroom border, it creates alternatives to the typical teaching and learning that is often isolated in classrooms from the application of that learning. Such reaching out also serves to reduce the tension between centralized control of education and the participation of the local population in its own teaching and learning. Often referred to as community schools, La Belle and Verhine (1981) reviewed a number of these programs and found that they represented efforts: to foster educational access, to facilitate the transition between study and work, to serve as community centers, and to strengthen nationalism and socioeconomic development. While these community oriented programs must reflect the general mission of the nation state, their bias is simultaneously to look inward and thereby respond to community needs and interests as a parallel to the interests of the state.

In the first instance (that is, community schools for educational access) the emphasis is more on providing schooling opportunities than on serving local needs and conditions. The Harambee Schools in Kenya, the CNEC schools in Brazil, and the Barrio High Schools in the Philippines can serve as examples. They have all been nationwide efforts to foster community voluntarism and self help for the provision of secondary education. Schools for the advancement of learning, the second type of community school identified by the authors, includes British Primary Schools, Family Schools in Argentina, and the Israeli Kibbutzim. Here the emphasis has been on having adults and children participate together as learners based on the assumption that individuals are educated most effectively when they interact with material that has the potential of immediate application in their own community. The third type of community school, this one intended to foster the transition from study to work, can be seen in the Village Polytechnic Movement in Kenya, the Brazilian National Apprenticeship Service of Industrial Training, and the combination of study and work in Eastern Europe and other communist countries like Cuba. These models have in common the preparation of youngsters for productive work in the community through both the provision of work experience and the pursuit of chosen careers.

A fourth type of community school places an emphasis on using schools as community centers. This approach views the school as an institutional focal point from which a variety of community services can emanate. Examples include School Community Centers in England, Cultural Missions in Latin America, and Unesco's Fundamental Education Program. Running throughout these last three examples is an emphasis on either the use of the school plant for social, cultural, and recreational purposes or using the school as a base for technical experts and school personnel attempting to foster social change. Finally, there are community schools used for national development schemes, including raising national identity and consciousness among students and members of the community, encouraging the use of the school as an agency of community change and development, and preparing youngsters to occupy economically productive roles in the community and nation. Community schools for nationalism and socioeconomic development have most often been associated with a national leader who wished to decolonize education, promote indigenous culture, and generate local and national change in ways meaningful to a peasant agrarian society. Such schools were associated with Mahatma Gandhi in India, Julius Nyerere in Tanzania, and Mao Zedong in China.

While these examples indicate the existence of community-based schooling within a variety of nation states, the authors who describe them note that they should not be thought of as operating independently from central government control. Instead, such schools can be considered successful only when the wider society, through political, cultural, and social patterns, is prepared both to assign the school such responsibility and to support its efforts.

NONFORMAL EDUCATION

As the school reaches further into the community, it more closely resembles the educational patterns associated with out-of-school educational activity. The term *nonformal education* was introduced in the late 1960s to signal a need for creating out-of-school responses to new and differing demands for education.

Although there has always been some attention placed on out-of-school education and on acknowledging the importance of community resources for teaching and learning, the new term helped to legitimate this attention.

Although nonformal education may be a substitute for schooling when schools do not exist, it should not be conceptualized as yet another strategy to provide schooling to a population. Nonformal education programs are not like schools because they do not receive or deliver the same medium of exchange—credits, grades, and diplomas that are recognized and sanctioned by the society's most legitimate and formal system of teaching and learning. At the same time, however, the fact that there may be more than one type of credit and diploma used in a society as a medium of exchange does not suggest that one type of education may have greater or lesser impact on selected learnings.

While available evidence fails to distinguish clearly between formal and nonformal education in all societies, such divisions do appear typical. Even in preliterate societies, the ethnographic information available indicates that both formal and nonformal education can usually be found. Initiation rituals, for example, constitute a type of systematic educational effort in preliterate societies, such rituals being characterized by systematic organization, an identified setting, specially designated teachers, definitive timing, a fixed curriculum, and other practices not unlike our own schooling system. As to nonformal instruction in these societies, occurring outside of the initiation rituals yet apart from the family, one might include the passing on of the society's history, music, and dance as well as hero stories and folklore by older playmates and non-kin adults.

During the 1970s in much of the Third World, nonformal education became a more frequent programmatic alternative for some youth and adults who were either unserved or poorly served by schools, or who needed to supplement the schooling they already received. In these instances, nonformal education often assisted in bringing educational services to a rapidly growing population that could not be adequately addressed through schools that had to be built, equipped, and staffed through a complex economic, managerial, and political bureaucracy. Nonformal education has also demonstrated some utility for youth and adults in responding to societal problems involving health, nutrition, unemployment, food production, and so on, that tend to characterize Third World concerns.

In the more industrialized countries, nonformal education has also been of potential use in meeting educational demands. For children and youth it provides specialized artistic, academic, basic-skills and sports instruction, peer-group activity through clubs and camps, and political and religious socialization. Throughout these activities, parents and youngsters look to nonformal education programs as a means to complement or supplement schools and in some instances to provide competing points-of-view. For adults, nonformal education has often meant a means for individual and social development, health and safety instruction, and job training.

The Control of Nonformal Education

Some nation states restrict local groups in their sponsorship of nonformal education programs unless the programs serve to maintain or enhance the goals of the state. This is common in many centralized communist countries, such as the Soviet Union and Cuba, as well as in authoritarian states like Germany under Adolf Hitler or Chile under Augusto Pinochet. Since such control is so dominant, schools and nonformal education programs tend to complement one another. Even when the state does not monopolize nonformal education, however, it may be a major sponsor of such activity, thereby extending the government's influence beyond the formal school. Such a complementary effort may foster common, society-wide life-styles, political ideology, and nationalism as important values for the welfare of the society as a whole. In the United States, for example, such organizations as the Boy Scouts and Baseball Little League are national efforts operating with the explicit support and approval of the national congress.

In societies where the state is not a primary nonformal-education sponsor, it is often the community, family, religious organization, private business, or other special interest group that becomes the most important facilitator of such programs. In these cases the goals and activities of formal and nonformal education are more likely to be distinguishable because various sponsors are able to retain and preserve either unique cultural attributes or deliver prescribed skills and knowledge. Whether the orientations of formal and nonformal education are similar and complementary or dissimilar and supplementary, therefore, depends on whether public and private initiative is transformed into viable programs. Where space is available, nonformal education may extend the influence of parents rather than of the state. In much of the world, for example, parents and children have the freedom to practice the religion of their choice or to participate in competing political organizations. Such openness would not be found, however, in such countries as Chile, China, South Africa, or Romania during much of the 1980s, as the totalitarian regimes in those nations prohibited the use of any form of education for passing on competing cultural, political, or economic doctrines.

Even if sufficient freedom is available, however, other conditions must also be present for nonformal education to reach a large sector of a given population. Primarily, these conditions revolve around the values held in a society that support systematic out-of-school instruction and learning as well as the extent to which access to programs is realistic and feasible for differing population groups. For example, race, ethnicity, social class, and sex are important variables in assessing participation rates in nonformal education, especially when that participation is voluntary and may involve some costs to the consumer. Some have argued that nonformal education is often used to reinforce a consciousness of kind as particular programs of instruction are oriented to middle and upper socioeconomic levels, religious or ethnic group,s and genders. For example, only those individuals with higher incomes are typically able to afford music instruction or academic tutoring for their children. Another fact is that the primary sponsors for Boy and Girl Scouts in the United States are church groups. And with regard to gender, particular athletic groups are oriented to males or females. In each instance, the backgrounds of participants are prepared in ways which reinforce prior socialization or anticipate behaviors which are valued by a particular segment of society.

The localized and decentralized nature of much of nonformal education in those countries where it is sanctioned carries with it not only these patterns of potential discrimination along socioeconomic, ethnic, and gender lines, but it also has other drawbacks. One of these is its lack of relative legitimacy when it attempts to provide credentials and certificates which are comparable to school diplomas for access to the work force. High school and college diplomas, for instance, are often used as surrogate measures of achievement or skills assumed necessary for entry into the job market. Nonformal education offers few such symbols of preparation that have widespread recognition or acceptance beyond a local region.

While not all nonformal education programs suffer in this regard, the fact that many compete explicitly with formal schools in providing preparation for gaining access to the world of work and are perceived as less than equal in quality and curricula, means that they struggle to achieve their goals. Moreover, some have argued (Bock & Papagiannis, 1983) that because of this lack of legitimacy, nonformal education designed to prepare individuals for access to the opportunity structure does a disservice to learners. This is especially the case with entry level workers from lower socioeconomic backgrounds who pursue nonformal education and find that their future mobility is limited because of the lack of perceived value attributed by others to their educational experiences (La Belle & Verhine, 1975). This lack of legitimacy, for example, may be seen in many nonformal technical-education programs —perhaps in construction, service, or clerical occupations— which provide the requisite skills to get an individual a wage-earning job. The nature of the job, however, may offer little prospect for future income or status mobility. In effect, irrespective of an individual's knowledge or skills, the lack of school credentials may lock the person into a lower-level and dead-end position.

Nonformal Education: Process and Pedagogy

Where nonformal education does not have to compete head-on with formal schooling, it can fare somewhat better. For example, for individual entrepreneurs like farmers or small businessmen, nonformal education might deliver skills and knowledge that has direct utility to their daily activity. In this way, there is no reason for nonformal education to feed its former students into the opportunity structure in a way which favors formal schools and their awarding of diplomas. Similarly, nonformal education may have utility in some countries for facilitating social change through highly participatory or grass roots efforts at the local level.

One such example, referred to as *animation rurale* and used over the last two decades in Senegal and Niger (Moulton, 1983), is intended to create bottom-up institutions that evolve from village-level development projects into national organizations, thereby allowing the peasant population economic and political self-direction. The program is based on the assumption that local village representatives, known as *animateurs*, can be used to train fellow villagers in farming, marketing, health care, and sanitation. While a number of local community-based projects have emerged from this effort, the goals of linking local participation and the creation of local institutions with those at the national level are reported to have fared less well.

Included in this nonformal-education and social-change category are a wide variety of literacy, consciousness-raising, and community-development activities, typically dealt with from both an individual or psychological and group or sociological perspective. At the individual level, a common strategy is to develop pedagogical methods and instructional products to enhance the learner's skills and knowledge. Experiments with photographic novels, games, theater, critical discussion, and reflection on one's position in society, comic books, radio, television, and many other forms of electronic and print media have been used to achieve these basically psychological goals. A classic use of such materials occurred among rural peasants in Ecuador in the mid-1970s as an emphasis was placed on developing an awareness of the individual participant's reality, self-worth, and literacy and numeracy skills appropriate to the rural dweller's needs and interests. For numeracy and literacy skills, for example, use was made of dice and cards bearing letters or numbers, number and word bingo, and mathematical roulette. Self-expression activities were constructed around drama, puppets, rubber stamps, and community newspapers. For consciousness-raising and reality awareness, a game called *hacienda*, based on the North American game of *Monopoly*, was used to simulate a rural village setting in which issues of land ownership and relations with local authorities are confronted. Other awareness materials included photonovels or magazines (portraying villagers dealing with the strife and struggle characteristic of village life) and cassette recorders, which villagers used to record music and dialogue, with the completed tapes edited for radio broadcast (Evans, 1975). While the creative use of these materials is what makes the project so unique, their impact varied to a large extent on the way the facilitator implemented the program and the nature of the group participation (Laosa, Alkin, & White, 1975).

Beyond the basically psychological approach to change, there is the more sociologically oriented strategy that emphasizes the linkages among individuals, institutions, and the biophysical environment rather than the internal psychology or skills of the individual. Usually the attention here is directed to social structures, institutions, and social units, and the problem is to work on behalf of lower socioeconomic-status populations through coordinating, altering, or radically transforming these phenomena. Group-oriented strategies often combine instructional products for information transmission, consciousness raising, or skill training with some form of community organization.

The most radical of these types of programs seek to create revolutionary political and economic change, often through guerrilla movements. Found throughout the world, this kind of conflict-oriented action usually accompanies a preparation program involving a particular ideological doctrine, literacy and basic skills, and military preparation, all of which are carried out through nonformal programs. The timing of these movements usually accompanies a perception that there exits little or no opportunity through existing institutions for achieving social justice and equality. Further, this kind of perception finds fault with, among others, inegalitarian opportunity structures, the disappearance of local and popular cultures, political corruption and illegitimacy, repression, government terrorism against members of the opposition, and a lack of opportunity to participate in decision-making within authoritarian regimes. Usually the programs involve preparation of a leadership or vanguard group, expansion of this group by recruiting and preparing large numbers of urban workers and peasants, and some form of violent conflict with those in power.

As Castro came to power in Cuba in the late 1950s, for example, he established a vanguard group in the rural area and began recruiting and training the peasantry. Nonformal education was used in military training to foster ideological commitments to the movement. And through the use of the mass media, nonformal methods were used to keep the urban population apprised of the activities and status of the transformation. In the Nicaraguan guerrilla campaign in the 1970s, the Sandinista revolutionaries established a clandestine radio network as a means of popular mobilization, and in El Salvador in the 1980s the opposition used television sets broadcasting guerrilla-produced video tapes of past successful military actions as a means to recruit individuals to support the revolution (La Belle, 1986).

While many people aspire to use nonformal education to achieve greater equality and access for the poor and disenfranchised, the outcomes of such efforts are typically less dependent on the methods and strategies adopted and more on the history and experiences of a community, nation, and region, on the problems and issues to be resolved, and on the kind of future that individuals wish to create. Further, while it may be popular to champion the cause of the poor to increasingly determine their own destiny, more powerful economic and political interests are likely to shape if not determine the outcomes of such programs. This argument suggests that in the absence of involving some action among dominant groups on behalf of the poor, relatively little of substance will likely occur. Therefore, it may very well be that providing skills and information to the poor through nonformal education so that individuals might act in their own interests politically and economically is necessary for change to occur, but they may just as easily result in conflict and frustration.

For instance, no matter what people's economic desires may be or how hard they work, unless they have access to land, credit, transportation, or some other means of translating that work into productive outcomes, they will potentially remain subject to the demands of more powerful economic interests. In the political arena, a specific example of conflict and frustration is found in what appeared early-on to be successful grass-roots collective political action in mainland China during 1989, but which ended in the use of military force to put down the challenge to those in power. A contrasting example with more positive outcomes was seen in Eastern Europe in 1989 and 1990 as the combination of power and leadership from the top, with organization and movement among the population at the community level, promised greater freedom in the future.

PROSPECTS FOR DELIVERY SYSTEMS

We have argued that it is worthwhile to view education as a broad-based concept which touches all aspects of life and involves all of our institutions and media. Broken into informal, formal, and nonformal modes, education as a concept reflects a sometimes planned and reinforcing, but oftentimes parallel and conflictual, set of interactions across time and space. Purposely orchestrating and integrating these educational modes is not only difficult, if not impossible under certain circumstances, but it is also likely to change the nature of each mode. Thus, as one makes efforts to have educational interventions reinforce and complement one another, there is a tendency to centralize, shape, and standardize informal and nonformal approaches such that the spontaneity of informal teaching and learning may be lost and the adaptability and flexibility of nonformal education may give way to the batch-processing and standardization associated with schools. The trade-off, however, may be to get schooling to attend more to what goes on outside of classrooms, to build formal education more on the experiences of learners in everyday life, and to transfer what goes on in schools to individual and societal problem-solving.

There is also benefit in envisioning these educational modes as being controlled by different interests in the society, each balancing the other as particular periods of time and issues emerge. Thus, the family, while it cannot control all of the informal educational influences in society, nevertheless invests heavily in the early years to lay a foundation of values and behaviors. As schooling emerges as the vehicle of the dominant group and the nation state, other interests, such as the church or a political party, have an opportunity to organize and articulate their goals through nonformal means. Thus, if a society provides freedom for the manifestation of all of the educational modes, there is the potential for an open market-place of ideas and a varied set of opportunities for teaching and learning.

Where possible, however, there seems to be a natural movement toward integration of the three educational modes. And whatever form learning takes, many are realizing that informal and nonformal education are powerful contributors to human growth and development and cannot be left unrecognized in favor of schools. The consensus among educators today appears to be that educational strategies must be comprehensive, be creative, and, where there is some consensus about the nature of society and participation in it, be complementary. In the absence of reinforcing what goes on in families and out-of-school programs through school curricula, while making simultaneous efforts to adjust the nature of all three, there is a real potential for having learners succeed on the street corner but fail in school and as productive citizens. In the United States this has become apparent because of the increasing numbers of youngsters who leave school early and are at risk for a variety of health, psychological, and sociological problems. Many believe that such characteristics are associated with changing family structures and a general lack of involvement and support in communities for the goals of schools. In Third World countries, a lack of funding to build schooling on the industrial model remains a driving force to link up resources, wherever they may be found, for educational purposes.

Thus, in those places where the educational modes come closer together, we may see a systematic effort to define what each mode can do best. For example, schools might well concentrate on the academic aspects of education, leaving to informal and nonformal modes such areas as vocational preparation and the passing on of ethnic, religious, and community values. This narrowing of focus in formal schooling might well be accompanied by new competition among schools to attract a populace that can exercise greater choice among institutions they might attend. Likewise, should a narrowing occur in role and function among modes, considerable complementarity might be found between families and nonformal-education agencies, especially when the agencies are separated from the central control of the state.

We also see in the future an obvious increase in the importance of technology across all modes of education, whether driven by quality, fiscal, or efficiency considerations. Over all, however, education will remain a labor-intensive process reliant on highly qualified professionals, and each locale and political unit will have to determine the best mix of delivery systems to employ.

REFERENCES

Anzalone, S. (1988) *Educational hardware for primary education in developing countries: A review of the literature. BRIDGES Education Development Discussion Paper.* McLean, Va: IIR.

Bock, J. C., & Papagiannis, G. J. (Eds.), (1983) *Nonformal education and national development.* New York: Praeger.

Cohen, R. A. (1969) Conceptual styles, culture conflict, and nonverbal tests of intelligence. *American Anthropologist*, 71: 828-856.

Coombs, P. H., & Ahmed, M. (1974) *Attacking rural poverty: How nonformal education can help.* Baltimore: Johns Hopkins University Press.

English, P. C. (1988) Back-to-school with distance learning. *Community, Technical, and Junior College Journal*, 259 (1): 36-39.

Evans, D. R. (1975) An approach to nonschool rural education in Ecuador. In T. J. La Belle (Ed.), *Educational alternatives in Latin America: Social change and social stratification* (pp. 169-184). Los Angeles: UCLA Latin American Center.

Gonzalez, J. (1980) A history of the radio mathematics project. In J. Friend, B. Searle, & P. Suppes (Eds.), *Radio mathematics in Nicaragua* (pp. 3-38). Stanford, CA: Stanford University Press.

Henry, J. (1960) A cross cultural outline of education. *Current Anthropology*, 1 (4): 267-305.

La Belle, T. J. (1981) An introduction to the nonformal education of children and youth: Presidential address. *Comparative Education Review*, 25 (3): 313-329.

La Belle, T. J. (1982) Formal, nonformal and informal Education: A holistic approach to lifelong learning. *International Review of Education*, 28: 159-175.

La Belle, T. J. (1986) *Nonformal education in Latin America and the Caribbean: Stability, reform, or revolution?* New York: Praeger.

La Belle, T. J., & Verhine, R. E. (1981) School-community interaction: A comparative and international perspective. In D.Davies (Ed.), *Communities and their schools* (pp. 211-268). New York: McGraw-Hill.

La Belle, T. J., & Verhine, R. E. (1975) Nonformal education and occupational stratification: Implications for Latin America. *Harvard Educational Review*, 45 (2): 160-190.

La Belle, T. J., & White, P. S. (1980) Education and multiethnic integration: An intergroup relations typology. *Comparative Education Review*, 24 (2, Part 1): 155-173.

Laosa, L. M., Alkin M. C., & White, P. (1975) *An evaluation of nonformal education in Ecuador. Final Report AID/TA-C-1124* (4 Vols.). Los Angeles: Center for the Study of Evaluation, UCLA Graduate School of Education.

Layne, A. (1985) Education and intergroup relations in Haiti. In J. N. Hawkins & T. J. La Belle (Eds.), *Education and intergroup relations: An international perspective* (pp. 87-105). New York: Praeger.

Melmed, A. S., Ellenbogen, B., Jamison, D. T., & Turniansky, U. (1982) Everyman University in Israel: the first two years. In H. Perraton (Ed.), *Alternative routes to formal education* (pp. 215-249). Baltimore: Johns Hopkins University Press.

Moulton, J. (1983) Development through training: Animation rurale. In J. C. Bock & G. J. Papagiannis (Eds.), *Nonformal education and national development* (pp. 25-91). New York: Praeger.

Nakamoto, J. M., White, P. S., & La Belle, T. J. (1985) Education and white-mestizo/Indian relations in Peru. In J. N. Hawkins & T. J. La Belle (Eds.), *Education and intergroup relations: An international perspective* (pp. 60-89). New York: Praeger.

Resnick, L. B. (1987) Learning in school and out: The 1987 presidential address. *Educational Research*, 16 (9): 13-19.

Spaulding, S. (November, 1986). *Technology, Education, Information and the Development Tasks Ahead.* Paper presented at the symposium on "Applications of Electronic Publishing in International Development: Cross Cultural Implications of Electronic Information Exchange" sponsored by New York University Institute for Intercultural Training and the Society for International Development, New York.

Unesco (1985) Distance education in Asia and the Pacific. *Bulletin of the Unesco Regional Office for Education in Asia and the Pacific*, (No. 16). Bangkok: Unesco.

Urch, G. (1985) Kenya: The emergence of an educated elite. In J. N. Hawkins & T. J. La Belle (Eds.), *Education and intergroup relations: An international perspective* (pp. 221-244). New York: Praeger.

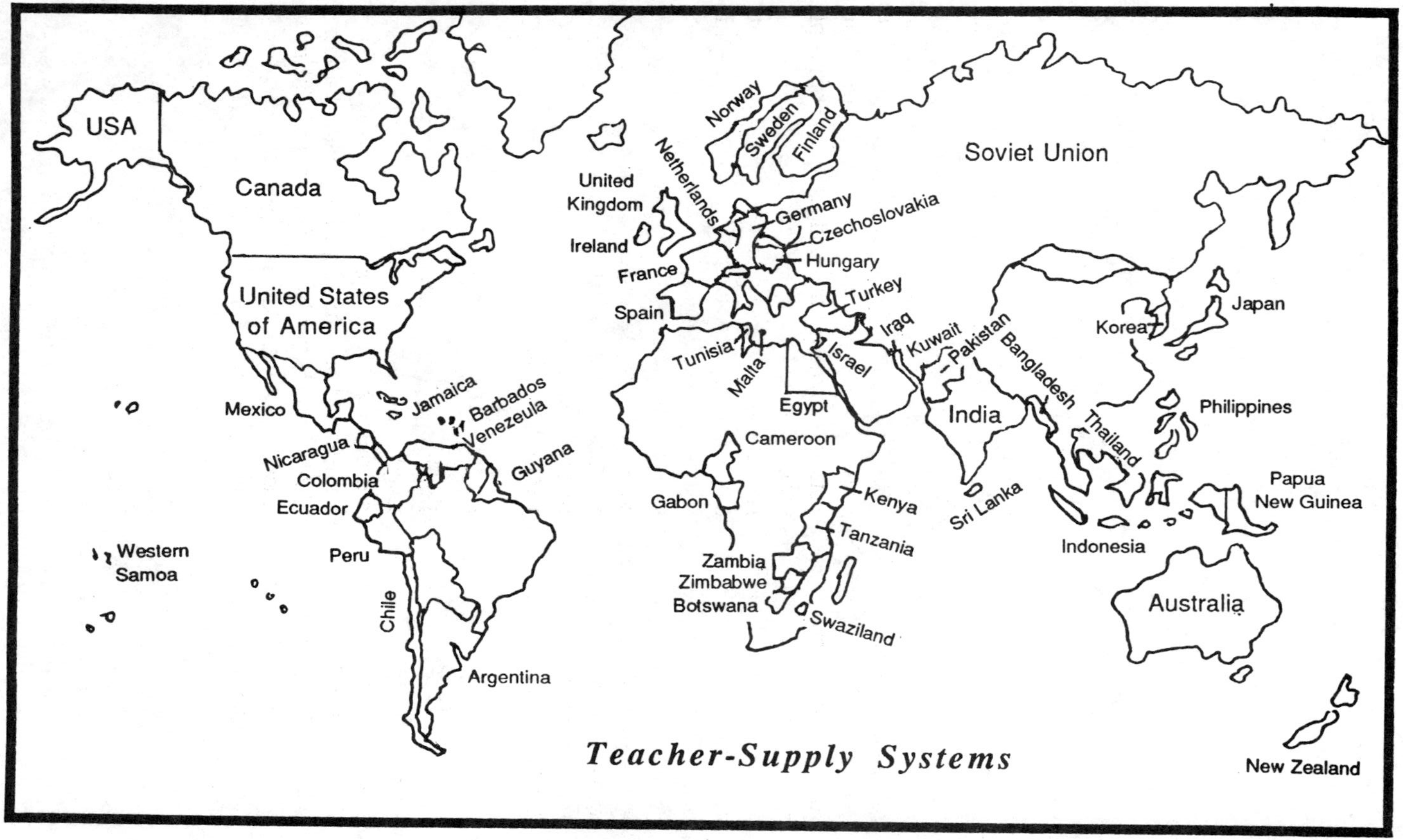

Teacher-Supply Systems

CHAPTER 7

Teacher-Supply Systems

How do school systems provide effective teachers?

R. MURRAY THOMAS

Descriptions of how nations furnish the schools with instructional personnel often focus exclusively on the preservice training of teachers. However, picturing a personnel-supply system in such a restricted manner can lead to a serious misunderstanding of the complex conditions involved in adequately staffing educational programs. One way to remedy this narrow perception is to conceive of the teacher-supply system as comprised of seven stages, extending from the initial recruitment of potential trainees to the final retirement of people from the profession. This chapter is organized according to such a scheme.

The stages are those of: (1) recruiting candidates, (2) admitting applicants to preservice education, (3) providing preservice education, (4) placing graduates in jobs, (5) providing suitable working conditions, (6) furnishing inservice education, and (7) retiring personnel from the education system. In the inspection of each stage, I identify ideal goals for the stage, note issues commonly encountered, and illustrate how education systems have sought to resolve such issues. Throughout the discussion, ways that societies have dealt with each stage are illustrated with examples from around the world.

DEFINING THE IDEAL TEACHER

Underlying any plan for providing instructional personnel is a conception of the traits that comprise the ideal teacher. Because each stage of the supply system is intended to contribute toward this ideal, it is appropriate at the outset to identify what those characteristics should be. As a starting point, consider a typical definition of the ideal teacher, one devised by the Indonesian Ministry of Education as a guide for that nation's teacher-education programs. According to the Indonesian proposal, a well-prepared teacher has a secure command of (1) the subject matter to be taught, (2) the teaching-learning process, (3) classroom management techniques, (4) the use of instructional resources and media, (5) educational foundations (psychological, philosophical, sociological, historical), (6) ways of directing teaching-learning interactions in the classroom, (7) how to assess students' progress, (8) the roles of guidance and counseling, (9) functions of school administration, and (10) the implications that educational research holds for improving instruction (Soedijarto, 1989: 88). Three further attributes that usually appear in such general descriptions are those of (11) a suitable personality, (12) good character, and (13) strong motivation to perform well.

Although such a definition of attributes serves as a useful starting point for designing a teacher-supply program, it fails to recognize that the detailed nature of the attributes can vary from one type of instructional assignment to another. For example, the specific traits desired in a teacher of preschool children are not identical to those desired in a university professor of physics or foreign languages. The skills required of a teacher of mentally-retarded children are not entirely the same as those needed by a secondary-school football coach. Thus, in addition to a statement of general attributes desired in effective teachers, the formulators of a teacher-supply system need to supplement their general definition with more detailed descriptions of characteristics needed by the various types of teachers that staff education programs.

Not only can different teaching positions call for diverse specific traits, but as education systems evolve, new responsibilities may be assigned to the schools, thereby requiring additional teacher skills. For example, under Finland's School Act of 1985, a teacher was expected not only to promote children's command of traditional subject matter but also to foster pupils' general personality development so that the young would become "mentally balanced, physically fit, responsible, autonomous, creative, peace-loving, cooperative citizens and human beings" (Niemi, 1987: 310). At the same time that these expectations were set forth, curriculum planning was decentralized in Finland. Thus, decisions about the detailed curriculum were removed from the nation's central Department of General Education and assigned to local authorities, with teachers expected to play an active role in deciding what would be taught. In effect, the 1985 School Act generated new problems of:

> preparing teachers to face all the challenges created by the school reforms and by the changes which society continuously requires. [Teachers] still have to be prepared to teach lessons, but they now are also assumed to be planners, decision-makers, flexible co-workers, and active participators outside the traditional classroom as well. Beyond this, they need to have adequate personalities to encourage pupils of different kinds (Niemi, 1987: 311).

In summary, then, a society's conception of which characteristics of children the schools should foster will help determine the traits needed by an efficient teacher. These traits, then, can be regarded as the principal outcomes to result from a teacher-supply system. Our seven stages of the teacher-supply process are intended to ensure that such attributes are acquired and maintained throughout a teacher's career.

At each stage in the following analysis I propose one or more standards which that phase should provide if the system is to produce the most effective instructional personnel. In other words, the standards are goals that a given stage is designed to achieve. A supply process would be operating at maximum efficiency if all of the standards were met. However, it is obvious that no system operates at its top potential, because each one suffers problems which result from conditions that impede progress toward the standards. The nature of such problems and of techniques educators adopt to solve them are noted throughout the discussion.

STAGE 1: RECRUITING CANDIDATES TO PREPARE AS TEACHERS

The first step toward providing an excellent corps of teachers is that of attracting from the general population the largest possible number of people who have the talents, interests, and opportunities to make them first-rate educators. Two standards are proposed for implementing this step.

The Pool of Candidates

1.1 *The Large-Pool-of-Candidates Standard.* "Far more candidates apply for admission to preservice teacher-education programs than can be accepted."

Underlying this standard is the assumption that the larger the source of candidates, the better the chance that programs can select those applicants who give high promise of becoming effective teachers. The smaller the pool, the more likely the programs must accept students who will not become high-quality teachers. The size of the pool is governed by factors that influence standard 1.2.

Vocational Information

1.2 *The Vocational-Information Standard.* "All potentially suitable candidates know (A) the nature of teacher training and of teaching as an occupation, including the profession's advantages and disadvantages, and (B) how and where to apply for appropriate preservice education."

According to standard 1.2, whether potential candidates seek to enter teacher training depends to a great extent on how attractive they perceive teaching as a life's work and on how well they understand procedures for entering a training program.

Among the variables that affect individuals' interest in teaching are the occupation's (1) prestige, (2) monetary or material rewards, (3) non-material rewards, and (4) working conditions.

The prestige of an occupation can be viewed as the overall level of regard or respect generally held in a society for people in that occupation. Such regard depends on a variety of characteristics of the vocation, including the skills required (such as mental versus physical), amount of training needed, degree of control over other people, size of material income, type of service to society, and more. Studies of occupational prestige in a variety of countries —representing both industrialized and traditional agricultural societies— have shown that there is great similarity among peoples in the level of prestige they impute to occupations common to their societies (Thomas, 1962). Medical doctors, high government officials, university professors, and scientists are universally ranked near the top. Technicians, skilled craft workers, and people operating small businesses are around the middle of the prestige scale, and manual laborers who have little or no training are near the bottom. While all members of a society do not agree precisely about where a given occupation belongs on the scale, there is still a general consensus about the level of regard in which different occupations are held. Likewise, it is recognized that a person's identity (who he or she is judged to be and how much respect he or she deserves) is partially a function of that person's occupation. As a result, the society's rating of the prestige of being a teacher can affect the level of an individual's interest in seeking to enter the profession.

Two surveys of occupational prestige from the Indonesian island of Java illustrate the relative placement of teachers on occupational-prestige hierarchies. One survey consisted of asking 939 high-school students in a city of over one million residents to rank 30 occupations in terms of their prestige. Of the three types of teachers in the list, *college professor* was ranked second from the top (surpassed only by physician), *high-school teacher* was thirteenth, and *elementary-school teacher* was twenty-first (Thomas & Soeparman, 1963). In the second survey, 96 respondents in three widely separated villages agreed almost entirely with each other on the ranking of 59 occupations. The top five occupations, in descending rank, were: physician, college professor, judge, civil engineer, and attorney. School principal was number 12 and elementary-school teacher was 22. The five lowest-ranking occupations were barber, blacksmith, tenant farmer, shoe repairman, and pedicab driver (Thomas, 1975: 82-83). It is worth noting that the elementary-school teacher was placed relatively higher by the villagers (rank 22 out of 59) than by the city high-school students (rank 21 out of 30). In the villages, where the overall education level of the respondents would be lower than among the families of the city high-school students, the position of elementary-school teacher was seen as more desirable than in the urban center. Occupational prestige, in effect, is partially affected by the variety of occupations in the local social setting.

In terms of status, the relationships of the several types of educational positions in the Indonesian studies are similar to the relationships in other societies. That is, the higher the grade-level of a teacher's assignment, the greater the prestige of the position. For example, a study in Zimbabwe of secondary-school students' vocational ambitions showed that 45% did not want to enter teaching. Of the remaining 55%, nearly 40% wanted to become secondary-school instructors and only 15% wished to teach in primary schools

(Chivore, 1986: 252).

As noted above, the general prestige of an occupation represents a composite of diverse factors. At least three of these factors can be of particular importance in affecting a person's decision about whether to enter teaching. First is the amount of material income the job will provide. The more adequate the income, compared to other vocations a person could follow, the larger the number of candidates who will seek to enter teaching.

A second factor is the set of non-material rewards the occupation can yield. A person who is a social idealist —whose reward comes from giving service to society and affecting others' lives in a positive way— can find teaching a highly appealing way of life, even when the monetary rewards are limited. Frequently a student whose life has been enriched by one or more teachers will, out of admiration and gratitude, choose also to become a teacher in order to enrich the lives of others in a similar manner.

A third factor, closely linked to the second, is the style of life that teaching represents. Some youths are eternally curious. They enjoy the pursuit of knowledge and of new skills. They like to manipulate ideas and search out the meaning of the universe and of life. Thus, at the end of adolescence, as they face the task of choosing a career, they view teaching as a vocation that permits them to continue a way of life that has brought them pleasure as students. And in judging whether they would like the life-style of various vocations, youths are in a better position to judge teaching than they are to judge most occupations, since they have spent years closely observing teachers at work.

Throughout the world, a universal complaint has been that the most capable secondary-school graduates tend not to enter teacher training. One reason has been the relatively low level of income the occupation yields. Another has been the lack of intellectual challenge offered by the subject-matter of the primary and lower-secondary grades. A third has been the difficulty that teachers may encounter in coping with student disobedience.

The case of Turkey illustrates an historical pattern which has shown a decline in the ability of a nation to attract its most promising youths into the teaching profession. Murray (1988) reports that during the regime of Ataturk (1923-1938), who was the founder of modern Turkey, teachers were viewed as prime agents for reforming society.

> As a result, during Ataturk's period the best, high-achieving students were sent to teacher-training colleges, where they were given scholarships and other incentives. Turkish teachers experienced their golden age during this period, not only financially but also morally. However, after the death of Ataturk, teachers gradually lost their privileged status. Political events between 1960 and 1980 resulted in limits being placed on educational influence in order to reduce competition in political matters. The teaching profession became a less attractive occupation for college students. Today

> teachers in Turkey face many problems, such as low salary, low status, heavy demands made upon time, over-work, less than sophisticated physical facilities, lack of opportunity to improve professional knowledge and effective performance, and finally, no job security (Murray, 1988: 6).

Murray's study of applicants to four-year and two-year teacher-education programs in 1982 and 1986 revealed that most students who entered teacher training had low grade-point averages from high school and that over the four-year period the quality of such applicants had declined. In 1982, 33% of the entrants were in the upper-grade-point range of 61-80, but in 1986 only 13% were in this upper range, while the 56% in the lower grade-point category of 41-60 in 1982 had increased to 81% by 1986. Likewise, among students who took the nation-wide college-entrance test, in 1986 a lower percentage ranked teacher-training as a desirable major field of study than had been the case in 1982; and the two-year teacher-preparation program was considered far less desirable than the four-year program (Murray, 1988: 9-10).

Officials in education systems may adopt several techniques for enhancing the prestige of teaching and thereby attracting a larger pool of candidates for training. The incentives include scholarships and financial grants for those enrolling in teacher-preparation courses, guaranteed employment upon completing training, brochures and films illustrating the interesting life of students who are in teacher-education settings, the preparation of newspaper articles or radio and television programs featuring teachers engaged in admirable activities, and widely publicized awards for superior teaching performance.

The pool of teacher-training applicants is also expanded when officials provide means of informing a wide range of youths and adults about how and where to apply for admission to a preservice program. The methods can include notices sent to secondary-school guidance counselors, newspaper articles, representatives of teacher-education institutions visiting secondary schools with slide shows or videotape presentations focusing on teacher preparation, and radio or television programs describing teacher-training opportunities.

STAGE 2: ADMITTING CANDIDATES TO PRESERVICE TEACHER EDUCATION

The process for determining the entrance requirements for preservice teacher training can be guided by two questions:

(1) What are the characteristics needed by teachers to perform adequately in their first teaching job? This question identifies the competencies teachers are to have upon graduating from the training program.

(2) Which of the specified characteristics can be produced within the preservice education program? This question identifies the curriculum focus.

When both questions have been answered, it will be apparent that only a portion of the characteristics from question one will be cared for in the answer to question two. In other words, the two, four, or five years of a typical preservice-training system can hope to provide only a part of the competencies needed by a beginning teacher. The remaining competencies are ones that applicants should already possess when they enter the program. Those competencies become entrance requirements. For example, fluency in speaking, reading, and writing the school's language-of-instruction is needed for teaching adequately. Most preservice programs are not designed to produce such fluency. The best that the program can be expected to do is to refine the basic language skills that students bring to their preservice experience. Therefore, a given level of language competence must become a requirement for entering the program. Likewise, conditions of good health, of aptitude for learning (general intelligence), of general knowledge about the social and scientific world, of computational competence, of values ("good character"), and of customs may also be expected of applicants, since such competencies are not to be part of the preservice curriculum.

Evaluating Applicants

2.1 *The Candidate-Evaluation Standard.* "The program uses evaluation procedures that yield accurate assessments of the entry characteristics that candidates are expected to bring to the teacher-preparation program."

Teacher-training programs vary in the methods they use for estimating the entrance competencies of applicants. In most nations, applicants to programs preparing primary-school teachers must have completed secondary school and then submit to an interview with a selection committee. Wherever teacher training is at the post-graduate university level, applicants may be required to have finished their undergraduate study at a specified level of successsubmit letters attesting to their good character. In Finland, candidates for both primary- and secondary-dvhool teacher preparation are required to pass a scholastic aptitude test and are interviewed to determine whether they appear highly motivated to be teachers and are fond of children and adolescents (Niemi, 1987: 311).

STAGE 3: PROVIDING PRESERVICE TEACHER EDUCATION

The five standards at Stage 3 are designed to foster the efficient preparation of teacher-education candidates to perform in their initial teaching posts at an acceptable level of effectiveness.

Teacher-Education Objectives

3.1 *The Appropriate-Objectives Standard.* "The instructional objectives of the preservice program are comprised of studies deemed most valuable in equipping teachers for their instructional roles."

The pattern of studies intended to meet this standard will vary somewhat from one teacher-education system to another. However, one typical pattern is that recommended at the 15th session of the Standing Conference of European Ministers of Education in Helsinki in 1987. The ministers, representing a broad array of European nations, proposed that:

> —Initial training (at least three years and at university level) should be based on broad and sound general education. It should give teachers the intellectual basis needed to meet new challenges in their future work in schools and to select what is essential knowledge from the mass of available information.
>
> —Emphasis should be placed in initial training on:
>
> (1) giving student teachers the personal and social skills (for communication, adaptability, creativity, self-confidence, and empathy) needed for classroom management, team work, and relating to parents;
>
> (2) teaching practice and knowledge of the school system and how it works;
>
> (3) mastery of subject disciplines and understanding of how subject knowledge can be selected, organized, and transmitted, i.e. the didactic preparation of the material to be taught;
>
> (4) philosophical reflection about values and their transmission to young people in pluralist European societies.
>
> —Teaching practice should form an integral part of initial training and aim to ensure a smooth transition from training to the job so as to avoid the widely reported problem of discouragement and inability to cope on first encounter with classroom reality. Beginning teachers should be given strong support and guidance.
>
> —Initial training should provide a minimum degree of familiarity with relevant educational research findings and methods and with such subjects as guidance and counseling, education for intercultural understanding, new technologies, special education, human rights and democratic citizenship, European and global awareness, and health and safety education (Council for Cultural Cooperation, 1989: 6)

The foregoing description represents rather well the main features of a great number of the world's teacher-education systems. However, it is also the case that there is considerable variation from one teacher-training system to another in their specific goals, length of study, course offerings, and methods of instruction. The diversity among preservice programs can be suggested by illustrative cases from Hungary, India, France, and Great Britain.

Hungary

In Hungary, teachers are trained either in universities or in teachers colleges. When prospective teachers enter the university, they take courses in two subject-matter fields as well as courses in education. The pair of subject-matter fields can form such combinations as physics and mathematics, Hungarian language and English, or the like. The students' education courses begin the first and second years with classes in educational foundations (general psychology, educational psychology, theory of education) and they progress over the five-year program into increasingly practical studies, including observations in schools, both inside classrooms and in such extracurricular settings as youth organizations and hobby clubs. The fourth year involves learning instructional methods in the two subject-matter specialties that each student has studied over the years. To provide intensive direct teaching experience, the fifth year places the candidate in a school as a full-time intern under university supervision (Cropley & Dave, 1978: 73).

India

Developing nations whose high rates of poverty and illiteracy are accompanied by serious shortages of educational personnel often adopt nontraditional modes of teacher education in order to staff classrooms. A case in point is a method of training teachers to instruct out-of-school primary-level pupils in India's Maharashtra state. The government of India has committed itself to providing universal primary education among its population of 850 million. However, over half of the nation's primary-aged children are not in school, with girls representing the bulk of those not attending. In the early 1980s, a survey showed that 95 percent of the population had been provided full-time primary education facilities within walking distance of 6- to 11-year-old children.

> At the beginning of each school year (around June/July) enorolment drives are organized. Many names are entered on the rolls. In a few months, from about 100 children enrolled in Grade 1, nearly 55 drop out. The position is better in urban areas but much worse in rural areas, where 80 percent of India's population lives, and where only about 15 percent of pupils reach Grade 4 (Naik, 1983: 61-62).

It was apparent to government officials that poverty was the chief reason for the poor holding power of the full-time school, since children in school all day could not contribute to the economic support of the family. Therefore, most of India's states started evening or late-afternoon part-time classes for the 9-to-14 age group. By the mid-1980s in Maharashtra state there were 51,045 full-time schools and 1,162 part-time classes. To solve the problem of providing part-time teachers, education authorities and village leaders created a pilot project which involved selecting adults for 90 of the classes and paying them 50 rupees per month. Forty-six of the teachers were farmers, 10 were laborers, and the rest artisans or unemployed. Of the 24 women in the group, all but two were housewives. Among the 90, most had studied beyond grade 7, whereas 27 were below this level. Only two of the 90 had annual household incomes of more than 5,000 rupees. The others, mainly from the 'backward' castes, had considerably less, so that the extra 600 rupees a year for teaching was an attractive incentive.

The teacher-training program was a combination of preservice and inservice. For one week within every six-week period, the trainees walked to a central village to attend classes from 11 a.m to 5:30 p.m., then returned each evening to their respective villages to teach under the supervision of one or two members of the project staff. Training was aimed at improving teachers' subject-matter knowledge, skills in organizing nonformal primary classes, and methods of instruction.

> Training is conducted through group work in which the trainers and trainees discuss problems and prepare materials. Emphasis is laid on building up the trainees' self-confidence and self-esteem. They are sensitized towards their new roles as stimulators of community education and development. They are helped to prepare improvised materials, write out their work plans, and prepare reports from a research angle.... A circulating library is organized for the teachers in each project area. It contains fiction, informative books, a science journal in the local language (Marathi), and one popular children's magazine (Naik, 1983: 65).

France

In France, an innovative approach to teacher education was created at the Institut de Formation Pédagogique et Psychosociologique in Paris. Central to the Institut's plan was the conviction that teachers should be prepared to adapt themselves over their life span to changes in society and in their own educational roles. More precisely, initial teacher education should equip participants to:

> (a) develop a harmonious personality (positive self-image, psychological stability), basic competencies (skill in observing, reading, expressing oneself), cognitive abilities (research analysis, synthesis, critical judgment, evaluation, self-evaluation), socio-affective abilities (communication, listening, comprehension, understanding); (b) adapt to real life (flexibility, adaptability); (c) assume functions and responsibilities in a creative and critical spirit, (d) work harmoniously in teams in all environments; and (e) participate not only in the local, but also in the national and international community (bilingualism, etc.) (Cohen, *et al.*, 1984: 29).

The program designed to accomplish these ends was founded on the belief that the teacher's task is "not so much to inculcate knowledge, but rather to create conditions that will enable pupils to develop all the capacities" for learning and for personal growth (Cohen, *et al.*, 1984: 31). To put this philosophy into practice, the Institut not only provided classes in traditional subject matter but paralleled such studies with group work, self-directed investigations, and self-evaluation activities intended to enhance the future teacher's personality and potentials. In other words, developing the creativity and personal-social skills of teacher-education candidates was accorded as much attention as were subject-matter knowledge and pedagogy. From their earliest days in the program, students' time was distributed between (a) observing and participating in schools and youth clubs at all levels and (b) studying at the Institut in work groups, seminars, and resource centers. The program also emphasized education's international dimension, with considerable attention given to bilingual education. In the latter phases of their study, students pursued student-teaching both in France and abroad. Those going abroad taught in such places as the United States, Great Britain, Canada, Ireland, Mexico, Switzerland, and Spain while living with local families.

Great Britain

Our fourth illustration is not an example of a specific teacher-education program. Rather, it is a set of observations by a pair of British educators who studied programs for educating teachers to work with gifted students. Cropley and McLeod (1986: 132) concluded that professional training for such teachers needed to consist of successive stages ranging from undergraduate to post-graduate preparation because:

> —Curricula in teachers' colleges and university education departments are crowded to the extent that they can, at most, provide only a single course on the special needs of all exceptional children, together with one, possibly two, additional senior undergraduate electives.
>
> —Teachers of the academically exceptional should ... have demonstrated ability to teach in a regular programme, which means that in-depth specialized preparation has to be delayed until a few years after preservice preparation.
>
> —A significant trend has developed whereby degree programmes in education of the gifted are increasingly offered at the postgraduate rather than at the undergraduate level, which means that they are not available to all teachers.

Although the foregoing examples fail to represent all the forms that pre-service training can assume, they do illustrate something of the diversity among programs.

Suitable Instructional Methods

3.2 *The Appropriate-Methods Standard.* "The instructional methods used in the teacher-education program are ones that efficiently: (A) carry students toward mastery of the objectives of the subject-matter fields in which they specialize and (B) not only teach instructional principles (theory), but also require students to demonstrate their skill (application) in applying the principles."

One of the serious problems that teacher-preparation programs in all nations have faced is that of successfully effecting students' transition from (a) knowing pedagogical theory and subject-matter information to (b) applying such knowledge in classroom teaching. Three popular ways of thus implementing student progress from theory to practice have been those of (1) microteaching, (2) practice teaching, and (3) participation in community activities.

Microteaching

The microteaching procedure consists of a novice teacher conducting a short segment of a lesson with a small group, such as four or five learners rather than an entire class. The novice's performance is recorded on videotape so that he or she, along with a teacher-education supervisor, can later view the segment and analyze the strengths and weaknesses of the presentation. Typically the aim of microteaching is to improve the trainee's skill in posing questions for a class, responding to pupils' answers, clarifying issues, encouraging pupils to offer more than one-word answers, and promoting pupils' self-assessment and self-directed learning.

The principal advantages of microteaching have been identified as those of placing students in a real teaching situation, yet one in which the complexities of a regular classroom are reduced (small number of learners, short lesson, short preparation time required). The technique focuses on the accomplishment of specific tasks, such as the practice of instructional skills, mastery of certain curriculum materials, and the demonstration of teaching methods. Furthermore, the feedback of information to the student teacher is immediate and graphic and provides for direct discussion of the performance with colleagues and supervisors.

The microteaching approach was created at Stanford University in the United States in the early 1960s. A survey of student-teaching practices in the U.S. near the close of that decade revealed that over 50% of all teacher-education programs in the country were using microteaching in some degree (Allen & Ryan, 1969: viii). By the close of the 1980s, microteaching was being applied around the world wherever video-recording facilities were available.

Practice Teaching

The activity referred to as *practice teaching* or *student teaching* consists of a teacher-education student giving instruction to a regular classroom of pupils. The amount of such direct teaching experience can vary from one or two lessons to an entire year of full-time or half-time service in a school. In effect, there are dramatic differences in the amount of actual teaching experience that candidates receive in teacher-education programs. However, the general trend has been toward increasing the amount of time students engage in practice teaching.

In the typical program, students spend several weeks in a classroom, guided by tutors in the training institutions and by cooperating teachers. The guidance mostly consists of discussion prior to teaching, occasional observation by tutor or cooperating teacher of the student teaching, and a post-teaching discussion when the tutor or cooperating teacher comments on the student's performance. Much of the student's time on extended practice goes on without this guidance, and in many schools students are used as surrogate teachers who, after a brief induction into the school, operate independently and teach without the direct supervision of the cooperating teacher. The guidance that is given is rarely related to any body of pedagogical principles and mostly consists of practical advice from a corpus of craft know-how developed over time by teachers (Stones, 1985: 4862).

Participation in Community Groups

With increasing frequency, teacher-education programs have engaged students in community activities as a mode of direct teaching experience. Such a plan was illustrated in our earlier example of the French Institut de Formation Pédagogique et Psychosociologique, where teacher-training candidates were assigned to work in youth clubs in addition to their practice teaching in classrooms. This trend toward more community and extracurricular participation has been stimulated by educators' interest in (1) affording teacher-training students experience with diverse types of learners in diverse settings, (2) contributing to community development through nonformal-education programs, and (3) providing leadership for youth organizations that offer constructive activities for the less privileged members of the community.

An international survey of out-of-school activities showed that the greatest amount of participation involved literacy programs, particularly in such developing nations as Argentina, Bangladesh, Chile, Ecuador, Egypt, Kuwait, Nicaragua, Pakistan, Tanzania, Thailand, and Venezuela. General community-development projects (health practices, family planning, farming methods, recreation, marketing) were the object of out-of-school assignments in Barbados, Guyana, Indonesia, New Zealand, Scotland, and Sri Lanka (ILO/Unesco, 1983: 52-53).

Student-Support Incentives

3.3 *The Student-Support Standard.* "The likelihood that students will continue in preservice training and will master the program's objectives is enhanced by provisions that enable them to devote their full time and energies to their studies."

Nations, as well as institutions within a country, vary in the type and amount of support offered students in teacher-preparation programs. The nature of such support is indicated by the following examples (ILO/Unesco, 1983: 9-10). Financial allowances, adjusted to the income levels of teacher-training candidates, are available in Australia, Colombia, West Germany, Hungary, Italy, and the Netherlands. Free board and room, along with monetary stipends, have been furnished in Bangladesh, France, East Germany, Guyana, and Jordan. Tunisia, in addition to free living accommodations, offers free tuition and medical care. Students receive salaries in Barbados, Malta, and India, with the Indian provision including free medical aid and travel facilities. The Soviet Union's Ukrainian republic has provided grants, hostel accommodations, free travel, and free access to sports facilities and artistic activities. Scholarships, grants, and loans are available to teacher-training applicants in Canada, Gabon, Indonesia, Israel, Norway, Papua New Guinea, the Philippines, Sweden, the United Kingdom, the United States, and Venezuela.

In summary, many countries provide special incentives to encourage able candidates to enter and remain in teacher-preparation programs. However, the value of the incentives differs markedly from one nation to another.

The Length of Preservice Training

3.4 *The Length-of-Study Standard.* "The amount of time candidates spend in the program is sufficient to equip them with the knowledge and skills needed to begin teaching at an acceptable level of efficiency."

A survey of 104 nations has revealed that the length of preservice programs ranges from one to five years (ILO/Unesco, 1983: 9-12) What the length of study will be depends on several factors. One is the level of a country's socio-economic development. National education systems, in the early phases of their evolution, typically can afford to provide no more than minimal preservice teacher training. Subsequently, as the system matures and the society's ability to finance education advances, increasingly more preservice study is required.

A second factor influencing length of preservice training is the amount of preparation deemed necessary for teaching at different grade levels. Less training is usually required for nursery-school and kindergarten teachers than for those who will teach in the elementary grades. Secondary-school instructors are typically expected to have more training than primary-school teachers, and college instructors are required to have the most formal preparation of all.

The following examples from an International Labour Office and Unesco survey in the early 1980s illustrate training programs of different lengths in representative nations (ILO/Unesco, 1983: 8-12).

At a relatively low level of teacher preparation, preschool and primary teachers have been trained in three-year secondary schools (normal schools) in such nations as Indonesia, Nicaragua, and Tanzania. However, Indonesia has recently moved the training to primary-school personnel into post-secondary teachers colleges.

At a more advanced level of preparation, graduates of secondary schools can enter a two-year course to train as primary-school teachers in Argentina, Colombia, Guyana, Kenya, Papua New Guinea, and Tanzania. A three-year college-level course has been the standard program for primary-school teaching in Canada, Chile, Cyprus, France, and the Federal Republic of Germany. In Cameroon, candidates can complete a three-year program that leads to a bachelor's degree and certification to teach in a junior-secondary school.

Four-year college-level programs for primary-school teaching have been conducted in Cuba, the German Democratic Republic, Peru, the Philippines, the United Kingdom, and the United States. Some nations offer more than one level of training; Colombia provides a four-year program as well as the two-year course mentioned above. A great range of countries prepare the bulk of their secondary-school teachers in four-year college-level programs. These nations include Canada, Cuba, both East and West Germany, Hungary, Indonesia, Iraq, Japan, the Netherlands, Nicaragua, the Philippines, the United Kingdom, and the United States.

Five-year programs that award both a university degree and certification to teach in senior-secondary schools are standard fare in many countries, including Cameroon, Malta, Peru, and Venezuela.

A one-year post-graduate course in professional studies for candidates with university degrees has been offered, usually for secondary-school teachers, in Australia, Bangladesh, Egypt, France, India, and Sweden. Such a course has sometimes also been provided for the official certification of primary teachers in Australia, France, the United Kingdom, and the United States.

The general pattern of development in all nations has been to increase the level of training as soon as the current teacher-supply system has been able to staff nearly all classrooms with at least minimally-prepared teachers. Such a development occurred in Finland in 1979 when the government began increasing qualification standards so that all future primary-school teachers (grades 1-6) became obliged to obtain a master-of-education degree (requiring about four-and-one-half years' preparation) and all secondary teachers were obligated to obtain a master-of-arts degree (about five or six years' preparation) (Niemi, 1987: 311).

Assessing Preservice-Education Outcomes

3.5 *The Evaluation Standard.* "The program constantly evaluates students' progress and uses the results of the evaluation for:

"(A) diagnosing students' learning difficulties and offering them ways to remedy the difficulties,

"(B) judging the effectiveness of the instructional program so its weaknesses can be corrected,

"(C) verifying that successful students have mastered the program objectives,

"(D) identifying students who should be eliminated from the program."

These judgments are typically based on (1) an inspection of student teachers' written lesson plans, (2) observations of student teachers' performance in directing a class of pupils, and (3) the newly graduated teachers' evaluation of their preservice experience.

An example from Finland illustrates the use of this third approach. A revised Finnish preservice teacher-preparation program was instituted following the passage of the 1985 School Act that placed additional planning responsibilities on teachers. To help the university faculty estimate how adequately the preservice program equipped prospective teachers to perform their roles, graduates were asked to evaluate their preparation. The respondents reported:

> that they had not yet received enough training to enable them to differentiate instruction sufficiently to meet the individual needs of large numbers of pupils, to handle pupils who had problems, to keep in touch with parents, and to make plans for the whole teaching period. All these abilities and qualities have become very important since the Act of 1985 (Niemi, 1987: 311).

In most nations, a student's successful completion of preservice training is accepted as evidence of the individual's qualification to teach. However, in some regions a student not only must graduate from a training program but must also pass tests administered by some central authority. For example, in the United States, the state of California requires graduates to pass the *California Basic Skills Test* to verify that prospective classroom teachers have a sufficient command of written English and mathematics to serve as suitable models of literate adults. Candidates must also demonstrate detailed knowledge of professional-education research and practices by passing the *National Teacher Examination* or its equivalent.

STAGE 4: FILLING TEACHING POSITIONS WITH QUALIFIED CANDIDATES

It seems obvious that not every teacher-education graduate will fit equally well into all possible teaching positions. Therefore, the aim of a nation's teacher-placement system is to locate available candidates in the positions for which they are best suited. This applies both to newly graduated teachers and to experienced educators who are leaving one position for another or who are reentering the profession after having left it for a period of time.

4.1 *The Proper-Match Standard.* "The teacher-placement system achieves a good match between (A) the sort of teacher needed in a given school and (B) the characteristics of the candidate who is placed in that position. In effect, the elements of the education system are coordinated in a manner that ensures efficient articulation among the number of students, the number of qualified teachers, and the available facilities and supplies."

In most countries, the general criteria to be considered in recruiting and placing teachers are determined by public authorities, who typically cast their standards in the form of regulations or official circulars. The authority may be the central government (Argentina), provincial officials (Australia, Canada, West

Germany, the United States), or local bodies (Japan, the United Kingdom). In some nations (Colombia, Czechoslovakia, New Zealand, Sweden) teachers' unions participate in setting the standards.

Educational administrators, in their effort to achieve a proper match between candidates and teaching posts, may depend on several sources of evidence. In virtually all cases, academic and professional-education qualifications are the principal bases for appointment.

> A few countries will accept candidates with qualifications below the set minimum, but usually on a temporary basis only and usually subject to a requirement of undergoing training or special observation during a trial period. In addition, many countries require evidence of physical and mental fitness, and in some cases evidence of aptitude for teaching as well. Several require teachers to be of their own nationalities. A number impose examinations, written or oral; these are in some instances competitive. In many countries screening and interviews form important parts of the recruitment process.... Other requirements frequently mentioned are evidence of good character, good morals...and respect for the established order.... France requires teachers to have discharged their military service obligations before recruitment (ILO/Unesco, 1983: 14).

Deviations from the officially approved teacher-placement process are often required when there is a mismatch between the number of teaching positions to be filled and the supply of properly trained candidates. For instance, in Zambia during the early 1970s the failure of the country's teacher-college building program made it necessary to employ an increasing number of untrained teachers, which resulted in the proportion of untrained teachers reaching the "unacceptably high level of 13.3%" of the nation's teaching corps. In addition, heavy reliance had to be placed on the recruitment of instructors from outside the country, so that only 1 out of every 10 secondary-school teachers was a Zambian (Ministry of Development Planning and National Guidance, 1971: 25).

STAGE 5: PROVIDING WORKING CONDITIONS THAT PROMOTE QUALITY PERFORMANCE

The pair of standards proposed for this stage concern the quality of the working environment and the rewards the society provides for teachers.

A Satisfactory Working Environment

5.1 *The School-Condition Standard.* "The school system furnishes teaching conditions which optimize the likelihood that teachers will apply the best instructional techniques of which they are capable."

Conditions implied in this standard include teacher-induction provisions, the ratio of teachers to pupils, the instructional materials available, the physical condition of the classroom, time for the teacher to prepare lessons and to evaluate pupils' progress, the quality of supervision provided by the headmaster, and more.

The term *teacher induction* "refers to the formal initiation of newly trained teachers into the profession and by which they come to be, at a basic level, professionally competent and personally at ease.... There is a general consensus that [this process may require] one to three years" (Tisher, 1984: 113-114). Whereas new teachers in virtually every school system have often received some measure of informal help from their more experienced colleagues, regular provisions for induction did not become widespread in such countries as Great Britain, Australia, and New Zealand until the 1970s. Since then, formal induction programs have become increasingly popular, though frequently limited to certain schools and in an experimental format, as has been the case in North America (Tisher, 1984: 114-115). The main objectives of such provisions are typically:

1. To extend the teachers' knowledge about the school and the educational system and how both function;
2. To increase the teachers' awareness and comprehension of the complexities of teaching situations and to suggest alternative ways of coping with these complexities.
3. To acquaint the teachers with support services and resources within the school and the region;
4. To help the teachers (generally through counselling activities) to apply knowledge they already posses, or could obtain for themselves, to the daily tasks or problems which confront them (Tisher, 1980: 81).

The approaches employed in induction programs can include: an orientation visit to the school prior to the beginning of classes, a reduced teaching load (fewer class hours per week, smaller classes), released time to visit other classes or other schools, and special conferences and workshops (as short as one hour or as long as several days). The conferences are conducted by experienced colleagues or specialists from outside the school. In addition, printed materials for new teachers provide information about conditions of employment, available facilities, and school rules and administrative procedures (Tisher, 1984: 115).

Attractive Incentives

5.2 *The Adequate-Incentive Standard.* "The rewards provided for teachers should be sufficient to maintain a high-level of teacher morale and dedication to the job."

The rewards for teaching can be material or nonmaterial, official or unofficial, and they vary from one society to another. The most obvious material reward is money. How well money serves to attract and retain teachers of high quality depends to a great extent on (1) how adequately teachers' incomes compare with incomes in other occupations and (2) what standard of living the teacher's income will support.

Money, in the form of immediate salary, is not the only material compensation teachers can receive. Other material rewards may include medical and dental care, a retirement pension, life insurance, free housing, a food allotment, clothing, transportation facilities, educational expenses, the opportunity to purchase goods at discount price, and free tuition for the teacher's children to attend school. A variety of factors can determine which of these forms of remuneration will be found within a given society. For example, In Swaziland, teachers are provided housing rent free. But the government has suffered difficulties in keeping up with the house-construction schedule, so that two problems arise —either not enough teachers can be hired or else those who are hired but are not given rent-free houses tend to cause unrest in the ranks of the profession (*Fourth national development plan*, 1983: 255).

Nonmaterial incentives that may motivate teachers to remain in the profession and provide dedicated service include a position of high respect in the eyes of the community. To illustrate, in our earlier example of evening primary-level classes in India, the part-time teachers, who were mostly farmers or housewives during the daytime, "seemed happy with the 'white-collar' status conferred on them by the teaching job. It enhanced their prestige in the community" (Naik, 1983: 64). In effect, people from lower social classes are likely to see a career in teaching as a more attractive route to improved social status than are people from upper classes.

The phrase *official rewards* is used in this discussion to mean those types of remuneration that are the stated conditions of employment. In contrast, *unofficial rewards* are kinds of compensation that are not part of a contractual agreement but which teachers can acquire because of their profession. The most common perquisite of this type is payment for privately tutoring pupils outside of school hours.

In a shadow zone between official and unofficial rewards is the practice in some regions of local school personnel levying special fees on families, then dividing the fees among the school staff. Such assessments may appear at various stages in pupils' school careers. They are typically given labels designed to legitimate their use —entrance-application fee, book-use fee, recreation fee, school-support fee, examination fee, and the like.

Other incentives are improvements in teachers' working conditions. For example, the Jamaican development plan for 1978-82 not only provided salary increases for teachers in remote, rural, and depressed areas but also provided improvements in the rural infrastructure, such as roads, electricity, and housing through collaborative efforts of the Ministry of Education and other government agencies (National Planning Agency, 1978: 103).

A substantial amount of evidence supports the observation that poor working conditions for teachers contribute to poor academic success of students. For instance, a study in Zimbabwe (Chivore, 1988: 75) led to the conclusion that well-qualified teachers were attracted to secondary schools which provided "decent [living] accommodation, as well as facilities in the form of specialist rooms, furniture, offices and equipment...and pupils' performance was relatively satisfactory." Schools without such facilities failed to attract properly qualified instructors. Instead, they had to accept ones who had substandard credentials, "with the result that pupils at these schools performed badly in their final examinations."

Guaranteed job security is a further working condition that can encourage teachers to remain in the profession. One device for providing such assurance is the adoption of teacher-tenure rules which typically specify a number of years that a newly hired teacher is on probation. During this period an individual can be dismissed on rather slight evidence of unsatisfactory performance. When the probation time has passed and the teacher has been judged adequate, he or she is awarded tenure. Personnel with tenure status cannot be terminated without the submission of a host of evidence that they have been grossly incompetent, negligent, cruel, or immoral.

Job security can also be enhanced by membership in trade unions or professional associations aimed at promoting the welfare of their members. In an ILO/Unesco (1983: 21) survey of the status of teachers in over 100 nations, very few countries reported restrictions on the right of teachers to join a union. A number of countries (Czechoslovakia, Gabon, Indonesia, Kuwait, Thailand) have only one union for teachers to join, whereas others (the United Kingdom, the United States) have multiple unions that compete with each other for members. In most provinces of Canada union membership is either automatic or compulsory. Japan permits teachers in the public sector to form organizations to improve their working conditions, but the government does not recognize these bodies as trade unions.

If a large percentage of a region's teachers belong to a union, and if the members are willing to engage in mass action (public demonstrations, work stoppages, election campaigns), they can exert effective political pressure on both the government and parents. In the array of mass labor actions reported throughout the world each year, many involve teachers' efforts to improve their job security, income, and working conditions. For example, in 1989, demands for salary increases were underscored in Greece by instructors abandoning their classrooms and in Britain by professors refusing to administer final examinations. In France, union members assailed the government for according supplemental pay for extra services rather than increasing all instructors' pay.

STAGE 6: PROVIDING UPGRADING OPPORTUNITIES FOR INSERVICE TEACHERS

Many members of the general public, and some educators, still hold the outmoded belief that teachers' formal education is over when they graduate from a preservice training program. However, the dominant conviction in modern education systems is that preservice studies merely launch the neophyte into the teaching profession with enough skills to perform at a minimally acceptable level. The beginning teacher is not yet a master of the trade, but still needs further education in order to extend and refine instructional skills and to keep up with new developments in the field. As the European Ministers of Education proposed in their 1987 conference: "The initial [preservice] and inservice education of teachers should be viewed by all those concerned as an integrated whole, a form of permanent education" (Council for Cultural Cooperation, 1989: 6). As a result of such a conviction, inservice training has become a widespread, integral part of teacher education throughout the world.

The two standards applied to inservice-training provisions concern the nature of teacher qualification and the forms that inservice education assumes.

The Nature of Quality Upgrading

6.1 *The Quality-Enhancement Standard.* "The education system improves and maintains the quality of instruction by providing for upgrading the official and unofficial qualifications of teachers."

The specific aims of inservice programs can vary from place to place. One of the most common aims, particularly in developing nations, is to increase the proportion of officially qualified teachers in the school system. When speaking of *qualified* teachers, we should recognize the distinction between *official qualification* and *operational qualification*. An officially qualified teacher is a person who has fulfilled the conditions required for receiving a professional credential or license as a teacher. This typically means completing a preservice-education program. In contrast, operationally-qualified teachers are ones who perform satisfactorily as instructors, whether or not they have a certificate or license. Obviously, when people are awarded official qualification, they are assumed to be operationally qualified, even though this is not always so, since it is apparent that some graduates of teacher-education programs turn out to be ineffective when they face a classroom of students. On the other hand, there are also people who lack official qualifications but who still perform as satisfactory instructors. They have an intuitive sense or reasoning skills that equip them to teach well. The assumption, however, is that they would be even better teachers if they did complete the usual preservice requirements. Therefore, inservice programs are designed to qualify teachers both officially and operationally by supplying unlicensed teachers with official qualifications and by improving the operational effectiveness of all teachers.

The ILO/Unesco (1983: 55) survey identified four distinct objectives of inservice or further-education programs —(1) completing the training of officially-unqualified teachers, (2) improving or broadening the skills of qualified teachers through study for higher degrees; (3) updating teachers' skills to cope with changes in subject-matter and methods resulting from educational reforms, and (4) providing all teachers with the opportunity to keep abreast of innovation in their subjects and in teaching methods.

An example of an effort to raise teachers' official qualifications is reported in the Swaziland national-development plan for the mid-1980s.

> The number of qualified teachers [in secondary schools] has shown a steady increase from 811 in 1978 to 1,172 in 1982. As a result, the proportion of the total secondary school teaching force that was qualified rose from 76 to 78 percent in the period 1978-1982. However, there were still a large number of unqualified teachers in the secondary schools: 329 in 1982. The shortage of qualified teachers was particularly acute in the fields of mathematics, science, and technology —subjects important to the development of the country. This continued utilization of unqualified teachers was associated, in part, with the explosion of enrollments at the secondary level (*Fourth national development plan 1983/84-1987/88*, 1983: 247-248).

The Suitability of Inservice Programs

6.2 *The Program-Supply Standard.* "The education system furnishes inservice-education programs that (A) are the ones most needed for improving instruction, (B) are sufficiently convenient to attract the teachers who could profit most from the experience, and (C) are conducted efficiently."

Inservice programs assume many forms. The most common type consists of a presentation aimed at a large group of participants, with the participants either meeting in a central location (such as a school auditorium) or receiving the instruction via mass-communication media (newsletters, correspondence courses using the mail service, radio, television). Inservice-education sessions that are comprised of prepared presentations to an audience can vary from a one-hour session to instruction over a period of weeks or months.

Despite the popularity of lectures and demonstrations for large groups, studies of such practices have cast doubt on their effectiveness. Bell and Peightel (1976: 11) reviewed research on inservice-education schemes and concluded that "Group approaches treating all teachers alike are less likely to accomplish their objectives than programs offering individualized training for different teachers."

In an effort to categorize the growing number of inservice centers in the United States, Bell and Peightel (1976: 18-19) proposed a four-fold scheme. The first three types of programs in the scheme differ in administrative structure but all offer training in a variety of subject-matter fields. The fourth type focuses on one subject field (such as science, language arts, social studies, the arts) or on a single level (such as preschool teaching). The four are labeled (1) *consortium*, consisting of three or more cooperating institutions or organiza-tions, (2) *partnership*, involving two cooperating institutions or organizations, (3) *autonomous center*, conducted by a single sponsoring unit, and (4) *special focus program*, concentrating on a limited aspect of teaching.

In response to the call for more long-term, individualized training opportunities, officials in a variety of nations have been providing the foregoing types of regional centers. For instance, in the Southern Africa nation of Botswana, the government's 1985-1989 national development plan called for the construction of nine new education centers and the upgrading of three existing ones.

> When completed and properly staffed, they will have the capacity to organize residential courses of two-week duration for 2,500 teachers and non-residential courses for another 1,800 teachers annually. Combined with the facilities at the Teacher Training Colleges and the University, it is estimated that there will be adequate facilities to cover the inservice training needs of all primary and secondary school teachers during [the sixth national-development program]" (Ministry of Finance and Development Planning, 1985: 146)

In order to render inservice education both convenient and attractive, education officials have adopted a diversity of practices. The case of Indonesia illustrates this point. Beginning in the early 1970s, the Indonesian government assigned 1,200 faculty members from teacher-training institutions to form 120 mobile inservice-training teams throughout the island nation. Each team was supplied either a four-wheel-drive van or a motor launch equipped with such instructional media as film projectors, charts, science kits, and teachers' guidebooks. In every school district, the teams stopped at a central school where teachers from surrounding villages gathered for a three-week workshop on the use of the nation's newest textbooks. By means of this approach, within less than five years more than 90,000 teachers had been upgraded. In addition, the Ministry of Education sponsored teacher-upgrading radio programs that were broadcast to 100,000 teachers on the island of Java and in nine remote outer-island provinces four times a week, 20 minutes a day (Postlethwaite & Thomas, 1980: 90).

Frequently inservice schemes are organized in a way that produces a *multiplier effect*, as in Botswana, where "Head teachers, senior teachers, and education officers drawn from various districts undergo an intensive inservice training program, and then organize similar programs for other teachers in their districts" (Ministry of Finance and Development Planning, 1985: 146-147).

In Israel, the efficiency of a mutiplier-effect program for introducing primary-grade teachers to a new Hebrew-language curriculum was demonstrated in a comparison between two approaches to curriculum implementation in 165 schools. The first approach involved staff members from the nation's curriculum-development center each working directly with an individual teacher to explain the theory and procedures of the new curriculum. In the second approach, a member of the center's staff worked with one teacher —called a *mediator*— who was then responsible for introducing the new system to five other teachers in the mediator's own school. The mediator approach proved far more popular with teachers, enabled them to solve implementation problems more adequately, used central-staff members' time more economically, and resulted in better pupil progress than did the program in which one staff member worked directly with one teacher at a time (Eden, 1978: 70).

Developing nations which have relatively small populations, financial constraints, and a limited supply of educational experts often depend on more developed countries for advanced teacher-education programs. For instance, Western Samoa, as a South-Pacific Island nation with a population of 170,000 and a restricted economy, has included in the government's periodic national-development plans a provision for sending selected teachers to Australia to upgrade their instructional skills and to develop fields of specialization (Economic Development Department, 1980: 67).

STAGE 7: RETAINING EFFECTIVE TEACHERS AND ELIMINATING INEFFECTIVE ONES

It is clear that some people who enter the teaching profession are far more satisfactory than others. Some are truly excellent, so it is in society's best interest to keep them on the job. But at the other end of the effectiveness scale, there are ones who not only waste their students' time but may even be destructive by teaching distorted or outmoded beliefs or by damaging students' self-confidence and enthusiasm for learning. The two standards proposed at this stage address issues of rewarding teachers who are masters of their profession and removing ones who are deemed unsuitable.

Rewarding Meritorious Teaching

7.1 *The Reward-for-Merit Standard.* "The education system provides sufficient benefits to retain effective teachers in the profession throughout their productive lives. The more meritorious the teacher, the greater the benefits provided."

The meaning of the term *sufficient benefits* often differs from one individual to another. For some, it means material rewards, such as an increased salary, health and accident insurance, opportunities for advanced study, and promotion to a position of greater responsibility or higher status. For others it means the nonmaterial satisfaction of improving the lives of young people and of making a positive contribution to society.

The results of a study by Farrugia (1986) of the attitudes of 186 teachers in Malta indicated that most teachers' (76%) greatest satisfaction derived from passing on values and knowledge to others, influencing young people, and teaching their favorite subject. Teachers' chief complaints about their occupation were not monetary, since only 10% cited poor pay and working conditions as sources of dissatisfaction. Rather, their main frustrations derived from non-material conditions —students' lack of interest and motivation to learn (42%) as well as the combination of administrative interference in the instructional process, lack of appreciation by parents and authorities, and school politics (42%). Farrugia (1986: 230) concluded that his findings:

> support the hypothesis that, for the majority [of teachers], the intrinsic rewards derived from pedagogical interaction sustain their occupational commitment in spite of the frustrations and disappointments in the material sphere. Teachers' malaise appears to result from the tension between these factors. However, the material aspects, such as claims for higher salaries and better conditions of work, attract more public exposure than satisfaction with pedagogical achievements.... Consequently, the Maltese public becomes more aware of teachers' complaints about the material aspects of their work than of their sources of intrinsic pedagogical satisfaction or frustration.

In seeking to derive constructive implications from his results, Farrugia (1986: 227) suggested, "It would appear that if the educational authorities adopted a less critical attitude toward teachers' work, and took steps to lessen administrative over-control, two outstanding sources of teachers' frustration would be removed." In effect, rewards for meritorious service can properly include a greater quantity of personal and public expressions of appreciation for teachers' contributions and a reduction of criticisms of teachers' performance.

In the case of Turkey, Murray (1988: 14) has proposed that keeping good teachers in the profession can be fostered by the school system's providing greater opportunities for professional growth and career development, such as summer courses for teachers that involve professors from foreign countries who introduce improved instructional methods. "Conversely, Turkish professors of education, cooperating in a teaching exchange program, could benefit from opportunities to collaborate with foreign colleagues regarding recent research findings and educational trends. Yet another possibility is to involve the wider community. Industrial cooperation might be sought as a means for obtaining financial support for progress in particular areas of education in which industry has a vested interest. Such support could entail providing consultants and equipment for instructors" (Murray, 1988: 14).

Removing Teachers from the Profession

7.2 *The Teacher-Removal Standard.* "The education system provides means for removing unsatisfactory teachers from the classroom and for retiring ones whose long service warrants the reward of a pension and freedom from further teaching responsibilities."

There are various reasons that teachers leave their current positions or abandon the profession entirely. In most cases they depart of their own volition to seek a better paying job, to be relieved of frustrating work conditions, to protect their health, to enter a more challenging occupation, or —in the case of women— to concentrate on the tasks of motherhood. Furthermore, many veteran teachers depart because their long years of service have earned them the right to retire with a pension. In contrast, some teachers are so incompetent or harmful that they deserve to be dismissed.

Consider, then, the issue of dismissal. School systems in every nation identify kinds of behavior for which teachers can be discharged. The rules and the disciplinary sanctions for infractions are often regulated by law. Sometimes the rules are laid down at the national level, but in other instances they are set locally. In Sweden each county has its own disciplinary code, while in Hungary and the Soviet Ukrainian Republic the code is set within the individual school. The types of offenses for which teachers can be dismissed can vary substantially from one school system to another. Typical causes are gross neglect of duty, sexual misconduct, being convicted of a crime, and abuse of students. In many nations, teachers can also incur disciplinary action for expressing unorthodox views in the classroom on politics, religion, race, and sexuality.

A probationary period following a teacher's initial appointment is required in numbers of school systems, with the period generally lasting one or two years. In many systems, probation policies apply to all schools, or at least to all public institutions. However, Colombia and the Philippines require a probationary period only in private schools. During this time the neophyte is on trial and liable to dismissal on the grounds of less evidence of incompetence —or at least with fewer legal formalities— than would be necessary with teachers of longer service, that is, ones who have achieved tenure status.

The interval of probation in Czechoslovakia and Scotland is officially considered to be a time for providing new appointees help and encouragement rather than for testing their abilities.

> In contrast, the Canadian Teachers' Federation refers to complaints among its members that supervisory practices are more judgemental than helpful and that this tendency, together with a tendency to give new appointees the most difficult assignments, is aggravated by the threat of teacher redundancy, which affects first teachers with least seniority (ILO/Unesco, 1983: 14).

Now to the matter of voluntary retirement. In virtually all countries, teachers who have completed an extended period of service are furnished a pension when they retire. A standard for old-age benefits recommended by the International Labour Organisation has been that teachers who complete 25 or 30 years of service should receive a pension at least equal to 40% of their previous earnings. Some school systems provide at this recommended level, some offer lower benefits, while others exceed the 40% standard.

> Luxembourg pays five-sixths of final salary and Sweden 75-80% after 30 years' service. Venezuela pays 80% after 25 years. In Italy, after 40 years' service a teacher may retire at age 65 with 94.4% of final gross salary. Colombia pays up to 75% of final gross salary and allowances.... Mexico and Nicaragua have paid up to 100% of previous earnings, but averaged over the last three years in the former case and the last five in the latter. In Jamaica, payment of the pension ceases if the recipient is declared bankrupt, or sentenced to a term of imprisonment (ILO/Unesco, 1983: 34).

With our overview of the seven stages of teacher supply now complete, we turn to a series of estimates about what might be expected in selected portions of the teacher-supply system in the years ahead.

PROSPECTS FOR TEACHER-SUPPLY SYSTEMS

Present-day societal conditions, in advanced industrialized countries and in developing nations alike, portend both encouraging and discouraging prospects for the task of providing a sufficient number of high-quality teachers to staff the world's education systems. The nature of such prospects can be estimated for preservice/inservice teacher-education and for the recruitment/retention of high-quality teachers.

Preservice and Inservice Programs

In the case of preservice and inservice programs, one of the most encouraging developments in recent times has been the creation of improved teacher-education instructional procedures, particularly those procedures that employ electronic media.

Videotape cameras and playback equipment —already widespread in North America, in Europe, and in a variety of East and Southeast Asian countries— are also increasingly affordable in teacher-training programs of developing nations. As a result, the use of such media can be expected to advance rapidly over the coming years. Once the original equipment has been purchased, the cost of producing training materials suited to local conditions is quite modest. Videotaped real-life events are far more graphic than verbal descriptions for introducing teacher-education students to exemplary classroom instructional methods, to ways of conducting field trips, to procedures for handling discipline problems, to the preparation of science projects, and to techniques of carrying out teacher-parent conferences. Videotaping also enables teacher-education students, along with their supervisors, to analyze the students' performance in microteaching sessions as well as in their practice teaching assignments.

Broadcast radio and television can be expected to play a more prominent role in the preparation of teachers over the coming years. Of the two media, the greater potential for accurately depicting teaching procedures is offered by television's combination of sight and sound. However, radio's low cost for both producing programs and receiving them suggests that radio will continue to be the more popular of the two, especially in developing nations. As in the past, broadcasts will continue to be used primarily for inservice rather than preservice education.

Teacher-training applications of electronic computers will expand rapidly. A substantial portion of the academic content of typical teacher-education programs can be cast in the form of self-instructional lessons that students pursue individually on microcomputers. Such content includes the material usually provided in textbooks and lectures on educational theory, instructional practices, principles of evaluation, comparative education, psychological and sociological foundations of teaching, and more. Not only can such lessons be suited to each student's individual learning rate, but they can offer continual feedback to the learner about how well the student has grasped each segment of the lesson.

Computers have also revolutionized the storage and retrieval of research results, so that, via telephone lines or satellites, microcomputers in teacher-training facilities can, within a few moments' time, furnish staff members and students a great host of up-to-date information about educational problems and solutions from around the world. This potential, now available primarily in advanced industrial societies, can be expected to extend into developing societies in keeping with both the pace of technological progress and the nations' ability to afford the required equipment. One hopeful trend in the field of communications media is that the growing competition among manufacturers stimulates a decline in the cost of equipment, thus rendering such devices increasingly affordable for teacher-education programs, even for ones with only modest financial resources.

Another recent trend that will likely continue into the future is the increased concern among teacher educators for furnishing preservice-training students a greater amount of practical experience before they graduate. This means more weeks of practice teaching, more work with youth groups and in community projects outside the school, and more microteaching.

A further development that can be expected in the years ahead is an increase in the amount and quality of inservice education. Teacher educators world-wide appear to recognize that preservice training is not enough to equip a teacher to perform effectively. Inservice education is at least as important, and in many cases more important, than preservice training.

In contrast to the foregoing positive trends are several discouraging prospects for the future. Perhaps the most distressing is the low level of financial support furnished for both preservice and inservice teacher education in many nations. As economic problems mount in so many countries of Africa, Latin America, much of Asia, and Eastern Europe, teacher-preparation programs can expect to suffer funding cutbacks. This will bring a deterioration of equipment, a shortage of textbooks, a decrease in the time and effort that faculty members dedicate to their teaching jobs as they seek elsewhere for supplementary sources of income, and a reduction in the financial resources students need to stay in school.

Teacher Recruitment and Retention

In many nations, the prospect in the near future for attracting more capable youths into teacher-training and for retaining competent teachers in the profession are rather dim. This pessimistic prediction is founded on two observations about monetary rewards and about teaching conditions that are likely to obtain over the coming years.

The first is that in numbers of countries, young people will view teaching as an unappealing career because teachers' salaries do not compare adequately with salaries in occupations requiring comparable preparation. The committee that conducted the ILO/Unesco survey (1983: 143-144) concluded that an adequate salary is " the principal, if not the only means of attracting entrants of the necessary caliber and retaining them.... In 15 of 32 countries [that have been studied]...the starting salaries of primary school teachers are 10% or more (in nine of them over 20%) below the average level of earnings in manufacturing industry... [and] in a considerable number of countries cost-of-living adjustments have not kept pace with the rise in the cost of living."

The shortage of qualified teachers can vary from region to region within a nation, from urban to rural areas, and from one subject-matter field to another. Rural schools in some nations suffer from a shortage of well-qualified teachers, whereas in other nations the schools of crowded and economically depressed ghetto areas of large cities have difficulty attracting well-prepared personnel. Properly trained mathematics, science, and vocational-education instructors are frequently in short supply, since graduates with backgrounds in these fields can find better-paying employment elsewhere. Such shortages are likely to continue in the future.

A further adverse condition, in addition to inadequate salaries, is the negative attitudes that some students display toward their studies and toward school personnel. In industrialized and developing societies alike, certain schools enroll a substantial quantity of students who lack motivation to learn and who disrupt classroom activities. Teachers often resign from their position —or abandon the profession entirely— because of the frustrations met in trying to instruct such pupils. These conditions appear to be found most often in societies that implement compulsory-education laws while, at the same time, limit the disciplinary measures that school authorities are permitted take, with the result that numbers of reluctant, antagonistic learners continue to populate classrooms.

The degree to which the foregoing adverse conditions will exist in the years ahead will vary markedly from one society to another. But it should be clear that those school systems which provide the least adequate remuneration for teachers and the least favorable teaching climate can be expected to attract and retain the poorest supply of competent teachers.

REFERENCES

Allen, D., & Ryan, K. (1969) *Microteaching.* Reading, MA: Addison-Wesley.

Bell, H., & Peightel, J. (1976) *Teacher centers and inservice education.* Bloomington, Ind.: Phi Delta Kappa.

Chivore, B. R. S. (1988) Factors determining the attractiveness of the teaching profession in Zimbabwe. *International Review of Education*, 34 (1): 59-78.

Chivore, B. R. S. (1986) Form IV pupils' perception of and attitude toward the teaching profession in Zimbabwe. *Comparative Education*, 22 (3): 133-153.

Cohen, R., *et al.* (1984) French case study. In L. H. Goad (Ed.), *Preparing teachers for lifelong education* (pp. 27-46). Oxford: Pergamon.

Council for Cultural Co-operation (1989) *Trends in European educational systems —and overall picture.* Strasbourg: Council of Europe.

Cropley, A. J., & Dave R. H. (1978) *Lifelong education and the training of teachers.* Oxford: Pergamon.

Cropley, A. J., & McCloed, J. (1986) Preparing teachers of the gifted. *International Review of Education*, 32: 125-136.

Economic Development Department (1980) *Western Samoa's fourth five-year development plan 1980-1984* (Vol. 1). Apia: Government of Western Samoa.

Eden, S. (1978) Implementation of innovations in education: A case study in curriculum planning. *Studies in Educational Evaluation Monograph Series*, (Serial No. 2).

Farrugia, C. (1986) Career-choice and sources of occupational satisfaction and frustration among teachers in Malta. *Comparative Education*, 2 (3): 221-231.

Fourth national development plan 1983/84-1987/88 (1983) Mbabane: Government of the Kingdom of Swaziland.

ILO/Unesco (1983) *Joint ILO/Unesco committee of experts on the application of the recommendation concerning the status of teachers.* Geneva: International Labour Office.

Ministry of Development Planning and National Guidance (1971) *Second National Development Plan.* Lusaka: Republic of Zambia.

Ministry of Finance and Development Planning *National development plan 1985-1991* (1985) Gaborone: Republic of Botswana.

Murray, K. B. (1988) Profile of the new generation of teachers in the Turkish educational system. *International Review of Education*, 34 (1): 5-15.

Naik, C. (1983) India: Extending primary education through nonformal approaches. *Prospects,13* (1), 61-72.

National Planning Agency (1978) *Five year development plan 1978-82.* Kingston: Government of Jamaica.

Niemi, H. (1987) The changes in curriculum, assessment, and learning strategies in Finnish schools. *International Review of Education*, 33 (3): 307-315.

Postlethwaite, T. N., & Thomas, R. M. (1980) *Schooling in the ASEAN region.* Oxford: Pergamon.

Soedijarto (1989) *Menuju pendidikan nasional yang relevan dan bermutu* [Toward relevant and high-quality national education]. Jakarta: Balai Pustaka.

Stones, E. (1985) Student (practice) teaching in teacher education. In T. Husen & T. N. Postlethwaite, *International Encyclopedia of Education*, (Vol. 8, pp. 4862-4867). Oxford: Pergamon.

Thomas, R. M. (1962) Reinspecting a structural position on occupational prestige. *The American Journal of Sociology, 67* (5), 561-565.

Thomas, R. M. (1975) *Social strata in Indonesia.* Jakarta: Antarkarya.

Thomas, R. M., & Soeparman, S. (1963) Occupational prestige: Indonesia and America. *Personnel and Guidance Journal*, January, pp. 430-434.

Tisher, R. P. (1984) Teacher induction: An international perspective on provisions and research. In L. G. Katz & J. D. Raths (Eds.), *Advances in teacher education, Vol. 1* (pp. 113-123). Norwood, N.J.: Ablex.

Tisher, R. P. (1980) The induction of beginning teachers. In E. Hoyle & J. Megarry (Eds.), *World yearbook of education 1980: Professional development of teachers.* London: Kogan Page.

SECTION III:

INFLUENCES ON EDUCATIONAL OPERATIONS

It is clear that in every society a large number of conditions affect the educational opportunities available to the populace. Several ways that such conditions can influence the nature of education systems are inspected in the four chapters that comprise Section III. The section is not designed to recognize all influential factors. Rather, it is intended to identify only a few conditions and to illustrate their possible effects on the educational fate of the citizenry.

The initial chapter (*Educational Equity*) introduces the issue of "proper educational opportunities." Then chapters 9 (*Language*) and 10 (*Economics*) inspect two of the key societal conditions that influence the conduct of education. Language was selected to illustrate one of the characteristics of culture that affects both the form that instruction will assume and the chance that some learners will profit more than others from educational offerings. Other key cultural characteristics that could be analyzed in detail, but that receive only passing mention in this volume, are such factors as religion, family organization, moral attitudes, gender roles and relationships, and social-class structure.

Economics, as a condition, was chosen to illustrate a vital element both in supporting a nation's educational activities and in defining the goals to be pursued by the education system as it helps prepare manpower for the society's job market. Another crucial element that affects the support of the education and determines the goals of schooling is the society's political structure. No single chapter of the book has been dedicated to an analysis of political influences. Instead, throughout the volume the effect of politics is recognized in connection with the topics of nearly all chapters.

The fourth chapter in this section (*Comparative Education Research*) addresses the issues of (1) what kinds of international comparative studies have been carried out on educational structures and practices and (2) what influence such research has apparently exerted on the conduct of education.

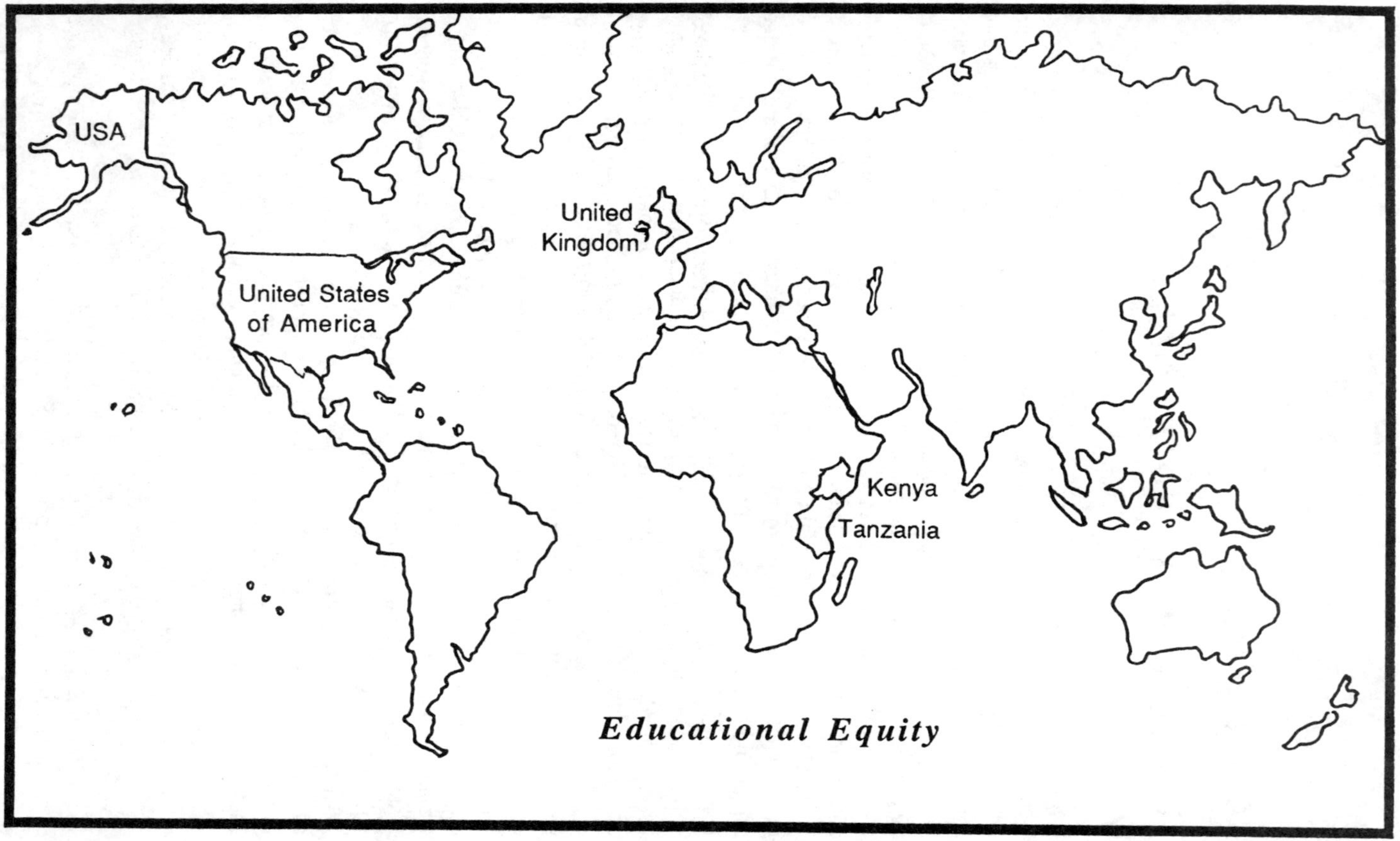
USA
United Kingdom
United States of America
Kenya
Tanzania
Educational Equity

CHAPTER 8

Educational Equity in Cross-National Settings

How do nations build educational bridges and dismantle educational barriers?

BEVERLY LINDSAY

> We have made progress...in dismantling barriers to the full participation of minorities in American life. But we have a long way to go. Some of the more difficult barriers to full participation by minority young people are not obvious. Among those who make it into four year colleges and universities, attrition rates are unacceptably high. This calls for a new understanding and a more creative approach to the barriers to success faced by minority youth (Commission on Minority Participation in Education and American Life, 1988: v).

While the preceding quote focuses on the United States, barriers to educational equity exist throughout the developing and developed world. Access to education is limited. For example, in 1985, only 41% of females and 59% of males were enrolled in primary education in low-income countries. In East Africa, at the close of the 1980s the official literacy rates were 35% in Kenya and over 70% in Tanzania, while less than 20% of youths of secondary-school age are in school. In England, about 89% of secondary-age youth attended school; yet only about 20% had advanced to the fifth and sixth form where they would be prepared for university education. In the United States, only 76% of African-American and 65% of Hispanic youth graduated from high school in the mid-1980s compared to over 90% of European Americans (Lockheed & Verspoor, 1989; Office of African Affairs, 1989a, 1989b; McKenna & Best, 1989; Commission on Minority Participation in Education and American Life, 1988: 8).

Such data clearly reflect a lack of equity in access to education in these societies. And because the causes of inequity can vary from one setting to another, a central issue educators face in providing appropriate learning opportunities is that of ascertaining the nature of the barriers to equity in specific countries and regions. Once the barriers have been identified, the next challenge is to determine how they can be dismantled and bridges to fair opportunities constructed.

Undergirding these two issues are five fundamental questions. What historical and sociocultural factors help fashion educational goals and opportunities in different regions? What features of educational equity are identified by policymakers and by persons directly affected by educational equity? How does the identification of different salient features lead to policies and programs for enhancing educational equity? What measures help determine the effectiveness of policies and programs designed to build opportunities for those adversely affected by inequities? And from inspecting illustrations focusing on specific regions of the world, what cross-national lessons can be extracted?

The following exploration of these questions focuses primarily on England, the East African nations of Kenya and Tanzania, and the United States. Analytical techniques identified with qualitative and policy research and evaluation will be employed in presenting data. Such methods explicitly recognize, and are designed to account for, various perspectives and premises regarding the same phenomena. Indeed,

> phenomenology emphasizes that groups of people...have systematically different views of reality and consistently different ways of interpreting. The phenomenologist assumes that people take action in the world based on their ideas and beliefs about the way the world is, in light of their notions of what things mean (Dorr-Bremme, 1985: 68).

Hence, the ostensible "objectivity" and detached distance of quantitative research and evaluation is not the mode of this chapter (Wiley, 1989: 9).

The major dimensions of this chapter involve: (1) portraying various perspectives of educational equity at different times and in different regions; (2) explicating some overarching purposes of secondary and higher education in relation to sociopolitical and economic conditions shaping educational equity; (3) analyzing various manifestations of educational equity or inequity —access, enrollment, attendance, retention, attrition, and completion rates; (4) examining policies and programs designed to ensure educational equity; (5) discussing evaluation methods to ascertain policy and program effectiveness, and (6) presenting continuing issues that influence educational equity.

PERSPECTIVES ON EDUCATIONAL EQUITY

So far in this chapter we have been using the word *equity* as if it had a universally agreed upon meaning, but such is not the case. Thus, to provide a sound foundation for our analysis of equity issues it is important to examine meanings assigned to the term.

In its most simplistic form, *equity* could be said to mean *equality*. But exactly what this equality should involve has not always been made clear.

One dimension of the equality question has concerned the *who* of equity. Whose welfare and perspective are the focus of attempts to improve educational equity? In most instances, the *who* are people that have had learning opportunities denied them because of their membership in a particular group, and not because they, as individuals, lacked the aptitude, motivation, or character traits needed to succeed in an educational program. The most obvious categories of educationally disadvantaged groups are defined by racial, ethnic, gender, social-class, or religious criteria. The nature of these groups varies from one society to another. Members of a given racial group who suffer educational disadvantage in one society may experience educational equity when they enter another society. Females in one nation may have greater educational opportunities than those in another. Thus, in analyzing educational inequity in a given society, it is important to identify which groups in the society are victims of educational discrimination.

A second dimension concerns which aspect of the educational process is the object of discussion. As educators, parents, and political activists have struggled in recent decades to specify what they intend by *equity*, their conceptions appear to have changed somewhat. Attention centered first on *equal access* to schooling, then shifted to *equal quality of educational settings*, and advanced to *equality of educational outcome*. As we trace this progression over the past four decades, we recognize that from the late 1950s through the 1970s, the term *equal educational opportunity* rather than equity was often heard in the United States and England. Ensuring access to public schools and higher education institutions was particularly a goal desired by racial minorities in both countries. In Africa during this same period, access was a paramount concern for indigenous peoples who, for the most part, had been unable to attend schools and colleges under European colonialism. Therefore, from England, to East Africa, to the United States, racism —as the systematic discrimination and subjugation of people due to alleged biological characteristics— was the chief barrier to educational equity.

By the 1970s and 1980s, the focus of educational opportunity shifted so that conditions within educational settings were taken into account. A quality environment was to be a part of the equity equation. For example, in the U.S., African-American and Hispanic educators, parents, and students asserted that learning opportunities would be greater if the linguistic and sociocultural backgrounds of minority public-school students were taken into account. In other words, equity meant proper learning opportunities once the students were enrolled. At the higher-education level, financial-aid packages would help provide the desired access so that American minority students, whose financial resources were extremely limited, could focus their primary attention on pursuing their studies. In African countries, governments' motivation to provide more favorable educational provisions was linked to plans for national development. Thus, educational opportunities were expanded for female students and minority ethnic groups, in particular, to enter the fields of business, economics, science, and technical studies. Development of a nation's infrastructure would result through such increased individual career diversity. In East Africa, the need for skilled workers in a variety of fields supported the call for broadened educational access to various fields of study. Yet, domestic and international economic conditions prevented additional expenditures on education which already exceeded one-third of national revenues. In a sense, societal economic conditions stifled educational equity throughout the 1980s.

Another shift occurred in perceptions of equity as demographic trends in the late 1980s caused many scholars and policymakers to observe even more clearly that educational equity was linked to a society's economic conditions. In the U.S., the book *One-Third of a Nation* (Commission on Minority Participation in Education and American Life, 1988: 3) reported that in the mid-1980s over 20% of the American school-age population were from ethnic minorities. By the year 2000, that proportion would rise to one-third, producing the group who would comprise the major net additions to the American labor force. Failure to provide educational opportunities for one-third of a nation was judged to have herculean social and economic costs. Similar conclusions were being reached in England, where the numbers of minority youth were also increasing. Thus, to both majority and minority students and policy makers, educational equity increasingly meant the opportunity to complete programs successfully. The diploma, degree, or other formal credential (symbolizing program completion) became the ultimate symbol of equity —equality of educational outcome across the subgroups of society.

The following discussion presents statistics that illustrate the extent of educational equity in the three geographic regions — England, East Africa, and the United States. As we delve cross-nationally, what will emerge is that educational equity reflects a continuum. Secondary-education enrollment and access to post-secondary educational opportunities are significant in light of racial, social class, and economic conditions in England. The focus in Kenya and Tanzania is on secondary education and higher education, the levels at which persons obtain skills that may be directly applicable to national development. In the United States, virtually everyone has the opportunity to pursue secondary education, although many minorities do not finish this level. (In some areas of California, for example, about 50% of Latino or Hispanic students do not complete high school [Morning Edition, National Public Radio, December 13, 1989]). But not everyone in the U.S. enjoys a fair opportunity to advance beyond high school, so that our discussion of equity in the U.S. concentrates on the higher education arena for Americans. The matter of who completes baccalaureate and graduate or professional degrees is of particular importance for questions of equity because policymakers who can effect educational change and equity are ones who have university and professional education.

PURPOSES OF SECONDARY AND HIGHER EDUCATION

With the foregoing perceptions of equity in mind, we turn now to the purposes of advanced education in our representative countries.

England

The mid-1940s ushered in a new era of education in England (Bruce, 1985: 164-165; Holmes, 1985: 1; Jones, 1985: 24-27). The ending of the second World War permitted the opportunity for more attention to be devoted to education. Emerging salient issues which were linked to education during the next twenty or so years included: developing and strengthening economic and political relations with other Western nations and within the colonies; preparing a domestic work force; and presenting the opportunity for some form of secondary education for all youth. To most educators and many political leaders, the provision of secondary education for all youth was the primary issue. However, it was clearly linked to other fundamental questions.

Redeveloping the economic structure and its components was a central issue immediately after World War II. This meant producing a work force capable of meeting the demands for rebuilding a domestic industrial society and forging economic linkages with other developed nations while simultaneously extracting economic benefits from its colonies. Although not always stated explicitly, there was an emerging consensus among education's policymakers that different types of education for students could help address these and other societal goals. In this light, the 1944 Education Act must be examined.

The Act was based on the view that three stages of education —primary, secondary, and further— should be available to students based upon their academic ability and not their parents' ability to pay. The massive introduction of the "11-plus" examination at the conclusion of primary education was designed to determine students' aptitude for attending one of three types of secondary schools —grammar, secondary-modern, or technical. A liberal education, steeped in the arts and sciences, would be appropriate for future business, industrial, and government leaders through grammar schools. The secondary-modern school would be an extension of general education. And for most other students, educational training of a vocational or technical nature through technical schools would enable them to fit efficiently into various occupational niches (Holmes, 1985: 2). The nature of the 11-plus exam and the type of preparation needed to succeed on it meant that the perpetuation of British social-class, racial, and cultural distinctions would be transmitted through the educational system. Educational equity would not be prevalent.

By the 1960s and 1970s, numerous economic and sociopolitical changes had occurred domestically and internationally which impacted the English educational system. The immigration of diverse ethnic and racial groups changed the demographic profile of the work place and schools. By the late 1970s, about 5% of the population were recent immigrants, with the Irish, West Indians, and Indians constituting the largest groups (Watson, 1985: 67). There were also other prominent forces for change, such as, the direct extraction of economic resources from independent nations (that is, former colonies) had declined, and the demands by the indigenous work force to participate more fully in the democratic process had increased (Bruce, 1988: 383-384).

Although the 1944 Education Act was intended to furnish greater educational opportunity for all, it still contributed significantly to inequities. The Act solidified a tripartite publicly-financed secondary-education system —grammar (academic), secondary-modern (general), and technical (vocational). [In addition, Britain has traditionally maintained numerous prestigious, privately controlled academic schools, incongruously referred to as *public schools*. The nation's social elite have usually attended such institutions.] The three types of publicly-funded schools largely existed until the mid-1960s. And during this period, the growing notion of the *comprehensive secondary school* evolved. Comprehensive schools, offering both academic and vocational curricula, enrolled children from 11 to 18. The watershed for the change in school types came with Circular 10/65 issued by the Department of Education and Science in 1965 when the secondary-modern schools would hereafter become *comprehensive* by offering vocational as well as academic studies (Holmes, 1985: 16). Since that time, comprehensive, grammar, and technical schools have been found in most parts of England. The real emergence of comprehensive schools occurred in the 1970s. Authorities intended that elitism based on class and race and perpetuated through the multifaceted approach would be lessened through comprehensive schools.

The key distinction between the two periods is observed through attempts to broaden access to secondary education without the adverse effects of tracking students into a particular type of school and curriculum. Under the old system, secondary-school selection was usually made at 11 with limited opportunities for change at 13 and 15 or 16 years of age. By the 1980s, the vast majority of secondary students attended some type of comprehensive secondary school, whereas through the mid-1960s only about 25% of the students were enrolled in secondary grammar schools which provided the potential for college or university study (Holmes, 1985: 16; Judge, 1984: 3).

Educational access by the mid-1980s meant that nearly 90% of English secondary-age youth attend school. However, this statistic still belies the fact that the upper tier, the sixth form of secondary school, is for the very privileged. This level caters to no more than 20% of the age group who have the credentials for secondary study to the Advanced-(A)-level examinations leading toward university matriculation (Office of European Affairs, 1989: 3-4; McKenna & Best, 1989: 3). Since the 1940s, privately-controlled schools (Britain's *public schools*) have provided a four- to six-year academic curriculum leading to potential university education. In this regard, the privately-controlled *public schools* and the publicly-supported *grammar schools* have been analogous; both have catered to the educational and social elite.

According to Broadfoot (1985: 7-8), public examinations are a "peculiarly English disease" which serves as a major mechanism for preventing educational equity, in terms of access to schooling. Examinations are formalized procedures, distinct from the classroom, that enable successful candidates to receive a certificate or diploma. Through the 1970s, secondary students in academic tracks in comprehensive schools and grammar schools took the General Certificate of Education (GCE) "Ordinary" or O-level examination after approximately four years of study. This examination focused on several subjects. If successful on the test, students could try the "Advanced" or A-level examination about two years later wherein they generally concentrated on two or three subjects to qualify for university matriculation. From 1965 onward, the Certificate of Secondary Education (CSE) was taken by students in other tracks who were not "qualified" to take the O-level examination. CSE students would leave secondary schools with a certificate, rather than with a failure on the O-levels.

Proponents of the examinations have contended that the tests enhance student motivation, maintain academic standards, and serve as a fair basis for selecting students for further education. However, evidence does not suggest that examinations are consistently utilized in this fashion. Considerable criticism has emerged regarding the several forms of secondary examinations. Some of the criticism has focused on (a) the social bias in favor of white upper and middle-class students to the exclusion of working-class and racial-minority students, (b) tests' inaccuracies and poor record of accurately predicting students' future success, and (c) an overemphasis on an academic approach to learning (Broadfoot, 1985: 9). When they are preparing for and taking the examinations, students can be "cooled out" of the academic courses in comprehensive schools and eventually from academic postsecondary options (Holmes, 1985: 19).

In summary, significant attempts have been made in England over the past three decades to improve access to educational opportunity for all segments of society. However, inequities continue to exist. All children and youths do not enjoy the same chance for schooling in keeping with their potential abilities.

East Africa

The present-day nations of Kenya and Tanzania had been British colonial territories until the early 1960s. Kenya achieved political independence in December 1963. Tanzania was formed by merging Tanganyika and Zanzibar in April 1964. As a result, these newly freed East African nations reflected political and economic initiatives of the British Parliament and private industries. During colonialism, their education systems functioned primarily for the benefit of the colonial rulers rather than for Africans. Operating under the colonial motto that the "masters' children were to remain masters in the government," the colonial rulers determined the level and type of education that Africans would receive. The educational system that was developed by the British government clearly reflected racist, segregationist policies, with Europeans trained as supervisors and leaders and Africans trained as servants and laborers (Cheru, 1987: 34; Kahama *et al.*, 1986: 177). Although missionary schools existed, they differed little from government schools since neither were linked to comprehensive African development or to the enhancement of indigenous cultural heritage. Indeed, some Africans believed the missionary schools merely cooperated with European settlers by providing a second-rate education intended to force Africans into roles of laborers (Andambi, 1984: 2; Cheru, 1987: 34; Rono, 1988: 6).

After World War II, some attempts were made to furnish greater opportunities for Africans through the application of the 1944 English Education Act in East Africa. However, when the 1944 Act, with variations of a tripartite structure (academic, general, and vocational education), was transferred to the colonies, it still did not provide secondary education for large numbers of Africans (Lindsay, 1980: 276; Rono, 1988: 6). Specifically, the educational system was designed to limit access to secondary education via stringent examinations and high African attrition rates. Thus, only two of every 100 African children entered secondary school. As a consequence, few East Africans moved into professional employment that would contribute to national development (Cheru, 1987: 41). As late as 1964, a Kenyan survey of high-level manpower revealed the acute shortage of Africans practicing domestically in professions: 36 doctors, 20 electrical engineers, and 17 university professors (Republic of Kenya, 1972). In Tanzania two years before independence, there were only 70 Tanganyikan Africans with university degrees. Despite the limited access to education, Africans continued to envision formal education as the means to an independent country and to status equivalent to that of Europeans. In essence, educational equity was a paramount goal.

After independence, the new governments began reviews of their educational systems. The 1964 Report of the Education Commission, better known as the Ominde Report, was most influential in the Kenyan review process. The Ominde Report addressed Kenyan educational problems and stressed the changing sociopolitical objectives of education. As a result, several national aims were identified in conjunction with education: national unity, national development, social equality, individual development and self-fulfillment, development of cultural heritage, and African socialism (Cheru, 1987: 7; Jomo Kenyatta Foundation, 1973: 1-3).

During the First Development Decade, the Ministries of Economic Planning and Development and of Education provided rationales for emphases on secondary and tertiary or higher education (Sifuna, 1983: 481). Factors which influenced the importance given to secondary education included: the need to create and increase a high-level national "elite" who could replace foreign personnel who had directed administrative and commercial tasks; the need to increase personnel in such fields as agriculture; and the sociopolitical pressures from the community to expand long-denied higher education. Thus, Kenya's immediate educational goals were to produce local human resources and education for national development.

Like Kenya, Tanzania was confronted with innumerable problems of development during the first decade of independence. Hence, the Ministries of Finance, of Development Planning, and of Education issued development plans stressing the role of education, particularly primary and some secondary education, to meet basic human resource needs and to provide terminal education for students. The capstone educational policy (articulated in 1967 by former President Julius Nyerere), *Education for Self-Reliance* (ESR), received favorable domestic and international acclaim. Key ESR principles included (a) developing an *ujamma* or socialist outlook, particularly the tenets of equality and brotherhood which entail collective responsibility in all areas of activity, (b) equipping learners with knowledge, skills, and attitudes for tackling societal problems, and (c) enabling learners to appreciate and develop a Tanzanian culture that perpetuates the national heritage. Especially notable was a general prescription for reconstructing national culture through the educational system (Tanzania, United Republic of, 1984: 1-3; Saunders & Vulliamy, 1983: 355-356).

Several years later in Tanzania, a document known as the Musoma Resolution further declared the importance of socialist attitudes toward work via the integration of practice and theory from primary to higher education. While the original Musoma Resolution was soon modified, it still served as a basis for expanding the role of primary and adult education (Cooksey, 1986: 183-191; King, 1986: 2-3). Linking economic development to a socialist state was continually reiterated in education as evinced in government documents pertaining to education. Thus, socialism and education for self-reliance became Tanzania's twin goals.

In short, during the first decade of independence, both Kenya and Tanzania articulated plans for linking education and national development via the formal education system's role in manpower or human-resource development. Both countries presented these goals in terms of cultural values indigenous to Africa —African socialism in Kenya and *ujamma* in Tanzania. Education for self-reliance, however, would be a more integral part of the cultural and political milieu in Tanzania than African socialism was in Kenya. Such indigenous value systems emphasized equity, which must be kept in mind as we explore dimensions of African educational equity.

Prior to independence, Kenya's educational focus had been on primary education. After independence, there was a structural change from eight years of primary education for Africans to seven years in the 7-6-3 plan. Under this 7-6-3 organizational structure, students received seven years primary (standards 1-7), six years secondary (Forms I-VI), and three years university education. By the mid-1980s, 83% or about 4.5 million Kenyan children attended primary schools. However, only 500,000 were enrolled in secondary schools. About 26,000 students were enrolled in the four public universities in the late 1980s (Office of African Affairs, 1989a: 2).

In Tanzania, basic primary education has been emphasized since independence, resulting in the official literacy rate of nearly 75%. Primary-school enrollment increased from 53% of the age cohort in 1975 to 72% in 1985. Secondary school enrollment virtually remained the same between 1975 and 1985, hovering between 3 to 5% of the age group. However, since 1987, growth above primary education has been officially encouraged. About 5,000 students were matriculants at the University of Dar es Salaam by the close of the 1980s (Office of African Affairs, 1989b: 2; UNESCO, 1987; Tanzania, United Republic of, 1986: 43).

In both countries, enrollment in postsecondary institutions has been quite limited —less than 1% of the age cohort, and particularly limited for females. At the university level in Tanzania, for example, women graduates were about 11.5% in the 1970s. Although the percentage of women increased at the beginning of the 1980s, it steadily declined afterwards. In 1981, 24% of the undergraduate enrollees were women, 21.2% in 1982, 19.6% in 1983, 18.9% in 1984, and only 16% by 1985 (Kahama *et al.*, 1986; Tanzania, United Republic of, 1986). There were no notable enrollment increases among women in other segments of higher education to offset their decline in the university population. In short, less than 20% of students in tertiary institutions were women, and they were primarily studying liberal arts subjects.

In East Africa, as in England, the secondary-school examination system and curriculum have proven to be critical hindrances to educational equity. Essentially, the secondary-school examinations have served as screening devices to determine which students can enter the universities and secondary-school teacher-training institutions. After independence, the East African Certificate Examination (EACE) was administered after four years of secondary education while the East African Advanced Certificate Examination (EAACE) was administered after six years of secondary education to the select few who had passed the EACE. During the 1970s, each country began administering its own examinations. These country examinations focused on the liberal arts and sciences. Thus, the *de facto* curriculum emphasized such academic studies, despite official pronouncements encouraging vocational and agricultural subjects.

Consequently, many students left secondary school ill-equipped with requisite skills for the labor market. Both individual and national development were stifled.

United States of America

After World War II, the United States moved into a period of economic expansion. Comprehensive secondary education became available for virtually all Americans of European heritage. Federal legislation was passed to enable returning military veterans to pursue higher education and enter the various professions. Such legislation was consistent with general purposes of American education, which included: revitalizing the economy, providing for participation in the democratic process, meeting human needs by improving the quality of people's lives, and expanding educational opportunities (Commission on National Challenges in Higher Educatioin , 1988: 1-15) However, these provisions often eluded ethnic and racial minorities since the American legal system prevented their participation.

Prior to 1954, educational segregation of racial groups was legal in the United States. As a result of disadvantaged racial groups' challenging segregation through the courts, in 1954 the nation's Supreme Court, in the case of Brown versus Board of Education, declared that official or *de jure* segregation in public schools was unconstitutional. The decision extended to all tiers of the formal public education system. Although this official decision had been reached, contemporary practices and institutional structures often served as barriers that excluded African, Hispanic, Asian, and Native Americans. Educational equity was not to be evident. In the late 1950s and early 1960s, federal military units were called upon to enforce desegregation in such postsecondary institutions as the Universities of Alabama, Georgia, and Mississippi. By the mid-1960s, such force was no longer necessary.

Yet, few racial minority students and professionals were present on predominantly white college campuses, in major businesses, and in social and public agencies. As part of comprehensive social legislation of the 1960s, the United States Congress passed the Civil Rights Act of 1964 as an attempt to prohibit discrimination due to race, color, religion, sex, or national origin in employment policies and practices. Related to this Act was Executive Order 11246, issued in 1965 by President Lyndon Johnson. This order prohibited federal contractors from discriminating on the basis of race, color, religion, and national origin. The order was amended in 1968 by Executive Order 11375 to include discrimination based on sex (Raffel, 1979: 110-111; Moore & Wagstaff, 1974: 73-74; Bailey, 1978: 75).

As a result of these executive orders, affirmative action plans were introduced to promote fair treatment for those groups "who would in the ordinary course of events be victimized by discrimination" (Swinton, 1978: 111). When affirmative action plans were initiated on college campuses, they included not only employment practices for staff, but recruitment and admission policies for minority students. What *affirmative action* meant in these institutions was the development of programs for recruiting minority-group students, faculty, and staff in proportions that would approximate the percentages in which such minority groups were found within the nation's general population or within a state or geographicla region.

In 1970, the Legal Defense Fund of the National Association for the Advancement of Colored People (NAACP) filed suit against the then Department of Health, Education, and Welfare (HEW) in the case of Adams versus Richardson (Haynes, 1978). The suit was filed on behalf of students who attended public colleges that segregated and discriminated on the bases of race and on the part of taxpayers whose taxes were being expended by HEW in the form of grants to public colleges. Grants to institutions practicing discrimination were prohibited under Title VI of the 1964 Civil Rights Act. The suit stated that "HEW has declined to exercise its jurisdiction under Title VI with respect to institutions of higher education" (Hayes, 1979: 3). Title VI was not being enforced in a variety of states, primarily ones in the South where the majority of African-American students resided. Ultimately 19 states were required to submit plans for dismantling dual systems of higher education, one for whites and one for blacks.

Despite such legal and judicial decisions, educational equity was not the norm for minority Americans. For instance, while over 52% of the European Americans who began college in 1980 had completed the baccalaureate degree by 1986, only a quarter of African and Hispanic Americans had earned the degree. Within the general American population, about 25% of whites (between 25 and 34 years of age) had completed four years of college in 1980; this figure remained constant through 1988. For African Americans, only 12.4% and 13% (of the population between 25 and 34) had completed this level of education in 1980 and 1988, respectively. The picture was even bleaker for Hispanics, of whom only 8.9% and 11.9% in 1980 and 1988 had completed four years of college (Magner, 1989: A-36; National Center for Education Statistics, 1989: 53).

Another indicator of the extent of educational equity is the actual number of advanced degrees awarded to minority Americans. Statistics from 1977 are compared to 1985. In 1977, 20,017 doctoral degrees were awarded to European-American men compared to 15,017 in 1985. For white women the figures were 6,819 in 1977 and 8,917 in 1985. African-American men earned 766 doctoral degrees in 1977 and only 561 in 1985. For women, the numbers rose slightly from 487 in 1977 to 593 in 1985. Hispanic men earned 383 doctoral degrees in 1977 and 431 in 1985. Women earned 139 degrees in 1977 and 246 in 1985. For Native Americans, very few degrees were earned: 95 in 1977 and 119 in 1985. Of these 67 were awarded to men in 1977 and a meager 28 in 1985

(National Center for Education Statistics, 1989: 68). Similar statistics are evinced for first professional degrees in fields such as law, medicine, dentistry, and veterinary medicine. In 1987, only 7.5% of the medical school graduates were minority Americans.

What becomes evident is the acute decline in degrees awarded to African-American and Native-American men. (While doctorates awarded to white men decreased, evidence does not indicate that their career options have become limited). Although there has been an increase in the number of doctorates and professional degrees earned by minority women, the overall numbers are still quite small. The immediate beneficiaries of educational equity are European American women. Such women are increasingly attending undergraduate, graduate, and professional schools and remaining until graduation. Retention rates for minority Americans are not favorable. For example, only 27% of Hispanic students who enter college as freshmen ever graduate. The quality of the academic environments, as evinced in increased racial harassment and the absence of academic support programs for minorities, are not conducive to retention. Hence, high attrition becomes the norm. According to Marable (1989: 24), "academic apartheid has intensified. Well-meaning white college administrators have perceived the issue as a `Black' problem. The white university must accommodate our needs and interests...if the underlying factors which provoke racial harassment are to be addressed."

To sum up, we can say that *access* to secondary and higher education has become law in the United States. Yet, *outcomes* show that minorities have not achieved equal proportions of completion when compared with the white American majority. This is due in part to the conditions of learning within educational institutions.

POLICIES AND PROGRAMS FOR EDUCATIONAL EQUITY

Public policies may be viewed as the plans of action to accomplish goals of national and state governments. Legislation, judicial decisions, or executive actions are the bases for public policies which are often influenced by economic and fiscal considerations (Klein, 1987). Indeed, the previous section highlighted some continuing and emerging policy issues pertaining to educational equity. Within higher education, policies are overall procedures or methods designed for program administration. Policies translated into practice become programs. To be effective, policy implementation should be based upon a comprehension of the major dynamics which affect program implementation, that is, national, state, institutional, and individual roles and perceptions. In an ideal sense, policies are based upon underlying philosophical premises which should permeate the milieu of the educational system.

England

In 1987, the British Conservative government proposed an education bill which some scholars termed the most radical educational measure since the 1944 Education Act. This Bill became an Act in 1988, due to considerable efforts by Conservative legislators who wanted the central government to address educational problems that were not being addressed by educators and the local education authorities (LEAs). The role of the central government through the Department of Education and Science would be increased dramatically (McLean, 1988: 1-2; Miller, 1988a: 1-2; Miller, 1988b: 1-3; University of Exeter, 1988: 1). Opponents asserted that innovation would be stifled by drastically curtailing the powers of the LEAs. A notable example is the Inner London Education Authority (ILEA), which has often been in the forefront of plans for educational innovations, including those to enhance educational equity.

The Act, in effect, expanded some education policies which were introduced in 1986. It provided for a uniform national curriculum consisting of programs, subjects, and student attainment targets which would account for up to 80% of pupil time during compulsory schooling up to age 16. English "public" schools were exempt from the national curriculum, thus permitting them to continue catering to the privileged. New secondary-school polices were introduced that would provide for a more comprehensive curriculum and a new examination. The General Certification of Secondary Education (GCSE) was introduced for 16-year-olds as the examination to replace the GCE and CSE. Its proponents asserted that it provided a fair method of assessing knowledge and skills garnered in a comprehensive secondary-school curriculum. This examination should enable students to pursue higher education opportunities or to enter the labor market. Part of such direct intervention in the curriculum and schools also represented an attempt to address the need to provide skilled youth for the increasing demands of a technological and information society. It would remain to be seen whether greater educational equity would actually result for racial and cultural minorities and for working-class students via these new provisions which were not designed originally to promote equity *per se*.

Changing demographics mean that minorities have come to comprise 30 to 40% of some secondary-school enrollments —a substantial pool for higher education and the labor market. Yet, the numbers of all 16- to 18-year-olds are decreasing. For example, by 1994 the number of 16-year-olds would be expected to decline from 802,000 in 1981 to 532,000 (Libby & Hull, 1988: 9-10). Hence, secondary schools and higher-education institutions would be called on to become more responsive to all youth, and especially to minority youth. Some concrete programs have been introduced to accomplish this goal.

Access courses have been designed to bridge the gap between secondary schools and higher education. Specifically, such courses are to facilitate the entry to universities or polytechnical institutions for nontraditional students, that is, those students from ethnic minorities (especially persons of African descent), working-class youth, and women who face particular barriers to further and higher education. Access courses are characterized by the absence of formal secondary-education requirements, recognition of prior experiential learning, a needs-based and negotiated curriculum, guaranteed progression on to specified higher-education courses, and higher-education staff-involvement in organizing and teaching access courses (Further Education Unit, 1987). These courses actually provide a "first chance" for some nontraditional students.

Libby and Hull (1988: 10) have identified ways colleges will need to respond to the needs of nontraditional students. Special education needs (SEN) is one category for such students. Since 1978, many students who would have failed to gain access into higher education have matriculated and are having some of their needs addressed. Academic-support programs, including counseling and advising, are furnished by colleges and polytechnical institutes located in urban areas. Offering courses via open learning or independent courses has also provided accessibility.

Secretary of Education and Science Kenneth Baker proposed methods to increase the participation rate of 18- to 20-year-olds in colleges and universities. He set the goal of improving the participation rate from 13% to at least 30%. Moving toward U.S. American admissions patterns would help attract working class, ethnic and racial minorities, and women (Walker, 1989: A37). In essence, more students would enter by nontraditional routes as universities designed flexible admission criteria, particularly criteria not based primarily on secondary school examinations.

In sum, the equity problem in the British educational system became quite pronounced in the application of the 1944 Act. It perpetuated privileges for the elite class at the expense of the majority who did not have fair access to higher education. Some remedies may result from the 1988 Act which focused on secondary education, but also bore resource implications for higher education.

East Africa

Given the needs for national development and individual and family aspirations for education, two major policies for educational reform were introduced in Kenya and Tanzania in the 1980s: educational restructuring and the manpower-needs approach to national development.

In the 1970s the Kenyan Minister for Education established a major committee to examine educational policies, and the group produced the 1976 Report of the National Committee on Educational Objectives and Policy, better known as the Gacathi Report. Recommendations of the Gacathi Report and of a University Task Force in 1981 led to the restructuring of Kenya's educational system. In January 1985, Kenya shifted from the 7-6-3 English model to the present 8-4-4 one which, in essence, is a variation of the model evident throughout much of the United States. Eight years of primary, four years of secondary, and four years of university education are characteristic of the present design. The rationales for supporting the new 8-4-4 model suggested that it would provide: (a) a more comprehensive and relevant curriculum, (b) a more equitable distribution of educational resources, (c) greater emphasis on technical and vocational training, (d) appropriate assessment and evaluation, (e) increased opportunities for further education and training, and (f) a greater sense of national unity (Kenya, Republic of, 1984: 1, 2).

Students of the new 8-4-4 system took the Kenya Certificate of Secondary Education Examination (KCSE) for the first time in 1989. The KCSE covers a comprehensive range of subjects as prescribed in the national secondary curriculum —communication (including English, Kiswahili, and foreign languages), mathematics, science, humanities, applied education (including agriculture and industrial education), and physical education. National assessments in academic and applied subjects, along with continuous evaluation by teachers, were intended to enable students to develop skills which are immediately useful upon leaving school or in further education. Providing more educational access and comprehensive education for all students was a key goal of the innovation.

In Tanzania, a salient factor influencing the need for restructuring education was the realization in the early 1980s that many features of *ujamaa* and education for self-reliance simply had not worked. The cultural and sociopolitical realities were not integrated with national economic conditions and family and individual aspirations. That is, the small percentage of students in secondary schools (only 3% to 5% of the age group) and perceived inequities were the realities. Thus, in 1984, the Tanzanian Presidential Commission Report on Education (Urch, 1989) was approved by the ruling party and government. A manpower-needs approach would be used in preference to the social-demands approach. Scientific and technological growth would be promoted along with vocational education. Hence, the curriculum and assessment would need modifications to accommodate the manpower-needs plan. Overwhelming agreement existed among the Ministry of Education and senior university and college administrators that a top priority was intensive training for preservice and inservice secondary teachers to address manpower and national-development needs.

The country's leaders recognized that national development is virtually impossible without highly skilled professionals in science, mathematics, and technical fields. Hence, fiscal resources have been targeted in these areas for the remaining years of this century to enhance the prospects for national development (Tanzania, United Republic of, 1982; Tanzania, United Republic of, 1986). Women are not well represented in some of these areas. As stated previously, less than 20% of Tanzanian university matriculants are women. In short, policies designed to promote national development and educational equity must clearly incorporate plans to include systematically the participation of women. A comprehensive secondary curriculum and testing on a variety of subjects should help enable females to compete more equally with their male peers who study in scientific and technical fields.

United States of America

The volume *One-Third of A Nation* asserted that leadership is perhaps the most crucial factor for minority advancement in the United States. The American president, legislators, and college and university presidents would have pivotal roles. Such leaders would need to recognize their interdependence and decide that attention to the total education system and its impact on minorities should be among their highest priorities (Commission on Minority Participation in Education and American Life, 1988: 24-28).

Keith (May, 1987: 11) and Clewell and Ficklen (June 1986: 52-55) have described how leadership by top university administrators is a key ingredient in effective policy implementation to increase minority participation at the institutional level. For example, the performance-evaluation of senior-line administrators (vice-presidents, deans, and directors) should be directly linked to their units' success in recruiting students and faculty, graduating minority students, and tenuring and promoting minority faculty and professional staff. Policies of accountability are essential components for administrators who ultimately affect changes to enhance educational equity.

Admission criteria should be reexamined for minority students. Blackwell (1981: 255-256), after analyzing selection criteria for graduate and professional schools, has pointed out that it is often asserted that minorities are not "qualified" for post-baccalaureate programs because their scores are lower than their white male peers. Yet, data indicate that the mean grade-point-averages (GPA) and Law School Aptitude Test (LSAT) scores for minorities matriculating in the early 1980s were comparable to those for white males in the middle and late 1960s. Keen competition had forced GPAs and LSATs to be higher over the two decades. But surely it cannot be argued that white males who graduated in the middle and late 1960s could not complete law school and become attorneys. Similarly, Nettles' research (1989: 12) indicates that Scholastic Aptitude Test (SAT) scores tend to overpredict the performance of African Americans. When SAT scores project that African-American and European-American students are likely to earn grades of *A*, and they are otherwise comparable, the African Americans will get lower grades. What this strongly suggests is that there are conditions in the college environment —in the learning-support system and in racism— which influence grades. Thus, SAT scores are not as salient as typically envisioned.

Research and evaluation data evince several recurrent themes regarding means of altering components of the college structure to provide viable support services for minority students so attrition is lessened and graduation prospects enhanced. Major components of the college structure include orientation, counseling, tutoring, housing, the role of majority and minority faculty, and extracurricular activities. For example, orientation sessions (which may be conducted throughout the freshman year) can provide students with assurances of belonging, the opportunity to learn what their programs require, and detailed information on academic and personal resources for assistance. The latter is of particular significance, since academic programs are often inadequate or connote negative stigma. Those developmental studies programs which provide remedial education for large numbers of minorities, in contrast to programs enrolling both majority and minority students, are often viewed negatively.

One policy which appears to have enhanced educational equity is the AHANA (Afro-American, Hispanic, Asian, and Native-American) program at Boston College where 12.5% of the students have been minorities. College officials have been convinced that the program's name, AHANA, helps attract students in contrast to some term that would clearly emphasize minority status in the sense of *minority* meaning "less than." AHANA has offered students a range of services, from tutoring to personal and academic counseling. The program is situated in a house where a variety of extracurricular activities also occur. Prior to the plan's inception, the graduation rate for minorities was only 17%; by 1989 it had reached 75% (Dodge, 1989: A38). While it cannot be argued definitively that AHANA was the sole factor in the improved retention and graduation rates, students have credited it with being an influential force.

Changing the learning environment to adapt to minority students' needs is another policy and program consideration. Several strategies have been incorporated into various programs. Extending the time for students to complete their degrees to four-and-a-half or five years has been one strategy. Employing and tenuring faculty who devote their energies solely to teaching rather than partially to research has been another. Finally, changing curriculum requirements to permit more flexibility in students' studies has been a further means to foster educational equity.

While initial access to education is the foundation on which virtually all other opportunity structures rest, equity only begins with access. According to Sudarkasa (1987: 4-13) and Marable (1989: 24-25), college curricula usually reflect little of the cultural diversity and pluralism characteristic of American society. Moreover, even less evident are the perspectives, scholarship, and creative works of minority scholars in the social and physical sciences and the arts and humanities. For example, Africans are strategically omitted from presentations of scientific, technological, and political developments that characterized the Age of Discovery or the Middle Ages —the period that provided the foundation for the Industrial Revolution. Ignoring minority contributions is tantamount to relegating them to inferior status since, after all, people are inferior if they were incapable of making contributions. Thus, minority students and scholars at institutions as diverse as Stanford, the University of California (Berkeley), American University, and the University of Miami have helped incorporate courses on minorities or Third World people into the core curriculum requirements for the baccalaureate degree. Such courses are taught by both minority and majority scholars.

In speaking of the centrality of policies pertaining to equity, a former secretary of education stated that American society has not moved far enough in its efforts wherein the government and universities can be uniform in the administration of policies. Some policies, such as affirmative action, can be justified philosophically and politically for a test of fairness if "we can say a certain group exits (in its present condition) because of past policies that have denied opportunity" (Bell, 1987). This perspective highlights the dilemma facing academe, especially since majority students and faculty often contend that they are now the victims of reverse discrimination. That is, some majority-group individuals claim that, with affirmative-action opportunities furnished for minority groups, equal educational opportunities are not now available to members of the majority population. If ensuring educational equity for all is the humanistic goal, then in the intermediate range, this means recognizing that centuries of racism have not been erased so that some dislocations may occur for European Americans as minorities are given due attention —particularly minority males— in the quest for educational equity (Bell, 1989: 12). But the larger principle of equality, however, must ultimately be preserved so that individuals are judged on the basis of their personal characteristics rather than on their gender, ethnicity and origins, religion, or social-class status.

EVALUATION AND EDUCATIONAL EQUITY

What emerges from the preceding discussion is the identification of culture-specific and generic factors affecting educational equity in England, East Africa, and the United States. The illustrations have included the roles of public and education policies and programs, examinations, curriculum, admissions criteria, and support programs in pursuit of equity. Observing the design and implementation of policies and programs, which address this variety of factors attempting to enhance educational equity, necessitates a succinct examination of the roles of evaluation.

If the "purpose of evaluation is not to prove but to improve" (Stufflebeam *et al.*, 1971), then it is important to identify an array of evaluation paradigms or components thereof to help ascertain policy and program effectiveness. Naturalistic/qualitative methods, case and multiple-case studies, and thematic paradigms which integrate the conceptual and practical appear particularly appropriate for assessing educational equity.

As stated in the initial part of this chapter, naturalistic or qualitative evaluation is characterized by the attempt to understand social phenomenon and meanings shared among participants within the culture. This type of evaluation can be "messy" since deduction and induction and interpretations of different world views occur simultaneously. But the method helps ascertain whether minority students, educators, and parents perceive educational equity in secondary schools and colleges, in contrast to what are articulated as the ostensible purposes and outcomes by the majority decision-makers. Moreover, qualitative or naturalistic evaluations are particularly appropriate when approaches and "treatments may be individualized and focused on programs [that] are tailored...to persons receiving service" (Institute for Program Evaluation, 1983; Yin & Heald, 1975: 374-375). Flexible admissions criteria —including access courses and various ways of determining the weight of such tests as the GCSE, SAT, or LSAT —for nontraditional and minority students in England and the United States are examples of evaluations for the purpose of providing individual services.

Single or multi-site case studies attempt to assess a phenomenon in its contextual totality. Generalizations can be made from multiple case studies (Goetz & LeCompte, 1984; Patton, 1982; Yin, 1982). Such studies lend themselves to examining various stages, strategies, causal processes, and barriers. Multi-site studies can address the same issues or questions in several settings (Firestone & Herriott, 1984). Hence, the findings from different sites may be integrated to form a comprehensive perspective. For example, examining the roles of support programs for minority students in England and the United States may provide some comprehensive perspectives on increasing student retention.

Multi-site case studies could enable comparative educators and researchers to help ascertain if the new 8-4-4 system in Kenya is adapted sufficiently to the African context. Or, might the system promote some of the negative features of the American structure in which minorities can be tracked into restricted curricula and remedial classes via standardized tests? Multi-site evaluations can stimulate cross-national dialogues between Africans, Americans, and British educators that might help ensure the transference and adaptation of positive features which contribute to educational equity.

According to Stufflebeam *et al.* (1971), there are four conceptual components to discern in evaluation: context, input, process, and product. Context evaluation aids in the planning of an ongoing program. It seeks to discover discrepancies between possible actions and likely results, that is, comparing actual and intended program outcomes. When planning and designing academic-support programs or major curriculum alternations, planners find context evaluation to be appropriate. Input evaluation aids decision-making when a key concern is that of making program goals operational. What should be added to or deleted from a program are key concerns.

Process evaluation serves the day-to-day decision-making needs. It provides feedback to the producers and managers of the program to monitor the operations and detect and predict potential problems of implementation. The level of fiscal and human resources, logistics, interpersonal relationships, and communications can be garnered through this form of assessment —often identified as formative evaluation. Requesting more resources can be made via this evaluation process. Understanding the multiple roles of minority and majority faculty in academic advising and student assessment are parts of process evaluation.

Product evaluation measures and interprets program attainments or outcomes. It focuses on the extent to which goals have been achieved, a form of summative evaluation. Thus, ascertaining whether students who study the new comprehensive curriculum and take the new GCSE in England or the KCSE in Kenya are able to pursue a variety of postsecondary options, compared to the old systems, could be examined through product evaluation. Perhaps the results will be comparable to those witnessed in the United States, where comprehensive secondary curricula have existed throughout the 20th century. But *de facto* tracking of racial and ethnic minorities has precluded a range of postsecondary options in comparison to those available to white students.

Evaluation provides responses to fundamental questions and issues regarding policies and programs to enhance educational equity. For example, what are the continuing impetuses within education institutions to design programs that increase access and retention of under-represented groups? What processes help ensure that scholarly perspectives of minority groups are incorporated into the curriculum? What is the relative importance of less tangible factors, such as the perspectives of minority and majority students and the racial and class prejudice of teachers and administrators, in affecting educational outcome? As such issues are explored, we observe that integrating policy and program implementation with evaluation helps build bridges leading to the avenues of educational equity.

PROSPECTS FOR THE FUTURE

Peering into the educational and social crystal balls of countries as diverse as England, Kenya, Tanzania, and the United States is risky, at best. But this peering does provide the opportunity to be at the forefront to address ongoing changes affecting equity. It would appear that the three following salient issues will continue to dominate the realm of educational equity as we move into the 21st century.

Matching Rhetoric with Reality

The first and most fundamental of these issues is that of matching rhetoric with reality. The stated and ostensible purposes of education eloquently reflect premises of the national and federal constitutions in the respective countries.

Nevertheless, exclusion, attrition, and omissions in education belie the eloquence. In English and American secondary schools and colleges, minority males —those of African, Hispanic, and Native-American descent— will likely continue to be excluded and to experience disproportionately high attrition rates compared to males of European descent. For minority women, access may remain constant, at its present low participation rates, or may increase in limited instances. Yet on two levels, access and attrition conditions will not bode well for minorities.

On the one hand, there will be continuing economic disparities for English and American ethnic and racial minorities. The absence of competitive skills gained via secondary schools and colleges will mean that unemployment, underemployment, and limited opportunities to enter blue- and white-collar occupations will be the reality. Poverty will abound. On the other hand, harsh psychological burdens will be prevalent, since poverty has a tremendous psychological impact. For the few minority females who successfully complete higher education, the severe paucity of "suitable" male partners will take a psychological toll, despite some valiant offers that these women graduates make to be androgynous and to explore alternative life styles.

In Kenya and Tanzania, limited access to quality education will continue for rural and ethnic-minority youth. Thus, as in England and the United States, economic disparities will be more pronounced between urban and rural residents and between the affluent and those living in abject poverty. The benefits of national development plans will not be enjoyed by such disadvantaged groups.

In the U. S. and English education systems, it is likely that descriptions of the contributions of ethnic and racial minorities to those societies will continue to be omitted from curriculum materials. As a result, educational equity for both minority-group and majority-group youth will not be fully realized. For minority youth, the omission means the perpetuation of the myth that their contributions were nil, while majority educators and students will continue to believe the myth and thus continue to attribute negative stereotypes to minorities. Neither group will be able to examine those roles and contributions of all which can enhance humanistic conditions for everyone in contemporary society. In East Africa, omissions from the curricula are not as glaring as during the colonial era and in the early years of political independence. However, accurate accounts of the current roles of indigenous Africans and illustrations of contributions of minority groups in England and the United States should be integrated into the curricular content of the four countries, thereby enlightening students, educators, and the general populace.

Promoting the Use of Modern Technologies

The second salient issue affecting educational equity will be the roles of Africans and minority-group English and Americans in promoting the use of contemporary and future technologies. A prominent illustration is the use and impact of computers. It is virtually impossible to communicate today in England and the United States —other than in face-to-face conversation— without the aid of some type of computer. International communication occurs via computer linkages throughout the world. African nations' development will be aided to the extent that domestic and international computer usage occurs.

Minority English and American youth, more often than their white peers, attend secondary schools in which there are either no computers or the use of computers is limited. In effect, innovations are not usually introduced to minority youth. Instead, they may be the recipients of out-dated technologies, as was the practice during the years of racial segregation when only second-hand or dated textbooks and curriculum materials were provided for American minorities and Africans. Increasingly it is becoming necessary for employees in such societies as those of the United States and England to be able to operate a computer, even in entry-level or menial positions in such businesses as fast-food restaurants. Computer literacy is becoming even more of a prerequisite to functioning in offices and white-collar positions.

Political and Economic Conditions

Changes in domestic and international political and economic conditions form the third set of factors affecting educational equity. Recent studies indicate that, despite a continuing attrition rate, more American minority youth are graduating from secondary school than ever before. Yet, fewer are matriculating at colleges. In 1989, about 30% of African-American youth from working-class backgrounds attended college, compared to nearly 40% in 1976. For middle-class youth, about 36% entered colleges in 1988 compared to approximately 53% in 1976. The picture was particularly abysmal for African-American men —only 28% attended in 1988 compared to 53% in 1976 (Wingert, 1990: 75).

While some of the reasons for the declining attendance rates have been discussed earlier in this chapter, a further major reason is the conservative political and economic climate in the United States in recent years. For example, the financial-aid provisions that the U. S. Congress and the executive branch have enacted are limited to only the lowest-income applicants. Students from working-class and middle-class families are excluded. Yet, for many minorities, being part of the middle class is, at best, a very precarious position —only one or two months away from low-income status. In the future, "financial need" will have to be defined more broadly if minority youth are to experience educational equity through college attendance.

Of particular concern to American youth is the shifting of emphasis away from the central government and onto state and local governments for designing and enforcing measures of educational opportunity. American history has clearly demonstrated that state and local institutions have continually lagged behind in providing equal educational opportunities for minorities. Perhaps the positive strides that were made at the federal level in the 1960s and 1970s can be can be transferred successfully to state and local governments. But creative pressures exerted by minority educators and parents will likely be needed to help ensure educational equity.

From an American perspective, it appears rather ironic that England is currently moving toward centralization of curriculum construction in an effort to help guarantee uniform quality in educational conditions. Yet, this move occurs under a conservative Tory Party which has not seemed overly concerned with educational equity. The driving force behind this move is apparently not so much a concern for the plight of minorities as it is a desire to make the nation more competitive on the international economic scene. Perhaps this ironic twist may provide further seeds for educational equity, since some policy makers assert that local education authorities have parochial perspectives. But the approach may be tempered if successive appointees to the post of Minister of Education and Science continue to be made from among the ranks of the Tory party.

Critics have suggested that shortcomings of educational efforts in East Africa are often the result of the direct transfer of features of Western societies that are unsuitable in the African setting. One such feature is the economic dependence of East African societies on the West. If educational equity is to be dispersed throughout East Africa, it will be necessary for the dependency relationship to be changed into one of economic and sociopolitical interdependency. Because Kenya and Tanzania are still in a state of national and educational development, they can profit in the future from examining closely features of Western education that foster inequities and thereby can more readily avoid adopting such features. A reexamination of traditional and emerging East African educational goals and practices may provide new paradigms that build bridges between socioeconomic conditions and educational institutions that can lead to boulevards of equity.

REFERENCES

Andambi, M. (1984) *The launching of the 8-4-4 education system.* Nairobi: Kenyatta University College, Bureau of Educational Research.

Bailey, R. (1978) *Minority admissions.* Lexington, MA: D. C. Health.

Bell, T. (1987, June 24) Comments made at the University of Georgia Seminar on Educational Policies, Athens, GA.

Bell, D. (1989) Legal scholars explore contemporary impact of Brown decision. *Black Issues in Higher Education*, 6 (18): 12-13.

Blackwell, J. (1981) *Mainstream outsiders: The Production of the black professionals.* Bayside, NY: General Hall.

Broadfoot, P. (1985) Comparative perspectives on the reform examinations. In K. Watson (Ed.), *Key issues in education: Comparative perspectives* (pp. 7-17). London: Croom Helm.

Brown vs. Board of Educatrion

Bruce, M. (1985) Teacher education since 1944: Providing the teachers and controlling the providers. *British Journal of Educational Studies*, 33 (2): 164-172.

Bruce, M. (1988) Making the grade or marking time? *Phi Delta Kappan*, 69 (5): 383-384.

Cheru, F. (1987) *Independence, underdevelopment, and unemployment in Kenya.* Lanham, MD: University Press of America.

Clewell, B., & Ficklen, M. (1986) *Improving minority retention in higher education: A search for effective institutional practices.* Princeton, NJ: Educational Testing Services.

Commission on Minority Participation in Education and American Life (1986) *One-third of a nation.* Washington, DC: American Council on Education.

Commission on National Challenges in Higher Education (1988). *Memorandum to the 41st president of the United States.* Washington, DC: American Council on Education.

Cooksey, B. (1986) Policy and practice in Tanzania secondary education since 1986. *International Journal of Educational Development*, 6 (3): 183-202.

Department of Education & Science (1965) Circular 10/65

Dodge, S. (1989) A center helps minority student solve academic, social problems. *The Chronicle of Higher Education*, 36 (13): A38.

Dorr-Bremme, D. (9185) Ethnographic evaluation: A theory and method. *Educational Evaluation and Policy Analysis*, 7 (spring): 65-83.

Firestone, W., & Harriott, R. (1984) Multisite qualitative policy research: Some design ad implementation issues. In D. M. Fetterman (Ed.), *Ethnography in educational evaluation.* Beverly Hills, CA: Sage.

Further Education Unit (1987) *Access to further and higher education.* London: Department of Education and Science.

Goetz, J., & LeCompte, M. (1984) *Ethnography and qualitative design in education research h.* Los Angeles: University of California, Center for Study of Evaluation, Monograph Series in Evaluation No. 8.

Haynes, L. *A critical examination of the Adams case: A source book.* Washington, DC: Institute for Services to Education.

Haynes, L. (Ed.) (1979) *An analysis of the Arkansas-Georgia statewide desegregation.* Washington, DC: Institute for Services to Education.

Holmes, B. (1985) *Equality and freedom in education: A comparative study.* London: Allen & Unwin.

Institute for Program Evaluation (1983) *The evaluation synthesis.* Washington, DC: General Accounting Office.

Jomo Kenyatta Foundation (1973) Curriculum guides for secondary schools (Vol. 2). Nairobi: Author.

Jones, C. (1985) Education in England and Wales: A national system locally administered. In B. Holmes (Ed.), *Equality and freedom in education: A comparative study* (pp. 24-62). London: Allen & Unwin.

Judge, H. (1984, September) *Teacher education in England and Wales.* Paper presented at the meeting of the National Commission for Excellence in Teacher Education, Minneapolis.

Kahama, C., Maliyamkond, T., & Wells, S. (1986) *The challenge for Tanzania's economy.* London: James Curry.

Keith, L. (1987, May) *Blacks in higher education in the 1980s: An assessment.* Paper presented at the annual conference on minorities, Athens, GA.

Kenya, Republic of (1972) *Ministry of Commerce and Industry.* Nairobi: Government Printer.

Kenya, Republic of (1984) *8-4-4 system of education.* Nairobi: Government Printer.

King, K. (1986) *Evaluating the context of diversified secondary education in Tanzania: Preliminary comments.* London: University of London Institute of Education.

Klein. S. (1987, April) *The role of public policy in the education of girls and women.* Paper presented at the annual conference of the American Educational Research Association, Washington, DC.

Libby, D., & Hull, R. (1988) The LEA, the college, and the community. In B. Kennedy & D. Parkes (Eds.), *Planning the FE curriculum: Implications of the 1988 Education Reform Act.* London: Further Education Unit.

Lindsay, B. (1980) Educational testing in Kenya. *Journal of Negro Education,* 49 (3): 274-288.

Lockheed, M., & Verspoor, A. (1989) *Improving primary education in developing countries: A review of policy options.* Washington, DC: The World Bank.

Magner, D. (1989) Colleges try new ways to insure minority students make it to graduation. *The Chronicle of Higher Education* , 36 (13): 1.

Marable, M. (1989) Beyond academic apartheid. *Black issues in higher education,* 6 (19): 24-25.

McKenna, F., & Best, J. (1989) *Schooling America.* State University, PA: Division of Educational Policy Studies, College of Education.

McLean, M. (1988, March) *Educational reform in industrial market economies: Corporatist and contract strategies.* Paper presented at the annual conference of the Comparative and International Education Society, Atlanta.

Miller, H. (1988a, March) *Global education policies.* Paper presented at the annual conference of the Comparative and International Education Society, Atlanta.

Miller, H. (1988b, March) *Structure and policy changes: Illustrations from higher education: The British case.* Paper presented at the annual conference of the Comparative and International Education Society, Atlanta.

Moore, W., & Wagstaff, L. (1974) *Black educators in white colleges.* San Francisco, CA: Jossey-Bass.

National Center for Education Statistics (1989) *The condition of education 1989* (Vol. 2). Washington, DC: U.S. Department of Education .

National Public Radio (1989, December 13). *Morning edition.*

Nettles, M. (1989) Black and white students' college performance in majority white and majority black academic settings. In *Title VI regulation of higher education: Problems and progress.* New York: Teachers College Press.

Office of African Affairs (1989a, January) *Country data: Kenya.* Washington, DC: U.S. Information Agency.

Office of African Affairs (1989b, January) *Country data: Tanzania.* Washington, DC: U.S. Information Agency.

Office of European Affairs (1989, January) *Country data: Britain.* Washington, DC: U.S. Information Agency.

Patton, M. (1982) *Practical evaluation.* Beverly Hills, CA: Sage.

Raffel, N. (1979) Federal laws and regulations prohibiting sex discrimination. In E. Snyder (Ed.), *The study of women: Enlarging perspectives of social reality.* New York: Harper & Row.

Rono, P. (1988, March) *Education reforms in Kenya in the independence period.* Paper presented at the annual conference of the Comparative and International Education Society, Atlanta.

Saunders, M. & Vulliamy, G. (1983) The implementation of curricular reform: Tanzania and Papua New Guinea. *Comparative Education Review*, 27 (3): 351-373.

Sifuna, D. (1983) Kenya: Twenty year of multilateral aid. *Prospects*, 13 (4): 481-492.

Stufflebeam, D., *et al.* (1971) (Eds.) *Educational evaluation and decision making.* Itasca, IL: F. E. Peacock.

Sudarkasa, N. (1987). Racial and cultural diversity is a key part of the pursuit of excellence in the university. *AAHE Publications: Bulletin: News and Information*, 39 (6): 42.

Swinton, D. (1978) Affirmative action in a declining economy. In C. Smith (Ed.), *Advancing equality of opportunity: A matter of justice.* Washington, DC: Howard University Press.

Tanzania, United Republic of (1986) *Basic education statistics in Tanzania (BEST) 1981-1986.* Dar es Salaam: Ministry of Education.

Tanzania, United Republic of (1984) *Basic facts about education in Tanzania.* Dar es Salaam: Ministry of Education.

Tanzania, United Republic of (1982) *Educational system in Tanzania: Toward the year 2000.* Dar es Salaam: Ministry of Education.

UNESCO (1987) *World education at a glance.* Paris: UNESCO Office of Statistics.

University of Exeter (1988, March). *Agenda number 154.* Exeter: Author.

Urch, G. (1989) *Educational technology and third world development: A Tanzania case study.* Paper presented at the annual conference of the Comparative and International Education Society, Cambridge, MA.

Walker, D. (1989) British cabinet minister calls for recognition to create an American-style university system. *The Chronicle of Higher Education,* January 18: A37.

Watson, K. (1985) *Key issues in education: Comparative perspectives.* London: Croom Helm.

Wiley, E. (1989) Stereotypes, prejudice hindering Hispanic women in academia. *Black Issues in Higher Education*, 6 (2): 1, 8-9.

Wingert, P. (1990) Fewer blacks on campus. *Newsweek,* January 29: 75.

Yin, R. (1982) The case study crisis: Some answers. In E. House, *et al.* (Eds.), *Evaluation studies review annual* (Vol. 7). Beverly Hills, CA: Sage.

Yin, R., & Heald, V. (1975) Using the case survey method to analyze policy studies. *Administrative Science Quarterly*, 20 (Fall): 371-381.

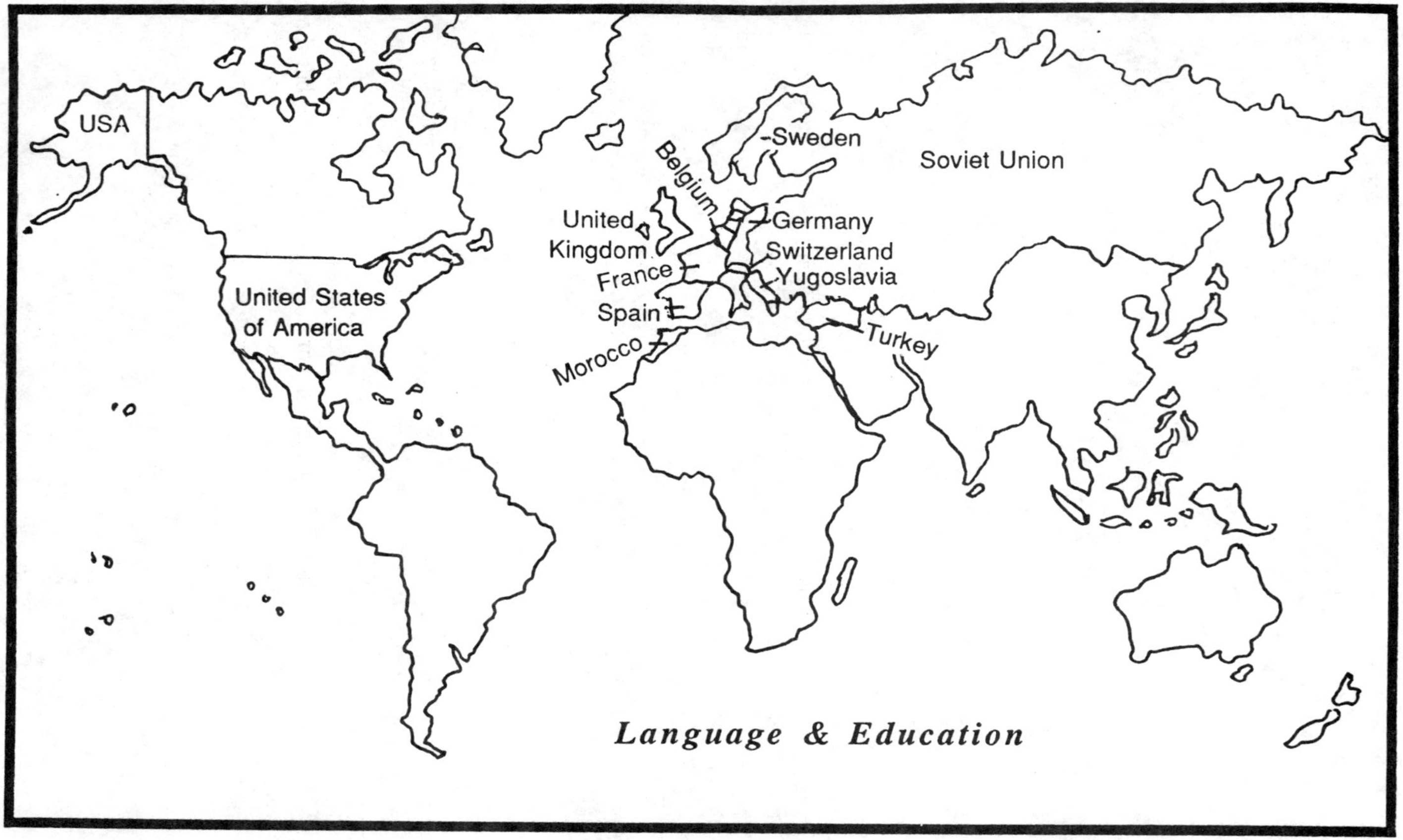
USA
United States of America
United Kingdom
France
Spain
Morocco
Belgium
Sweden
Germany
Switzerland
Yugoslavia
Turkey
Soviet Union
Language & Education

CHAPTER 9

Language and Education

In the world's education systems, what is the status of language as a goal and as an instrument for learning?

LESLIE J. LIMAGE[1]

The whole notion of modern-day education is founded on two assumptions about language. The first assumption concerns language skills as desired outcomes of education —language as a goal. The second concerns language skills as instruments in the process of education —language as a learning tool. More precisely, the assumptions are:

Assumption 1: Language as a Desired Educational Outcome The most important means of communication among people is spoken and written language. The more skillfully people use language, the more adequately they can manage their social relations, their occupations, their role as citizens, and the expression of their feelings. Thus, a central task of the education system is to promote learners' ability to speak, to understand speech, to read, and to write at least their native tongue and, preferably, as many other languages as may significantly contribute to their welfare.

Assumption 2: Language as an Instrument for Learning With rare exception the effectiveness of education depends primarily on the ability of the learners to understand speech and to express themselves orally (oracy) in the language that is used for instruction. And beyond the earliest years of childhood, success in an education system also typically depends on the learners' skill in reading and writing (literacy) in the instructional language, since the content of education is so often conveyed in printed form and so often requires written responses from the learners. Therefore, students who lack sufficient literacy skills not only fail to progress adequately in the language-arts portion of the curriculum, but they usually fail in the other subject-matter areas as well, particularly in those areas in which reading and writing are essential, such as mathematics, the physical sciences, and the social sciences.

In view of the foregoing assumptions, the central question addressed in this chapter needs to be set in a very broad context. As will be seen, the choice of languages in different learning settings involves the complex interaction of a large number of factors. And political, economic, and social concerns can easily preempt purely pedagogical ones. As William Mackey has pointed out: "All languages are equal only before God and the linguist" (Mackey, 1984: 43).

Therefore, we shall look successively at a number of broader issues in which the choice of language of instruction is embedded. First of all, we need to have some understanding of the literacy situation in the world. Secondly, we should examine the political and economic climate in which decisions about educational investment are being made. Thirdly, we need to have some understanding of what is meant when we talk about *literacy* and *illiteracy* in a comparative and international perspective. This understanding then enables us to inspect more closely the role of language policies in specific countries and groups of countries. Only then are we in a fairly knowledgeable position to review the impact of language choice on an individual's enhanced participation in society. Finally, we can ask ourselves, what are the prospects for various language policies to evolve which successfully respond to individual and group priorities?

THE LITERACY SITUATION IN THE WORLD

The Unesco Office of Statistics regularly analyzes the literacy situation in the world as well as a number of other indicators of participation in education. In November 1989, it completed such an analysis. Table 9-1 illustrates the major findings. The number of adult illiterates (15 years old or above) in 1985 was estimated at 965 million, with the worldwide illiteracy rate 29.9% of all adults. That figure was expected to decrease to 962.6 million by 1990. Thus, the numbers should continue to decline slowly. Yet if past trends continue, there will still be 942 million illiterates in the year 2000, representing 22 per cent of the adult population. In this same year, all but 23.5 million of the 942 million illiterates will be found in the developing countries. The decrease in the absolute number of illiterates will be observed only in developing countries of Eastern Asia (which includes China), in Latin America and the Caribbean, and in the industrialized countries.

The world illiteracy rates were also projected to decline from 29.9% in 1985 to 26.9% in 1990 and to 22% in 2000. However, there is considerable variation in the extent of this decline between different groups of countries. For example, between 1985 and 2000, the rate in Sub-Saharan Africa is expected to drop 18.8 percentage points compared to 16.4 percentage points for the Arab States, 6.3 for Latin America and the Caribbean, and approximately 12 points for both Eastern and Southern Asia.

In the developing countries in 1990, adult illiteracy rates were highest in Southern Asia (53.8%), followed by Sub-Saharan Africa (52.7%), Arab States (48.7%), Eastern Asia (24%), and Latin America and the Caribbean (15.2%). This ranking is expected to remain valid in the year 2000, although individual rates will likely decrease.

Table 9-1

Adult Illiterates and Illiteracy Rates for Both Sexes
Years 1985, 1990, 2000

*Adult Illiterates** (in millions)*	*1985*	*1990*	*2000*
World total	965.1	962.6	942.0
Developing countries	908.1	920.6	918.5
in the regions of:			
Sub-Saharan Africa	133.6	138.8	146.8
Arab States	58.6	61.1	65.8
Latin America and the Caribbean	44.2	43.5	40.9
Eastern Asia	297.3	281.0	233.7
Southern Asia	374.1	397.3	437.0
Developed countries	57.0	42.0	23.5

*Illiteracy Rates** (percentages)*	*1985*	*1990*	*2000*	*% Decrease 1985-2000*
World total	22.9	26.9	22.0	—7.9
Developing countries	39.4	35.1	28.1	—11.3
in the regions of:				
Sub-Saharan Africa	59.1	52.7	40.3	—18.8
Arab States	54.5	48.7	38.1	—16.4
Latin America and the Caribbean	17.6	15.2	11.3	—6.3
Eastern Asia	28.7	24.0	17.0	—11.7
Southern Asia	57.7	53.8	45.9	—11.8
Developed countries	6.2	4.4	2.3	—3.9

Note: The foregoing are preliminary results. Countries and territories with less than 300,000 inhabitants have not been taken into account. Some countries are classified at the same time as Sub-Saharan Africa and as Arab States.

*Adults = those age 15 and over

**Percent of population over age 15 that are illiterate

Source: Unesco Office of Statistics, 1989

In 1990 the illiteracy rates were estimated to be higher than 40% in 49 countries, 30 of them in Sub-Saharan Africa. If this trend is not modified, in the year 2000 there will still be 33 countries in the same situation, 22 of them in Sub-Saharan Africa.

These figures do not distinguish between men and women who are illiterate. Invariably, however, women have higher rates of illiteracy, and the differences in percentage points between the sexes are quite large in Africa and Asia (21 points in 1985) but much smaller in Latin America and the Caribbean (4 points). These figures on adult illiteracy in the world do not take account, of course, of the more than 140 million school-age children who have never attended any formal or non-formal educational institution. Nor do they take account of a similar number of children who drop-out prior to completing four years of primary schooling. Further, they make no reference to the uncalculated numbers of children who have seen the quality of their primary schooling severely eroded as a result of persistent economic austerity.

[Note: Unesco statistics are based on figures provided by governments of its member states. They are usually based on census data. Thus, the Office of Statistics may be using data collected at different times in different countries. The census information may be based on a simple question, such as "How many people in your household can read or write?" What is meant by literacy and illiteracy may be different or unclear. Therefore, it is important to recall that these figures should be treated with caution. They do not provide a valid ranking of countries and are only roughly comparable. They indicate broad trends; the methodology to project these trends is constantly being refined.]

THE CHANGING POLITICAL AND ECONOMIC CLIMATE

This brings us to the political and economic climate worldwide and how it affects the quality and quantity of educational provision. Doing so helps us to situate efforts to ensure the development of a fully literate world. Looking back, we find the 1960s and early 1970s were a period of optimism concerning the value of education to enhance the life chances of all young people. The world enjoyed a period of enormous educational expansion as well as innovation in the form of compensatory measures to ensure equality of opportunity. The democratization-of-education movement guided major policy shifts in both industrialized and developing countries. But with the onset of economic recession about 1974, governments began looking more closely at the social sector as a whole. Education loomed up as the most probable area for saving. Why education? As Keith Lewin of the University of Sussex (United Kingdom) in a study for Unesco has pointed out:

> Social sector spending is more likely to be under domestic control than, say, debt servicing and is therefore more immediately susceptible to government action. Second, as one of the largest segments of social expenditure, it presents itself as having the greatest potential for substantial savings. Third, where economic policy favours a diminution in the role of the state and limitation in the services that it is responsible for, social services as a whole are likely to be vulnerable. Finally, where short-term planning horizons are dominant, it is those sectors which have long lead times and long-term benefits that appear least attractive (Lewin, 1986: 223).

These views continue to dominate policy making in numerous industrialized and developing countries.

The 1980s were particularly hard on the poorest countries, indeed on poor people everywhere. In more than half of the least-developed countries, per pupil expenditure on primary education declined in real terms to the point that the education systems are on the verge of collapse. A Unesco study appearing in 1990 shows that primary education enrollment is dropping in one out of every five developing countries. In some African nations, primary-school student numbers declined between 1980 and 1985 by as much as one-third. Policies to restructure economies, devised to deal with the debt crisis, are contributing to this educational deterioration. Even when inflation is taken into account, educational spending per primary school student has declined over the last decade in half of the world's countries.

The quality of education is also suffering. For example, two-thirds of the teachers in developing countries currently receive lower salaries than they did in 1980. Class sizes have expanded. It is more common to see 60 pupils in a classroom in Africa than the exception. In a number of developing countries, there is evidence that parents no longer perceive school attendance as valuable. This state of affairs was not the case during the 1960s and early 1970s, even in developing nations. In those earlier decades, Sub-Saharan Africa alone doubled its school enrollment from 20 to 46 million pupils.

The current climate has been described by Eric Hewton in *Education in Recession* (Hewton, 1986) as one in which a "cutback culture" prevails in the industrialized countries. There is ample evidence to show that most of the support systems put in place in the 1960s have been seriously cut —remedial education, compensatory programs, and school meals. Class sizes have increased in the industrialized nations, especially in the early elementary grades and lower secondary schooling. In effect, it is these critical years for basic-skill acquisition which have been most hard hit.

Each continent has a growing body of literature recording the waste of untapped human potential. In Latin America, structural-adjustment policies have led to what is called a "lost generation". Hence, it is not surprising that broad literacy projections reflect the fact that the world is not progressing at the same pace as in the preceding period

On the other hand, the geopolitical climate of the world is changing rapidly before our eyes. The growing trend towards cooperation between the United States of America and the Soviet Union opens up opportunities for governments to reconsider national priorities. The movement of Western Europe towards the elimination of many economic and legal barriers in 1992 and the rapid changes taking place in Eastern Europe are providing new possibilities to re-adjust national goals. Throughout the world, countries can now seriously consider reductions in arms expenditures and can place education back on national agendas for high-level public commitment. It is also timely that the United Nations declared 1990 International Literacy Year. Unesco and the other agencies of the United Nations system, the World Bank, and numerous bilateral and multilateral aid agencies have prepared major strategies to assist countries in providing better and more educational opportunity.

LITERACY/ILLITERACY IN INTERNATIONAL PERSPECTIVE

Having set the stage for analyzing the role of language choice for basic skill acquisition, we should now look more closely at what the international literature tells us about definitions of literacy and illiteracy. The definitions can be grouped in three broad categories: those which view literacy as a set of basic skills; those which view literacy as the necessary foundation for a higher quality of life; and those which view literacy as a reflection of political and structural realities.

For gathering the literacy statistics with which we began this chapter, Unesco provided the following guidelines to its member states in the 1978 "Unesco Revised Recommendation Concerning the International Standardization of Educational Statistics."

> The following definitions should be used for statistical purposes:
>
> (a) A person is literate who can with understanding both read and write a short simple statement on his everyday life.
>
> (b) A person is illiterate who cannot with understanding both read and write a short simple statement on his everyday life.
>
> (c) A person is functionally literate who can engage in all those activities in which literacy is required for effective functioning of his group and community and also for enabling him to continue to use reading, writing and calculation for his own and the community's development.
>
> (d) A person is functionally illiterate who cannot engage in all those activities in which literacy is required for effective functioning of his group and community and also for enabling him to continue to use reading, writing and calculation for his own and the community's development.

This attempt to give some guidance to the international community in order to have globally accepted definitions has proved difficult to apply. The guidelines were intended to be used in the collection of statistics either through a national census or through a standardized test. In many countries, the guidelines have simply proven unusable. Countries such as Canada and the United States usually refer to grade-level or number of years of schooling as a reflection of literacy levels. Other countries, particularly in the developing world, look to school enrollment indicators to give some idea of how many people have been given at least some opportunity to learn to read and write. Each of these types of indicators has its shortcomings. When literacy skills are measured by grade-level, it is usually assumed that a standardized test can be used to evaluate a reading level associated with a particular grade. However, these tests have been strongly criticized as arbitrary and insufficient when they are the sole criterion for measuring attainment (Anderson *et al.*, 1985; Owen, 1985).

School-enrollment indicators also provide incomplete information. They do not adequately reflect how many children repeat a year of schooling, how many children drop-out along the way, or anything about the quality of the instruction they receive (Coombs, 1985).

Another approach to defining literacy was introduced by Unesco in the late 1960s and early 1970s with the Experimental World Literacy Programme (EWLP). The term *functional literacy* became associated with work-oriented programs. Indeed, the EWLP was conceived as a special program for specific groups of adults in a number of developing countries. The idea behind the program was that developing countries could usefully follow in the path of the industrialized nations. There were necessary stages of development in capitalist societies. When certain sectors of the economy reached what was called the "take-off" stage, they were ready for special attention. If developing countries could not afford to educate all their adults, they should focus on those adults working in the productive sectors; to provide literacy instruction would make them even better workers. The net result of the program in 11 countries was generally disappointing (Unesco, 1976). One of the key ingredients of a successful literacy program had been neglected, that of learner motivation. Workers in the sectors selected for the experimental program could see no direct advantage to themselves in becoming more "functional" to their employers. Hence, the term *functional literacy* as used in such a context took on a specific ideological connotation. It was perceived as a method of creating a more efficient work force without concern for the needs and goals of individuals.

In the latter 1980s, the term *functional literacy/illiteracy* led to another set of difficulties which illustrates the problem of discussing literacy in an international setting. A large number of industrialized countries have been reluctant to recognize that there are sizable numbers of young people and adults in their populations who are either completely illiterate or who possess very little mastery of the written word. Countries such as Canada, the United States, and Great Britain have been addressing this problem in various degrees for many years (Hunter & Harman, 1979; Limage, 1986, 1990). Countries such as France, the Federal Republic of Germany, and the Nordic nations only officially recognized this issue in the early and mid-1980s. Indeed, many people in these and other industrialized countries have found it difficult to accept the idea that nations which have had obligatory schooling for more than one hundred years can possibly have illiterates in their populations (Limage, 1975, 1990). In addition, there is a strong reluctance for people to look at what is going on in schools which might affect children's learning, or that affect their *not* learning, as the case might be. In France, for instance, it was always assumed that the millions of immigrant workers who resided in the country provided the only possible illiterate population. Courses were created from the late 1960s onwards called "alphabétisation de travailleurs migrants". [*Alphabétisation* in French means "literacy tuition.") In reality, these courses were, and remain, "French as a second or foreign language." In many cases, the immigrants have been literate in their first languages but not in French. But to add to the confusion, when the French government officially recognized in an official report in 1984 (Espérandieu, *et al.* 1984) that native French speakers might be illiterate, they used a newly-created word for the purpose: *illettrisme*. This new word was intended to distinguish French illiterates from immigrants and also to show that people who had been to school for some period of time had a different kind of illiteracy than those who had never attended schools. An enormous controversy continues in France as one vocabulary is used for French people and another for immigrants from the Mediterranean Basin countries and Africa.

The other French-speaking countries do not use separate words for literacy/illiteracy when referring to immigrants and nationals or when referring to literacy problems in the developing countries. Nonetheless, the issue has reached the forum of international organizations such as Unesco. At the 1989 General Conference of Unesco, many representatives from developing countries denounced the use of one vocabulary for the industrialized nations and another for their own country (Limage, 1990). They rejected the idea that it is more noble or different to be illiterate in an industrialized country than in a developing one. The term *functional literacy/illiteracy* (*illettrisme* in the French case) was being used in the General Conference documents to refer to the industrialized countries and *illiteracy* on its own referred to the developing nations. As a result, the author of this chapter, as a member of the International Literacy Year Secretariat of Unesco, is engaged in a systematic review of terminology to be used in the international discussions as an effort to produce terminology which will not prove insulting to individuals, communities, or groups of countries, a task necessary for making international comparisons fair and meaningful.

Another illustration of the complexity of talking about literacy took place among the four international agencies organizing the World Conference on Basic Education for All (WCEFA), held in Thailand in 1990. Unicef, Unesco, the World Bank, and the United Nations Development Programme have sought to make education once more the national and international priority as mentioned earlier in this chapter. The four have been concerned both with improving and expanding primary education and providing basic skills for all adults. Literacy and numeracy are viewed as part of a larger concept —*basic education*— whose precise characteristics have continued under debate.

For the purposes of our discussion of literacy in this chapter, however, we propose one advanced by Hunter and Harman (1979) in *Adult Illiteracy in the United States*. Literacy, then, becomes:

> the possession of skills perceived as necessary by particular persons and groups to fulfill their own self-determined objectives as family and community members, citizens, consumers, job-holders, and members of social, religious, or other associations of their choosing. This includes the ability to obtain information they want and to use that information for their own and others' well-being; the ability to read and write adequately to satisfy the requirements they set for themselves as being important for their own lives; the ability to deal positively with demands made on them by society; and the ability to solve the problems they face in their daily lives.

This type of definition leaves it to the individual to set goals and decide what role literacy will play in his or her life. It does not place in the hands of an employer or an institution the decision about what it is to be *functional*. The definition is very much in tune with successful literacy campaigns and classes. For example, the guiding principle behind most adult literacy provision in the United Kingdom since the 1975 awareness-raising campaign has been to let the learner set goals, pace, and content (Limage, 1975). Indeed, since examinations of all types can lead to stress for the learner, most perceptive adult educators have avoided testing when possible. When funding of programs depends on such evaluation, however, programs have had to compromise. As recently as late 1989, three British groups —the Adult Literacy and Basic Skills Unit, the Training Agency, and the British Broadcasting Corporation— created communications and literacy programs leading to certification that requires testing. The organizations proposed that the time is now right for certain groups of people with limited basic skills to undertake a course and obtain some kind of diploma which may help them find a job or improve their career opportunities.

LITERACY EFFORTS: THE APPROACHES

Our discussion of the implications of literacy definitions for international perspectives leads us to a brief overview of the kinds of efforts intended to reduce the illiteracy figures mentioned in the beginning of this chapter.

The Universal Declaration of Human Rights, adopted by the United Nations on December 10, 1948, declares in its Article 26:

> Everyone has the right to education. Education shall be free, at least in the elementary and fundamental stages. Elementary education shall be compulsory. Technical and professional education shall be made generally available and higher education shall be made equally accessible to all on the basis of merit.

A number of other conventions, recommendations, and declarations have appeared since that time, attempting to further define the right to learn. Broadly speaking, however, literacy efforts have been two-pronged: the expansion and improvement of primary education and adult literacy provision. Although some countries have attempted to address the issue of illiteracy as a continuum for children and adults alike, many others have kept the discussion of schooling separate from that of adult education. In addition, international trends set by funding agencies which hold the debt of many developing countries prevent these countries from establishing their own priorities. When, for example, funding agencies promoted investment in higher education rather than primary schooling or adult basic education, many developing nations placed their scarce resources in higher education (Coombs, 1985).

Setting priorities for investment has strong implications for the type of literacy effort which will be undertaken. The agencies that promote the improvement and expansion of only primary education consider that it is better to provide basic skills for the young. They contend that adults might not be successful learners, and eventually illiteracy will be eliminated by the passing of the older generation. But as we saw earlier in this chapter, the quality of primary schooling is in serious jeopardy as a result of deteriorating economic conditions. Even in the industrialized countries, expenditure per pupil is not increasing as it did during the 1960s and early 1970s.

A second approach to literacy provision is the targeted attack which was illustrated earlier by the Experimental World Literacy Programme and its work-oriented plan. This approach is still used when adequate resources and high-level public commitment are lacking. Such is very clearly the case in industrialized countries which are increasingly turning towards the voluntary or private sector to fill in the gaps left by public provision. Countries with a strong history of charitable activity and volunteer work, such as the United States and the United Kingdom, are quick to respond to this type of program. But the ability of small-scale projects or programs to deal with the complex problem of illiteracy is necessarily limited.

A third approach to eliminating illiteracy is the mass campaign. In the 20th century, the Soviet Union undertook the first such program. In general, with such a scheme, literacy is seen as a means to a larger set of political, social, and economic goals. As Harbans Bhola has put it, the mass campaign is a declaration of "business not as usual" (Bhola, 1984). Entire populations are mobilized, so that all are involved in the learning process in some way. Literacy is presented as part of a package which promises tangible change in the quality of life for the entire society. In Cuba, the slogan was "Each one teach one". In Viet Nam, the literacy campaign was part of the struggle for independence, first from France and later in the war with the United States. In the Soviet Union, both social change and nation-building were involved. Hence, literacy instruction was carried out in more than 50 languages spoken there, and alphabets were created for a number of languages that had a purely oral tradition.

For all these approaches, the role of the language of instruction is critical to the effectiveness of learning opportunities. In the following pages, we look first at language policy from a top-down perspective across a range of countries and then turn our attention to the classroom.

LANGUAGE POLICIES: THE RANGE OF CONTEXTS

If one were to take an international and historic perspective on language-policy formulation and implementation, it would appear that developing rather than industrialized nations have paid the greatest attention to the status of official languages. This trend is especially true for the period since World War II when the decolonization process began in earnest. Few industrialized nations (with either a market- or planned-economy orientation) have found it necessary to re-assert existing language policies or to formulate new ones. It is thus common-place that choosing official languages has historically been associated with nation-building or with attempts to develop a sense of national unity. This is the case in both officially monolingual states and multilingual ones.

The focus of this section of the chapter is on the range of national responses to cultural and linguistic diversity. Two groups of countries are examined. Within each group, specific contexts are given greater attention. The first group have a monolingual language policy, or at least give a central position to a dominant language. These countries range from the most restrictive one for policy purposes, the Federal Republic of Germany, through France, the United Kingdom, Spain (where major change has occurred in recent years), and finally to Sweden (with its historic commitment to preserving cultural identity). The second group is comprised of countries that accord institutional recognition to multilingualism —Belgium, Switzerland, the Soviet Union, and Yugoslavia.

Monolingual Hegemony in Western Europe

One of the foremost scholars of language policy and planning in an international context, E. Glyn Lewis, once wrote:

> Where we are faced with the choice between equally sacred claims and values, what, as teachers and citizens, can we do? Tension does not entail conflict unless we will it so. We accept tension and so promote pluralism. The latter is not only governed by a number of principles but it also engenders at least one principle which, while valuable in itself, ensures that tension and the intrinsic conflict of values is creative rather than destructive. This principle is tolerance... (Lewis, 1978: ix).

It is precisely that level of tolerance that we are examining when we look at nations in Europe where there is at least monolingual hegemony if not actual official monolingual policy.

The Federal Republic of Germany

One might locate language policy in the Federal Republic of Germany (FRG) at one end of a spectrum. Although, for practical purposes, there is regional dialectal diversity in terms of German speakers, overall there has been little reason in modern times to question the validity of maintaining German as the only official language of the country. In the early 1960s, however, the FRG began to compensate for migrant workers from several Mediterranean Basin countries —Morocco, Turkey, and Yugoslavia, in particular. At that time until today, such migrants in Germany have been perceived as resolutely temporary guest laborers or *Gastarbeiter*. Educational as well as language policy has barely addressed the special needs of the migrants' children when the workers' families have reunited (Limage, 1984, 1985a; OECD, 1984).

In fact, over the years, Turkish, Yugoslav, and Moroccan children of migrant workers have been born in Germany and raised attending German schools. Although migrant parents may well have viewed their stay in Germany as temporary, economic reality has meant that return to their homelands has primarily taken place as a result of unemployment and forced departure. Studies have shown that migrant children have higher professional aspirations than German nationals of similar socioeconomic backgrounds, but regardless of performance in school, they cannot expect to attain other types of jobs than those held by their less-educated parents (Limage, 1984, 1987).

In terms of language policy, the only possibility for these children to learn their mother tongues is provided as a result of bilateral agreements between countries of origin and the country of employment, the FRG. Such is also the case for the same type of bilingual instruction in other European nations (with the exception of Sweden, which is discussed below). Instruction in the mother tongue is paid for by the countries of origin and provided by teachers brought from those countries. The program involves an enormous financial sacrifice for migrants' original middle- and low-income countries that are already struggling to provide universal primary schooling and some expansion of secondary schooling in their homeland. The arrangement is, however, a political statement by both groups of countries. The nation of origin is indicating to its migrants that they are not abandoned, although there is little economic possibility for their return migration. The country of employment is indicating its "tolerance" of cultural and linguistic diversity by allowing such classes to take place in their public schools.

France

Clearly, extremely limited German acceptance of diversity is not the only policy response in Europe. A somewhat attenuated form is found in France which, for historic reasons, is also a resolutely monolingual country at the official level. However, in reality France is a linguistically and culturally diverse country which has had French imposed upon its diversity since the Revolution of 1789 (de Certeau *et al.*, 1975). The partisans of the Revolution sought to unify a linguistically and culturally diverse country, as well as to impart republican ideas in all official communications, through the use of the French language. Conflict for power among church, monarchy, and republican ideals were played out in a struggle in which the French language represented the values of liberty, equality, and fraternity. Later on, with the spread of literacy and the introduction of compulsory primary schooling, language policy still favored French over the regional languages, both to develop national unity and to lay siege to the so-called "obscurantism" of the church (Furet & Ozouf, 1977). Until quite recently, the effort to stifle the use of regional languages meant that speakers of Occitan, Corsican, Languedoc, or Catalan would be punished if they used those tongues in school or on the playground. In fact, at present these other languages are only taught by permission and under special conditions. The law governing language policy is that of January 11, 1951, which "favors the study and use of local languages and dialects within their own regions" (Falch, 1973). In other words, French policy tolerates instruction in regional languages only when there is a formally-expressed demand and in a specific context.

It should be recognized that France's national language minorities are not negligible in numerical terms. There are an estimated ten million speakers of Languedoc, 1.5 million Bretons who have at least some knowledge of their regional language, 260,000 Catalan speakers, 220,000 Corsican speakers, and 90,000 Basques. All of these groups have lived within historically recognized territories for hundreds of years (Lewis, 1981). The numbers of national minorities are augmented if we consider the migrant workers and their families in France —approximately four million migrants of the first and second generation that have come from a wider range of countries than those found in the FRG.

Beginning in the mid-1970s, however, much like Germany, France entered into bilateral agreements with the governments of Algeria, Morocco, Tunisia, Italy, Portugal, Spain, Turkey, and Yugoslavia to provide for instruction of the mother tongue in French public elementary schools, either during the school day or afterwards on school premises (Limage, 1984). Greater tolerance prevails at the level of secondary schooling. There has been a serious attempt to diversify foreign-language options at that level when student numbers are sufficient to warrant offering Arabic, Portuguese, Italian, or Spanish. Nonetheless, French language policy remains centralized and essentially monolingual.

Sweden

Moving along the spectrum, we turn to another monolingual country, Sweden, which has developed another response to diversity in its midst. Like the FRG and France, Sweden has a single official language and has been an important country of employment for migrant workers from the Mediterranean Basin. Sweden has, however, an over-arching historic tradition of institutional arrangements to protect and preserve its own cultural heritage and identity. This principle has been extended to the cultural and linguistic identities of migrant workers. The Swedish maintain their monolingual policy but also provide at government expense for the instruction in the mother tongue of children and adults of migrant origin. It is the only European country to do so (Limage, 1984). The social cost and benefits of respecting diversity are considered consistent with both tradition and the healthy development of Swedish society.

The United Kingdom

The situation in the United Kingdom places that nation partially outside the analytical spectrum adopted in this chapter. While bilingual education is institutionally recognized in Wales for both Welsh and English speakers, the rest of England gives much more limited official attention to the enormous linguistic diversity present as a result of Commonwealth migration and regional dialect usage. A recent report on *Improving Secondary Education* by the Inner London Education Authority (Hargreaves, 1984) noted that these schools served speakers for 147 different languages. The languages ranged from Bengali, Turkish, Gujerati, Spanish, Greek, Urdu, Punjabi, Chinese, Italian, and Arabic to French and Portuguese. Nonetheless, the report, which has been considered a critical and progressive one in British educational circles, emphasized the need to increase English-as-a-second-language provision in public schools and gave no serious attention to mother tongue-instruction. In view of cutbacks in that nation's educational expenditure, this policy is not surprising. What it does favor, however, is increased attention in the general curriculum to the cultural diversity of the school population for all children, including native speakers of English.

Spain

Probably the only European country to radically alter its language policy in recent years is Spain. With the close of the Franco-government era, Spanish educational institutions have been accorded considerable regional autonomy. In terms of an official language for international purposes, Spanish still dominates the scene. Within the country, however, matters of linguistic diversity by the central government have been assigned to the regions. The outstanding example of the revitalization of a previously clandestine language usage is Catalan. In the restructuring of the role of central government, the *Generalitat de Catalunya* took over responsibility for major educational reforms, including the introduction of bilingual Spanish/Catalan instruction throughout the region. Catalan, like the Basque language, was forbidden during the Franco regime. However, for centuries Catalan has been the vehicle of a rich cultural and literary heritage. During Fanco's reign, the language was maintained privately by the intellectual and industrial elite of the region in spite of severe restrictions. Prior to the Spanish Civil War of the mid-1930s, Catalunya was the site of enormous innovation in pedagogy, art, architecture, urban planning, and industrialization. The region remained an important industrial center to which migrants from poorer regions of Spain came throughout the Franco period. At present, in parts of the region, migrants from Andalusia and even parts of the Basque country are in the majority. Hence, in the region there are other Spanish dialects beyond the national Castilian Spanish, as well as an elite Catalan-speaking population. (Badia i Margarit, 1969). A bilingual-education policy was developed in post-Franco Spain as part of an effort to create a truly public education system separate from the system of state-financed but privately (primarily Catholic) owned schools which had existed previously. Hence, bilingualism was consistently associated with democratization in the post-1975 reforms. Since Catalan was, and remains, the language of upward mobility in the region, the introduction of schooling in Catalan encountered less resistance from native Castilian Spanish dialect speakers than would have been the case in other circumstances. Also, the prodigious effort required for retraining teachers on a voluntary basis and, in most cases, without financial assistance was made possible by the enormous popular support for educational and political reform.

It would be inaccurate to assert that the introduction of Catalan did not provoke any conflict. In the early stages, extreme demands, primarily at the university level, that all instructors use Catalan in their teaching met with serious resistance. At the primary-school level, however, careful language planning occurred and surveys were conducted on a class-by-class basis to decide which of several models of bilingual education would be most appropriate. The success of language-policy reform in Catalonia might be largely ascribed to the previous prestige of the Catalan language, to the association of the new policy with a whole host of democratization reforms, and to the central government's acknowledging the importance of Spanish regional diversity, even at the risk of greater political conflict.

It could be said that Spain has come the furthest of the European nations discussed in terms of recognizing linguistic diversity in an officially-monolingual country.

Institutionalized Multilingualism

While linguistic diversity appears to characterize all the countries of Europe to a greater or lesser extent, official recognition of such diversity has only been directly addressed in Belgium, Switzerland, the Soviet Union, and Yugoslavia.

Belgium

In comparison to the European countries discussed earlier, Belgium is a relatively recent and arbitrary creation as a nation state (Lagasse, 1982; Limage, 1985b). Its current institutional arrangements as well as their precariousness date back to problems which were not satisfactorily resolved in 1831 when the country's constitution was created. In fact, what one finds in Belgium today is a policy of territorial unilingualism. Flemish (closely related to Dutch) is the official language of the northern region; French is the official language of the southern region; and a small eastern region is officially German-speaking. Only the capital, Brussels, is truly bilingual. Native speakers of one language are not required to learn the other. Within the French-speaking region, Walloon, an indigenous language related to French, is spoken by fewer and fewer young people and is only used in university contexts where preservation of the cultural heritage is promoted, such as at the University of Louvain.

The Flemish and French-speaking communities appear constantly to be questioning the foundations of Belgium as a centralized state, thus reflecting a long-standing hostility based on economic disparities, religious differences, and separate cultural affinities. Within these tensions, a large migrant community, such as those in the Federal Republic of Germany and France, finds little sympathy for its special needs. Mother tongue and second-language provisions for migrants are similarly limited.

Successive governments of Belgium have been brought down because the linguistic autonomy of regions has not been coupled with the political autonomy considered necessary to hold the nation together (Lagasse, 1982).

For there to be a national consensus in the country, there basically needs to be a truly federal system of government, such as is found in Switzerland or in Yugoslavia. To illustrate, let us consider the Swiss and Yugoslav federations.

Switzerland

Switzerland consists of approximately 3.9 million German speakers (73%), 1.2 million French speakers (22%), 210,000 Italian speakers (3.9%), and 40,000 Romansch speakers or 0.7% of the population (Lewis, 1981). In each canton of

Switzerland, the area's dominant language is used and taught, while the other national languages are not obligatory, with the exception of three bilingual and trilingual cantons. The tensions found in Belgium appear singularly absent in Switzerland. On the other hand, if attention to migrant workers and their children's languages remains a touchstone in each of the European countries under discussion, Switzerland is no more tolerant than any of the others. Italian migrant workers outside the canton in which Italian is spoken cannot expect better professional or academic outcomes for their children than they could in France or Belgium.

Yugoslavia

Yugoslavia presents another way of recognizing a multilingual society. For historic reasons, recognition of regional linguistic and political autonomy has held the country together. Like Switzerland, Yugoslavia is a federation in which all nationalities are considered equal and all their languages official. The Yugoslav government goes a step further, however. According to its 1971 census, all inhabitants would be classified in two categories: those who state a nationality and those who do not. The stated nationalities include the national groups of Yugoslavians, Croatians, Macedonians, Montenegrins, Muslims, Serbs, and Slovenes. Nationalities of Yugoslavia, however, also include (as incorporated national minorities): Albanians, Bulgarians, Czechs, Hungarians, Italians, Rumanians, Slovaks, and Turks. Further, immigrant groups include Austrians, Germans, Greeks, Jews, Poles, Gypsies, Russians, Ukrainians, and Wallachians. By and large, a great percentage of each of the nationalities which has a region is found in its own territory, but all nationalities are found throughout the country as a whole, especially in industrial centers. Yugoslavia resolves this heterogeneity within a federated multilingual society by recourse to individual rather than group claims to linguistic recognition. In practice, then, education and other basic services are provided in the learners' mother tongue whenever sufficient numbers warrant such treatment.

The Soviet Union

No discussion of multilingual states would be complete without reference to the Soviet Union. Although language policy in the USSR has evolved since the 1917 revolution, it can probably be safely stated that the policy has evolved within unchanging parameters. As the most distinguished English-speaking scholar of Soviet language policy, E. Glyn Lewis, puts it, the parameters are the expansion and contraction of a single initial policy statement (Lewis, 1972).

The Soviet language position is, and will remain resolutely pluralist, and it responds to extreme linguistic as well as developmental diversity. The initial policy outlined in a Resolution of the Tenth Congress in 1921 stressed the dialectic relationship which was to underpin the creation of a socialist state. The dialectic is between the centralizing forces and the nationalist elements which are simultaneously encouraged:

(a) to develop and consolidate their Soviet statehood in forms appropriate to the conditions of national way of life of the various peoples;
(b) to develop and consolidate in the native language, justice, administration, economic and governmental bodies composed of local peoples who know the way of life and psychology of the local population;
(c) to develop the press, theatre, clubs and educational establishments generally, in the native tongue;
(d) to establish and develop a wide network of courses and schools, general as well as professional and technical, in the native language (Lewis, 1981: 350).

From its inception, the Socialist government perceived education as an important tool for creating the Soviet state. Given the enormous linguistic diversity of the population of the USSR, as well as the equally diverse levels of economic and social development, national languages were considered to be instrumental as vehicles for the new social ideas as well as for creating a sense of national identity. In fact, the first mass literacy campaign in the twentieth century was undertaken in many parts of the Soviet Union only after some 50 minority languages were cast in a written form. The tension or dialectic between the importance of an over-arching lingua franca, Russian, and the development of national languages to meet changing social and economic needs continues to this day. Scholars of Soviet language-planning identify periods of increased emphasis on centralization, or attempts to impose Russian as a lingua franca, and more liberal periods in which national languages were encouraged at all levels. As with the other federal multilingual countries, territorial rights in the Soviet Union have always been fundamental in the development of actual rights to education and public service in one's mother tongue. The populations without territorial rights have suffered most as a result, the Jews being the best-known case.

A first phase of Soviet language policy clearly favored pluralism for national and minority languages. In the late 1930s a second phase emphasizing centralism, as spelled out in terms of Soviet patriotism, meant an identification with Russian patriotism. After the repressive experience under Stalin, divergent views on language policy were once again aired under Khrushchev, who developed a strategy of returning power to national languages. He sought a balance between advocates of centralism —through increased use of the Russian language— and the supporters of linguistic pluralism. Under Brezhnev, however, some return to a more centralizing view gained considerable ground. In more recent times, Gorbachev faced unusual demands for linguistic and cultural rights in the republics.

The Soviet experience clearly illustrates the fact that major social change cannot occur without the full participation of society and, in the case of the USSR, of an extremely linguistically diverse society at that. Early Soviet policy provided mass literacy in the regional tongues and formal schooling as well as entire administrative infrastructures on a scale which remains unmatched elsewhere in the world. The creation of territorial rights, while at the same time moving other populations to settle in these territories, is a frequently criticized policy. However, it could be argued that many languages would have simply died out if that had not been the case, particularly in Central Asia. What has been seen is a lively development of literature and publishing in all the languages of the Soviet Union. The tensions between the use of Russian as the most powerful language of international and inter-republic communication and the use of national languages will never be eliminated. These tensions will continue to be played out within already defined parameters.

LANGUAGE POLICIES AND SCHOOLING

If we were to agree with the original assessment made by E. Glyn Lewis regarding the primordial importance of tolerance in dealing constructively with the inevitable tensions of cultural and linguistic diversity, then we might go on to state that maintaining a language through the education system is a political act. The political act, according to Lewis, is conditioned by an understanding of the social and political consequences of its maintenance. It may be that those consequences are intended to foster a critical and open pluralism or that they are intended to segment and isolate groups in a larger society. Let us consider these matters more closely.

Mother-Tongue Education: The Debate

A number of Unesco studies and a large body of international research attest to the educational value of instruction in a child's or adult's first language or mother tongue. Clearly, an individual is likely to learn faster and better if addressed in a language which she or he understands. The closer the language of instruction to the individual's first language, the easier is the process. At the other extreme, if the language of instruction is far removed from that of the learner's first language, even though the former is the official idiom of the country, the process will be just as difficult as learning a foreign language.

Another initial point must be made as well. We need to distinguish, as does Mackey (1984: 47) between "the art of reading and the uses of reading." He points out that literacy is most efficiently conveyed by the use of an alphabetized version of the individual's first language. The process may take a few months, or in the case of non-alphabetic scripts, such as Chinese, a number of years. Nonetheless, once the reading skill is acquired, it is transferable to reading in another language, although not automatically.

These two points being made, however, the debate about language of instruction is much more complex. We have seen that countries with a monolingual official language tend to view minority languages with varying degrees of tolerance for a range of reasons:

—The official language is intended as a unifying force in a country with numerous dialects and idioms.

—Scarce resources make it difficult to provide teaching and learning materials in several languages.

—The official language used in schooling represents the state's ability to establish the rule of law in a society.

—The need for economic development may take precedence over the preservation of cultural identity in some countries.

—Knowledge of the official language means access to a language of wider, possibly international communication and may hence be perceived as more urgent or important.

The list is in no way exhaustive. The choice of language for instruction and the length of instruction in a first language are the result of many considerations. The specific local and country context as well as the population concerned are first factors. It may be practically impossible to provide instruction in a specific language if the numbers in need are too few and resources too limited to provide the teaching expertise. This is true both in monolingual countries with sizable language minorities like the United States and in officially multilingual countries with serious safeguards of individual minority rights such as Yugoslavia (Rotberg, 1984; Mikes, 1984).

Another factor is whether the first language or mother tongue is viewed as a language of instruction for transition purposes at a later level. For example, in the United States, most so-called bilingual-education programs developed over the past 20 years are actually transitional programs. It was never intended that a Spanish speaker or a Vietnamese speaker receive more than initial instruction in the first language. The question has always been, in such learning situations, how soon should English be introduced and in what quantities. This is also the issue in developing countries, such as Nigeria in which experiments have been undertaken to use Hausa, Yoruba, and Arabic prior to instruction in English. Three major projects using other minority languages as media of initial instruction in Nigeria have been carried out over the past 20 years. Ayo Bamgbose (1984) reported the concern by parents that their children might be disadvantaged if taught in the mother tongue rather than in English, which is the language of wider communication. There was no clear-cut pattern as to the best point at which to introduce English across languages and regions of the country. In the final analysis, limited material resources dictated the choices made in the use of the mother tongue.

In the Spanish case discussed earlier, the hegemony of Castilian Spanish had a strong effect on Catalan efforts to introduce truly bilingual education. Miquel Siquan (1984) noted that Catalan is a minority language of high prestige in Catalonia. Usually a minority language does not have the status of being the language of social mobility. Nonetheless, in the introduction of Catalan into schools in the post-Franco era, it was found that Catalan native speakers mastered both Spanish and Catalan more effectively than Spanish native speakers mastered Catalan as well as their own language. Many factors contribute to this finding, the major one being that no out-of-school Catalan language-use is necessary in the Spanish speaker's daily life. Thus, although the educational facilities might be comparable both in schools with a majority of Catalan speakers and in schools with a majority of Spanish speakers, the results are not the same.

Then, what about the place of mother-tongue instruction in officially multilingual countries? Melanie Mikes states:

> Education in the mother tongue is the practical result of the Yugoslav model of multilingualism, which excludes any implication that one language may be inferior or superior to another. Education in the mother tongue has the effect of ensuring the exercise of human rights in general and the protection of national minorities in particular (Mikes, 1984: 12).

In spite of great language diversity throughout the world, a large number of children are able to receive their primary education in their mother tongue. But even in a country which goes to great lengths to protect the language rights of individuals, other considerations may enter into a parent's decision for a child's language of instruction. Not infrequently a language of wider communication will be chosen by parents for secondary schooling in place of the mother tongue. Indeed, looking internationally across countries with both monolingual and multilingual language policies, we recognize that many practical concerns are shared. What, then, are the future prospects for the promotion of education in the mother tongue as a key factor in ensuring a fully literate world?

FUTURE PROSPECTS: LANGUAGE AND LITERACY

At the beginning of this chapter, we looked at the literacy situation in the world and noted a concentration of illiteracy (as officially recognized) in certain regions. We also noted the disparity between access to education for women and girls and that for men and boys. In addition, these same regions, Africa and Asia in particular, are the most severely affected by ongoing economic austerity and indebtedness. And the quality of education has suffered as a result of these conditions. In that context, we might hazard some reflections on the prospects for mother-tongue instruction to promote universal literacy.

First of all, it seems clear that choice of language of instruction by decision-makers will remain essentially a political one. Where the prevailing climate in a country tends toward a conservative preoccupation with the presence and/or influx of speakers of languages other than the dominant one, mother-tongue instruction will be limited to transitional programs at best. This is clearly the situation in almost all English-speaking countries and in all the officially monolingual countries of Europe. It is not clear that the opening of economic and legal barriers within the countries of the European Economic Community (Common Market) in 1992 will initially affect languages of instruction in schools. Similarly, in the short-term, the major social changes occurring in Eastern European countries are too new to evaluate.

Also, as long as economic conditions dominate educational planning, it is probable that choices regarding educational investment will continue to be made based on expediency rather than on lessons learned about effective instruction.

The major lesson derived from all literacy efforts —be they formal schooling, campaigns, or targeted projects— is that success is based on three crucial factors: high-level national commitment, mobilization of human and financial resources, and popular participation. High-level national commitment means that education is essentially a public responsibility and governments should give it the necessary priority. Mobilization of human and financial resources means that governments should be able to allocate resources to the social sector, including education, on a greater scale than has been the case throughout the 1980s. Popular participation means that literacy is everybody's concern. Once a major public commitment has been made, there is a role for voluntary and community initiatives, private and business involvement, the press and television, and international cooperation.

It is not necessary that everyone has the same view of what constitutes literacy or that we all have a single model of how languages of instruction are best used in schools and in adult literacy projects. International comparisons will continue to provide a rich range of experience which can be adapted to local needs and aspirations. The interdependency of the world requires that we better be able to communicate with each other. Literacy and language learning are key ingredients to the quality of that communication.

REFERENCES

Anderson, R., *et al.* (1985) *Becoming a nation of readers. The report of the commission on reading, National Academy of Education.* Champaign, IL.: Center for the Study of Reading.

Badia i Margarit, A. (1969) *La llengua del Barcelonins.* Barcelona: Editions 62.

Bamgbose, A. (1984) Mother-tongue medium and scholastic attainment in Nigeria. *Prospects,* 14 (1): 87-93.

Bhola, H. S. (1984) *Campaigning for literacy.* Paris, Unesco.

Coombs, P. (1985) *The world crisis in education. The view from the eighties.* Oxford: Oxford University Press.

de Certeau, M., Julia, D., & Revel, J. (1975) *Une politique de langue. La Révolution francaise et les patois.* Paris: Editions Gallimard.

Espérandieu, V., Lion, A., & Bénichou, J. P. (1984) *Des illettrés en France.* Paris: La Documentation Francaise.

Falch, J. (1973) *Contribution á l'étude du statut des langages en Europe.* Quebec: Laval University Press.

Furet, F., & Ozouf, M. (1977) *Lire et écrire. L'alphabétisation des français de Calvin à Jules Ferry.* Paris: Les Editions de Minuit.

Hargreaves, D. (1984) *Report of the Committee on the Curriculum and Organization of Secondary Schools. Improving Secondary Schools.* London: Inner London Education Authority.

Hewton, E. (1986) *Education in recession.* London: Allen and Unwin.

Hunter, C. , & Harman, D. (1979). *Adult illiteracy in the United States.* New York: McGraw-Hill.

Lagasse, C.E. (1982) *La Contre-réforme de l'état. Panorama des institutions de la Belgique.* Brussels: Ciaco editeur.

Lewin, K. (1986) Educational finance in recession. *Prospects,* 16 (2): 215-229.

Lewis, E. G. (1972) *Multilingualism in the Soviet Union.* The Hague: Mouton.

Lewis, E. G. (1978) What are the international dimensions of bilingual education? In J. Alatis (Ed.) *International dimensions of bilingual education, Georgetown University round table on languages and linguistics.* Quoted in Foreword to E. G. Lewis (1981). B*ilingualism and bilingual education.* Oxford: Pergamon.

Lewis, E. G. (1981) *Bilingualism and bilingual education.* Oxford: Pergamon.

Limage, L. (1975) *Alphabétisation et culture: Etude comparative. Cas d'études: l'Angleterre, la France, la République Démocratique du Viet Nam et le Brésil.* Unpublished doctoral dissertation. Paris: University of Paris V.

Limage, L. (1984) Young migrants of the second generation in Europe: Education and labor market insertion prospects. *International Migration,* 22 (4): 367-387.

Limage, L. (1985a) Policy aspects of educational provision for children of migrants in Western European schools. *International Migration,* 23 (2): 251-259.

Limage, L. (1985b) Multilingual education provision in Belgium. In J. Hawkins & T La Belle (Eds.), *Education and intergroup relations: An international perspective* (pp. 293-314). New York: Praeger.

Limage, L. (1986) Adult literacy policy in industrialized countries. *Comparative Education Review,* 30 (1): 50-72.

Limage, L. (1987) Economic recession and migrant/minority youth in Western Europe. *International Migration*, 25 (4): 399-414.

Limage, L. (1990) Adult literacy and basic education in Europe and North America: From recognition to provision. *Comparative Education,*

Mackey, W. (1984) Mother tongue education: Problems and prospects. *Prospects*, 14, (1): 37-49.

Migrants' children and employment: The European experience. (1984) Paris, Organisation for Economic Co-operation and Development.

Mikes, M. (1984) Instruction in the mother tongues. *Prospects*, 14 (1): 121-131.

Owen, D. (1985) *None of the above*. Boston: Houghton Miffin.

Rotberg, I. (1984) Bilingual education policy in the United States. *Prospects*, 14 (1): 133-147.

Siquan, M. (1984) *Language and education in Catalonia. Prospects*, 14 (1) 107-119.

The experimental world literacy programme. (1976) Paris: Unesco.

Unesco Office of Statistics (1989, November) *The literacy situation in the world.* Unpublished report. Paris: Unesco.

NOTE

[1] The views expressed in this chapter are the responsibility of the author and in no way reflect those of the organization with which she is employed.

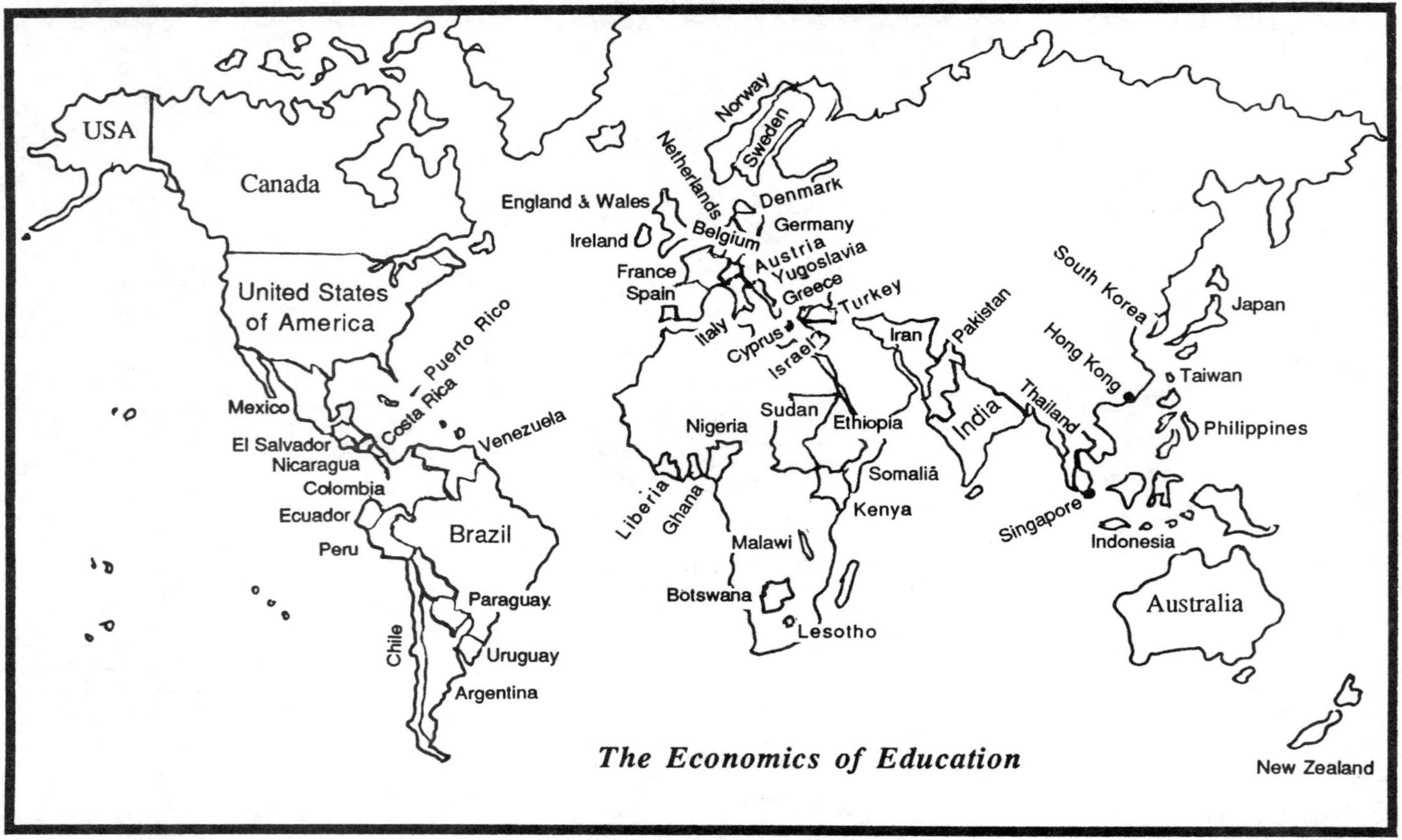
USA
Canada
United States of America
Mexico
El Salvador
Nicaragua
Costa Rica
Puerto Rico
Colombia
Venezuela
Ecuador
Peru
Brazil
Chile
Paraguay
Uruguay
Argentina
England & Wales
Ireland
Norway
Sweden
Netherlands
Denmark
Belgium
Germany
France
Spain
Austria
Yugoslavia
Greece
Italy
Cyprus
Turkey
Israel
Iran
Pakistan
India
Nigeria
Sudan
Ethiopia
Somalia
Kenya
Liberia
Ghana
Malawi
Botswana
Lesotho
South Korea
Japan
Hong Kong
Taiwan
Thailand
Philippines
Singapore
Indonesia
Australia
New Zealand
The Economics of Education

CHAPTER 10

The Economics of Education

What key economic issues concern educational planners?

MARK BRAY

The economics of education is a branch of economic theory which has long roots but which has only blossomed since the early 1960s. Several classical economists in the eighteenth and nineteenth centuries, including Adam Smith, Alfred Marshall, and John Stuart Mill, highlighted the importance of education as a form of investment; and in 1924 the Soviet economist Strumilin examined "the economic significance of national education" (Woodhall, 1987a: 1). However, the economics of education has only established itself as a firm discipline in more recent times.

This chapter can do no more than highlight the main issues in the field. Readers wishing to explore the subject in depth could usefully commence with the seminal books written by Blaug (1976), Cohn (1979), Psacharopoulos & Woodhall (1985), and Psacharopoulos (1987). Readers may also wish to examine key journals in the field, of which the most prominent is the *Economics of Education Review*.

The chapter has five main sections. They focus in turn on human capital theory, manpower planning, rate of return analysis, the role of vocational and technical education, and sources of finance for education. The final section pulls threads together in conclusion.

HUMAN CAPITAL THEORY

The concept of human capital underlies most economic rationales for investment in education. The importance of human capital was highlighted as early as 1776 by Adam Smith in his book *The Wealth of Nations.* He compared human capital with machines and other sorts of physical capital and noted that:

> A man educated at the expense of much labour and time to any of those employments which require extraordinary dexterity and skill, may be compared to one of those expensive machines. The work which he learns to perform...will replace to him the whole expense of his education, with at least the ordinary profits of an equally valuable capital (in Blaug 1976: 2).

Smith thus highlighted the importance of entrepreneurial and other skills for economic development. Some of these skills depend on personal aptitudes, but most can be cultivated through education and training.

Surprisingly little attention was paid to this concept during the next two centuries. The idea was rejuvenated in 1960 by Theodore Schultz in his presidential address to the American Economic Association (Schultz, 1961). His ideas partially inspired and were followed by a series of important works, including those by Denison (1962), Hansen (1963), and Becker (1964). These works have had a major impact on investment policies in both industrialized and less developed nations.

Part of the earlier failure to take full account of human capital arose from difficulties of measurement. The fact that physical capital was more easily quantified gave it stronger respectability and attention. Schultz also noted (1961: 2) that to some people the mere thought of investment in human beings was offensive:

> Our values and beliefs inhibit us from looking upon human beings as capital goods, except in slavery, and this we abhor.... [To] treat human beings as wealth that can be augmented by investment runs counter to deeply held values. It seems to reduce man once again to a mere material component, to something akin to property.

Suggesting that this attitude was illogical, Schultz turned to empirical analysis. He focused primarily on the USA, and set out estimates of the total stock of educational capital at various points in time. He found that the ratio of the stock of educational capital to the stock of physical capital appeared to have risen from 22 per cent in 1900 to 42 per cent in 1957.

Denison (1962) extended this work. His chief focus was the contribution of different factors of production to the Gross National Product (GNP) of the USA between 1910 and 1960. He found that the increase in GNP could not be completely explained by increases in the nation's labor force and physical capital, so turned to analysis of the unidentified "residual" factor in economic growth. He stressed the importance of improvements in the quality of the labor force through increased education, though also noted the significance of technological progress and economies of scale. Denison concluded that education of the labor force accounted for as much as 23 per cent of the annual growth of GNP in the USA between 1930 and 1960.

MANPOWER PLANNING

The work of Schultz, Denison, and others directly contributed to a wave of interest in manpower planning. In the Soviet Union, manpower planning had been a key instrument for central direction of economic and social development since 1928 (Hinchliffe, 1987: 315). In capitalist countries, however, manpower planning only became widespread in the 1960s. Subsequently, manpower planning failed to live up to many of its promises, and its image became rather tarnished. However, manpower planning has not been completely abandoned as an instrument for overall economic and social planning. Many governments feel that despite weaknesses in the techniques of manpower planning, its basic premises remain valid.

Development of Concepts and Techniques

The pioneering manpower planning project in the Western world was the Mediterranean Regional Project (MRP), launched in 1961 by the Organisation for Economic Cooperation and Development (OECD). The MRP sought to produce educational plans in a common conceptual framework for Portugal, Spain, Italy, Greece, Yugoslavia and Turkey (Parnes, 1962; Williams, 1987).

The MRP was based on a simple input-output view of the economy. Planners commenced by identifying a target GNP, and by subdividing the target by industrial sectors. A figure corresponding to average productivity of labor was then applied to each component, thus producing a forecast of labor requirements. The labor force was then classified by occupation. Finally, the occupational composition of the labor force was translated into national education requirements by applying a standard measure of educational achievement necessary to perform successfully in each occupation.

This procedure was later subjected to severe criticism, including by the OECD itself. The project's main evaluator (Hollister, 1965) showed that even the fairly similar countries participating in the original MRP exercise displayed major variations not only in the total employment needed to generate a given output but also in the occupational composition of this total. This finding cast considerable doubt on the appropriateness of the manpower planners' formulae.

Other objections to the MRP procedure focused on data requirements and availability. The procedure required extensive information, for example, on the extent to which individuals could move from one job to another and on the impact of technical change. Available information was rarely sufficiently accurate, detailed, or recent. Partly because of these problems, by the late 1960s MRP methods had largely been abandoned by the OECD countries, though they have remained in use in many less developed nations (Youdi & Hinchliffe, 1985: 258).

Another seminal work was a 1964 book written by Harbison and Myers. The book was global in orientation, and, as indicated by the authors in their foreword (1964: v), was "deliberately designed as a blueprint for action rather than solely as a scholarly academic exercise."

The authors divided the nations of the world into four groups, which they labeled underdeveloped, partially developed, semiadvanced, and advanced. The categorization was chiefly devised according to an index of human resource development, based, among other items, on primary and secondary school enrollment rates, the number of physicians and engineers per 10,000 people, and the percentage of the population in agriculture.

Noting correlations between the human resource index and per capita incomes, Harbison and Myers proceeded to recommendations for manpower development. They suggested, for example (1964: 72), that:

> a rough estimate for the average Level I country which seeks in ten to twenty years to reach the average development of Level II might be ... to try to double its primary enrollment ratio, to increase its secondary enrollment ratio about 4.5 times, and to increase its higher education enrollment ten times. To achieve this, it should probably devote about 50 per cent of its total funds for formal education to second-level schooling, about 20 per cent to higher education, and the remainder to primary education.

The Harbison and Myers book had considerable influence, both in international organizations and in individual countries. In many contexts the concepts were employed in conjunction with those set out by W. W. Rostow (1960), who had identified what he called a set of stages of economic development through which all countries had to pass if they wished to transform themselves from being "traditional" to having "high mass-consumption."

However, Rostow's hypothesis was later discredited. One objection was the implication that the goal of all developing nations is, or should be, to imitate Western European or North American models of high mass-consumption. These developed societies are very wasteful of resources, and they suffer many problems which the Third World would do better to try to avoid. Secondly, even if high mass-consumption were a desirable goal, its achievement for the majority of nations would be impossible. The present developed countries reached their position in large measure by exploiting other parts of the world. This option is not open to the developing countries. They have no colonies to exploit, and, except for the minority who are oil producers, the markets for their exports are both limited in size and controlled by the developed world. Other objections focus on the failure of Rostow's hypothesis to match the actual experience of many countries, and on its lack of empirical support (Bray *et al.*, 1986: 4-5; Fagerlind & Saha, 1989: 68-71).

The work of Harbison and Myers has also been discredited. Blaug (1976: 68), for example, asserted that the work "embodies virtually every mistake that it is possible to make in international comparisons of income and education." He challenged the weights that Harbison and Myers attached to specific components in their human resource index, noting that no rationale was presented for the weights, and suggesting that the weights might have been inserted to assist the analysis to reach pre-determined conclusions.

Harbison and Myers did warn that correlations between the human resource index and GNP per head did not necessarily imply causation. However, Blaug (1976: 69) pointed out that these warnings only appeared twice in 223 pages, and he suggested that the whole thrust of the book was contrary to such reservations. Blaug (1976: 70) was particularly critical of the Composite Index, which he considered "simply a red herring calculated to mislead readers into thinking that there are definite stages of educational development much like Rostow's stages of economic growth." Nevertheless, even Blaug conceded that Harbison and Myers had presented some useful advice on manpower planning.

Contemporary Perceptions and Practices

In retrospect it is obvious that many of the prescriptions for development advanced in the 1960s were over simplistic. This has led to widespread cynicism about manpower planning and associated techniques.

While many critics have pointed out what is wrong with manpower planning, however, it has been harder to present convincing alternatives. Especially in developing countries, governments are acutely conscious of the waste of resources represented by educated unemployment and misemployment. They are also conscious of bottlenecks in their economies, and of the need to train manpower for future technical change. As a result, many governments still collect data on employment trends and on projected training requirements, and they seek to build the information into their planning processes.

As one might expect, however, there are considerable differences between the practices of different countries. Even among developed capitalist countries there exists a sharp contrast between France, which centralizes data collection and seeks to build the information into its planning processes, and the United Kingdom, which has no single body responsible for manpower development and is more prepared to rely on market forces and the "social demand approach" (Harnqvist, 1987).

A contrast may also be drawn between Hong Kong and India. Authorities in the former have the advantage of a compact territory, a unitary government, and access to excellent data collection and processing facilities (Ng, 1987). Hong Kong's situation is very different from that of India, which is much larger in area and population, has a decentralized system of government, and has major problems of data collection and processing (Verma, 1985). It is not surprising that manpower planning is undertaken more enthusiastically and effectively in Hong Kong than in India. Even in Hong Kong, however, contemporary planners are more aware of the shortcomings of manpower planning than were their counterparts in the 1960s. They are also aware of the speed with which technology may make precise predictions quite inappropriate, and of the impact of political forces which influence the pace of migration and other factors.

RATE OF RETURN ANALYSIS

Rate of return analysis also builds on the concept of human capital, though it takes a rather different direction from manpower planning. Many of the early human capital theorists made specific reference to rate of return analysis (Hansen, 1963; Becker, 1964; Schultz, 1971), but the most striking proliferation of studies has occurred more recently. Within the literature, the work by George Psacharopoulos is generally the best known. Psacharopoulos' 1973 book was entitled *Returns to Education: An International Comparison.* Eight years later an article updated the figures and concepts (Psacharopoulos, 1981), and four years later another article presented a further update (Psacharopoulos, 1985).

The basic concept underlying rate of return analysis is that individuals with higher levels of education generally earn higher incomes. The higher incomes can be at least partly attributed to the education and to the human capital which it represents. By comparing the costs of education with the higher incomes obtained, it is possible to calculate a rate of return on investment. Comparison between the rates of return of alternative investments provides a guide for policy makers on whether it is economically desirable to increase expenditure on education.

One important distinction is between private and social rates of return. The private rate of return views the calculation from the viewpoint of the individual, whereas the social rate of return views it from the viewpoint of society as a whole. The two main factors causing divergence between private and social rates of return are education subsidies and income taxes. When education is free or highly subsidized, the private rate of return will tend to be higher than the social one because the individual does not have to pay the full costs of education but still receives considerable benefits. When income taxes are imposed, on the other hand, the benefits accruing to the individual are less than those accruing to the society as a whole.

Calculation of Rates of Return

Figure 10-1 illustrates the rate of return concept, and compares the costs and benefits of investing in university education with the costs and benefits of not doing so. A similar diagram could be created to compare secondary with primary education, or primary with no education.

Statistical analyses show that by going to university, individuals significantly increase their chances of higher annual salaries after graduation. The area B, therefore, represents the extra economic benefit that the individuals can gain. However, if the individuals had not gone to university, they could have commenced work at an earlier age. The earnings foregone, represented by the area F, must therefore be considered a cost to be set against the benefit. Thirdly, the individuals will encounter some direct costs from study —fees, purchase of books, etc. These are represented by the area C.

Figure 10-1
Rates of Return to Increased Education

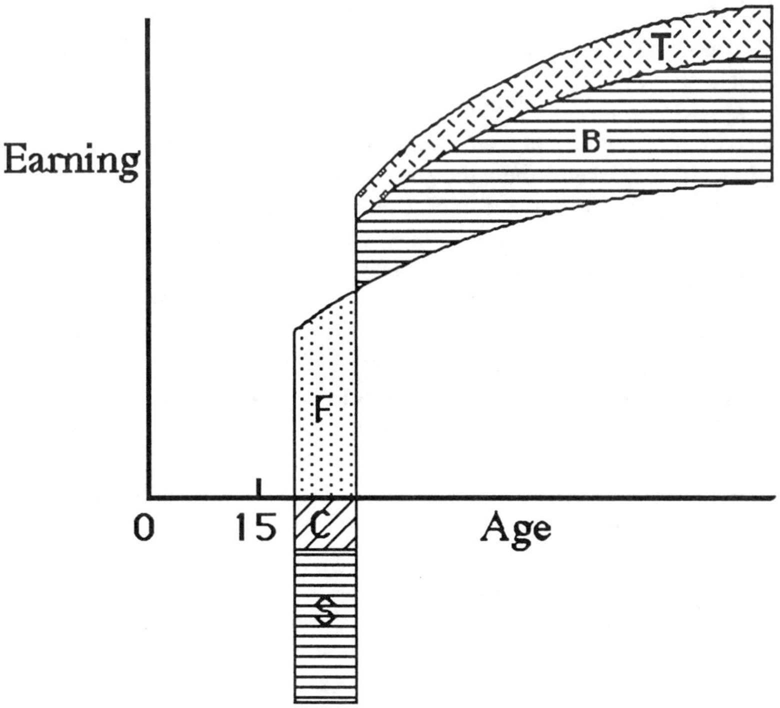

Comparison of costs and benefits in this way permits calculation of the private rate of return. The formula used would be:

$$\text{Private Rate of Return} = \frac{B - (F + C)}{(F + C)} \times 100.$$

Calculation of the social rate of return would take additional account of subsidies in the cost of education, represented here by the area S. It would also to allow for the taxation recovered from the individuals, represented by the area T. The social rate of return could then be calculated by the formula:

$$\text{Social Rate of Return} = \frac{(B + T) - (F + C + S)}{(F + C + S)} \times 100.$$

While the above procedure explains the basic concept, it admittedly is a simplification. A full calculation of rates of return would have to allow for such additional factors as:

Averages. Some individuals, of course, have higher incomes than others, even when they study the same subject. Also, some individuals incur higher costs than others, even when they study the same subject. For actual measurement of rates of return, a sufficiently large sample would be needed to create a reasonable average. This average would further allow for the fact that some individuals do not even seek paid employment after graduation but, instead, undertake unpaid work e.g. as housewives. It would also include allowance for dropouts, that is, of individuals who start courses (thereby incurring costs), but who do not finish (thereby probably failing to gain benefits).

Unemployment. In many cases, individuals are unable to gain jobs immediately after they graduate. As a result, the financial benefits from the extra study are delayed and reduced. It would be necessary to decide whether unemployment was actually a result of the education. If the individual would not otherwise have been unemployed, the lost earnings during the period of unemployment would be an additional cost to be set against the benefits.

Effects Other than Education. It is questionable how much increases in earnings are really attributable to education and how much they are due to such other factors as ability and socio-economic background. This has been a thorny problem in the economics of education. It is usual to make some allowance for the other factors, though, like Denison's "residual", it is difficult to know how much that allowance should be (Psacharopoulos 1987: 343-344).

Data on Projected Incomes. Ideally, rate of return analysis would be calculated on longitudinal data, calculating the actual incomes of specific individuals and aggregating them. However, in practice this is rarely possible. Instead, rates of return are generally calculated from cross-sectional data. When subsequently checked, these estimates do not always match reality.

Part-Time Earnings and Part-Time Study. The diagram in Figure 10-1 assumes that students study full-time, and that they do not earn any money during their period of study. In practice, this may not be true. Indeed, some students hold full-time jobs but then undertake part-time study in the evenings and on week-ends. For these students, the calculation would have to be adjusted. It would still have to show a cost of foregone leisure, although analysts find it very difficult to know what value to place on this.

Empirical Evidence and Its Implications

Considerable empirical evidence has been collected on rates of return. Table 10-1 presents a summary, by region and country type, of data collected by Psacharopoulos (1985). Table 10-2 presents a more detailed breakdown.

Table 10-1
Rates of Return to Education, by Region/Country Type (%)

	Social			Private		
Region/Country Type	*Prim.*	*Secon.*	*Higher*	*Prim.*	*Secon.*	*Higher*
Africa	26	17	13	45	26	32
Asia	27	15	13	31	15	18
Latin America	26	18	16	32	23	23
Intermediate	13	10	8	17	13	13
Advanced	na	11	9	na	12	12

na = not available, because of lack of a control group of illiterates.
Source: Psacharopoulos 1985: 586.

From the figures, several points emerge. First the majority of rates are high, and would probably compare favorably with most alternative forms of investment. The view of Psacharopoulos (1985: 591) is that:

> Underinvestment exists at all levels of education, especially in Africa. This proposition is supported by evidence that the social returns to education in the region are well above any plausible social discount rate used in project evaluation.

Second, rates of return are generally highest at the primary level. They are intermediate at the secondary level, and are generally lowest in tertiary education. This does not necessarily mean that tertiary graduates do not obtain significantly higher salaries than secondary school leavers. Instead it reflects the high cost of tertiary education. Primary education, by contrast, may generate modest benefits; but it usually has an even more modest cost.

Third, as might be expected, private rates of return are almost always higher than social ones. However, the extent of the divergence differs markedly, and is generally greater in less developed than in more advanced countries. While it is arguable that private rates of return need to be great enough to give individuals an incentive to undertake studies, it is also arguable that in many cases the subsidies are excessive. Psacharopoulos (1985: 591) recommends a general decrease in subsidies for tertiary education, thereby releasing resources for greater investment in primary education.

Table 10-2
Rates of Return to Education, by Country (%)

		Social			Private		
Country	*Year*	*Prim.*	*Secon.*	*Higher*	*Prim.*	*Secon.*	*Higher*
AFRICA							
Botswana	1983	42.0	41.0	15.0	99.0	76.0	38.0
Ethiopia	1972	20.3	18.7	9.7	35.0	22.8	27.4
Ghana	1967	18.0	13.0	16.5	24.5	17.0	37.0
Kenya	1971	21.7	19.2	8.8	28.0	33.0	31.0
Lesotho	1980	10.7	18.6	10.2	15.5	26.7	36.5
Liberia	1983	41.0	17.0	8.0	99.0	30.5	17.0
Malawi	1982	14.7	15.2	11.5	15.7	16.8	46.6
Nigeria	1966	23.0	12.8	17.0	30.0	14.0	34.0
Somalia	1983	20.6	10.4	19.9	59.9	13.0	33.2
Sudan	1974		8.0	4.0		13.0	15.0
ASIA							
Hong Kong	1976		15.0	12.4		18.5	25.2
India	1978	29.3	15.7	10.8	33.4	19.8	13.2
Indonesia	1978	21.9	16.2	14.8			
Pakistan	1979				14.6	6.7	9.4
Philippines	1977			8.5			16.0
Singapore	1966	6.6	17.6	14.1		20.0	25.4
South Korea	1980		8.1	11.7			
Taiwan	1972	27.0	12.3	17.7	50.0	12.7	15.8
Thailand	1972	63.2	30.9	18.4			
LATIN AMERICA							
Brazil	1970		23.5	13.1		24.7	13.9
Mexico	1963	25.0	17.0	23.0	32.0	23.0	29.0
Paraguay	1982	14.0	11.0	13.0			
Peru	1980	41.4	3.3	16.1			
Puerto Rico	1959	24.0	34.1	15.5	68.2	52.1	29.0
Venezuela	1984				32.5	11.7	20.6

Table 10-2 continued
Rates of Return to Education, by Country (%)

Country	*Year*	Social *Prim.*	*Secon.*	*Higher*	Private *Prim.*	*Secon.*	*Higher*
INTERMEDIATE COUNTRIES							
Cyprus	1979	7.7	6.8	7.6	15.4	7.0	5.6
Greece	1977	16.5	5.5	4.5	20.0	6.0	5.5
Iran	1976	15.2	17.6	13.6		21.2	18.5
Israel	1958	16.5	6.9	6.6	27.0	6.9	8.0
Spain	1971	17.2	8.6	12.8	31.6	10.2	15.5
Turkey	1968			8.5		24.0	26.0
Yugoslavia	1969	9.3	15.4	2.8	7.6	15.3	2.6
ADVANCED COUNTRIES							
Australia	1976			16.3		8.1	21.1
Austria	1981					11.3	4.2
Belgium	1960		17.1	6.7		21.2	8.7
Canada	1961		11.7	14.0		16.3	19.7
Denmark	1964			7.8			10.0
France	1976				13.5	10.8	9.3
Japan	1976	9.6	8.6	6.9	13.4	10.4	8.8
Great Britain	1978		9.0	7.0		11.0	23.0
Netherlands	1965		5.2	5.5		8.5	10.4
New Zealand	1966		19.4	13.2		20.0	14.7
Norway	1966		7.2	7.5		7.4	7.7
Sweden	1967		10.5	9.2			10.3
United States	1976					11.0	5.3

Source: Psacharopoulos 1985: 598-600.

Criticisms of Rate of Return Analysis

While rate of return analysis has a strong army of supporters, it also has many critics (Dore 1976, Klees 1986). The critics often commence by taking issue with the underlying notion that market forces arrange for people to be paid what they are worth: that a person's wage always accurately reflects a person's marginal product. In the words of Dore (1976: 92-93):

> It is hard to believe that because the social rates of return to higher education work out at 23 per cent in Mexico ... and only 6 per cent in the Netherlands ... an extra Dutch graduate would be likely to make a lesser real contribution to the welfare of his fellow men than an additional Mexican graduate. A much more likely explanation is that the political structure in Mexico and its class base perpetuates an inequality of income distribution in Mexico many times greater than that in the Netherlands.

In practice, it may be suggested, wage rates are determined much more closely by traditional differentials and the bargaining power of trade unions than by the marginal productivity of the individuals.

Secondly, rate of return calculations are always based on past data. A policy maker in Nigeria, for example, might look at Psacharopoulos' table and see a social rate of return from primary education of 23 per cent. But that was in 1966, and much has changed since then. The whole structure of employment has altered, and primary school leavers can no longer expect to secure the same sorts of jobs that they could obtain in the mid-1960s. Even if the figure were more recent, it would still be based on the past rather than on prediction of the future.

The third main objection is that rate of return analysis appears to present blocks of education as if they were uniform throughout the world and at all points in time. Many countries suffer acute problems of quality. A glance at Psacharopoulos' table would show policy makers high rates of return from investment in primary education. This implies that an increase in the number of primary school places would be a wise use of resources. In practice, however, rapid expansion of primary education could have disastrous consequences for quality, and could be almost entirely self-defeating. Nigeria's attempt to universalize primary education in the mid-1970s provides a very salutary experience in this respect (Bray 1981).

It was observed above that rate of return analysis has had powerful advocates in the World Bank. This institution has had sufficient financial influence and dissemination capacity to spread its message far and wide. More recently, however, there have been signs of movement away from such strong emphasis on rates of return. The analysis certainly has its uses; but it is best employed in conjunction with other instruments rather than as a tool on its own.

THE ROLE OF VOCATIONAL AND TECHNICAL EDUCATION

Another persistent debate concerns the role of vocational and technical education. Especially in less developed countries, education has frequently been criticized for being too academic. It is widely argued that academic schooling is irrelevant to the agricultural base of most developing countries, and that it causes inappropriate attitudes. One solution to this, it is suggested, is to "vocationalize" the school curriculum by incorporating a high percentage of technical work. Many advocates of vocationalization note high levels of unemployment, and argue that schools should teach practical skills in order to allow school leavers to become self-employed.

The 'Vocational School Fallacy'

While the vocationalization argument holds initial appeal, it does not always bear close scrutiny. To demonstrate this, it is useful to commence with a well-known article published in 1966. The article was written by Philip Foster, and was entitled "The Vocational School Fallacy in Development Planning".

Foster began by quoting the views of a respected economist, Thomas Balogh. These views, he suggested, were representative of those held by many others. The comments were made with specific reference to Africa, though could equally have had a wider focus. Foster suggested (1966: 142) that Balogh's views could be summarized as follows:

> Since between 80 and 95 per cent of Africans are dependent upon agriculture, the essential need in African education is the development of large-scale technical and agricultural programs within the schools at all levels: "The school must provide the nucleus of modern agriculture within the villages, and play a central role in the general raising of standards of living within the subsistence sector." Present educational facilities constitute an obstacle to rural progress because people are not trained for agriculture, and academic systems of formal education are the chief determinant of attitudes hostile to the practice of rural agriculture. Schools are regarded as primarily responsible for the flight from the rural areas to the towns.

Foster suggested that if there was anything surprising in Balogh's views, it lay not in their originality but in the degree to which they reproduced with virtually no modification a series of arguments that had been set out by colonial authorities at periodic intervals since the 1840s. Foster pointed out that the view supposed that schools were easily manipulated instruments for change, and ignored the impact of wider economic forces. Rather, he suggested (1966: 145), the failure of vocational education to become more popular was mainly the result of low demand for it:

> An examination of opportunities within ... [the European dominated] sector throughout the colonial period reveals that relatively there was greater demand for clerical and commercial employees than for technically trained individuals. Opportunities certainly existed in technical fields and in agriculture, but they were inferior to the other alternatives. Access to most of the highly paid occupations was, therefore, achieved through academic institutions.

Foster added that:

> Those who criticise the "irrational" nature of African demand for "academic" as opposed to "vocational" education fail to recognise that the strength of academic education has lain precisely in the fact that it is pre-eminently a vocational education providing access to those occupations with the most prestige and, most important, the highest pay....

While in the post-independence era political structures have altered, economic structures have changed much less. Although artisans and farmers can become quite prosperous, bureaucratic jobs usually yield incomes which are higher, more dependable, and unaffected by seasonal fluctuations. Consequently, bureaucratic jobs, which are chiefly acquired through academic education, are almost invariably considered more desirable. On the other hand, where the incomes of agricultural workers and artisans are significantly higher than those of white-collar workers, Foster pointed out that there is no shortage of recruits. It is therefore a myth to suggest that the formal school in itself makes its products unwilling to get their hands dirty. The real determinant of attitudes is the reward given to each type of training in the economy.

Contemporary Policies

While Foster's observations make considerable sense, the misconceptions which he attacked remain widespread. One reason is that Foster's article has not been read sufficiently widely! Policy makers in a broad range of countries continue to face serious unemployment and rural-urban migration, and they continue to view the school system as a vehicle which can help to solve problems independently of wider economic forces.

One recent book which surveys issues in an international context has been prepared by Lauglo and Lillis. In their introductory chapter, the authors (1988: 3) point out that contemporary interest in vocationalization transcends the divide between rich and poor countries and between different political systems. The issues are at the forefront of public debate in France, Sweden, and the United States as much as in Sierra Leone, Brazil, and Colombia (see also Keep & Mayhew, 1988, and World Bank, 1989). While of course the contexts of these countries differ markedly, certain issues continue to recur.

Among these issues is the question of self-employment. Some vocationalization initiatives have been founded on the assumption that introduction of woodwork, sewing, or other practical subjects in the secondary school curriculum will enable school leavers to become self-employed. However, this assumption has usually proved over-optimistic. First, schools cannot always allocate sufficient time to enable practical skills to be learned in depth. Second, and more important, effective self-employment requires additional skills which are rarely taught in schools. For example, self-employed workers must know where and how to obtain loans to purchase equipment. They also need skills in accounting and in negotiating payment for services (especially from relatives and friends who expect work to be performed free of charge). Self-employed workers must also be able to locate raw materials and judge appropriate prices for their products. Certainly many young people are capable of acquiring these skills and the complementary knowledge; but the pupils with the greatest ability often secure paid employment, leaving only the less capable youths to be pushed into self-employment.

Another recurring issue concerns the cost of vocational education. The need for specialist equipment, raw materials, and smaller class sizes inevitably raises unit costs; and the high costs are not always matched by good results. It was partly because of awareness of these high costs that the World Bank significantly modified its enthusiasm for vocationalization in developing countries (World Bank, 1989). Many analysts now assert that at the secondary level a good general education is a more cost-effective investment (Psacharopoulos & Woodhall, 1985: 314; White, 1988: 7).

Nevertheless, it is also obvious that vocational and technical education is essential for economic development. If it is not provided in general secondary schools, then it may be provided in specialized post-secondary institutions or on the job. Hong Kong, for example, has a well-resourced set of technical institutes which are operated by the government and have been deliberately designed to meet projected skill needs for economic growth. In contrast, Japan has a strong reputation for company-sponsored on-the-job training. Employees in Japan have strong loyalties to the companies which employ them, and the fact that individuals are more likely to remain with their employers for a complete working life-time makes the companies more willing to invest in training (Sako & Dore, 1988).

SOURCES OF FINANCE FOR EDUCATION

Analysis of sources of finance forms another important sub-branch of the economics of education. The role of private schooling is particularly controversial. Other debates focus on the role of fees in publicly-funded institutions and the operation of student loans.

The Role of Private Schooling

Many people are ideologically opposed to private schooling, asserting that it is elitist and socially divisive. Others argue that privatization strengthens market responsiveness to the consumers' needs and improves efficiency. During the 1980s the voice of the pro-privatization lobby gained considerable strength.

Table 10-3 shows the proportion of pupils in private schools in a variety of countries. The table must be treated with caution, for classifications of private education vary. Not all private schools are commercial enterprises: many are operated by churches and other community organizations, often with large government subsidies. The latter situation partly explains the very high proportions in Ireland and Hong Kong, for example.

Even with allowance for variations in meaning, the table indicates a wide range in the extent of private schooling in different countries. It also shows that private schooling tends to be more widespread at the secondary than at the primary level.

James (1988) notes two main situations in which private schooling is prominent. The first is one of excess demand, where governments have insufficient resources to meet all public aspirations. This situation has become increasingly common in developing countries, where rapid population growth has been coupled with economic austerity (Coombs 1985: 136-70). Secondly, private education may provide an alternative type of education. In some countries the public has become increasingly critical of the uniformity and standards of the public school system. This has increased pressure for privatization in the USA and Hong Kong, for example (Coleman, 1981; Hong Kong, 1988).

The economic arguments about privatization may take either side. The chief argument in favor is that privatization promotes the responsiveness of school systems to their consumers. Advocates assert that privatization also promotes efficient use of resources. On the other hand, economists may argue that in some cases education should be highly subsidized or free of charge in order to allow optimum use of human resources. If talented but poor pupils were excluded from school by the existence of fees, it is said, then society as a whole would fail to benefit fully from their talents.

Table 10-3
Percentage of Students Enrolled in Private Schools

ADVANCED INDUSTRIAL COUNTRIES	*Primary*	*Secondary*
Australia	10	26
England & Wales	5	8
France	15	21
Germany	2	9
Ireland	98	91
Italy	8	7
Netherlands	69	72
New Zealand	10	12
Sweden	1	2
USA	18	10

AFRICAN AND ASIAN COUNTRIES		
Hong Kong	92	72
India	25	49
Indonesia	15	34
Kenya	1	60
Nigeria	31	45
Singapore	35	28
SOUTH AMERICAN COUNTRIES		
Argentina	17	30
Brazil	12	43
Chile	17	20
Colombia	15	47
Ecuador	17	30
Paraguay	15	33
Peru	13	13
Uruguay	16	16
Venezuela	11	21
CENTRAL AMERICAN COUNTRIES		
Costa Rica	3	6
El Salvador	4	29
Mexico	5	26
Nicaragua	12	43

Note: Data are for varying years between 1973 and 1980.
Source: James 1988: 96.

A related argument is that education has certain "spill-over" effects. Universal literacy, for example, facilitates general communication; and the extension of education has implications for public attitudes and aspirations. Recognizing these externalities, economists often argue that governments should subsidize education for the poor in order to reduce the danger of private underinvestment.

Should Education be Fee-Free?

The debate about privatization overlaps with another debate about school fees. In most parts of the world, the concept of fee-free education has been generally accepted as a laudable social goal. Among the best-known expressions of this philosophy, with the implied global approval emanating from the body which issued it, is the 1948 United Nations Declaration of Human Rights. Article 26 of the Declaration states that:

> Everyone has the right to education. Education shall be free, at least in the elementary and fundamental stages. Elementary education shall be compulsory.

However, the widespread philosophical shift in favor of privatization has been accompanied in some quarters by a shift in favor of fees, even in government-owned institutions. The United Nations declaration does not have universal support, and is not based on completely sound logic (Bray, 1987; Lewin with Berstecher, 1989)

Among the most striking shifts in philosophy is that of the World Bank. The Bank is part of the United Nations system, and until the mid-1970s appeared to accept the view of its parent body set out in the 1948 declaration. In the last decade, however, World Bank officials have increasingly recommended imposition of fees. Their rationale has partly been based on the severity of financial pressures, which in some countries have made it simply impossible for governments to provide fee-free education.

Paradoxically, the World Bank also recommends imposition of fees in order to improve equity. Jimenez and Tan (1985: 19), for example, reported that in Pakistan only 3 per cent of the eligible population was enrolled in higher education but that they consumed nearly 30 per cent of total educational expenditure. Since the students who attended higher education institutions tended to be from relatively prosperous families, the heavy subsidies for higher education seemed to benefit the rich more than the poor.

An equity argument for charging fees may also be employed at the primary level. Birdsall (1983), for example, has argued in favor of charging fees in order to extract resources from the rich to benefit from the poor. She admits, though, that the policy can only work under four conditions: (a) when the extra resources are used to improve quality and to build schools nearer the homes of disadvantaged children, (b) when the elasticity of demand of the rich is high enough to ensure increased revenues following introduction of fees, (c) when the positive effect of the increase in quality and/or the lowering of distance is stronger in absolute terms than the negative effect of the increase in fees, and (d) when increased revenue is sufficient to improve quality and to provide a larger number of school seats. As Eicher (1984: 140) comments, these conditions are "very stringent indeed".

Nevertheless, the challenge to the generally accepted notion that free education is always desirable has become powerful. The World Bank is an influential organization, and its views have a strong impact. At the tertiary level, an increasing number of governments in both industrialized and less developed countries are replacing student grants by loans. Student loans are not without pitfalls, but when well organized and administered they can work effectively and equitably (Woodhall, 1987, 1989).

TRENDS AND PROSPECTS

In a 1985 paper Mark Blaug, one of the key figures in the development of the economics of education, reviewed the state of the discipline as he saw it. The 1960s, he suggested, was the heyday of the discipline:

> those were the days when Denison's sources-of-growth accounting was generally believed to have demonstrated the precise quantitative contribution of education to economic growth, when Gary Becker's *Human Capital* (1964) was widely acclaimed as opening up new vistas in labour economics, when every discussion of educational planning revolved around the respective merits of the "social-demand approach", the "manpower-requirements approach", and the "rate-of-return analysis". Those were, in short, the "golden years" of the economics of education when no self-respecting Minister of Education would have dreamed of making educational decisions without an economist sitting at his right hand (Blaug, 1985: 17).

Blaug observed that the 1970s were characterized by much less self-confidence. Earlier prescriptions for development had proved less efficacious than had been anticipated. Attention in many quarters turned from quantity to quality of education, and in this sphere economists were considered less useful than psychologists and psychometricians.

Nevertheless, the economics of education as a field of study did not die out in the 1970s. On the contrary, the decade brought vigorous development and growth. Empirical research greatly improved the knowledge base and deepened awareness of the complexity of options facing policy-makers. During the 1970s, moreover, the profession began to adopt much stronger comparative dimensions.

This trend has continued during the 1980s. The specialist journals have contained a steady flow of articles reporting new insights and findings from a wide range of countries. Much of this work has been conducted by scholars in universities, but a great deal has also been done by staff of such institutions as the World Bank. Thus, while the status of the economics of education might have diminished during the 1970s, it was restored during the 1980s. In most countries economists are again at the right hand of Ministers of Education, their role given particular status by the severity of economic crisis which has been a widespread affliction.

Lest this become a cause for complacency, however, it must be recognized that economists of education remain ignorant about many areas. Their interpretations conflict, and many prescriptions are still based on assumptions rather than empirical evidence. An important critique by Klees (1986: 606) argues that perspectives have also been too narrow and one-sided. "The current majority positions do not even ... acknowledge, let alone consider or understand, other points of view." Klees is especially critical of the dominance of neoclassical perspectives, e.g. on rates of return analysis. He highlights the neglect of radical and institutional perspectives, of which one particularly valuable contribution is consideration of costs and benefits to different groups rather than to some fictitious "society as a whole".

Nevertheless, from the viewpoint of comparative education it is worth noting a positive evolution within the last 15 years. In 1977, Hansen wrote an article entitled "Economics and Comparative Education: Will they ever meet? And if so, when?" His survey of the literature on the economics of education found significant comparative research in only three topics: the education-earnings relationship, returns to human capital, and the education-economic growth relationship. Comparative dimensions of other topics, he suggested, had been seriously neglected. Among the specific topics he identified were estimates of the effects of schooling on earnings and of educational production functions, manpower planning, educational finance, and equality of educational opportunities.

Were Hansen to repeat his review today, he would find a marked change. There is of course much more to be done; but comparative dimensions have at least been introduced to all the topics Hansen identified, as well as to many others.

REFERENCES

Becker, G. S. (1964) *Human capital: A theoretical and empirical analysis, with special reference to education.* New York: National Bureau of Economic Research.

Blaug, M. (1976) *An introduction to the economics of education.* Harmondsworth: Penguin.

Blaug, M. (1985) Where are we now in the economics of education? *Economics of Education Review*, 4 (1), 17-28.

Birdsall, N. (1983) *Strategies for analysing user charges in the social sectors.* Washington: The World Bank, Country Policy Department.

Bray, M. (1981) *Universal primary education in Nigeria: A study of Kano State.* London: Routledge & Kegan Paul.

Bray, M. (1987) Is free education in the Third World either desirable or possible? *Journal of Education Policy*, 2 (2), 119-129.

Bray, M., Clarke, P, & Stephens, D. (1986) *Education and society in Africa.* London: Edward Arnold.

Cohn, E. (1979) *The economics of education.* Cambridge: Ballinger.

Coleman, J. (1981) Public schools, private schools and the public interest. *The Public Interest*, 64 (1), 19-30.

Coombs, P. H. (1985) *The world crisis in education: The view from the eighties.* New York: Oxford University Press.

Denison, E. F. (1962) *The sources of economic growth in the United States and the alternatives before us.* New York: Committee for Economic Development.

Dore, R. (1976) *The diploma disease: Education, qualification and development.* London: George Allen & Unwin.

Eicher, J. C. (1984) *Educational costing and financing in developing countries: Focus on Sub-Saharan Africa.* Staff Working Paper No.655, Washington: The World Bank.

Fagerlind, I., & Saha, L. (1989) *Education and national development: A comparative perspective* (2nd ed.). Oxford: Pergamon.

Foster, P. J. (1966) The vocational school fallacy in development planning. In C. A. Anderson & M. J. Bowman (Eds.), *Education and Economic Development* (pp. 142-163). Chicago: Aldine.

Hansen, W. L. (1963) Total and private rates of return to investment in schooling. *Journal of Political Economy*, 81 (2), 128-141.

Hansen, W. L. (1977) Economics and Comparative Education: Will they ever meet? And if so, when? *Comparative Education Review*, 21 (2/3), 230-246.

Harbison, G. H., & Myers, C. A. (1964) *Education, manpower and economic growth*, New York: McGraw-Hill

Harnqvist, K. (1987) Social demand models. In G. Psacharopoulos (Ed.), *Economics of education: Research and studies* (pp. 315-323). Oxford: Pergamon Press.

Hinchliffe, K. (1987) Forecasting manpower requirements. In G. Psacharopoulos (Ed.), *Economics of education: Research and studies* (pp. 356-363). Oxford: Pergamon Press.

Hollister, R. G. (1965) *A technical evaluation of the Mediterranean Regional Project.* Paris: Organisation for Economic Co-operation & Development.

Hollister, R. G. (1967) A technical evaluation of the O.E.C.D.'s Mediterranean Regional Project and conclusions. In J. A. Lauwerys, G. Z. Bereday, & M. Blaug (Eds.), *The world year book of education 1967: Educational planning* (pp.161-70). London: Evans.

Hong Kong, Education Commission (1988) *Education commission report no.3.* Hong Kong: Government Printer.

James, E. (1988) The public/private division of responsibility for education: An international comparison. In T. James & H.M. Levin (Eds.) *Comparing public and private schools: Institutions and organisations* (pp. 95-127). Brighton: The Falmer Press.

Jimenez, E., & Tan, J.P. (1985) *Educational development in Pakistan: The role of user charges and private education.* Washington: The World Bank, Education & Training Department.

Keep, E., & Mayhew, K. (1988) The assessment: Education, training and economic performance. *Oxford Review of Economic Policy*, 4 (3), i-xv.

Klees, S. J. (1986) Planning and policy analysis in education: What can economics tell us? *Comparative Education Review*, 30 (4), 574-607.

Lauglo, J,. & Lillis, K. (Eds.) (1988) *Vocationalizing education: An international perspective*. Oxford: Pergamon.

Lewin, K. with Berstecher, D. (1989) The costs of recovery: Are user fees the answer? *IDS Bulletin*, 20 (1), 59-71.

Ng, S. H. (1987) *Technological advances and training: A case study of Hong Kong*. Hong Kong: New City Cultural Service.

Parnes, H. S. (1962) *Forecasting educational needs for social and economic development*. Paris: Organisation for Economic Co-operation & Development.

Psacharopoulos, G. (1973) *Returns to education: An international comparison*. Amsterdam, Elsevier.

Psacharopoulos, G. (1981) Returns to education: An international update and implications. *Comparative Education*, 17 (3), 321-341.

Psacharopoulos, G. (1985) Returns to education: A further international update and implications. *Journal of Human Resources*, XX (4), 583-604.

Psacharopoulos, G. (1987) The cost-benefit model. In G. Psacharopoulos (Ed.) *Economics of education: Research and studies* (pp. 342-347). Oxford: Pergamon Press.

Psacharopoulos, G., & Woodhall, M. (1985) *Education for development: An analysis of investment choices*. New York: Oxford University Press.

Richter, L. (1984) Manpower planning in developing countries: Changing approaches and emphases, *International Labour Review*, 123 (6), .677-692.

Rostow, W. W. (1960) *The stages of economic growth*. Cambridge: Cambridge University Press.

Sako, M., & Dore, R. (1988) Teaching or testing: The role of the state in Japan. *Oxford Review of Economic Policy*, 4 (3), 72-81.

Schultz, T. W. (1961) Investment in human capital. *The American Economic Review*, 51 (1), 1-17.

Schultz, T. W. (1971) *Investment in human capital: The role of education and of research*. New York: The Free Press.

Verma, M. C. (1985) Review of skilled-manpower forecasts in India. In R.V. Youdi & K. Hinchliffe (Eds.) *Forecasting skilled manpower needs: The experience of eleven countries* (pp. 194-210). Paris: International Institute for Educational Planning.

Williams, G. (1987) The OECD's Mediterranean Regional Project. In G. Psacharopoulos (Ed.) *Economics of education: Research and studies* (pp. 335-336). Oxford: Pergamon Press.

White, M. (1988) Educational policy and economic goals. *Oxford Review of Economic Policy*. 4 (3), 1-20.

Woodhall, M. (1987a) Economics of education: A review. In G. Psacharopoulos, (Ed.) *Economics of education: Research and studies* (pp. 1-8). Oxford: Pergamon Press.

Woodhall, M. (1987b) *Lending for learning: Designing a student loan programme for developing countries.* London: The Commonwealth Secretariat.

Woodhall, M. (1989) (Ed.) *Financial support for students: Grants, loans or graduate tax?* London: Kogan Page.

World Bank (1989) *Vocational education and training in developing countries: Policies for flexibility, efficiency and quality.* Washington: The World Bank.

Youdi, R. V., & Hinchliffe, K. (Eds.) (1985) *Forecasting skilled manpower needs: The experience of eleven countries.* Paris: International Institute for Educational Planning.

CHAPTER 11

Comparative Education Research

What are the methods and uses of comparative education research?

GARY THEISEN & DON ADAMS

As described in chapter one, comparative education is typically concerned with education questions in an international or cross-cultural context. Considerable controversy exists concerning the appropriateness of particular methodologies, the relevance of some disciplinary skills, and the relative importance of different substantive themes. Embracing a heterogenous set of intellectual and professional objectives and activities, comparative education is the product of many disciplines and can lay claim to no single conceptual or methodological tool that distinguishes it clearly from other sub-areas in education or the applied social sciences. The adjective *comparative* helps to narrow the focus; however, the term lacks precision. The ambiguity contributes to the multi-faceted character of comparative education research.

THE NATURE OF COMPARATIVE RESEARCH

We make comparisons many times every day. For example, we routinely compare jobs, food, sports teams, political positions, books, cars, children, schools, and teachers. These comparisons may be in terms of value, quantity, quality, efficiency, beauty, ideology, or on any of a multitude of criteria or characteristics. We compare to make choices, to engage in debate, to better understand ourselves, our lives, and the environment about us. Comparison can help us to understand, to extend our insights, and to sharpen our perspectives. If we wish to know something well, many writers tell us, we must examine it in comparison. Some argue that there is a liberating quality about comparison which "...represents a quest for enlightenment, and thus...is one of the most fruitful ways of thinking. It helps to rid us of inherited fossilized notions, and enlarges our visual field " (Dogan & Pelassy, 1984: 9).

The examples above suggest that comparison is integral to the process of cognition and perhaps latent in all human thought. Social scientists tell us that it is a universal method of the social sciences. "Thinking without comparison is unthinkable. And in the absence of comparison, so is all thought and scientific research" (Swanson, 1971: 145). Levy flatly states: "All scientific analysis is a subset of the general set entitled comparative analysis" (Levy, 1970). Yet the pervasive quality of comparison in every day life and in "science" disguises the fact that comparative research is complex and controversial. When and under what conditions is it appropriate to make comparisons? How do we distinguish between trivial, everyday comparison and comparison which adds to research-based knowledge? Are there important differences between the orientations of most comparativists and most non-comparativists, and do these differences have significant methodological implications? (Ragan, 1987: 2)

Comparative research that is rich in detail is usually focused on individual cases. Large-scale surveys that produce highly aggregated data from many countries can provide breadth, but they are often frustratingly deficient in detail. In the former the reliability of findings is often questioned; in the latter, validity. The comparative education conceptual literature suggests that there are indeed traps and tradeoffs in the science and art of comparison.

Formal comparative research, as contrasted with everyday ad hoc comparison, is expected to meet the acknowledged standards set for scientific research. That is, it should be planned, problem focused, theory driven (or with expectations of contributing to theory), and undertaken with an explicit methodology. Comparative research is designed to extend systematically our knowledge, thereby to meet informational needs through the formation of generalizations and by offering explanations of perceived relationships and logical patterns.

The nuances of meaning of the terms "comparative research" and "comparative method" are likely to continue to be debated; however, the trend is to view comparison as most fruitful when the process, problem, or event being examined is interpreted within a describable social context. Comparative research that is designed to formulate generalizations and explanations asks such questions as "Does the relationship hold in another country or another cultural setting?" Or, less frequently, "Does it hold in another historical period?" These investigations allow the researcher to focus on attributes of the total social system, such as, how the education and economic sectors are interrelated, how the social-economic characteristics of communities affect schooling, and how the social status of occupations like teaching are determined by value systems.

Comparative education research, like all research, reflects the disciplinary training of the researcher and the prevailing preferences among the range of available models, theories, and world views. The disciplines in which comparative educators have been trained are readily apparent in the literature they produce. For example, researchers with training in anthropology often focus on cross-cultural comparisons and use participant-observation research techniques. The disciplines of sociology, political science, and economics often lead researchers to make cross-national comparisons that rely on data and information obtained from survey techniques using questionnaires and interviews.

Disciplinary distinctions explain only some of the variety within the comparative field. Contemporary comparative education research has entered a period of methodological, theoretical, and paradigmatic diversity reflecting trends apparent in most of the social sciences. For example, the emergence of pluralism as a conceptual theme emphasizing multiple paths to development in comparative research counter-balanced the decline in primacy of the functionalist world view that emphasizes an orderly, evolutionary view of change. Theories of radical change that stem from both Marxist and neo-Marxist theories have also influenced comparative research, particularly since the 1960s. The subjectivist models of knowledge and change found under such labels as phenomenology, hermeneutics, or more broadly, interpretism, in their formal application have only recently been given significant application by comparative education researchers.

PROBLEMS IN COMPARATIVE RESEARCH

The difficulties in undertaking comparative research are many. Perhaps the most persistently inhibiting constraint on researchers is the cultural value system of which they are a part. Examining the work of sociologists, Dogan and Pelassy (1984: 9) observe:

> Every researcher, even a comparativist researcher, belongs to a culture, and that can limit his or her capacity to perceive. These blinkers have not been easily recognized. Sociologists from the West have been slow to realize that they were taking their own measures for universal ones. For a long time, classic comparisons have implicitly incorporated the idea of progress, tending to consider each political system according to the place it occupied on an imaginary scale, leading inexorably to development, democracy, or even 'Westernization'.

There are also difficult conceptual and measurement problems associated with comparative research. Many educational concepts do not have equivalent meanings across social or cultural groups or even across nations. The word *college*, for example, has definitions that include "a degree-granting institution of higher education," "a secondary-level school," and "a loose collection of faculty with similar academic concerns."

Our experience and training limit our range of perspectives and drive the formulation of our research questions. The primary task of a comparative researcher is to identify an acceptable level of conceptual equivalence across cases regarding the idea, institution, or process being studied. The second task focuses on measurement. Both highly structured data-gathering techniques (such as questionnaires), and less structured ones (such as participant observation), are subject to comparability problems. The more obvious, more easily manipulated stumbling blocks include comparable linguistic translations, standardization of statistical information, uniform administration procedures, and temporal equivalency. Of even greater importance is ensuring that the indicators chosen to describe a concept, event, or relationship do not distort the "meaning" of what is being measured and thereby encourage false inferences to be drawn from the comparisons (Theisen, 1984).

The consequences of cultural-bias, conceptual, and measurement problems are well documented in comparative research. These problems are not unique to a single discipline or methodological approach. As noted earlier, some researchers focus exclusively on a few cases using qualitative research methods to capture the complexity and detail of what they are observing, including the rich subtleties of culturally-specific meanings. But such richness in description and analysis is typically provided by limiting the number of cases which can be studied. The observations may be valid in the particular context in which they are observed, but they provide meager evidence to support their generalizability.

Other researchers who employ large numbers of cases to support their generalizations sacrifice the "thick description" that close observation over long periods of time can provide. Good researchers realize that each approach is a valuable tool in the comparativist's methodological bag. Their application is not an "either-or" dilemma, but rather an issue of suitability. Methods must be matched to purpose. Comparative research methods are not mutually exclusive; they are complementary.

CATEGORIZING COMPARATIVE EDUCATION RESEARCH

In order to demonstrate better the variety of investigations undertaken by comparative researchers, we systematically reviewed articles published in one major journal in comparative education, the *Comparative Education Review* (*CER*). All articles from 1957 through 1989 were examined, even though many issues of the journal were specific to a single country. All the articles were included because they fell into at least one of the thematic areas describing comparative education (see the next section). The research examined was classified into one of four different categories: (1) analytical research; (2) descriptive research; (3) evaluative research; (4) exploratory research [Table 11-1].

Analytical Research. The purpose of analytical research is to increase understanding of how variables relate to one another, how those relationships can be changed, and how the relationships vary across individuals and settings. The aim often is to examine components of an educational system or program and to specify functional or cause-and-effect relations and outcomes. Analytical research may also focus on an actor or a set of actors in an attempt to explain roles and behavior. Typical questions asked in this type of research are: "What are the functional relations between variables A and B?" and "Why does a system, institution, or actor behave in a particular way?"

Table 11-1

Criteria for Classification of Comparative Research

Research Type	*Typical Questions*	*Purpose of Research*
Analytical	What are the explanations for relationships between components?	Description of roles.
	Why do actors or systems behave in the way they do?	Specification of cause- and-effect relations or explanation of relations and consequences.
Descriptive	What is the current status of the phenomena?	Description of phenomena or conditions.
	What are the relationships between variables?	Description of relations between variables.
Evaluative	Is program A better or more cost effective than program B?	Judgment of the merit, value, or worth of any given program or technique.
	Is the program or policy appropriate for a particular context?	Interpretations useful for decision making.
Exploratory	What issues pertaining to roles, relationships, and processes exist which are worthy of examination by other modes of research?	Generating new hypotheses or questions.
	What models, paradigms or methods might be useful in designing future research?	Exploration of relationships and functions with potential for other in-depth research.

Descriptive Research. Descriptive research is distinguished by "the general procedures employed in studies that have for their chief purpose the description of phenomena, in contrast to ascertaining what caused them or what their value and significance are" (Good, 1973). In descriptive research, investigators attempt to answer questions that require an accurate, sometimes detailed depiction of the subject under study. A researcher reports on the way things are, or as they are perceived to be (Gay, 1987). As Thomas has stated in Chapter 1, "The term descriptive study can be applied to a work that does no more than delineate the components of an educational operation and the connections among the components."

Evaluative Research. The evaluative method of research is used to test a particular social science hypothesis or a principle of professional practice (Rossi & Freeman, 1989: 38). Evaluative research investigates the issues concerning the merit, value, or worth of educational techniques or programs (Borg & Gall, 1989). It may be undertaken to assess the appropriateness of program changes, to identify ways to improve the delivery of interventions, or to meet the accountability requirements for demonstrating progress that are imposed on educational initiatives by donor groups that fund them. Evaluation has utility for planning and policy formation, for testing innovative ideas on how to deal with individual and community problems, for deciding whether to expand or curtail programs, or for supporting a decision to fund one program as opposed to another.

Exploratory Research. The purpose of exploratory research is to generate hypotheses or research questions rather than to test propositions or find "answers." In their exploratory efforts, researchers examine the utility of new paradigms for organizing or studying data that describe a process or product. Exploratory studies may synthesize and extrapolate data to define issues that need further analytical, evaluative, or exploratory research. In contrast to searching for cause-and-effect or functional, dependency relations, exploratory researchers try to identify, for example, associations that have not yet been recognized or understood among educational actors, relationships between educational interventions and the educational system, or ones between the educational system and its environment.

Table 11-2 indicates major shifts of emphasis in the research themes and objectives represented by articles in the *Comparative Education Review* over a 33-year period. Relative increases in analytical research, evaluative research, and exploratory research are accompanied by decreases in descriptive research. A number of interpretations might explain this trend, but most likely the shift exemplifies changes that have taken place in the types of research skills employed and thematic priorities emphasized in comparative education over the past three decades. For example, sophisticated, empirical social-science methods have been much more integrated into the training of recent cohorts (1970s and 1980s) of scholars engaged in comparative education research than in earlier cohorts. Secondly, the data reflect a shift in the type of problems emphasized in comparative education. The recent concerns of the field are instrumental —they deal with questions of implementation, planning, and decision making. More will be said about this shortly.

Table 11-2

Research Methods Used in the Comparative Education Review —1957-1989

Research Type	*1957-1967* n	%	*1968-1978* n	%	*1979 1989* n	%
Analytical	10	3%	25	10%	33	12%
Descriptive	269	86%	158	61%	124	45%
Evaluative	4	1%	48	19%	61	22%
Exploratory	31	10%	25	10%	60	21%
Total	314	100%	256	100%	278	100%

n= 848

Further analysis of the contents of the *CER* and other journals devoted to comparative research in education could be helpful in understanding the changing nature of comparative education and, indirectly, the uses of comparative studies. How research and the logic employed in analysis is structured could illuminate how different conceptual paradigms affect the content and results of research. The categories we employed in our cursory analysis are neither all-inclusive nor terribly precise. Other typologies might include, for example, theory building and policy orientation.

ESTABLISHING RESEARCH AGENDAS

The traditional distinctions between the terms *basic research* and *applied research* do not apply as well to the social sciences as they do to the physical sciences. Basic research consists of activities designed to provide answers to questions that may or may not have an immediate impact on the design of policy or the formation of programs dealing with the subject in question. Basic research is knowledge driven. Applied research is solution driven; it is designed to produce information that will abet the cause of reform or provide evidence about the success or failure of policies and programs already in place. Most comparative education research, whether applied or basic in design, ultimately informs policy and decision makers about concepts, strategies, and applications that bear on current educational practices.

The tendency for comparative education research to be applied stems from several factors:

—Although some scholars would argue that education is itself a discipline, it can more readily be described as a field to which other disciplines, such as economics, politics, sociology, psychology, and history, are brought to bear. Research that may be described as basic, pure, or theoretical takes place first and foremost within the context of the discipline. Comparative education is, however, not without its basic researchers and conceptual tacticians; for example, see the texts of Bereday (1964) and Holmes (1981).

—Education is one of the most public of arenas for research and program change. Teachers, administrators, and researchers operate within the brightness of light focused on performance and accountability. Research is generally supported that enlightens persistent problems of low levels of student and teacher performance, and that identifies action-oriented policies and practices that are linked to improved learning. Moreover, there is in comparative education a long tradition of research focused on issues surrounding the borrowing and exchange of educational ideas and practices across national boundaries.

—Accountability has become the watchword of educational investment. Taxpayers want to know how well the schools that they are supporting are performing and how these institutions can better enhance the life-chances of the students in them. Cross-national studies of achievement are a practical manifestation of the concern that government leaders have about the performance of their nation's school systems vis-á-vis those in other countries.

—Efficiency and equity issues have forced school systems to conduct self-examinations of how well resources (both fiscal and human) are being utilized and how evenly distributed they are on the basis of race, gender, and other ascriptive characteristics such as handicaps and special abilities.

The question of whether a particular piece of comparative education research should be classified as basic or applied is of less interest than the recognition that all research is driven by a real or perceived belief that its results will make a difference in both our immediate and larger world of activities and relationships. Comparative education research addresses a wide array of problems, issues, and themes which resist easy classification. The following general thematic genres describe the framework under which most comparative research conducted in the past three decades can be classified.

Comparative Theory

Theory, either directly through the framing of research questions or indirectly through the implicit assumptions of the researcher, has influenced all comparative research. However, the explication of a particular theoretical approach and the comparison of educational explanations from multiple theoretical perspectives constitute unique lines of research. Among the theories most prominently employed in comparative education are the following:

Functionalist Theories. Such theories draw from mainstream social science and tend to explain social change as a gradual process of structural differentiation and specialization. They have been widely influential in comparative education research: human capital models (Bowman and Anderson, 1968 pp 113-31), modernization models (Inkeles and Holsinger, 1974), and production-function models (Leigh & Simmons, 1975; Heyneman & Loxley, 1983). These theories generally treat education as a good that benefits the individual and that contributes to the public weal.

Marxist and Neo-Marxist Theories. Conceptions deriving from the dialectical materialism of Karl Marx assume that tensions and contradictions between groups and classes in society are always present and, when sufficiently intense, set the stage for radical change. Education is viewed as a means of legitimizing social and economic inequities and of maintaining stasis in the existing social structure (Carnoy, 1974).

Dependency and World Systems Theories. Such theories emphasize the interdependence of countries and the tendency of core, industrialized nations to influence or control "peripheral," less industrialized ones. Education in periphery nations reflects the hierarchial relationships and dependent linkages to the economy and culture of the core nations (Wallerstein, 1979; Arnove, 1980). Some comparative scholars have suggested that a world knowledge system exists, with scholars, academics, and professionals from the periphery linked to the center in a web of inequality (Altbach, 1978).

Interpretist Theories. Functionalist, Marxis,t and dependency theories often share a view that reality is concrete and is defined by tangible, empirically-defined facts. Interpretist and humanist theories emphasize the subjective nature of reality and the need to study educational systems in terms of what education means to those who participate in the process, namely the individual students and teachers (Berge *et al.*, 1973; Popkewitz, 1984).

Conceptually, all of these major theoretical trends owe their origins to the work done in other social science disciplines, but the application of them to multiple education settings in order to understand better the education-society nexus has been a unique contribution of comparative educators.

Global Education

A much older concept —that of global education— gained renewed popularity in the 1960s and 1970s as a result of two decades of international and domestic violence and social upheaval. Peace and global understanding, it is assumed, can be facilitated by researching and disseminating information on cross-cultural common denominators and by exploring differences among customs, beliefs, and socialization in a comparative, objective fashion. The lessons learned from the efforts of comparative educators have now found their way into much of the core international curricula in the social science disciplines. The principles of balanced observation and interpretation of data within the context of social, historical, and economic fact have led not only to a better understanding of how different education systems work, but also to a better appreciation of the mutual interdependency of all the peoples of the world.

Development Education

Development education is, in a sense, the logical outgrowth of global education. It emphasizes the application of pedagogical tools and training techniques to inform better the large segments of the community, both domestic and international, that are not acquainted with international issues, whether the issues pertain to schooling matters or not. Most universities offer at least one course on development education, and organizations such as the Society for International Development have outreach and extension services to promote this objective. Comparative education researchers have contributed to these efforts through the gathering, organization, and presentation of data describing how other social systems and their institutions, including education, are linked to our own.

Comparative Education

Our use of the term *comparative education* here refers to research activities aimed at thoroughly documenting the characteristics of different national education systems in terms of organizational structure, goals, and pedagogical processes. As noted by one of the senior scholars in the field, "In order to understand an educational system, and the society in which it is embedded, one must be able to answer: Who gets educated; For how long; and Why?" (P. J. Foster, personal communication). In the post-colonial period of the 1950s, and 1960s, comparative education researchers produced a wealth of literature describing and analyzing Western and developing-country educational systems. It is upon this groundbreaking work that documents such as *The Encyclopedia of Comparative Education and National Systems of Education* (Postlethwaite, 1988) have been constructed. As basic social science theories have been elaborated in the past two decades, so have analyses and interpretations of education systems improved.

Education in Developing Countries

In the latter part of the 1970s and throughout the 1980s, the bulk of funded research efforts focused on the developing countries (Coombs, 1985). These activities have been principally applied in nature. Several reasons account for this focus:

—More than a billion adults in the world are illiterate, the majority of those in developing countries; one in five has no opportunity to go to school, even if it were within the individual's economic means to do so.

—Only about 40% of African children complete primary education, despite primary schooling's proven social and individual payoffs.

—Governments in developing countries spend approximately $60 billion annually on education. Yet in many countries it takes an investment equivalent to 10 or more years to produce a graduate from a five-year primary cycle.

—Four-fifths of the world's children live in developing countries.

The imperative to conduct research in developing countries is simple: ways must be found to transform the bulk of the world's population into a literate and numerate majority. The social and economic futures of all of the world's population depends on the development of a sustainable self-sufficiency. Because most governments are already spending as much as their budgets will realistically permit on education, because of the high dropout and repetition contributing to the inefficiency of developing world education systems, and because of the low and declining quality of schooling in these countries, innovative solutions must be found to stem the erosion of an educated human resource base. Investigations to identify the sources of investment inefficiencies, to strengthen planning and management, and to test the application of technology to alleviating the problems of low access to and poor quality of instruction have been the hallmark of comparative research during the past decade.

The reason for identifying these various "themes" within the comparative education framework is to call attention to the fact that the field has multiple consumers of research, each category of user possessing different needs that are shaped by differing objectives and views of what the field needs to accomplish. As in any social science field, form should follow function. Comparative research must be understood in terms of what its designers hope to accomplish with it, and the methodologies that one is free to employ and that are best suited to the objectives. The question of *what* is to be studied and *how* must also be examined from the perspective of the resources that are available to implement the research.

SPONSORSHIP OF RESEARCH

Research costs. It costs in at least three ways. First, there is the direct outlay of funds necessary for travel, printing, reproduction, field staff, and more. Some methods are more expensive than others. Some questions require a much more elaborate set of preparations and data collection activities than others. Research conducted in a library, or in places where the cost of living and of labor is low, may be funded out of the researcher's own pocket. It is increasingly difficult, however, for researchers to conduct first-hand field work without some sort of institution-based financial support.

Second, the indirect costs of research are also high. A university may pay a faculty member's salary while that individual is conducting an investigation, but if the results do not directly benefit the university through acclaim for the researcher and through recognition of the relevance and importance of the findings, institutional support will wane. All researchers must ask the question, "What am I giving up by engaging in this study? Are there other, more important questions that could be explored?" Comparative researchers must also ask whether the sites chosen for comparison or for primary focus are the best ones to answer the questions that need to be addressed. Comparative studies frequently represent a tradeoff between what is best and what is feasible.

Third, empirical research, especially that involving the collection of primary data in developing countries, poses a cost burden on the ministerial and university officials who participate as collaborators. Top-level researchers and administrators are in very short supply in most developing countries. Research and development activities that involve a collaboration of scholars from outside and from within the country require those officials to invest time and effort to make the research activities successful. Such investments may require them to subordinate other activities, some of which may be critical to the functioning of the educational system. Research collaborators thus have the responsibility not only to ask how important the proposed investigation is to them, but also how important is it relative to other tasks and responsibilities that may be neglected as a result of the research effort.

Comparative education research is sponsored in a great variety of ways. Some is built upon the solitary commitment of effort and resources of a single individual. Most often, however, comparative research is supported through government funds or donor agencies. Students of comparative education need to examine the source of funding because research sponsorship and research focus are very closely connected. The following examples illustrate this point:

Independent Research. University scholars are sometimes fortunate enough to secure small faculty-development and area-studies grants to pursue a topic or to write an article that is of particular interest to them. Rarely do these funds exceed the equivalent of a semester's salary plus incidental research expenses. The limits of funding impose de facto restrictions on the type of question that can be investigated and on the methodologies (library vs. field research, primary vs. secondary data analysis) that can be employed. Research of a non-applied or "basic" nature is most likely to be conducted under this type of sponsorship.

Government-funded Research. Almost all senior education officials in countries around the world are concerned about the performance of their school systems in both absolute and relative terms. Policy makers are interested in comparing educational districts and even schools to identify differences in academic performance, to spot inequities in the distribution of learning resources (including schools, texts, and teachers), and to target reform initiatives on geographic and substantive areas where they are most needed. In relative terms, decision-makers want to know if their investments are generating returns comparable to those being realized in other countries. Are the students of country X performing as well as those in country Y in mathematics, science, or the like? If not, how can comparative research shed insights into the sources of the discrepancies? Such questions are important, for in an increasingly global economy the long-term advantages that may accrue to nations with a superior human resource base are of both economic and political importance.

Donor-funded Research. In 1988 two billion dollars of the approximately 160 billion spent on education in developing countries was provided by donors. In proportion to the total, it is a modest amount. However, in light of the low value taxpayers place on foreign assistance, especially in the United States, it is imperative that donor officials demonstrate that: (a) resources devoted to educational development are being wisely and effectively used and (b) benchmarks are created against which progress in increasing the numbers of children with access to quality schooling can be measured. The donor community supports comparative education research both within and among countries. The findings are used to maximize the impact of scarce resource investments, to design more effective, sustainable education activities, and to monitor and evaluate progress towards country-defined objectives. Whenever appropriate, results are used cross-nationally to replicate the conditions for success enjoyed in some countries and to avoid the conditions that led to failure in others. The largest source of funds for comparative-education research, almost exclusively applied and problem-oriented, is international donors. However, even in agencies such as the United States Agency for International Development (USAID), which spent approximately $160 million on education in developing countries in 1988, only 3.5 percent of that total was marked for research.

Examples of Funded Research

In the past decade several large-scale comparative research activities have captured the attention of comparative educators, political decision-makers, and funding sponsors. Each of these efforts represents different perspectives on research objectives and methodologies. The following three examples illustrate the form that such studies can take. The first two illustrate cross-national projects. And though the focus of this book is on international comparative studies, it is useful at this point to recognize that broad-scale research can also be conducted within a given country. The third of our examples draws attention to one variety of such within-country investigations.

Studies by the International Association for the Evaluation of Educational Achievement (IEA)

The IEA Studies were conceived in the 1970's as a means of comparing the performance of students in selected subjects across national boundaries. The designers of the studies were acutely aware of the contextual and pedagogical differences that existed among education systems. Their work over the past two decades has led to significant breakthroughs in the development of valid cross-cultural measures of student achievement. Researchers have developed sampling methodologies that account for significant internal variation in countries but yet allow for generalization across countries. Sophisticated analytic techniques have been created that permit comparisons across national samples despite problems of missing and occasionally unreliable data, variations in curriculum content and pedagogical style, and differences in the organizational structure of school systems.

IEA findings have been instrumental in calling to the attention of politicians and key educators the large and growing differences across nations on basic achievement-test data. Officials in the U.S. Department of Education, for example, are alarmed by test results that show U.S. secondary students ranked 14th on mathematics scores among the 15 nations with equivalent measures (Altbach, 1987). U.S. ninth graders ranked 13th out of 17 nations on science achievement tests (IEA, 1988).

The IEA studies are not without their critics. Some have argued that the cross-national collection of achievement data fosters a climate of "olympic gamesmanship" with regard to schooling (Inkeles, 1979). Others have noted that in the effort to make the studies comparable across nations, methodological and content sacrifices have been made at the expense of a more complete understanding of variations within individual countries, variations that, if more carefully researched, might better inform national policies designed to improve the education status of children (Theisen *et al.*, 1983).

Despite these criticisms, the IEA activities have made significant contributions to the methodologies and analytic tools available to comparative-education researchers. The studies have also called to the attention of key education and political actors the substantial differences that exist among the educational systems of the world in terms of the academic achievement they produce. IEA studies have shed light on why some of these differences occur and have highlighted a range of inefficiencies in the schooling process. The legacy of IEA investigations is the lesson that countries learn not only from the successes and failures of others, but that the emerging global community requires that nations be concerned with parity of pupil performance as they improve their systems according to indigenous norms and standards.

The BRIDGES Project

The Basic Research and Implementation for Developing Education Systems project (BRIDGES) was a five-year cross-national research effort funded by USAID and focused on developing countries. Implemented by Harvard University and sub-contractors, the effort represented a novel approach to advancing educational reform and development.

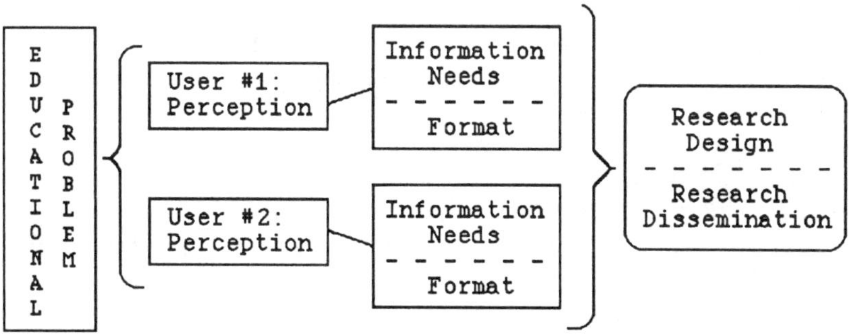

Traditional comparative research projects often begin with the question "What do I think the education community needs to know about problem x in order to ameliorate that problem?" Usually the results, when obtained from an investigation, are fed to decision-makers in the form of reports. The BRIDGES project was designed to integrate the user's need for particular types of knowledge and information into research questions: "What kinds of information do decision-makers need and use in making key policy determinations?" "In what format is information most readily used and applied by these officials?"

In consultation with ministry officials from developing countries, the BRIDGES staff defined five sets of variables subject to manipulation by shifting educational policies:

—instructional materials
—teacher characteristics
—learning technologies
—learning facilities
—information use

The researchers then reviewed the educational and social science literature from industrialized and developing nations to document what was already known about the behavior of each of these sets of variables separately or in combination with other variables. The items were then examined to determine how much they influenced educational achievement and efficiency. The objective was to identify what policy implications consistently appeared across the country reviews. This comparative analysis led to one of three conclusions:

1. The research that had already been conducted on these variables was relatively complete and further investigations were unlikely to reveal new and different conclusions. Recommendation: Do not expend further resources on researching these topics.
2. There are significant gaps in the research literature on a particular topic, but further investigation is unlikely to lead to insights that can be enacted by either policy change or resource reallocation. Recommendation: Acknowledge that the problem exists, but leave further investigation and intervention to others.
3. Gaps that exist in the comparative literature are substantial, they focus on key issues, and they can be addressed by further research. Recommendation: If the findings have a high probability of being used by decision-makers and planners as previously defined by the survey of key officials, proceed with the research.

It is important to note that the BRIDGES model of comparative research is decision-oriented. It is characteristic of efforts funded by many international donors in that it is highly applied (that is, focused on immediate action), and it attempts to draw on the lessons learned from investments in other countries with comparable socio-economic and cultural settings. The comparability of country settings is always problematic because of a large number of factors affecting educational conditions, including cultural variations, organizational differences, political structures, and administrative traditions.

Projects by the National Council of La Raza

The National Council of La Raza exists to improve life opportunities for more than 20 million Americans of Hispanic descent. The Council conducts applied research, policy analysis, and advocacy on behalf of all Hispanic Americans. It publishes such studies as *Literacy in the Hispanic Community* (Vargas, 1988) and *The Education of Hispanics: Status and Implications* (Drum, 1986). Using standard research techniques and statistical measures, the reports identify inequities among racial/ethnic groups in the United States in terms of student enrollments, achievement, and access to resources. The studies are comparative in the sense that they examine student populations for systematic differences in performance and the determinants of those differences within and among groups. Comparisons may be made across states, occupation categories, and genders. The Council is an example of the way special interest groups can use scientific research to identify and legitimize needs for social and educational reform.

Funding Considerations

Given the shortage of funds to conduct cross-national studies, it is not surprising that researchers are increasingly looking to constellations of countries that share similar characteristics as the units of their analysis. For example, Sub-Saharan African nations, although quite different in their cultural heritage and historical traditions, share similar contemporary educational profiles and face very nearly the same economic constraints to development. Research findings that inform decision-makers in one country about the application of technology to improve access to school by rural populations, for example, might well have strong comparative relevance in neighboring countries. A constant challenge is to sort out those cultural and organizational differences that might facilitate or impede the transfer of knowledge across educational settings. A second challenge is to design dissemination and utilization strategies which may have an impact on the policy-making processes of those countries committed to educational reform.

Not all donor agencies fund purely applied research efforts or activities that are cross-national in scope. Organizations such as the International Development Research Center (IDRC) in Canada also support relatively small-scale research and development activities by indigenous researchers. IDRC's activities and comparable investments made by both large and small donors are important to enhancing the research capacities of scholars and practitioners in developing countries. Donors of all sizes have niches to fill in support of establishing the research foundations necessary to ensure a self-sustaining, self-analytic capability that is the basis for developing a sound, equitable, and efficient education system.

LINKING COMPARATIVE-EDUCATION RESEARCH TO EDUCATIONAL AND SOCIAL CHANGE

Comparative-education research over the past three decades has demonstrated that a clear distinction exists between information that is gathered by researchers and the knowledge that is produced from that information. Information may be random and disconnected. For example, data that are produced for annual statistical reports are rarely used for planning and design purposes. Yet those same data, if placed into a logical, analytic framework and integrated into routine decision-making can form a knowledge base that may be used to improve the educational system.

The link between research and educational and social change rests on:

—the degree to which research-based knowledge is integrated into the formation and implementation of national and local educational policies,

—the quality of the decision-making and analysis used in addressing policy issues,

—the validity and reliability of the research that constitutes the knowledge base,
—the appropriateness and timeliness of the knowledge to the issues that need to be addressed.

Comparative research, in the best of circumstances, is cumulative over time, across locales (whether those be national or district boundaries), and across disciplines. Studies that have the greatest impact and relevance are those which integrate ideas and facts into observations that examine education as a total process, not as a disaggregated set of discrete pedagogical or policy-making activities. Teachers, parents, and officials act within the context of multiple social and economic pressures; studies that ignore this complexity, diminish their influence on social change.

Knowledge-building through comparative research has, in the past, too often focused on differences between and within educational systems. Over the past thirty years, however, researchers have observed that the similarities across systems —primarily in terms of objectives, problems, and constraints— are equally striking. These similarities, many of which are noted elsewhere in this volume, argue for the application of comparable, albeit not uniform, research methodologies across educational systems. Quantitative and qualitative methods are called for which take into consideration the complexity of each case and, at the same time, attempt to examine the same issue in multiple settings. The challenge to comparativists is to sort out those influences which are culture and context specific from those which are not.

In the final analysis, educational systems vary in structure, purpose, and accomplishments, despite their similarities. Regardless of the best intentions of researchers, knowledge will not always be used by policy-makers and education managers in ways that are most instrumentally rational and effective. In many instances, established education policies may be in direct contradiction to the changes suggested by a study's findings, so that the research will be ignored. A further point is that the effectiveness of research should not be measured by the immediacy of its impact. Comparative studies can stimulate dialogue and provide the framework for:

—enhancing the accountability of decision-makers by making policy options and their attendant outcomes public,
—increasing the rationality of decision-making by making a variety of options and anticipated results available to key education officials, and
—identifying new educational possibilities, new mixes of educational resources and interventions to achieve desired goals.

In summary, comparative researchers can have substantial impact on educational change by:
—carefully targeting their intended audience and policy-making clientele,

—examining education from a holistic, cross-sectoral perspective,
—presenting findings in terms of options, written in the context of the political, financial, and educational tradeoffs associated with each of them,
—disseminating findings in a manner and focus that will capture the interest of decision-makers and that will inform their deliberations, and
—providing critiques and assessment of current and past attempts at educational reform.

These conclusions taken together represent a departure from the less proactive posture that many comparativists have demonstrated in the past. What, then, are the implications of these recommendations for future research activities?

FUTURE TRENDS IN COMPARATIVE RESEARCH

In the years ahead, controversy is likely to persist among scholars and practitioners over the technical conditions necessary to allow meaningful comparison. Each of the variety of theoretical perspectives and methodologies has its advocates and detractors. Yet, driven largely by nearly universal demands for educational reform and efficiencies, comparative research offers excellent prospects for facilitating change.

Despite the ambiguity characterizing the concept of comparison and the limitations of comparative methodologies, comparative research has contributed incrementally to our understanding of educational systems and processes. The wealth of data, information, and knowledge that has accumulated on most of the nations of the world has stimulated a new era of cross-national borrowing. Comparative studies have helped us learn something of the complexities in the diffusion of innovations across nations. The influence of cultural paradigms, ideologies, and theoretical perspectives has been imprinted on both the design of research and the interpretation of results. Progress in the conduct of studies has introduced us to the intricate and often tortuous process of linking new knowledge to decisions and thus has helped to dispel much of our earlier naivete about linear, "rational" planning. We have unlearned some of our earlier preconceptions about the consistency of relationships between educational inputs and outputs and have developed newer, more realistic sets of hypotheses regarding significant inputs.

New developments in communications technology, the opening of political borders, and the growing importance of developing world economics will keep comparative research in the limelight in the foreseeable future. The field is likely to grow in importance and in the frequency with which it is utilized. We estimate that these three areas of change will influence comparative research in the following ways:

Communications

Technology now provides decision-makers with tools to assemble and analyze data with speed and efficiencies never known before. The use of micro-computers to produce annual statistical reports and the construction of databases that will inform those reports will make more data available to more people. Systemic codification of data will make it easier to check for inconsistencies and easier to make longitudinal and cross-sectional comparisons. Because databases are readily distributable in micro-computer format, they are also likely to be accessible to increasingly large numbers of people —both practitioners and scholars. Public review of data may lead to greater accountability, and to an exploration of wider policies options.

Video-disc and computer technologies, and international communication tools such as the fax, will increase the speed with which research findings can be disseminated and the ease with which libraries of research materials can be collected and shared around the world. These developments will be of greatest importance to scholars and educators in developing nations who lack sufficient resources to conduct their own research and who have limited access to current educational references. These developments may help to shrink the distance between "center" and "periphery" researchers.

Political Change

The walls surrounding Eastern European nations literally and figuratively have been disintegrating. Countries in Latin America, South Asia, and Africa have been attempting to diagnose and solve their political, economic, and educational problems. In these situations, comparative researchers will have the opportunity to reassess the reliability and validity of country statistics on schooling and will be requested to assist in developing a better understanding of the organizational and operational structure of those systems. By the year 2000, we anticipate that researchers will devote considerable effort to the development and implementation of a select number of comparable education indicators across all nations. Comparative researchers will be instrumental in improving the quality of educational data in both the public and confidential domains. Descriptions of national educational systems will expand and improve; they will also become more complex. As researchers grow more aware of the multitude of ways that education is linked to social, political, and economic forces and to changes in other social sectors, they will employ new, more broad-based, and long-term criteria in evaluating the effectiveness of existing programs and policies and in estimating the possibilities of new areas.

Economic Resources

The global economic crisis is forcing educators to address the need for improving the quality of its potential work force and the need to achieve greater efficiency and effectiveness in the use of resources allocated to developing that human resource base. The 1990s promise to be the decade of "Education for All" (EFA, 1989). The EFA charter calls for an 80% primary school enrollment rate for all of the countries of the world by the year 2000. To not succeed is to jeopardize the well-being of all nations. Comparative educators will contribute to this quest by:

—continuing research on ways to improve access to, and the quality of, educational services.

—examining policies and programs that work in certain countries and inspecting the contextual factors that are necessary to ensure their application elsewhere.

—Investigating how to strengthen the linkage between education and work.

—Scrutinizing "optimal" mixes of public and private support for education under different conditions and of appropriate balances of resource allocation among primary, secondary, and tertiary levels of education.

Comparative studies will not be limited to these issues in the next decade but will be heavily influenced by them. Researchers will also be extending work already done in areas in which significant progress has been made. The more general questions include:

Transfer of Knowledge

1. What kinds of tools and methodologies are especially effective in transfering knowledge across cultural, social, and linguistic boundaries? For what kinds of knowledge are these methods most productive?

2. What organizational and social characteristics facilitate the institutionalization of knowledge and of methods produced by comparative research?

3. What kinds of information are most needed by scholars and practitioners to understand and improve educational systems and the achievement of individual students? In what format is this information most usefully presented?

Implementation of Change

1. How do decision-making processes vary across educational settings? What do those variations imply for the collection, analysis, and presentation of the information that we seek?

2. When, how, and at what levels have successful education interventions been accomplished? How do these efforts inform new initiatives in both the industrialized and developing nations?

3. What do the experiences of the newly-industrialized countries (Korea, Singapore, Taiwan, and others) mean for the educational choices of nations embarking on similar processes of change?

4. What new organizations, cross-cultural or global in scope, need to be created to fulfill the various research and development objectives identified earlier in this chapter?

Conceptual Integration

1. How can more fruitful dialogue be promoted between the various theoretical camps of researchers? How can the ever more sophisticated methodological tools available to comparativists be harnessed to inform better the programs of donors and governments?

2. How well does theoretical and conceptual evidence mesh in informing issues such as the centralization/localization debate that will play major roles in shaping education policy in the 1990s and 21st century?

CONCLUSION

If the state of comparative research can be summed up in two words they are *balance* and *integration*. Balance is required in the interplay of disciplines and methodologies that are brought to bear on education issues. Balance is necessary in the application of conceptual models to issues. Balance is required between our efforts to generalize and our desire to isolate characteristics that are unique.

Integration means that we must meld the research and experiences of scholars the world over in order to gain a better, more multi-faceted picture of educational problems and innovative solutions. Integration is necessary to fuse research with practice; research resources are too scarce to be able to afford to do otherwise.

Comparative education research has generated an enviable pool of knowledge in the past three decades. The next decade promises to be an exciting period of quantitative growth and qualitative improvement.

REFERENCES

Altbach, P. G. (1978) The university as center and periphery. *Journal of Higher Education,* 3, Autumn: 157-169.

Altbach, P.G. (1987) Special issue on the second IEA study. *Comparative Education Review*, 31 (1): 7-158.

Arnove, R. F. (1980) Comparative education and world system analysis. *Comparative Education Review,* 24 (1): 48-62

Bereday, G. Z. F. (1964) *Comparative methods in education.* New York: Holt, Rinehart, & Winston.

Berger, P., Berger, B., & Kellner, H. (1973) *The homeless mind.* New York: Vintage.

Borg, W. R., & Gall, M. D. (1989) *Educational Research.* New York: Longman.

Bowman, M. J., & Anderson, C. A. (1968) Concerning the role of education in development. In M. J. Bowman, *Readings in the economics of Eeducation* (pp. 113-131). Paris: UNESCO.

Carnoy, M. (1974) *Education as cultural imperialism.* New York: David McKay.

Coombs, P H. (1985) *The world crisis in education: The visions for the eighties.* New York, Oxford.

Dogan, M., & Pelassy, D. (1984) *How to compare nations.* Chatham, NJ: Chatham House.

Drum, L. (1986) *The education of Hispanics: Status and implications.* Washington, DC: Policy Analysis Center, National Council of La Raza.

EFA (1989, September) *World charter on education for all and framework foor action to meet basic learning needs. Working Draft B.* New York: Education for All.

Gay, L. R. (1987) *Educational Research.* Columbus: Merrill.

Good, C. V. (Ed.) (1973) *Dictionary of education.* New York: McGraw Hill.

Heyneman, S., & Loxley, W. (1983) The effect of primary school quality on academic achievement across 29 high- and low-income countries. *American Journal of Sociology,* 88 (6): 1162-1194.

Holmes, B. (1981) *Comparative education: Some considerations of method.* London: George Allen.

IEA (International Association for the Evaluation of Educational Achievement) (1988). *Science achievement in 17 countries.* Oxford: Pergamon .

Inkeles, A. (1979) National differences in scholastic performance. *Comarative Education Review,* 23 (3) :386-407.

Inkeles, A., & Holsinger, D. (Eds.) (1974) *Education and individual modernity in developing countries.* Leiden: E. J. Brill.

Leigh, A., & Simmons, J. (1975) *The determinants of school achievement in development countries: The education production function. World Bank staff working paper no. 201.* Washington, D.C.: World Bank.

Levy, M. J. (1970) Scientific analysis is a subset of comparative analysis. In J. C. McKinney & E. A. Tiryakinn (Eds.) 1970. *Theoretical sociology.* New York: Appleton-Century-Crofts.

Popkewitz, T. (1984) *Paradigm and ideology in educational research.* New York: Falmer.

Postlethwaite, T. N. (Ed.) (1988) *The Encyclopedia of Coomparative Education and National Systems of Education.* Oxford: Pergamon.

Ragan, C. C. (1987) *The comparative method: Moving beyond qualitative and quantitative strategies*. Berkeley: University of California Press.

Swanson, G. (1971) Framework for comparative research: Structural anthropology and the theory of action. In L. Valier (Ed.), *Comparative methods in sociology: Essays on trends and applications* (pp. 141-202). Berkeley: University of California Press.

Theisen, G. (1984, March) *Comparative educational analysis: The measurement of meaning and the meaning of measurement.* Paper presented at the meeting of the Comparative and International Education Society, Houston, TX.

Theisen, G., Achola, P., & Boakari, F. (1983) The underachievement of cross-national studies of achievement. *Comparative Education Review,* 27 (1): 46-68.

Vargas, A. (1988) *Literacy in the Hispanic community.* Washington, DC: Policy Analysis Center, National Council of La Raza.

Wallerstein, I. (1979) *The modern world system.* London: Academic Press.

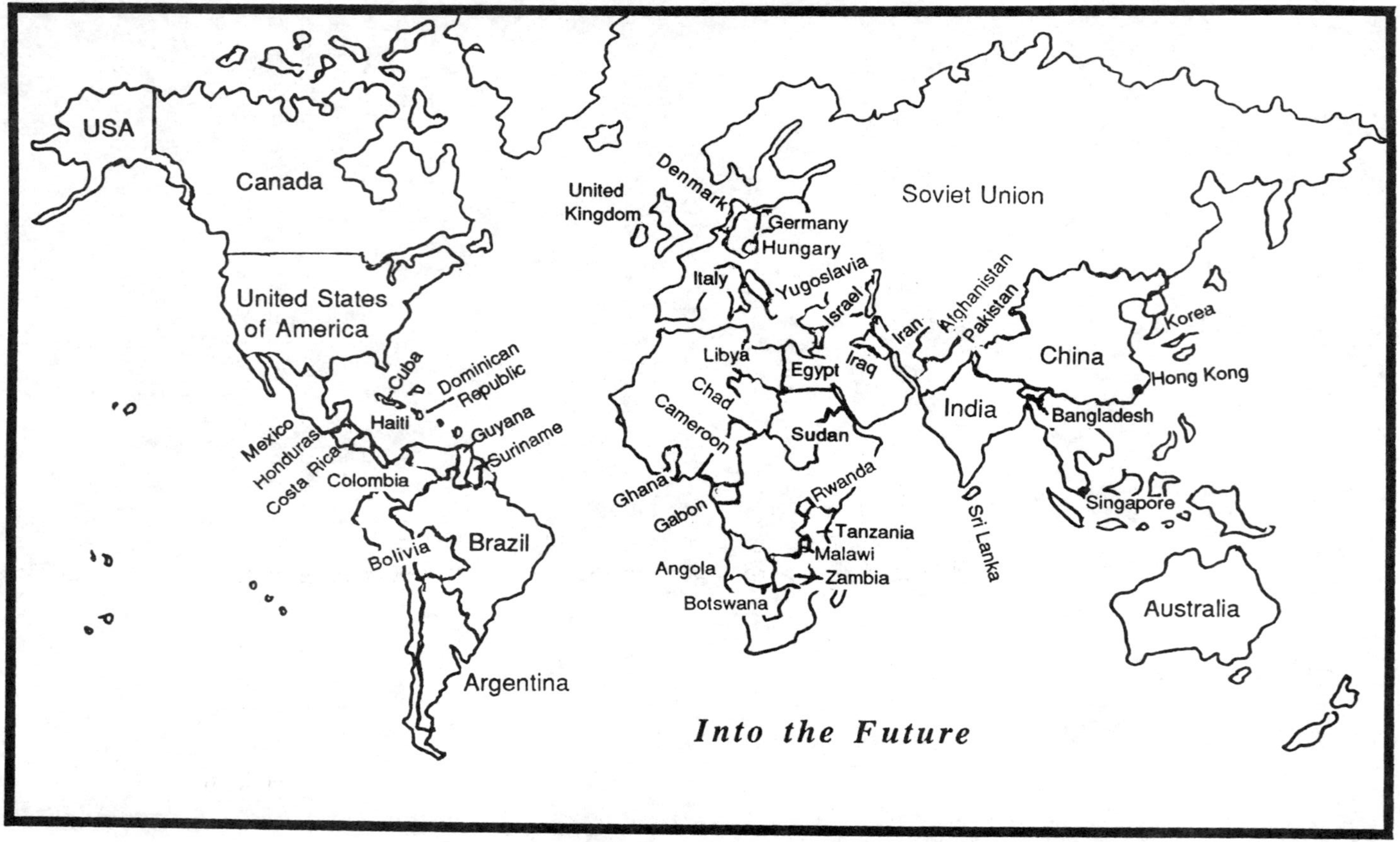
USA
Canada
United States of America
Mexico
Honduras
Costa Rica
Cuba
Haiti
Dominican Republic
Guyana
Suriname
Colombia
Bolivia
Brazil
Argentina
United Kingdom
Denmark
Germany
Hungary
Italy
Yugoslavia
Israel
Soviet Union
Iran
Afghanistan
Pakistan
Iraq
Libya
Egypt
Chad
Cameroon
Sudan
Ghana
Gabon
Rwanda
Tanzania
Malawi
Zambia
Angola
Botswana
India
Sri Lanka
China
Korea
Hong Kong
Bangladesh
Singapore
Australia
Into the Future

CHAPTER 12

Postscript — Into the Future

What developments may appear in the decades ahead?

R. MURRAY THOMAS

To supplement the estimates of future prospects found in Chapters 2 through 11, this final chapter offers additional speculation about education in the years ahead. The extensive first portion of the chapter contains conjecture about the likely influence of three societal conditions on educational operations. The brief second part of the chapter offers a prediction about the future of international comparative education as a field of study.

A LIKELY FUTURE FOR THE WORLD'S EDUCATION SYSTEMS

Three societal factors that will significantly affect the future of education are population-growth patterns, the use of natural resources, and technological innovations. The following pages furnish predictions about how these factors may develop in the decades ahead and about likely educational consequences of such developments. The speculation includes both an identification of educational problems and a description of measures that could be adopted for attacking the problems.

Population Growth and Distribution

Pondering the question of how well future educational provisions will keep pace with the world's population growth brings to mind Stephen Crane's poem about the man who pursued the horizon (McDonald, 1964: 15). Like the horizon, population growth for the coming half century will continue to speed far ahead of educational planners' ability to furnish suitable educational opportunities for the world's inhabitants. The nature of the problem has been dramatically reflected in demographers' population expectations for the 100-year period between 1950 and 2050. The world's inhabitants in 1990 were estimated at 5.32 billion. Demographers propose that this figure will more than double to 10.8 billion by 2050. In recent decades, both the absolute numbers of people and the rate of growth have been increasing: "It took only about 13 years for the world population to grow from 4 to 5 billion, whereas it took about a century and a quarter to grow from 1 to 2 billion" (Jamison, Johnson, & Engels, 1987: 1).

As Figure 12-1 shows, virtually all of the next half-century's increase will occur in developing nations, since the advanced industrial societies have by now nearly reached a steady state in growth due to family-planning practices and other social conditions that cause the developed countries to produce hardly more than enough children to replace their elders in the population. This means that the most serious educational problems associated with population growth will be suffered by developing societies.

Figure 12-1
World Population Increase

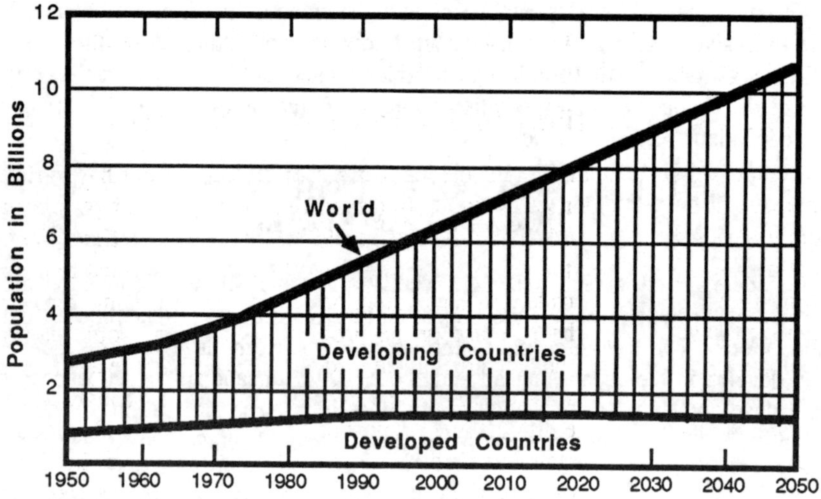

Source: Jamison, Johnson, & Engels, 1987: 1.

Whereas in 1950 two out of three of the world's peoples lived in developing nations, the faster growth rates in those countries has now resulted in three out of every four people inhabiting developing regions. Asia, as the world's largest land mass, contained half the world's population by the 1990s, while the other half was divided rather evenly between the the advanced industrial nations and the remaining developing societies (Jamison, Johnson, & Engels, 1987: 3).

> Birth rates have been declining throughout the world for the past several decades. Death rates have also declined, but as populations begin to have increasing proportions in the older ages, death rates are likely to rise. This is already happening in many developed countries. Among developing regions, vital rates are highest in Sub-Saharan Africa, while birth rates are lowest in Asia and death rates are lowest in Latin America. In spite of declines in

> fertility in the developing countries, the current birth rate of 31 per 1,000 population is more than twice the rate in the developed countries.... A continuing decline in the birth rate is expected in both developed and developing countries at least until the middle of the next century, as more and more couples control their fertility (Jamison, Johnson, & Engels, 1987: 7).

Such, then, are the general trends in world population growth. And while these gross figures are of some value for predicting educational consequences, additional information is required for speculating about the likely effects of population issues in specific regions and nations. Such information includes individual countries' recent (1) overall population growth rates, (2) mortality and fertility rates, (3) government population policies, (4) indices of the societies' economic capacity, and (5) migration patterns. We first illustrate these five factors as they are found in specific nations, then consider strategies for coping with the problems posed by such circumstances.

Population Conditions in Representative Nations

The contributions of individual societies to the world's population has varied markedly from one nation to another. For example, the number of people in certain developed nations declined during the 1980s (Denmark, East and West Germany, Hungary), and the populations of about 20 more are expected to drop during the 2020-2030 decade. In these countries, which are reaching zero or negative growth rates, the increase in the proportion of older people poses problems of employment, health care, housing, social insurance for the aged, and changed patterns of consumer demand. The trend toward an increasingly older population also forces the diminishing proportion of workers in the population to pay increasingly larger amounts to the support of the non-productive elderly.

In 2030, when two dozen or more developed countries experience zero or negative population growth, at least the same number of African and Middle-Eastern nations will still be growing annually at a rate of 2.5% or more. Among the world's major regions, the most serious growth problems are in Sub-Saharan Africa, where over two-thirds of the 25 countries with the world's highest fertility rates are located. Eight of the world's nine high-fertility countries are in Sub-Saharan Africa. The largest increases have occurred in Benin, Congo, Malawi, and Rwanda. "The only four African countries in this group that show any signs of decreasing fertility are Botswana, Kenya, Madagascar, and Uganda" (Jamison, Johnson, & Engels, 1987: 17).

Three of the factors which interact to affect a society's educational and social-welfare provisions are (1) the population growth rate, (2) the nation's economic vitality as reflected in the per-capita gross national product (GNP), and (3) the government's attitude toward population conditions. The 10 examples in Table 12-1 show how these factors may differ from one developing nation to another.

Table 12-1

Population Growth, GNP, and Government Attitude

Country	*Population Growth Rate*	*Per Capita* GNP ($US)*	*Government's Attitude toward Growth Rate*
Argentina	1.27%	2,350	Satisfactory
Bolivia	2.76%	600	Mortality rate too high, fertility rate too low
Bangladesh	2.67%	160	Mortality & fertility too high
China	1.39%	300	Mortality & fertility too high
Cuba	.75%	?	Satisfactory
Egypt	2.55%	760	Mortality & fertility too high
Gabon	3.45%	3,080	Mortality rate too high, fertility rate too low.
Iran	3.45%	?	Satisfactory
Libya	3.65%	?	Satisfactory
Mexico	2.20%	1,860	Mortality rate satisfactory, fertility rate too high

*Annual per capital GNP
Source: United Nations Population Fund, 1989.

First, compare the West African nation of Gabon (pop. 1 million) with Mexico (pop. 80 million). Gabon's annual growth rate of 3.45% is far higher than Mexico's 2.20%, yet the government of Gabon hopes to accelerate growth even more (decrease mortality, increase fertility), while the Mexican government seeks to reduce growth. This phenomenon can be explained by the rationales the two governments offer in support of their proposals. In Gabon:

> The policy to increase population size aims at counteracting acute labor shortages. Rural labor deficits have disrupted agricultural production which is a necessity. The current development plan stresses the need to mobilize all human resources to participate actively in achieving development goals" (United Nations Population Fund, 1989: 205).

The difficulty in providing agricultural workers in Gabon has resulted not only from the interaction of mortality and fertility rates, but also from migration from the countryside to the city. Urban population has been growing at 5.68% annually and rural only 1.75%. In a primarily agricultural country, 41% of the people have become city dwellers.

In contrast, the Mexican government considers continued population growth a detriment to the socioeconomic welfare of the nation as increasing numbers of people are unable to make a significant contribution to the economy, so they become a burden on the society. The government has incorporated population-control provisions into its programs of education, public health, agrarian reform, and rural development.

Next, consider two oil-rich Muslim societies, Iran and Libya. Both governments report satisfaction with growth rates that are the highest in Table 12-1. At a yearly increase of 3.45%, Iran's population in 1990 of 48 million will double in slightly less than 20 years, whereas Libya's 4 million people, at a growth rate of 3.65%, will reach 8 million in 19 years. The satisfaction expressed by both governments with these high rates derives from their confidence that oil sales can sustain rapid population rise and from their conviction that population size is an important factor in their nations' functioning as international political powers, particularly as agents in the spread of Islamic fundamentalism. The attitude of the Iranian government also reflects the country's experience during the Iran-Iraq war of the 1980s when many thousands of young men and women were needed in the armed forces. Thus, bearing more children became every family's patriotic duty. These ambitious rates of population increase, however, place a heavy burden on the nations' educational establishments to furnish buildings, teachers, and equipment to serve the rapidly expanding cohorts of learners.

Two other Muslim nations in Table 12-1 —Bangladesh and Egypt— have growth rates substantially lower than those of Iran and Libya, yet their leaders wish to reduce population increase. The official position of both governments is that the chief deterrent to socioeconomic development is excessive population growth. Thus, population-control measures are included in both countries' national-development plans.

The Bolivian government has never included a comprehensive policy toward population in its series of development programs that began in 1952. The government's desire to increase fertility rates is founded on a perception that more people are needed in rural areas (urban growth rate = 4.21%, rural 1.34%) and that too many people are emigrating from Bolivia.

Such countries as Cuba and China have succeeded in reducing population increase by means of family-planning education and incentives for people to have smaller families.

In summary, the pace of population increase in the decades ahead can be expected to vary markedly among nations as a result of different governments' policies, traditional attitudes of the populace toward issues of religion and of family size, and the condition of the nations' economies. Among the countries that will experience the most rapid growth are many which lack the financial ability to provide educational opportunities for the majority of their inhabitants.

As noted above, birth rates and death rates within a population are not the only factors affecting educational policy and practice. Migration is also a significant force. The two most important reasons people move from one place to another are to escape political oppression and to improve their economic welfare. The migration of large numbers of refugees fleeing from political conflicts has included the exodus of Ethiopians from Tigray Province into Sudan, of Afghans into Pakistan during the Soviet occupation of Afghanistan, of Chinese and Vietnamese into Hong Kong, of Jews from the Soviet Union into Israel, and of Africans into Botswana and Cameroon from neighboring countries. Political refugees and undocumented immigrants seeking better job opportunities are also viewed as a significant problem by a broad array of other governments, ranging from the United States and Canada to Costa Rica, Honduras, and India.

Such population shifts yield educational consequences for both the country the migrants enter and the one they have just left. In the country they enter, immigrants not only swell the ranks of those seeking educational services, but they also bring language skills and cultural traditions that may not fit easily into the practices of existing schools and nonformal programs. Obviously, the larger the number of immigrants and the more varied their characteristics, the greater the problems educators face in coping with learners' cultural diversity.

An important educational consequence for the country the migrants have left is the *brain drain* —the phenomenon of skilled, educated citizens abandoning their native land for better opportunities elsewhere. Present-day examples of developing nations that officially express concern with the brain drain are Suriname (which has suffered a net loss of 5 people per 1000 through migration), Chad, Ghana, Guyana, Haiti, India, and Iraq. Governments of advanced industrial countries may also complain about the loss of trained talent. A fear that skilled citizens will leave the country motivated the governments of the Soviet Union and other Eastern European nations to impose emigration restrictions until the end of 1989. Furthermore, officials in Great Britain have voiced concern about the exodus of university professors, particularly those moving to the United States.

The movement of people from one nation to another is not the only type of demographic shift that poses problems in educational planning. The worldwide rural-to-urban drift of populations produces a rising demand for school buildings and teachers in metropolitan areas and for social services intended to compensate for the conditions of poverty into which so many families slip when they move from the country to the city.

Table 12-2 displays comparisons of urban-versus-rural growth rates in a sampling of developing nations. In most cases, governments hope to stem the the rural-urban flow, but usually their efforts yield poor results. However, some nations, such as the People's Republic of China, have met with notable success by imposing strict sanctions on people moving into cities without permission.

Table 12-2

Urban Versus Rural Population Growth Rates in Developing Nations

Country	*Annual Urban Growth %*	*Annual Rural Growth %*
Afghanistan	5.84	1.82
Angola	5.57	1.68
Argentina	1.65	—.95
Brazil	3.19	—1.27
China	2.16	1.18
Dominican Republic	3.85	—.03
Iraq	4.46	.90
Malawi	7.38	2.69
Rwanda	7.60	3.08
Tanzania	9.59	1.31
Zambia	6.09	1.18

Source: United Nations Population Fund, 1989.

It is apparent from Table 12-2 that the population problems of Sub-Saharan Africa are not limited to high general growth rates. There is also a marked disparity between urban and rural rates, as migrants stream into the cities of Angola, Malawi, Rwanda, Tanzania, and Zambia in rapidly growing numbers. In Brazil, proverty-ridden sections of cities expand while the population of the nation's vast countryside declines. In such Middle-Eastern nations as Afghanistan and Iraq, rural peoples continue migrating to the cities in large numbers.

In summary, the foregoing review suggests the following population trends for the next half century:

1. There will be continued rapid increase in the world's population, with most of the growth coming in nations which suffer the weakest economic systems and which exhibit political instability.
2. Governments will differ significantly in their attitudes toward population control and in the effectiveness of their implementation of population policies.
3. Particularly in industrialized nations whose population growth has reached nearly a steady state, older adults will form an increasingly large proportion of the citizenry.

4. Migration rates from one country to another and from rural to urban areas will continue to rise as the rapidly expanded population of developing nations exerts more and more pressure on those countries' limited resources. The advance in the pace of migration will increase the socioeconomic and cultural diversity of the areas that receive the migrants.

All of the foregoing trends hold two kinds of implications for the world's educational establishments. First, education will be expected to serve as a significant instrument for altering undesired population trends. In other words, education will be the vehicle through which people acquire family-planning practices and learn the consequences of unconstructive population growth. Second, education systems, especially in developing nations, will be pressed to expand their facilities so as to care for more learners and for greater cultural diversity among the learners. Although industrialized countries will experience a reduced need for more educational facilities for the young, they will face a greater demand for educational services to adults, including the aged. The following paragraphs focus on measures that can be adopted in response to these demands.

Strategies for Coping with Population Problems

Factors that contribute to reduced fertility rates vary from one society to another. However, modern communication facilities and education, improved methods of contraception, and improved economic development have been among the more important influences enabling some developing nations to reduce fertility at a more rapid pace than was true in certain developed countries. "It took about 58 years for the total fertility rate to decline from 6.0 to 3.5 in the United States [between 1842 and 1900]. China accomplished the same changes in 7 years [1968-1975], while it took 12 years in Colombia [1068-1980] and in South Korea [1961-1973]" (Jamison, Johnson, & Engels, 1987: 13).

Among the modern communication media that contribute to population reduction are radio, motion pictures, and television, which serve as vehicles for teaching the general public about contraception, family-planning practices, and government incentives (such as free schooling for children of small families) and disincentives (such as public censure and higher taxes for large families) aimed at solving population problems.

As an example of coordinated population-control measures that a country may adopt, consider the case of Sri Lanka, a crowded island nation with limited space and limited natural resources. Although the annual growth rate by the end of the 1980s was only 1.32%, the government, in recognition of:

> the implications of excessive population growth on social and economic development,... has made a commitment to reduce the rates of growth and natural increase by expanding family planning services, promoting women's education and employment, raising the legal age of marriage, and, recently,

> by renewing its effort to combine sterilization with fiscal and monetary incentive and disincentive measures.... The levels of emigration are considered to be significant (3.3 per 1000) and satisfactory. The Government is implementing a repatriation programme [for past immigrants] and encouraging people to seek suitable employment in the [Arab] Gulf States" (United Nations Population Fund, 1989: 526).

Present trends indicate that the coming years will witness a marked increase in efforts both by governments and by international organizations to accelerate the adoption of population-control measures, with formal and nonformal educational agencies assigned a key role in promoting such measures.

Governments vary not only in the extent to which they wish to introduce population-reduction plans, but also in the degree to which they can successfully implement such plans. A nation highly successful in carrying through population reduction has been Singapore, which achieved a growth rate of 1.09% annually as a result of educational efforts and a series of strict social and economic disincentives that actively discouraged large families. By the mid-1970s the two-child family had been established as a social norm. In 1984 new measures —a set of incentives and disincentives— were introduced to encourage financially well-off and educated women to have more children and to encourage less-educated and poor women to have fewer children. The steps were intended to redress the typical "lopsided population growth" in which women in higher social classes have few children and those in the lower classes have many. A current objective of the Singapore government is to achieve a zero growth rate by 2030 (United Nations Population Fund, 1989: 518).

In the years ahead, the implementation of population-control methods promises to become increasingly efficient as experience gained in one country is transferred to other countries. The improvements that are expected will include more efficient educational methods.

The reduction of fertility rates is also fostered by steps that discourage teenagers from bearing children. In countries with the highest incidence of fertility, the birth-rates among teenage girls are nearly 10 times the rates in countries with the lowest fertility rates. However, the problem of teenage pregnancies is not limited to developing countries. For example, in the United States in the 1980s adolescent girls accounted for nearly half of all out-of-wedlock births in the nation, a rate much higher than that of other advanced industrialized countries (Romig & Thompson, 1988: 134; Jones, 1986: 228). Results of surveys conducted throughout the world are consistent with data from the United States in showing that high birthrates among teenagers are associated with low levels of educational attainment and with high rates of poverty and unemployment. The younger a woman was when she gave birth, the more likely it is that she came from an impoverished home (Zimmerman, 1988: 320). To cope with issues of teenage pregnancy, secondary schools in the United States offer three types of courses intended to help students make constructive judgments about sexual activity and parenthood. The first type, enrolling both boys and girls, consists of classes entitled *Family Life Education* or *Modern Living* that focus on such issues as choices of lifestyles, financial planning, occupational preparation, sexual behavior, and child-rearing practices. The second type, also enrolling both sexes, is typically called *Health Education*, with discussions of sexual matters comprising part of the course of study. The third variety is aimed at a more restricted clientele —pregnant adolescents and teenage mothers— with the classes often labeled *Teenage Parenting*. The stated goals are to help young mothers continue their education, control their fertility, and become better parents. A commonly used measure of the success of such efforts is the prevention of second pregnancies (Roosa, 1986: 316).

In regard to these problems of teenage pregnancy, the future is expected to find more school instruction and nonformal educational efforts designed to reduce the incidence of child bearing among adolescents and to provide opportunities for those girls who do become pregnant to continue their education.

A growing number of nations conduct programs entitled *multicultural education* aimed at improving relations among the increasingly varied religious, ethnic, and socioeconomic groups that comprise most societies. In a similar manner, *global-education* courses are designed to enhance understanding and constructive interactions among nations. Such programs are likely to increase even more rapidly in the future.

In view of the changing age structure of societies —and especially of societies with low growth rates— a greater future investment of educational resources can be expected for services to the middle-aged and the elderly. Lifelong education has become a byword in most modern societies, reflecting a commitment to furnishing learning opportunities for the entire population, an obligation that the increasing proportion of adult voting citizens are insisting that their governments honor in practice.

In summary, how well societies succeed with population control and with furnishing educational opportunities for all inhabitants clearly depends on a variety of conditions, including political stability, economic strength, government population policies (incentives and disincentives), individuals' attitudes about family planning, immigration rates, and educational provisions.

The Use of Natural Resources

Intimately linked to population growth are questions of how societies use natural resources, including human resources: Will there be enough food and shelter for all the inhabitants? Will the air to breathe, the water to drink, and the food to eat be of high quality, that is, of a quality that fosters good health and ample energy? Do people's present-day uses of the environment portend bright prospects for coming generations, or will a continuation of present patterns of use irreparably diminish future generations' life chances? Will the distribution of population and resources be such that people in all regions of the world can enjoy a fair chance to survive and prosper, or will resources be so unevenly apportioned that some peoples enjoy abundance —or at least have minimally adequate resources— while others suffer impoverishment? To what extent will the treatment of the environment by people in one region affect the fate of people in other regions? How are humans' uses of resources likely to influence the life chances of other species now on earth?

A review of recent trends in resource utilization and in the treatment of the environment indicates that there are already serious threats to the quality of life. Unless major changes are effected in how resources are employed, prospects for the future are grim indeed. As a World Bank report has pointed out:

> The links among poverty, environmental degradation, and population growth are often direct. As more and more people in poverty press upon limited natural resources in rural ares, they begin to deplete the stock of renewable resources. In South Asia the long-term deforestation of watersheds has caused severe erosion. Population pressure on the fragile land base in Africa and the Middle East has become serious. The arid and semiarid areas of the world are likely to face a crisis of water scarcity by 2000. Desertification and deforestation —often irreversible— have reduced the land available for agriculture, wildlife habitats, and recreation.
>
> But not all environmental degradation results from the pressure of population growth. Intensive use of hydrocarbons by high-income countries and deforestation in sparsely populated tropical areas are starting to have global effects. The same is true of the growing amounts of hazardous materials that are generated mainly by industrial countries. Some developing countries are experiencing serious air and water pollution (World Bank, 1989: 15).

There is widespread agreement among ecology experts that education is one of the most important instruments for correcting, or at least ameliorating, the damage that has already been done to the natural environment. It seems reasonable to assume that four types of knowledge should comprise the future content of formal, nonformal, and informal educational efforts. The four types are reflected in the following questions:

(1) What present-day environmental conditions threaten the quality of life on earth?

(2) If the forces producing such conditions continue unchanged, what consequences can be expected in the future?

(3) What steps can be taken to reverse, or at least to retard, the deterioration of the environment?

(4) What can individuals, such as students, do to alter the forces that endanger the quality of life?

Teaching about the Dangers and Their Causes

The type of curriculum content that serves to answer the first two questions is illustrated by the following examples of five environmental problems —the greenhouse effect, acid rain, deforestation, ozone destruction, and the disposal of waste.

The term *greenhouse effect* refers to the earth's atmosphere becoming increasingly hotter as short-wave radiation from the sun readily passes through the atmosphere to the earth, while at the same time the earth's longer-wave heat radiation is having an increasingly difficult time escaping out through the atmosphere. This problem of a growing imbalance between the heat received and the heat expelled by the earth is caused by an increase in atmospheric carbon dioxide, water vapor, methane, and other gases that absorb and block heat radiation rather than allowing it to pass into space. The main sources of such destructive gases are automobile exhaust fumes and the emissions of factory smoke stacks. Each year the world's 400 million automobiles discharge 550 million tons of carbon into the air. A number of consequences of continued high levels of emissions have been identified. Between 1965 and 1990, the average temperature in the tropics rose nearly one degree Celsius, so that the amount of water vapor over the equatorial Pacific increased by 20 to 30 percent. As the warming of the atmosphere continues to melt greater expanses of polar ice, thereby elevating ocean levels, the Mediterranean Sea is expected to rise 5 to 22 inches by year 2025, inundating such cities as Venice in Italy, Split in Yugoslavia, and Alexandria in Egypt. By the late 21st century the Mediterranean is expected to have risen more than six feet, thus flooding wide expanses of coastland. Already the higher water level around Australia has destroyed large areas of low-lying tropical forest (Allaby, 1990: 211-212).

Acid rain is the result of factories emitting sulfur dioxide fumes that combine with water vapor in the atmosphere to produce a sulfuric-acid form of rain which corrodes buildings, destroys plant life, and pollutes water ways. By the close of the 1980s, at least 14,000 lakes in eastern Canada were reported "acid dead", with another 300,000 damaged or vulnerable. The environmental interdependence of nations is reflected in the observation that half of the acid rain falling in Canada originated in the United States, while one-forth of the acid rain in the United States originated in Canada.

The massive destruction of forests (deforestation) and the depletion of plant life and of top soil in semiarid regions (desertification) in recent decades seriously threatens the worldwide ecosystem. The most dramatic instance of dangerous deforestation in the 1980s was the decimation of the vast Amazonian forests of Brazil, with some observers estimating that around 50,000 square miles of virgin forest were lost in 1988 alone (Allaby, 1990: 216). Not only is abundant plant life necessary for processing carbon dioxide to produce oxygen, but the earth's rainfall and temperature patterns are highly dependent on the continued vitality of forest regions.

The *ozone layer* or *ozonosphere* is the uppermost stratum of the atmosphere. Within this layer is found the greatest concentration of ozone. The layer extends from 8 to 20 miles above the earth's surface, with the heaviest concentration at an altitude of 12 miles. From the viewpoint of human welfare, a crucial function of the ozone layer is that of shielding the earth against ultraviolet radiation from the sun. Scientists have reported that the chlorofluorocarbon gases, used in such everyday products as refrigerants and fire extinguishers, have been rising into the upper atmosphere and depleting the ozone. The resulting 'holes" in the ozonosphere, detected over both the north and south poles, pose dangers to life that are as yet incompletely understood. One consequence, however, is increased danger of people developing skin cancer as a result of the higher incidence of ultraviolet light reaching the earth.

Population growth is accompanied by increasing quantities of waste products that derive from three principal sources —individual households, manufacturing plants, and such commercial operations as variety stores, business offices, markets, and restaurants. Deciding on how to get rid of the waste has become a major ecological problem, particularly in the world's rapidly expanding urban areas. The two most common ways of disposing of trash, garbage, human excrement, and chemical waste are to bury it in the earth or to pour it into waterways with the hope that it will quickly biodegrade, that is, decay into a form environmentally constructive rather than harmful. The damage resulting from unsuitable methods of waste disposal includes the spread of disease among humans and animals, contamination of potable sources of water, distortion of the earth's scenery, annihilation of plant and animal species, and depletion of natural resources required for human survival. The rate of such damage has been mounting rapidly in recent decades and can be expected to accelerate in the years ahead unless strong measures to remedy destructive disposal practices are soon adopted.

The foregoing sorts of knowledge, then, form appropriate ccurriclum content for informing learners about the extent and causes of the destruction of natural environments.

Teaching Ways to Combat Environmental Damage

The third question in our suggested list of curriculum guide-questions focuses on what students should learn about what can be done to preserve, reclaim, and enhance the quality of the environment. The following examples suggest the topics which this portion of the curriculum can profitably include:

1. Legislation. Government regulations set standards for the control of air and water pollution, the safe disposal of waste products, and the transporting and storage of dangerous substances, the cutting of forests, agricultural practices, and the like. Such legislation has been enacted at all administrative levels —local, provincial, national, and international. As an example at the international level, the European Parliament in 1989 voted to bring vehicle emissions controls into line with those of the United States by 1993. Furthermore, the European Commission in 1989 moved to take action against Britain in the European Court of Justice for failing to translate the 1985 Directive on Water Quality into national legislation and for the presence of excessive amounts of lead in water in Scotland and of nitrates in water in England. Similar action was also aimed at France and Belgium. At the same time, plans were laid to establish a Europe-wide code of labeling for consumer products to identify those least harmful to the environment (Allaby, 1990: 210).

2. *Incentives.* Governments, business organizations, philanthropic foundations, and international-aid bodies offer rewards to encourage the preservation of safe and attractive environments and to promote the reclamation of abused lands, waterways, and atmospheres. Such incentives include reduced taxes, good-citizen awards, gifts of cash or products, and public recognition through newspaper and television publicity. The use of combined negative and positive sanctions by an international organization was illustrated by (1) the World Bank's 1989 cancellation of a $500 million loan to Brazil for power-related projects (including the building of dams) and (2) the Brazilian government's abandonment of the project in favor of accepting a $400 million loan from the bank for projects related to energy conservation and the protection of indigenous peoples' tribal lands (Allaby, 1990: 210).

3. *Exploration and Invention.* Linked to legislation and incentives are the attempts of inventors to develop economically feasible substitutes for traditional energy sources and modes of disposing of waste. For example, air pollution resulting from the use of fossil fuels in automobiles, factories, and buildings can be reduced by the substitution of methanol in cars and solar energy systems for producing electricity and for heating buildings.

4. *Recycling and Reclaiming.* Among the most promising inventions are ways of recycling cast-off materials so they can be used constructively rather than cluttering the landscape and polluting the earth, atmosphere, and water. Successful programs of recycling paper, glassware, and aluminum cans have been adopted at an increasing pace in recent years. Systems of garbage disposal that turn the waste from households into fertilizer and other products have grown in popularity, especially in crowded urban centers of industrialized nations. Water purification facilities that reconstitute sewer water and desalination plants that remove the salt from sea water are increasingly adopted as sources of potable water in areas suffering drought and ones supporting large populations.

5. Education. The success of the measures described above depends to a great extent on how well people understand the relationship between the quality of life and the ways environments are affected by human actions. The success depends as well on how adequately people understand the ways the environmentally significant acts in one region affect the quality of life in other regions. Education systems —formal, nonformal, informal— bear the principal responsibility for promoting such understanding.

Our fourth curriculum guide-question concerned what students themselves might do to protect the environment. To foster students' participation in such constructive measures as those outlined above, education programs can usefully include descriptions of how, as a citizen, a student can take direct action. For example, students can learn how to evaluate a legislator's voting record, to write effective letters to political figures, to conduct peaceful demonstrations, to publicize either damaging or constructive actions of public officials and businesses, and to boycott ecologically destructive commercial ventures. In addition, students can improve their own daily treatment of the environment and organize campaigns to alter damaging practices within their school and community.

Summary

As governments and the populace grow increasingly sensitive to how critically the fate of humans and other species is threatened by deteriorating environments, the emphasis on ecological education is bound to expand significantly. Recent years have witnessed a marked addition of departments of environmental affairs in universities, of courses on ecological matters in colleges and secondary schools, and of units of study in social-science classes at primary and secondary levels. These trends can be expected to accelerate in the future.

Technological Innovations

The remarkable speed at which electronic computers and associated inventions have changed the lives of so many people during the past two decades suggests that we can hardly overestimate the way additional technological innovations may alter life over the next half century. Our best educated guess will likely fall short of envisioning the technological marvels that lie ahead. However, we can illustrate ways that presently available technology could readily affect educational practice in the near future. Our six examples focus on (1) the production of reading materials, (2) distance education, (3) individualized instruction, (4) educational administration, and (5) the conduct of research. The following applications move from the simplest to the most elaborate. In this context, *simple* and *elaborate* refer to the complexity of the equipment, the ease of keeping the equipment in working order, the training of personnel, and the cost of the equipment and its use.

Producing Reading Materials

Despite the recent expansion of electronic media throughout the world's education systems, books and allied printed materials will continue in the future to serve as education's most important instructional and administrative media. In the great majority of the world's classrooms, the most reliable indicator of what is taught is the textbook. In like manner, the most convenient source of information about the way the education system is administered is the collection of printed regulations and reports that governments issue to guide their education systems' daily operations.

For instructional purposes, the advantages of books and pamphlets over other media are so great that their continued popularity over the coming years is assured. Unlike computers and television receivers, books are easily carried from place to place, require no electricity, are not subject to mechanical breakdown, and can be used at the learner's own convenience. Thus, printed materials will continue to provide the core of instruction, particularly in developing societies.

However, what is new and very promising is the innovative technology for producing high-quality learning materials at low cost and suited to the needs of particular regions, schools, and classrooms. This recent technology is popularly known as *desk-top publishing* (Seybold & Dressler, 1987). Today, a teacher using a microcomputer, a photocopying machine, and a heavy-duty stapler can produce instructional pamphlets of professional quality. Advanced industrial nations provide such equipment for virtually every school. Developing countries are rarely so fortunate. Yet, they can at least equip the central ministry of education and regional offices with such items and, at those levels of the administrative hierarchy, can produce instructional materials.

From the viewpoint of simplicity and speed of production, it is more practical for a school system to publish short pamphlets —16 or 32 pages— than entire textbooks. A series of such pamphlets can comprise the text materials for an entire year-long course. Teachers or curriculum developers with a modicum of training in the writing of instructional materials can thereby adjust the reading matter to the local language, local geographical and historical conditions, and local value systems.

The process of composing a manuscript on a computer is far faster than writing by hand or with a traditional typewriter. Errors are easily corrected, paragraphs quickly moved from one place to another, spelling checked for accuracy, synonyms provided by the computer-program's thesaurus, and encyclopedia or dictionary information brought onto the screen in a moment's time. Charts and graphs are readily created and inserted into a narrative. And whenever an extended segment of a previously printed document is to be incorporated into the manuscript, the writer need not copy the document word by word. Rather, an electronic scanner will reproduce the document in a form suitable for the manuscript. And further conveniences of this type can be expected in the future.

The book you are now reading is partially a product of desk-top publishing. The authors submitted their chapters to the editor on microcomputer disks. The editor displayed each writer's work on the screen of his own microcomputer to cast the material into the form you now see. The final version was printed by the editor in *camera-ready* condition and sent to the publisher to be printed and bound. Such use of a microcomputer eliminates the need for print-shop typesetting and saves months in the process of issuing a book.

What this technology means for the immediate future is that reading materials of high quality can quickly be created to fit specific needs of particular instructional programs. Desk-top publishing places individual school systems and teachers in control of the content of their instructional materials. Since the technology is now available at a reasonable cost for even relatively poor nations, what is needed for the future are improved methods of training personnel in the creation of effective reading materials.

Distance Education

As noted in Chapters 3 and 6, one of the most promising innovations for extending learning opportunities to large and widely-dispersed audiences has been the development of distance-education technology.

In the years ahead, distance-teaching media —particularly radio and television— will be utilized with increasing frequency and sophistication to reach learners of all ages as a relatively low cost. Distance education is a viable means for upgrading teachers' talents as well as for offering the general population basic-skills instruction (reading, writing, speaking, calculating), general and vocational education (social sciences, natural sciences, occupational knowledge), and information on family planning and population control.

A continued expansion of *open-education* opportunities, as exemplified in the open-university programs described in Chapter 6, can be expected in the coming years to serve the needs of adults who wish to update their vocational preparation as societies come to depend increasingly on a technically-trained labor force.

Individualized Instruction

As nations progress in their ability to provide microcomputers for every classroom, opportunities increase for furnishing students instruction suited to their individual interests and learning rates. Not only have computers proven to be effective for drill activities (learning arithmetic combinations or foreign-language vocabulary words), but a growing array of programs have been developed to teach higher-level skills of analysis and problem solving in subject-matter fields ranging from the physical sciences to history, physical education, and psychology. One important advantage of well-conceived computer programs is that they give the student frequent, immediate feedback about how well he or she is mastering each step of the learning sequence. And when a segment of the sequence has been misunderstood, programs typically switch the student to an alternate explanation of the troublesome concept in an effort to remedy the learner's misconception.

Computers serve this individualizing function at all levels of the education hierarchy, kindergarten through the university. In a growing number of schools, primary-grade children begin creative writing on a computer rather than by hand, since the computer frees them of such tasks as painstakingly forming each letter and erasing mistakes. Once children learn the keyboard, they are freed to concentrate on the ideas they wish to express rather than on the mechanics of handwriting. As affordable voice-activated computers become increasingly available, pupils can dictate their thoughts into a microphone and have the resulting narrative appear in printed form on the computer screen.

Computers have also greatly extended the potential for people learning at home, either as homework for a class at school or as an independent self-improvement activity. A home microcomputer is rapidly becoming a common fixture in technologically advanced societies as well as in upper and upper-middle socioeconomic homes of many developing nations.

Progress in the use of computers and of such allied technology as compact disks is bound to accelerate in the future.

Educational Administration

Planning and implementing the conduct of a nation's education programs is clearly a very complex task. It requires a host of data-collecting and analysis, predictions about the future, supervision of ongoing activities, and assessments of how effectively the components of programs are operating. The ability of educators to carry out these functions has been greatly enhanced in recent years by the application of computers and of information networks utilizing telephone lines and communication satellites. As examples of three such administrative functions, we can briefly inspect the tasks of architectural planning, record keeping, and student assessment.

In the process of school construction, architects planning classroom buildings, laboratories, gymnasiums, and landscape patterns can avoid costly errors and save weeks of time by creating on the computer screen three-dimensional simulations of alternative designs that can be manipulated in ways which provide views from every perspective. Furthermore, the complex computations required for calculating the needed amounts of building materials, the strength and life-expectancy of building components (walls, roofs, beams, floors), and the costs of labor and materials can be produced by a computer far more accurately and infinitely faster than by hand. Such records, in their computer-stored form, can be transmitted to other regions of the nation via the telephone lines. Or a paper version of any record can easily be printed from the computer file, with an exact facsimile of the printout sent immediately over the phone lines with the aid of a relatively inexpensive *fax* attachment. If recent developments are valid portents of the future, then the use of electronic mail for educational purposes will grow at a rapid rate in the years ahead.

Within ministries of education, regional offices, and individual schools, the traditional rows of file cabinets are being eliminated as records are transferred to computer disks that take up a small fraction of the space required for file drawers.

The ease of assessing the operations of an education system is greatly enhanced by the application of computer technology. Ministries of education in industrialized and developing nations alike have been compiling test-item banks in which a large quantity of test questions for various grade levels and subject-matter fields are stored. The task of creating a test consists of drawing from the bank suitable items, which are quickly cast in the desired form of the test and printed out. After the tests have been administered, they can be scored electronically, and statistics about the success of different groups and individuals can be produced by the computer. School districts and individual teachers also develop specialized test banks. At an growing rate, particularly in higher education, students do not take a paper version of a test but, rather, they interact with a computer, which automatically scores their answers as they work through the items. These innovations in assessment techniques, and other inventions hardly envisioned today, will undoubtedly expand in the future.

Educational Research

Among all the areas of educational operations, that of educational research has perhaps profited the most from electronic innovations which contribute to greater efficiency at each stage of a typical scholarly investigation.

Early in a research process, as an investigator seeks to learn what advances have already been made in the field under study, computers linked into communications networks facilitate the task of surveying the literature in the field. From a computer terminal at one site, a researcher can discover the location and general contents of relevant books, journal articles, and theses in distant libraries. Or, as an alternative to contacting other libraries, an investigator using a compact-disk attachment to a microcomputer can find on a disk the abstracts of a quantity of pertinent articles and can immediately print those abstracts that are of particular interest. Furthermore, journal articles not available in the local library can be obtained immediately from most places around the world by means of a *fax* attachment to the telephone. In addition, one researcher can quickly correspond with a variety of others by means of electronic mail, that is, by means of a microcomputer linked into a communications network via the phone lines and satellites.

At the stage of generating new data about the research question at hand, investigators can use audiotape or videotape recorders for accurately collecting accounts of interviews, pupils' and teachers' classroom behavior, group-work activities, students' out-of-school social environments, and more. Whenever lessons are cast in the form of computer programs, students can study while seated at a computer terminal, with their work guided automatically by diagrams and reading material on the computer screen. At the same time, an accurate account of the learner's performance at each stage of the lesson is automatically recorded in the computer for later interpretation by the researcher.

After data have been collected, the results can be organized and analyzed by a computer with far greater speed and accuracy than would be possible if the researcher were working "by hand."

Finally, the task of creating a professional-quality printed report of the project is expedited through the use of a computer that functions as a word processor and a graphic-design instrument.

Summary

As the foregoing examples suggest, the field of technology provides some of the most promising possibilities for improving the efficiency of educational operations in the future. Technological innovations, when wisely used, offer the potential for enhancing the quality of education and extending learning opportunities to a wider range of populations than ever before. However, the greatest gains will likely be enjoyed by the more advanced industrialized countries which have the infrastructure (well-designed school buildings, reliable electricity, electronic-repair facilities), personnel-training programs, and economic capacity to supply and operate the new technology.

A LIKELY FUTURE FOR THE FIELD OF INTERNATIONAL COMPARATIVE EDUCATION

The quantity and quality of studies in international comparative education by the opening of the 1990s appeared greater than ever before. Participation in the world's leading comparative-education professional societies was high. The most prominent journals in the field were in good health at a time that subscriptions to many journals in the social sciences were declining. A growing variety of books on comparative-education themes was being published. Newspapers, television programs, and popular magazines increasingly featured educational developments from around the world. Such events herald a bright future for comparative education.

The reasons for the growing vigor of the field are fairly clear. Each year the earth becomes more populous and its inhabitants more interdependent. With increasing frequency, political and economic changes in one society affect the fate of people in other societies. And with the widespread availability of television and radio, people in all parts of the world become instant witnesses of distant events. As a result, people's cross-national awareness is expanding, extending to all facets of culture, including education. Hence, there is a ready audience for information about educational operations around the world and a growing corps of investigators interested in producing this information. In sum, the field of international comparative education seems bound to flourish in the years ahead.

CONCLUSION

This chapter has been dedicated primarily to three societal conditions that bear important implications for the future of the world's education systems —population growth, protection of the environment, and technological change.

Population increase poses two major problems for educators. First is the challenge to furnish suitable learning opportunities for all members of the society, a goal particularly difficult to achieve in nations that continue to register high growth rates. Second is the challenge to devise educational programs that convince citizens of the need for population control and that teach people suitable techniques of family planning.

The rapid deterioration of the earth's environments calls for instructional approaches that motivate the entire populace to support those conservation measures required for the survival of the species and for enhancing the quality of life.

Technological innovations offer hope that the educational challenges of population control and of managing the environment can be met. However, as Coombs remarked in his 1980s version of *The World Crisis in Education*::

> None of these gadgets, or all of them together, should be expected to perform educational miracles. They will not lessen the need for good teachers or for talented creators of good learning materials. But they have a high potential, if well used, for enhancing the productivity of teachers and and the motivation and learning achievements of students, and not least of all for greatly widening the access to learning for motivated learners outside of the schools (Coombs, 1985: 133).

The foregoing issues of population growth, the environment, and technology have been offered as illustrative concerns for educators and not as the only significant aspects of educational development that require decisions in the years ahead. Clearly there are many other matters that also call for the best efforts that educators and political leaders can muster. Numbers of these matters have been reviewed in earlier chapters —priorities among educational goals, choices of instructional methods and of delivery systems, the selection of assessment approaches, decisions about centralization and decentral-ization of educational governance, equity in access to educational opportunities, questions of language policy, problems of educational finance, and decisions most suitable roles for comparative-education research. In addition, a host of further concerns will continue to demand attention. These include questions of:

Relevant education. The issue is: Education for whom and for what purpose? "Should all students receive the same education, as this might be considered the most democratic and equitable? Or should students receive an education, especially at the primary and secondary level, which is largely adapted to the economic and social needs of the regions where they live?" (Spalding, 1988: 8).

Moral education. Which agencies in the society should be assigned responsibility for teaching moral values and and for monitoring the application of these values in the lives of children and adults? What should be the sources of the values that are taught?

Special education. Which individual differences among learners warrant special treatment, and in what form should this treatment be provided? For example, should children with mental and physical handicaps be placed in classes designed especially for their needs, or should they be in classes along with age-mates who display no such handicaps? Who should be responsible for paying the costs of special treatment?

Promotion policies. What criteria should be used to determine whether a pupil advances from one grade to the next in the schooling hierarchy?

> When as many as 50% or more of the children do not finish primary school [as is the case in many Latin American countries], can this be blamed only on the student or is the system at fault? ... One [solution] is the automatic promotion system, whereby students are promoted from grade to grade until they finish the primary cycle, no matter how they achieve in their school work. This approach can be a disaster if it is not accompanied by changes in the way the school curriculum works and by careful teacher training so as to prepare teachers to handle such a system (Spalding, 1988: 9).

International cooperation. What sorts of outside educational aid should developing nations seek, and under what conditions should they accept aid? What kinds of educational assistance should international bodies, such as Unesco and the World Bank, or should private foundations and individual nations furnish to other countries, and controls are these donors warranted in maintaining over the use of such help?

In summary, the future holds no lack of challenge for the education systems of the world. Scholars and practitioners who toil in the field of comparative education face both the opportunity and the obligation to contribute toward the solution of the host of problems to be met in the decades ahead.

REFERENCES

Allaby, M. (1990) Environment. In *1990 Britannica book of the year.* Chicago: Encyclopaedia Britannica.

Coombs, P. H. (1985) *The World Crisis in Education.* New York: Oxford University Press.

Jamison, R., Johnson, P. D., & Engels, R. A. (1987) *World population profile: 1987.* Washington, DC: U. S. Government Printing Office.

Jones, E. F. (1986) *Teenage pregnancy in industrialized counties.* New Haven, CT: Yale University Press.

McDonald, G. D. (1964) *Poems of Stephen Crane.* New York: Crowell.

Romig, C. A., & Thompson, J. G. (1988) Teenage pregnancy: A family systems approach. *The American Journal of Family Therapy,* 16 (1): 133-143.

Roosa, M. A. (1986) Adolescent mothers, school dropouts, and school based intervention programs. *Family Relations,* 35: 313-317.

Seybold, J., & Dressler, F. (1987) *Publishing from the desktop.* New York: Bantam.

Spalding, S. (1988) Prescriptions for educational reform: Dilemmas of the real world. *Comparative Education,* 24 (1): 5-17.

United Nations Population Fund (1989) *Inventory of population projects in developing countries around the world 1987/88.* New York: Author.

World Bank (1989) *World development report 1989.* New York: Oxford University Press.

Zimmerman, S. L. (1988) State level public policy choices as predictors of state teen birthrates. *Family Relations,* 37: 316-321.

Index